Pacific Cosmopolitans

Pacific
Cosmopolitans

A CULTURAL HISTORY OF

U.S.-JAPAN RELATIONS

Michael R. Auslin

Harvard University Press

Cambridge, Massachusetts · London, England

2011

Library of Congress Cataloging-in-Publication Data

Auslin, Michael R., 1967–

Pacific cosmpolitans : a cultural history of U.S.-Japan relations /
Michael R. Auslin.

p. cm.

Includes bibliographical references and index.

ISBN 978-0-674-04597-2 (alk. paper)

1. United States—Relations—Japan. 2. Japan—Relations United States.
I. Title.

E183.8.J3A927 2011

303.48'273052—dc22   2010051155

Once again, to Ginko and Benjamin
This too is a part of our story.

∽

And to the memory of my great-grandparents
and grandparents, who took their own voyage
across an ocean and encountered another culture.

Contents

Note on Names

THROUGHOUT THIS BOOK, Japanese names are rendered in traditional style, with the family name coming first and the individual's given name coming second. A number of famous individuals in the first and second chapters of this book are popularly known by their given names, as are the various members of the Tokugawa family. Thus, the warlord Toyotomi Hideyoshi is referred to as Hideyoshi, and Prince Tokugawa Iesato as Iesato. In addition, the terms *bakufu* and *shogunate* are used interchangeably to refer to the shogun's administrative structure, which functioned as a quasi-national government in Japan. *Edo* refers colloquially to the Tokugawa shogunate, in the way *Tokyo* is shorthand for the current Japanese government. Certain commonly used place names, such as Honshu or Tokyo, are rendered without diacritical marks.

Pacific Cosmopolitans

Introduction

O N A SWELTERING July morning in 1853, Japanese fishermen casting their nets in the wide waters of Edo Bay were startled to see a procession of fearsome ships round the headlands of the Uraga Channel. Two steam frigates and two sloops of war bristling with dozens of guns and nearly a thousand sailors appeared like an apparition out of the midday haze. Within hours, local samurai officials had been notified and were rowing out in their tiny shore boats to meet the behemoth armada. The unique relationship between Japan and America was about to begin.

Just a century and a half later, it is nearly impossible to imagine the thoughts racing through the minds of both the Americans and the Japanese that day. What little each knew about the other was more likely to be an amalgam of tales and hearsay than fact. Only a handful of Japanese had ever seen an American, and barely more than that in America had come into contact with any Japanese. Yet within just a few years of that fateful morning in 1853, Japanese and Americans would meet regularly, forming a relationship inconceivable to those first pioneers. And as they did so, they not only changed each other but helped, as well, to create the modern world.

* * *

Global history is largely the record of encounters between different cultures. Across the earth's surface and across centuries, societies small and large have embraced or rejected the ideas and ways of life of other groups. Some have survived these encounters, while many others have not, succumbing either through war or more peaceful absorption. Only in very recent times have some cultures actively attempted to engage with others, embracing exchange as a way to solidify political relations, develop their economies, defeat traditional enemies, or deepen their own cultural traditions. Among those thousands of exchanges, few have been as consequential and long-lasting as that between the United States and Japan.

This book explores the enduring cultural exchange between Japan and the United States. It does not pretend to be an exhaustive history of Japanese-American cultural relations, since such a study is impossible. Rather, this study uncovers the deep fascination in both countries with an exotic Other, a fascination that soon became a rigorous attempt to maintain permanent contact as well as to study and analyze the fundamental features of each country. This book focuses particularly on the organizations that developed to promote cultural exchange and the individuals who played major roles in those groups.

As a lens through which to view recent global history, this book shows how radically human contact has changed in just a few decades, thanks to technology and the rise of a consumer-oriented middle class. It also highlights uncomfortable realities about international relations, namely, that politics and economics are indelible aspects of cultural encounter and that any attempt to ignore them in favor of some elysian model of human relations misses the engines which drive contact and produce value that is material and nonmaterial alike. I am a firm believer in the importance of cultural exchange but recognize that it always has and always will play a subordinate role to the more traditional economic and political concerns of leaders in both countries.

Yet walk into any American college today, and you will find a class on Japanese studies. Within those classes the overwhelming majority of students grew up watching Japanese animation or reading *manga* comics produced in Japan. After class lets out, those students will often while away the hours playing Nintendo games in their rooms, while others will head to the gym for classes in karate or aikido. Back at home, their empty nester parents may be heading out in their Toyotas for a sushi dinner and then stopping at Crate and Barrel to pick up a shoji screen for the living room, where they'll diligently sip cancer-blocking green tea.

This powerful mix of Japanese cultural and commercial influences on American life is itself a pale shadow of a mirror lifestyle across the Pacific. In the past century and a half, the surface of Japanese society has become all but indistinguishable from Western, and specifically American, models. Tokyo teens line up outside McDonald's (Makudo) and Kentucky Fried Chicken (Kentakun) outlets, while their parents pick up cellophane-wrapped egg salad sandwiches at 7-Eleven before heading off to the office. The whole family will troop out to the latest Tom Cruise movie on weekends and often head to Hawaii for New Year's or the Golden Week break in May.

Such blatant stereotyping reflects important truths about a unique historical relationship. For much of the past 150 years, Japanese and Americans have been fascinated with each other's culture, just as they have been with other cultures, from China's to Great Britain's. Most nations form their closest international relationships with cultures with which they share ethnic ties or a long common historical experience. Thus, the United States remains a nation that looks first to Europe and particularly the Anglo-Saxon nations, while Japan has long recognized the profound Sino-Korean influences on its culture. American immigrant communities, from Germans to Ethiopians, maintain enduring cultural ties to their homelands and promote their native customs in numerous ways, just as Japanese continue to explore the impact of the traditional Chinese ecumene on the formation of Japanese society.

Yet in the case of U.S.-Japan relations, where no ethnic bonds or long standing ties existed, there was no natural constituency in either nation clamoring for close contact. Despite this, the modern path of both societies, but especially that of Japan, has been shaped by their transpacific engagement. The cultural interactions between Japan and America were of course just one part of a broader bilateral relationship guided. Commercial, political, and ultimately strategic concerns remained in the forefront of both countries' national policy. As important as these other concerns were, however, it was the cultural side of Japan that was most often experienced by upper- and middle-class Americans, while American models and awareness of life in the United States profoundly shaped modern Japanese sensibilities. As this book relates, moreover, the number of groups devoted specifically to U.S.-Japan relations was unique when compared with other national cultural organizations that had a global focus, such as the British Council or the Alliance Française.

The mention of those other organizations, however, reminds us that the century-and-a-half encounter between Japan and America was part of a much larger global historical process, one in which the trends of discovery, trade, commercialization, and technological progress helped foster the growth of modern, industrialized, middle-class societies. These trends transformed the way peoples across the globe have interacted with each other since the late nineteenth century, making our experience of world's fairs, international academic conferences, and endless tourism a wholly new era in human relations. For this reason, too, the U.S.-Japan relationship is of interest to students of international history.

It must be stressed at the outset that the cultural exchange between America and Japan did not follow a simple, linear pattern of growth. In Japan, for example, certain writers and activists throughout the nineteenth and twentieth centuries were vehemently opposed to the erosion of what they saw as traditional Japanese culture and mores by Western influences. Anti-Japanese racialist movements in the United States marred official relations for much of the early twentieth century. And four years of brutal war in the 1940s almost entirely stopped all cultural engagement. Yet the story of this century and a half is one of a steady increase in the formalization of cultural relations, the growth of complex exchange organizations, and the delicate balancing of private versus public interests in cultural encounter. These relations became just as important a facet of the overall U.S.-Japan relationship as did diplomatic negotiations or economic activity.

The history of U.S.-Japan cultural exchange therefore reflects the tension among three different groups of private actors: the cosmopolitans, those who believed that different cultures could learn from each other and thereby promote greater understanding and a sharing of cultural forms; the nationalists, who sought to protect their unique cultures from foreign contamination and yet also saw culture as a tool to be used in furthering state interests; and the internationalists, who sought to transcend national governments with supranational global governance that would end conflict. A final actor that influenced all three groups in various ways was the state, which ran its own cultural outreach and often sought to use private cultural exchange for its own purposes, both before and after the Pacific War.

Since the end of World War II, Japanese and American cultural exchange has become stronger than ever. Support from both countries' governments, as well as from corporations and major foundations in both countries, has led to an explosion of cultural exchange groups, academic studies programs, and traveling exhibitions across the Pacific. Some observers in both lands have criticized the politicization of cultural exchange, while others have called for more governmental funding in order to maintain the high level of activity. For many American and Japanese citizens, the opportunity to attend a Japanese film festival, visit an American art exhibit, or travel to each other's country has become an important part of their lives, and few think about the government, private, or corporate funds that help them pursue their very personal interests.

This constant exchange over the past 150 years has helped maintain close political relations between Tokyo and Washington and has supported powerful interest groups in each country. To a certain degree, critics are right to point out that culture and politics have become entangled, but such a blanket criticism misses the astonishing vibrancy of U.S.-Japan cultural exchange over the decades and the degree to which much of it was due to individuals acting with little thought of high-level diplomacy or economic profit. Through the decades, legions of Japanese and American individuals have committed themselves to learning about the other culture and spreading their knowledge through writing, teaching, or performing, thereby following in the footsteps of the first Pacific cosmopolitans, who struggled to find out about the shadowy lands across the waters.

CHAPTER 1

Shadows and Trinkets

A MERICA AND JAPAN first encountered each other as vague images shadowed by myth. Vast oceanic distances separated the two lands, and only tantalizing hints of exoticness washed up on each countries' shores during the eighteenth and early nineteenth centuries. Each was drawn to the other precisely by the allure of the unknown. In a time when Japanese were forbidden to travel overseas and when Americans were focused on building a new nation, each land played an insignificant role in the life of the other. Yet the shadowy images continued to intrude upon popular imagination over the decades. Eventually, as transpacific politics caught up both nations in its wide net, the mystique of the unknown was challenged by cultural explorers intent on finding trinkets, both material and psychological, to bring home.

Yet, to understand how these two nations reacted to each other, we must first know how they interacted with the world around them. While the intensity of their encounter would ultimately far outstrip the modest expectations each had for the relationship, neither encountered the other in a vacuum, nor did they separate their views of the other country from the way they saw the outer world. And though their transpacific ties would not only change both countries but would help propel each into its modern, international era, in the beginning their relations were simply the stuff of sea tales and myth, especially in the young United States. For Americans, as for the rest of the world, Japan in the nineteenth century was a sealed treasure house, the famed "Cipangu" of Marco Polo. In reality, that myth masked a vibrant Japanese interaction with the outside world, an interaction that would help Japan forge a new identity.

Japan: The Legend of Closure

Even today, the allure of Japan derives from a legend, an image that served Japanese and, later, Americans alike. This legend, of a secluded, mist-shrouded realm, in one way or another has indelibly marked the history of Japan, equating it with mythical places like Shangri-la. Foreigners and the Japanese themselves have fed the legend, and it has become common to treat Japan as somehow different from other countries. One can read in eighth-century Japanese imperial poetry a paean to the "eightfold enclosure" of clouds that protects the imperial land. Better known, of course, is the "divine wind," the *kamikaze* that not once but twice destroyed the invading Mongol fleets of Genghis Khan in the thirteenth century, thus sparing Japan the subjugation imposed on most of Eurasia. For centuries, such images have pulled foreigners to try and discover the truth about Japan.

What interested Americans, however, was a legend derived from a kernel of truth. When Commodore Matthew C. Perry arrived in Japan in July 1853, he was hailed back home as having "opened" a country closed to contact with the rest of the world for over two hundred years. The Japanese government of the time, the Tokugawa bakufu, had itself used the legend of its traditional isolation as a way to limit contact with undesirable foreign nations, particularly Russia, for decades. As the legend developed, however, the world accepted as fact that the Tokugawa bakufu had issued a series of seclusion edicts during the 1630s, in order to protect Japan from the ecclesiastical temptations of Christianity and to cement its own power after triumphing in a century-old civil war. These culminated in a prohibition on Japanese travel overseas and a complete ban on the foreign religion. This, of course, is true so far as the edicts go, but such an interpretation served its own ideological purposes independent of historical reality.[1]

The reality is that the Japan opened by Commodore Perry had never really been closed. To say that Japan was closed in 1639 is as arbitrary as saying that it was opened back up in 1853. In fact, Tokugawa Japan maintained a complex cultural relationship with the outer world, a relationship that prepared the country for the intensity of its encounter with the United States starting in the mid-1800s. Japan was tightly woven into the pre-twentieth-century East Asian regional system dominated by China, and throughout the centuries of Tokugawa rule Japan had a widespread encounter with foreign ideas and goods.

When the third shogun, Tokugawa Iemitsu, issued the last of the maritime edicts in 1639, Japan was already firmly embedded into the Chinese-centered regional trading system.[2] The climax of the sixteenth-century civil wars in Japan and the dawn of the Tokugawa era coincided with the sunset of the Ming dynasty (1368–1644). From the mid-fifteenth century onward, the Ming court had begun to pull back its relations with other countries, ending official overseas voyages and restricting access to China's ports. Yet China remained the hub of an expansive regional trading network, linking Arabian merchants with Southeast Asian markets and stretching its tentacles northward to Japan.

Japanese rulers and merchants participated in this trade, even through the disruptions of the civil wars. Ironically, it was during the battle-scarred sixteenth century that a consumer-oriented society firmly developed in Japan, a change driven in part by visionary warlords such as Oda Nobunaga (1534–1582), who lowered taxes on merchants and created free trade zones within his domains. Markets sprang up in pacified areas, and trade routes were protected by powerful warriors. During these years, a recognizably Japanese style of living developed, with commercially produced material goods becoming increasingly available even to commoners.

For centuries, Chinese goods had been seen as the height of sophistication and a symbol of one's wealth. Not surprisingly, then, as a consuming class emerged in Japan during the 1500s, there was a strong demand for recognizably Chinese goods, even if they were not high-value luxury items. Rich warlords may have lavished funds on Chinese ceramics and artistic works, but everyday items we now think of as "Japanese," such as soy sauce, tofu, tatami matting, and cotton clothes, were all imported from China or derived from Chinese examples.[3]

This flourishing regional trade, in which Japan was an increasingly active participant, was disrupted by at least three separate threats during the fifteenth, sixteenth, and early seventeenth centuries. The first threat, during the 1400s, was increased piracy along the Chinese coast. Bands of multiethnic raiders known as *wakō,* or "Japanese pirates," ravaged ports and trading entrepōts, hiding in myriad islands along the Japanese littoral. Despite repeated Chinese demands that the pirates be suppressed, the enfeebled Japanese military government, then headed by the Ashikaga family, was ineffective in restoring any long-term order. It would take until the end of the civil wars in the late 1500s for the samurai leader Toyotomi Hideyoshi (1536–1598) and the first Tokugawa shoguns to quell the pirates. The second threat manifested itself in the last decade of the sixteenth century. Hideyoshi, the peasant turned supreme military warlord of Japan, launched a devastating invasion of Korea in 1592, which he conceived of as the first step in ruling the known world, which was China. This needless war disrupted the long-standing Japanese-Korean trade in Northeast Asia. Not until Hideyoshi's death in 1598 was peace restored between the two nations. The final threat to the Asian trading network was the collapse of Ming China itself, from the assault by Manchu invaders in the 1630s to the crushing of final resistance in the late 1660s.

It was in response to these three regional disturbances that the fundamental feature of East Asia's international relations developed: the maritime restrictions system. The initial attacks by pirates resulted in the first trade limits set by the Ming court during the mid-fourteenth century. Foreign trade was almost entirely subsumed into the long-standing tradition of the tribute system. The tribute system had been perhaps the central foreign policy of Chinese dynasties back to the founding Han. It was an ideological conceit, positing a hierarchical relationship between China, represented by the emperor, and all foreign lands. Non-Chinese could participate in the system by acknowledging the emperor's superiority, receiving in return valuable commodities and cultural artifacts such as the Chinese calendar and the duty to use the current Chinese reign name: in short, participation in Chinese civilization.[4] The tribute system, which expanded during the Tang and Ming dynasties, codified the Chinese division of the world into two realms, the "civilized" (*ka,* or Chinese) and the "barbarian" *(i).* Chinese foreign affairs thus conveniently meshed deeply held cultural beliefs and cold-hearted policy. The Ming maritime restrictions of the mid-1400s were thus not an attempt to isolate China from the outside world but rather a clearly defined policy to try ordering foreign relations and to control their influence on domestic politics, economics, and culture.

The Japanese created their version of the maritime restrictions in the early 1600s in the light of Asian influences. The Japanese did not restrict their foreign relations because of a unique, culturally inspired abhorrence of foreign contact. Rather, the new Tokugawa leadership, worried about its domestic strength and desiring to be seen as all powerful, decided to imitate the most advanced policies existing on the continent. The Japanese policy was complementary to Chinese policy and held the same ends: to control, not sever, foreign relations and limit their domestic impact.[5] The restriction was also a part of the Tokugawa attempt to normalize relations with regional powers after the devastation of Hideyoshi's invasion of Korea and make Japan appear a benign state. This has been described as the "diplomacy of amity" of Tokugawa Ieyasu in the years immediately following his establishing the bakufu in Edo (modern-day Tokyo).[6]

That the restriction edicts were designed primarily for political purposes is clear from a brief look at their evolution and context. Starting in 1598, just three months after the death of Hideyoshi, Ieyasu acted in his capacity as one of the guardians of Hideyoshi's child heir to open trade with Manila through Portuguese Jesuit intermediaries. This soon expanded to trading relations with Annam (Vietnam), the rest of the Philippines, Cambodia, Spain, England, and Holland. Japan was an active participant in a global trade network, even if it played a minor role. The problem was that trade soon impinged on political stability.

Within fifteen years, the now-unrivaled Tokugawa bakufu began clamping down on threatening political behavior by Franciscan and Jesuit missionaries in Japan. Despite its apparent political supremacy, the bakufu had in reality established a de facto political equilibrium in Japan, recognizing that the most powerful feudal domains in the country were nigh autonomous. For their part, these domains, particularly Satsuma in southern Kyushu and Chōshū in western Honshu, acceded to Tokugawa control of foreign affairs and agreed to abide by certain domestic demands. In

the six-odd decades of direct contact with Christian missionaries, however, thousands of ordinary Japanese and several very powerful feudal
lords had been converted to Roman Catholicism, particularly in the
south, where the most anti-Tokugawa lands were located. For the newly
established Tokugawa, the Catholic intrusion was as much a cultural as it
was a political threat. New ideas of divinity and new ritual practices in
themselves were not so threatening, but the exclusive nature of the new
religion was a concern. When Buddhism had been introduced into Japan
a millennium previously, there was a brief political struggle between various ancient clans over political power, but as a religion, Buddhism had
very quickly proved its syncretic nature by doctrinally accepting the native religion, now known as Shinto.

Such was not the case with Christianity, which demanded the renun-
ciation of all other religion. Moreover, unlike Buddhism, Christianity was
intimately connected with the political power of the various European
states practicing one denomination or another, and protecting the influence and spread of Christianity often was the pretext for political or military intervention. In the context of Japan's civil wars, which were building
toward their climax, this raised the threat of Western intervention on behalf of their new coreligionists.

Thus, as part of a comprehensive policy to remove any potential threat
to the new government, the Tokugawa bakufu began to reduce the Christian influence. In 1613, all Christian missionaries were expelled. Yet, given
the possibility that missionaries would attempt to sneak in with traders,
three years later the Tokugawa restricted all foreign trade to the two ports
of Nagasaki and Hirado, both in Kyushu, the southernmost of the main
islands of Japan. In 1633 the number of trading ships from abroad allowed
each year was reduced, and a silk monopoly run through licensed whole-
salers was established. By 1636 the Catholic Portuguese were restricted to
Nagasaki and finally expelled altogether in 1639. The English having
pulled up stakes in 1623, this left only the Protestant Dutch among Western powers in Japan; in 1641 they were sent to Nagasaki, to the small, manmade island of Dejima in Nagasaki Bay, there to be kept virtual prisoners
for over two centuries.[7]

These evolving maritime restrictions had a domestic side as well. What
we now think of as the main props of the seclusion policy emerged in the

1630s, during the rule of the third shogun, Iemitsu. This grandson of Ieyasu is largely credited with stabilizing bakufu administration and giving the shogunate the general shape it would hold for the next two centuries. As clashes between Japanese and Westerners increased along with the growing overseas trade, Iemitsu in 1633 promulgated orders prohibiting Japanese from going abroad or returning home, on pain of death. Two years later, he prohibited all Japanese ships from going abroad and increased suppression of Christian teachings and again limited the presence of missionaries. In 1637 a major uprising of Christian converts erupted near Nagasaki, at Shimabara, and Iemitsu ordered a siege of the rebels after failing to defeat them outright. He was aided in the battle by Dutch traders, who had no qualms about flinging cannonballs from their ships at their besieged fellow Christians. All thirty-five-thousand-odd rebels, including women, children, and scores of masterless samurai, eventually were put to the sword. In the following year, 1639, Iemitsu completely proscribed Christianity within Japan. The bakufu then limited its formal foreign relations to Korea and the kingdom of the Ryukyus (Okinawa), both of which were allowed to send official embassies to Edo, and did so sporadically into the nineteenth century.[8] The Dutch and Chinese were accorded trading status only and kept tightly controlled at Nagasaki, the Dutch being allowed off their fan-shaped island only to be paraded before the shogun in Edo once every year (an event later scaled back to once every four years).

We have now worked our way back to the beginning and found the origin of the legend of Japanese seclusion. Those in the West conflated political and religious strictures with comprehensive isolation. That Christians were expelled, mutatis mutandis, must mean that no foreigners at all, save the imprisoned Dutch, were allowed in Japan, and thus no contact occurred with the West until the bulldog determination of the American Perry reversed centuries of tradition.

Here the historians' story of Japan's interaction with the world traditionally ended, at least until the arrival of Perry two centuries later. In both the narrative of the times, used by the Japanese for their own purposes, and our historical narratives created decades later, the political trumped the cultural, as well as the social and the economic. The Tokugawa political system is often upheld as a model of how politics creates the overall structures within which all other aspects of human life take place and how the state's monopolization of coercive power allows it to punish those who transgress the boundaries deemed necessary to protect that power. In this view, the feudal system, comprising mainly the caste or status system, and the semiautonomous domains kept Japanese society frozen in place until the West burst in and unleashed subterranean economic and social currents.[9] But while politics sets the frame, it cannot control all that occurs within that framework, and in the Japanese case, cultural interaction continued over the following two centuries.

During these generations, Japan was much like other premodern societies in its relative isolation and sporadic encounter with other cultures. Until the late nineteenth century, the vast majority of peasants and common folk around the globe were little exposed to direct cultural exchange. The global diffusion of religious beliefs and technology, startling when viewed from the vantage point of centuries, made but small ripples on the surface of the life of an individual or even on that of several generations. In terms of daily life, a French peasant on the eve of the Revolution knew as little about the world outside his village as did his Japanese counterpart, and both had just as little interaction with foreign cultures. Only in the nineteenth century did technology advance to the point where the most assertive civilizations could repeatedly and regularly reach hitherto "undiscovered" regions. The slow rise of literacy, even in Europe, eventually sped this process, while the transformative strength of international capitalism was limited to a few European nations. Viewed from this vantage point, early modern Japan, that is, the Japan of the seventeenth to nineteenth centuries, seems much more "normal" and the European intruders the "abnormal."

Yet if we measure by the yardstick of European global reach, Tokugawa Japan experienced a significant diffusion of foreign cultural elements compared with that of other nations at the time. Even so, this cultural encounter had a very limited domestic effect, beyond an equally circumscribed group of specialists; the bulk of the Japanese population enjoyed intriguing but largely superficial cultural encounters, much like the bread and circuses of ancient Rome.

Among the more memorable foreign encounters during the centuries of the Tokugawa era were the sporadic tribute missions sent by Korea and the Ryukyus. These spectacles fascinated Japanese commoners who caught a glimpse of the strangely garbed foreigners passing through their cities on the way to the shogun's capital. One defining feature of Tokugawa Japan was its extensive system of official roads and post towns, each of which comprised a minicity; this system of roads formed a national transportation artery along which foreign dignitaries could travel. Foreign embassies would sail to Kyushu, in the far southwest, and from there travel by road and coastal boat the five hundred miles to the shogun's capital of Edo. At each post town they passed through or lodged in, they drew ogling crowds. These sporadic "carnivals" played a role in defining for Edo-era Japanese their identity, at least in terms of material culture.[10] Popular prints show the foreigners in their distinct national garb as they carry the goods to be presented to the shogun, and these prints provided ordinary Japanese with a surface-level understanding of the differences of their daily lives from those of the privileged representatives of another culture. Similar scenes were played out when the "red-haired" barbarians, the Dutch, made their annual trek to the shogun's palace.[11]

Of rather more importance than the occasional and brief parade of Koreans or Ryukyuans was the pervasive presence of China, through its ideas and goods. For most of Japanese history, China represented "civilization" and the source of the most important of the cultural imports that by the Edo period had become totally naturalized. From *kanji,* the ideographic writing system, to Confucianism, the semiofficial ideology, and from painting to tea leaves, China for centuries had provided Japan with the benchmarks of what it meant to be an advanced society. Japanese scholars both admired and wrestled with China, attempting to find a place of pride for Japanese thought within the ocean of Chinese beliefs and writings that permeated the East Asian cultural sphere.[12] From a political standpoint, moreover, the maritime restriction policies of the 1630s themselves were designed to allow the Tokugawa government to participate in the regional Chinese-centered trade network. That network not only dealt with goods but also allowed the flow of ideas and people (mostly traders, of course) across borders.[13]

Like the Dutch, Chinese traders were restricted to the port of Nagasaki during the Tokugawa centuries. Unlike the Dutch, however, the Chinese lived not on a manmade island but in the city proper, a vicinage that became, perhaps, the prototype for later "Chinatowns" in Yokohama and Kobe. By the middle of the seventeenth century, there were as many as five thousand to ten thousand Chinese living in Nagasaki, comprising somewhere around one-sixth of the city's population.[14]

These merchants traded and brought with them goods that quickly entered the bloodstream of Japanese culture. Japanese cuisine was particularly affected by the regional trade with China. Culinary imports included the sweet potato and the pumpkin, as well as tea leaves (green tea until this time had been powdered), whose easy steeping led to the spread of tea drinking down to the common levels of society. These all became permanent staples of the Japanese diet, although the government soon encouraged farmers, through a program of import substitution production, to domesticate each of these goods. As the culture of tea drinking worked its way into every corner of society, commoners also began to use Chinese-style porcelain, thereby influencing the native pottery industry.[15]

Not only material culture was affected by the encounter with Chinese traders. As the resident Chinese in Nagasaki regularly held their traditional seasonal festivals, mainland folk culture, such as the dragon dance, spread to Japanese towns. Soon, it was de rigueur for Japanese festivals to have dancing "Chinamen" and dragons.[16] While these performances, unlike food and tea, were not part of daily life, they served nonetheless to define the image of the foreign and, even more importantly, to domesticate it.

The fascination such foreign objects held for Tokugawa-era Japanese is amply illustrated by the story of the shogun's elephant. Much like the famous giraffe of the Chinese emperor Yongle in the early 1400s, the shogun's elephant represented the power of the bakufu to bring the strange and exotic into everyday life yet also to contain it.[17] The great political figure of eighteenth-century Japan was the eighth shogun, Yoshimune. Brought to Edo as an adult to continue a shogunal line that no longer was producing heirs, Yoshimune was already the feudal lord of the domain of Kii and was known as an able administrator and reformer. Part of his reformist zeal extended to the importation of Western books on science, as we shall see shortly. Yet Yoshimune also was fascinated by less utilitarian forms of foreign culture.

In 1728, two Vietnamese white elephants arrived in Nagasaki. They were not part of an officially sponsored trade mission with China but were imported at the personal request of Yoshimune. Though one elephant soon died, the surviving pachyderm became a national sensation, "touring" Nagasaki, Kyoto, and Osaka while on its way to Edo. Demotic guidebooks, complete with woodblock prints, explained for fascinated townsfolk the travels of the elephant. Though Kyoto was merely the halfway point of the elephant's overland journey, it was there that the story climaxed. The emperor himself, a twenty-seven-year-old named Nakamikado, wanted to lay eyes on the beast. Yet no living being without proper court rank could be brought into the imperial presence. Thus, the Vietnamese elephant was duly granted the junior fourth rank, a senior position, and ceremoniously brought into the sacred precincts.

While amusing to the modern reader, the story powerfully shows the limits of the acceptance of the foreign in Tokugawa-era Japan. Not only was the elephant "naturalized," so to speak, but it was culturally tamed. The bestowing of rank, indeed the parade through Japan itself, signaled that this was no longer a wild beast and potential threat but rather another symbol of the universality of the shogun and, by extension, the emperor. It was this very taming of foreign culture, the dragon dances and elephants, the teapots and sweet potatoes, that symbolized the distinct limits of foreign encounter in early modern Japan.

Yet cultural encounter during the Edo period was not limited to foodstuffs or the domestication of the exotic. Of more import than the merchants plying their trade in Nagasaki were the numerous Chinese intellectuals who came to Japan's shores with the downfall of the Ming dynasty in 1644. These scholars brought with them philosophical ideas, such as Chu Hsi (Zhu Xi) Neo-Confucianism, as well as artistic techniques, literary traditions, architectural skills, printing technology, medical arts, and even martial arts.[18] Exemplary in this regard was the noted scholar Shu Shun-sui (1600–1682), who arrived in the domain of Mito in 1656. There, through his close collaboration with the scholar-lord Tokugawa Mitsukuni, Shu influenced Japanese Neo-Confucian thinkers such as Fujiwara Seika and Hayashi Razan. Shu also built the famous Confucian Yushima Shrine in Edo and laid out the equally well known Koishikawa garden on the Mito domain's Edo estate, both of which still exist in modern Tokyo, if reduced in size and splendor.[19]

The institutionalization of Neo-Confucian studies as the bakufu's official learning and the spread of that philosophy in the seventeenth and eighteenth centuries through the various domain and temple schools that educated samurai and commoner alike both testify to an important role for Chinese thought during the period of so-called seclusion. Yet, in the end, no aspect of this encounter was to change in any fundamental way the lives of Japanese during the Tokugawa period or the political, social, or economic bases of their society. Indeed, Chinese learning served precisely to buttress the ideological claims to supremacy of the Tokugawa family. Ironically, the most important aspect of this encounter was Chinese influence on the birth of Japanese "national learning" *(kokugaku)*, which was an intellectual movement in the eighteenth and nineteenth centuries that glorified Japan's native myths and literature and the position of the emperor, precisely in response to the pervasiveness of Chinese learning.[20]

The pervasiveness of Chinese culture and its influence on various aspects of Japanese life, however, was not the sum total of Japan's encounter with the foreign during the supposed years of isolation. For much of the Tokugawa period, but particularly starting in the mid-eighteenth century, a culture that no Japanese had ever directly seen played an increasingly important role in shaping Japanese visions of the world.

Shattering Boundaries: The Beginnings of Western Learning

Scholars have commonly ascribed the modernization of Japan to the importation of Western knowledge starting in the mid-nineteenth century. Unlike Chinese cultural imports, which were easily absorbed by the Japanese precisely because these forms were part of a centuries-long encounter with China, Western ideas and cultural forms came from a completely different civilization. When these forms, wrapped up in what was called Dutch or Western learning, were introduced into Japan, they acted much like a pathogen for which the host organism has no inherent immunity. Yet cultures are not biological entities, of course, and the Japanese actively analyzed and adapted these new foreign stimuli. Such was Tokugawa Japan's reaction to the knowledge brought by the Dutch traders imprisoned at Nagasaki.

Perhaps inadvertently, it was the Chinese who played almost as large a role as the Dutch themselves in importing Western information. Despite the bakufu's ban on all Christian paraphernalia, Chinese translations of Christian books were smuggled into Japan throughout the Edo period, primarily into Nagasaki. Many of the books were interdicted, but certainly some must have slipped through the censors' net. Not even the imperial precincts were safe from foreign threat, as forbidden texts were unearthed in 1771 in Kyoto, site of one of the oldest Christian communities before the proscription of the religion, and in nearby Osaka in 1698 and 1829.[21]

The Chinese did not deal solely in contraband, however. Much of Tokugawa Japan's knowledge of the outside world and specifically of the West came from Chinese geographical works or Chinese translations of Western books. As early as 1666, Chinese-derived atlases were introduced into Japan, and a fairly accurate cataloging of Asian lands existed in the Edo period. No fewer than eleven major collections, including the famous *Wakan sansai zue,* were introduced during the Tokugawa years.[22] The works of Chinese scholars such as Wei Yuan (Gigen; 1794–1856) played a particularly important role in the confused days leading up to and following Commodore Perry's arrival in 1853, with some works winding up in the hands of bakufu policy makers, such as Abe Masahiro.[23]

Yet the Chinese physically could carry only limited numbers of books and hence ideas. For a deeper penetration of Western culture into Japan, direct transmission from European countries was required, and that meant the Dutch. The bakufu approached Western knowledge as all governments do, with a bureaucratic mind-set that such information could help administrators create better policies. Bakufu leaders recognized almost immediately that the Dutch traders represented a unique source of foreign intelligence, and these leaders did not hesitate to exploit it. The Dutch factors (heads of the trading post) were required to submit an annual intelligence briefing on the state of Europe and the world. These *fusetsugaki,* as they were called, were far from objective or comprehensive analyses by disinterested bureaucrats, since many of the Dutch trading heads were relatively uneducated merchants more interested in keeping their Japanese hosts happy than in educating them about the world.

Nonetheless, these annual reports did allow bakufu policy makers to have a general level of knowledge of what we now term current events.

Dutch transmission of intelligence, however, was only part of the story. Of rather more importance was the scientific and artistic works the Dutch were commissioned to bring starting during Yoshimune's rule. As noted above, Yoshimune was a reformer, and he sought out Western books on astronomy, to perfect the lunar calendar for better agricultural yields, and medicine. Yoshimune's example allowed a small group of Japanese thinkers the chance to shatter the traditional boundaries of knowledge in Japan. As these scholars gained fluency in Western ideas, they continually pushed for greater access to Western sources of knowledge in the face of bakufu resistance. Gradually, but with surprising power, the influence of Western learning began to ripple through Japanese society.

The independent yet farsighted efforts of physicians such as Sugita Genpaku (1733–1817) to translate Dutch versions of German anatomical works meant a slow but steady revolution in the Japanese scientific worldview.[24] No longer was the human body conceived of as a microcosm of the Buddhist universe; rather, it was seen as a complex organic mechanism. This mind-set spurred advances in botany and agriculture as well, some of which were practiced by the shogunate's highest officials, such as senior councilor Matsudaira Sadanobu. In art, too, Dutch books had an important impact. The painter and polymath Shiba Kōkan (1747–1818), among others, gained knowledge of perspective, distance, and the use of chiaroscuro.[25] In science and art, Japanese thinkers were approximating reality better than they had in the past with only native and Chinese guides.

Starting in the late 1500s, with the arrival of Portuguese missionaries, accurate maps and atlases were provided to the bakufu. The Portuguese (soon followed by the Dutch and English) and the information they brought caused a radical change in the worldview of informed Japanese. No longer did they divide the world into the "three realms" of Japan, China, and India. The world now consisted of "myriad countries" *(bankoku),* each with a different people and customs.[26] A *"bankoku* boom" beginning in the mid-seventeenth century produced such works as the *Bankoku sōzu* (A Complete Map of the Myriad Countries; 1647), which listed forty different peoples of the globe; Ishikawa Yoshiyuki's complete world atlas, titled *Bankoku sōkaizu* (A Map of the Myriad Countries of the Whole World; 1688); Shitsuki Tadajirō's *Bankoku kanki* (Selected Views of the Myriad Countries; 1782), in which Shitsuki a translated a Jesuit atlas that provided astronomical and geographical information; and Morijima Nakayoshi's five-volume *Bankoku shinwa* (New Tales of the Myriad Countries; 1789).[27]

The bakufu also enlisted independent Dutch-learning scholars and Confucianists, such as Ōtsuki Gentaku, Takahashi Kageyasu, and Udagawa Yōan, appointing them to a new office for the translation of Western books and guiding their efforts. Their first commission was to translate the 1743 Dutch version of Noel Chomel's *Dictionnaire Oeconomique*, which was a compendium of European information on political economy. Takahashi and Ōtsuki already had a small archive from which to begin their research, for a few major works had already been translated during the seventeenth and eighteenth centuries. In the following decades, the Astronomical Bureau continued this trend, publishing books and making copperplate engravings of world maps. By 1800, Japanese geographers were nearly as knowledgeable as their European counterparts.

Given all these trends, it would be hard to argue that Japan was not affected during the Tokugawa years by its encounter with Dutch-mediated Western culture. The great scholar Donald Keene noted over half a century ago that by 1800 the Japanese were perhaps the best-informed people on earth about other lands.[28] True, much of that knowledge circulated among a fairly small segment of elites, but more than bits and pieces flowed down to the level of the commoners, winding up in broadsheets or secondhand atlases. Those with more direct access to Western information found that their understanding of the world, both the natural and the manmade, was slowly evolving. The "foreign," then, be it Chinese or European, was a constant presence in Tokugawa Japan yet appeared more as a shadow on the wall than as a concrete influence on daily life.

American Shadows: Reaching Out across the Pacific

To Japanese of the Tokugawa era, the "foreign"—if it did not mean Chinese or Asian—usually meant European. Yet very slowly, Japanese started becoming aware of another land, one on the other side of the globe, which seemed fantastical at first and later on became a consuming interest. Accounts of a land called Amerika came as early as 1708, in the burgeoning geographical works of the era. The very first mention was in a book called *Zōho ka-i tsūshō kō* (A Revised Study of Chinese-Barbarian Trade) by the Confucian scholar, astronomer, and geographer Nishikawa Joken (1648–1724). This book became one of the pathbreaking texts on foreign geography during the middle Edo period, driving a middle-class interest in lands beyond Japan.

These early mentions of America came as small parts of larger studies that often encompassed the whole globe. It took well over a century for America to rate its own study, but when it did, Japanese thinkers began to take more notice of the country. Aochi Rinsō (1775–1833), one of the leading Western-studies scholars, produced a two-volume work titled *Amerika-shi* (A Record of America), which was published in 1827, although possibly written earlier. Aochi, a colleague of the artist and scholar Watanabe Kazan, had been employed by the bakufu to compile various atlases, including the *Yochi shiryaku* (A Brief Record of the World) in 1828, which made him one of the small circles of officially sanctioned foreign-studies scholars. Drawing on Chinese and Dutch works, his *Amerika-shi* contained sections on North and South America, entries that were primarily geographical in nature, as well as a brief history of the exploration of the continents, including an account of Columbus and Amerigo Vespucci's travels.[29] Although much of Aochi's information came from Dutch atlases, it is unknown whether he and other Japanese scholars requested only such narrow geographic works or read broader treatments of American society and culture. Regardless, bits and pieces of information regarding Great Britain's colonies and later the new nation began filtering through Japanese geographical compilations and into the wider geographic imagination of Tokugawa-era readers.

Most of the information in books like *Amerika-shi* concerned geography proper and political economy: topography, crop varieties, and rudimentary political intelligence. Brief descriptions were often embellished with the wild products of the authors' imaginations. Very little, if anything, provided a glimpse into, or an understanding of, American society or culture, and there was just as little narrative. Nishikawa Joken's descriptions from 1708, for example, lacked not only firsthand knowledge but also any type of detailed information. Instead, his cursory treatment, admittedly the first, wrote that in America "men and women all [used] birds' feathers and the skins of tigers and leopards for clothing" and that "honey [was] exceedingly plentiful."[30] These first accounts of America highlighted Native American tribes and ways of life, while ignoring the small European colonies starting to take root on the eastern edge of the continent. Early Japanese readers, thus, were presented with idyllic scenes of exotic tribes living in a primordial wilderness, which was just the opposite of increasingly urbanized Japan.

Despite such deficiencies in knowledge, the volume of information on America available to Japanese steadily grew over the next century. It is not surprising that the market for studies on America exploded with the arrival of Commodore Perry, as six books about the United States appeared in the year after his Black Ships first visited Edo Bay. Yet even a decade before his arrival, starting in the 1840s, the Dutch began providing the Tokugawa bakufu with more accurate foreign information, as it became clear that Western powers, with Great Britain and America in the vanguard, were encroaching on East Asia, albeit from opposite directions. The Dutch, of course, were worried about losing their lucrative trading monopoly, but as they provided more intelligence to Japan's policy makers, Tokugawa leaders began to fear a strategic threat to their homeland.

Once the Dutch opened the information floodgates, the well-established Western-learning circles quickly began incorporating the information into their growing library of volumes on foreign affairs. Spurred on by an increasingly worried bakufu, a nascent Japanese national security and intelligence community grew in size, providing more sophisticated analysis to its consumers. A good example is the 1846 five-volume world atlas titled *Kon'yo zushiki,* by the Dutch-studies scholar Mitsukuri Shōgo (1821–1847). The extensive account of America in the *Kon'yo zushiki* contained detailed descriptions of each of America's regions, beginning with a "General Account of the American Continent" and ending with a "Short Biography of Washington."[31] By the eve of Perry's arrival, then, the most highly placed readers in Japan were starting to receive information about actual Americans, which was a far cry from the descriptions of mythical tribes in early books.

Despite this growth in accuracy, illustrations of or insights into American culture remained limited throughout the period preceding direct Japanese-American relations. The simple fact was that, when Tokugawa-era Japanese focused their eyes outside the shogun's realm, they did so by looking west, across China and Eurasia to Europe. Scholars such as Mitsukuri Shōgo or Aochi Rinsō focused most of their efforts on learning about the whole world or, when dealing with the West, with Europe. It was not just that the United States was a relatively small and isolated country but also that for over a century Europe had defined what the "West" was to Japan. Japan's direct connection to the Western world was through Holland, a European country, and it was European books and news of Europe's growing global power that defined the outer world to Japanese scholars and officials of the Tokugawa era. Indeed, of the 280 books on foreign issues published between 1616 and 1852 (the year before Perry arrived), at most two were devoted solely to America, while mention of the United States and the American continent was limited to a handful of broader works.[32] Neither breadth nor depth marked Japanese knowledge of the United States.

All that would change with the arrival of Perry in mid-1853. He was coming from a country that in its own way was becoming more and more interested in the secretive land across the Pacific but whose knowledge of Japan was largely outdated by over a century.

America: Revolutionary Expansion

If Japan's eyes were turned westward to Europe, then the young America's eyes had been turned eastward toward the same lands. As colonies that had been founded by European immigrants, the birth culture of the new society was a unique amalgam of Old World custom and a revolutionary approach to the creation of a future informed yet unhindered by precedent.[33] For Americans, as colonists or new citizens, their relationship to Europe was as complex as that of Japan's to China. Americans *were* Europeans; not only their identity but their entire social, cultural, economic, and political life were inconceivable apart from the mother countries, especially Great Britain. At the same time, of course, a growing sense of uniqueness and a desire to attempt a new experiment in self-governance had grown throughout the decades of colonial rule, propelling the disparate colonies toward declaring their sovereign autonomy.

With independence in 1776, America's relationship to the world was now unmoored from the past. The new nation would have to negotiate the creation of its own policies and the nurturing of its own interests, but again that could only be done through the prism of a shared cultural background.[34] That America was a multinational land was evident from its beginning and was a point of pride, though in reality ethnic tensions had long soured relations between different groups, especially in the slums of large cities like New York. In early America, "multinational" of course meant European countries or European colonies, from Sweden and Germany to Bermuda and the Antilles. Later waves of immigration in the early nineteenth century, of Irish and Scots, would rub the raw nerve of ethnic conflict, but again within a fairly bounded context of European commonness.

From the beginning, then, there was a unique twist to the concept of "foreign" in America. In a nation of immigrants, all its inhabitants were either foreign or descendants of those who recently had been foreign, including African slaves. This did not apply, of course, to the Native American tribes, who were continually pushed westward by the expansion of settlers across the continent. Moreover, the country had not only official foreign relations but also an ever-expanding informal encounter with other lands and peoples. It was a complex role, then, that the "foreign" played in the life of the young United States. For Japanese, such a role was as much cultural as political; for Americans, it was more clearly a political issue when foreign relations took place with countries from which the young republic's citizens largely came. It was a different story, however, when Americans began to discover Asia. If American eyes naturally turned eastward to Europe, Asia had to play a very different role in the creation of American culture and the myths that sustained it.

Americans first engaged Asia in the years just after declaring independence in 1776. Despite the Atlantic orientation and origins of the United States, there was from the country's beginning a Pacific sphere of interest as well. Trade pulled American society westward and served to spread European culture across the continent. The Northwest fur trade not only created vast American fortunes, such as that of the German immigrant John Jacob Astor, but also was the first important economic link between the eastern seaboard cities and the Pacific trading realm.[35] Within decades of American independence, the whaling industry, along with the expansion of key cities such as San Francisco, would steadily link Asia to American economic concerns on both coasts.

Beyond its symbol of economic potential, however, Asia also came to represent a powerful cultural mystique for Americans. It lay, in the American mind, beyond the end of a vast wilderness across a continent that itself was only slowly opening up its wealth to explorers, settlers, and traders. Beyond uncounted leagues of storm-tossed ocean, dotted by various isles that also could be linked to the great expansion of the nation, there existed an entirely new and unknown world of riches and tradition. The fact that Great Britain had forbidden trade with East Asia during colonial times, reserving it for the monopoly of the British East India Company, only made the region more appealing to Yankee merchants and explorers. Trade with the hitherto taboo realm was itself an exercise in American independence. But as a source of America's own cultural development, Asia at first was perceived to play no role.

Americans, like their European counterparts, first focused on Asia because of the whaling industry and the promise of trade with China. In 1784, just a year after the United States secured independence from Great Britain, a consortium of New York businessmen sponsored a trading voyage to China. Despite the success of this initial foray, the overwhelming bulk of American trade continued to be conducted with Europe, of course, and Asia was for decades but a promising backwater in U.S. economic activity. In fact, more than half a century later, in the early 1840s, U.S. imports from China stood at barely $5 million, a miniscule percentage of overall trade, and the basis for a continuing trade deficit with Peking, which refused to accept almost any goods from Western countries.[36]

Despite the tenuousness of these economic ties, those who traded with China found a fairly open field, and transpacific shipping became the origin of many an American fortune. More slowly, the "China trade" entered into American consciousness as a symbol of the exotic, a world of antiquity and wealth.[37] Mansions along the East Coast, from New York to New Bedford, Massachusetts, and as far inland as Litchfield, Connecticut, were raised on the proceeds of trade with China. Some of the nouveaux riche went even farther, ostentatiously displaying a connection with Asia that intensified as provincial American cities such as Boston prospered from trade and sought to showcase their wealth. A memorable description from Van Wyck Brooks gives the flavor of this display: "The Cushing house in Summer Street [Boston] was surrounded with a wall of Chinese porcelain. Peacocks strutted about the garden. The Chinese servants wore their native dress."[38] Silks, porcelain, ivory, and sandalwood carvings all took their place as valued objets d'art, testaments to the global reach and wealth of their owners, who were quickly becoming a major economic force in society.

The Pacific region trade network of which American merchants were becoming a part thus linked the world that lay beyond the settled part of the United States to the young country's political and economic centers on the eastern seaboard. Asia was incorporated into the American consciousness at an early stage, but also at a remove, due to distance as well as difference. As for Japan, this small island nation was but one part of the larger network, a land and an idea more or less indistinct in American minds from the idea of Asia as a whole.[39]

While it is true that, for most Americans, Asia served merely as a producer of luxury goods, for some of the young country's intellectuals, the region slowly became part of their larger world view and an object of learning that opened up new intellectual vistas far removed from their European origins. The colonists had brought with them to the New World a European-inspired outlook on the ordering of knowledge. Enlightenment ideals fired intellectuals, who were often also political thinkers. Benjamin Franklin, the most famous early American intellectual, founded the American Philosophical Society in Philadelphia in 1743, only eighty years after Britain's Royal Society first convened formally. Though perched on a perhaps tenuous strip of coast on the continent, the colonists were driven by a scientific curiosity as strong as that of their counterparts back in the homelands. To inquiring Americans, who were slowly expanding into the farther reaches of the continent, Asia was another field to be conquered, at least intellectually. Knowledge of Asia, then, played a part in the forming of America, even if in a minor role, for the new nation saw itself perched on both a geographic divide between east and west and an historical one between the American future and the European past. What would prove important before long was that these early seeds of knowledge about Asia would soon blossom into an American fascination with the Orient.

Yet when Americans thought about Asia in the eighteenth and early nineteenth centuries, they usually had China in mind. Indeed, that country was well known to American thinkers via various European writings, including the tales of Marco Polo and the musings of eighteenth-century philosophers such as Voltaire and Leibniz, both of whom praised Confucian ethics and the stability of China's politics, and Montesquieu, who criticized the despotism that underlay the Chinese political structure, in his attempt to champion European constitutionalism.[40]

Not surprisingly, perhaps, Americans approached China pragmatically, forgoing much of the theoretical speculation of European political thinkers but focusing on questions of science and trade that hit closer to home. One early example came in a 1768 publication of Franklin's stepchild, the Philosophical Society: "Proposals For enlarging the Plan of the American Society, held at Philadelphia, for Promoting Useful Knowledge." The goal being to foster the "Improvement of their Country, and Advancement of its Interest and Prosperity," the members of the learned society saw much to learn from China. They believed that America shared a similar environment with China as well as important "natural Produce," such as trees, ginseng, and silk. This similarity in turn led to hopes that native industry could be expanded, thus enriching the colonies.[41] Limited in usefulness as such studies were, they nonetheless showed the range of the American mind.

As American interest in Asia grew throughout the late 1700s, it was easier to come by information on China than on other Asian lands, due in no small part to the long Western fascination with the country and the historical significance of its imperial past. Yet even discerning readers might have been confused by a tendency to lump in the rest of Asia with writings on China, often giving just the thinnest of accounts of realms not under the sway of the Ch'ing emperors. For example, "Dissertation on the Chinese," which appeared in the *New York Magazine* in November 1792, contained a minute description of Chinese social, political, religious, and general cultural forms, discussing Buddhist philosophy and Chinese mythology and stressing China's intellectual links to India. Near its end, however, the article suddenly took up Japan, partially using Dutch surgeon Isaac Titsingh's famous descriptions of his recent stay in the country. Compared to the relative depth of analysis of Ch'ing society, the article's superficial treatment of the Tokugawa realm was limited to disproving the claims of the Japanese that they were not descended, at least ethnically, from China.[42]

China was, to some degree, a concrete place, known through various histories and accounts. Japan, however, was merely an image, one however that was coming to represent the exotic of Asia. Even during colonial days, many of the Asian products that American merchants imported from Britain were called "Japan" goods. Luxuries such as prints, lacquer ware, and silks were thus homogenized in the American mind. The vast majority of these items undoubtedly were of Chinese origin, since the amount of trade the Dutch conducted at Nagasaki could not have supported the level of exchange apparently reached even in the thirteen colonies. Nevertheless, in periodicals of the major trading cities, such as the *Pennsylvania Gazette,* advertisements appeared regularly during the 1760s and 1770s, hawking just such "Japanware" and testifying to the general level of supply and demand.[43] For most colonial consumers, then, "Japan" was an image constructed from the goods of a variety of Asian lands transported in the holds of merchant ships.

During these early years of America's engagement with Asia, writers used Japan primarily as a prop in larger debates, and their largely uninformed view of the country was positive or negative depending on the larger point they were trying to make. As much as Japan was a positive sign of the exotic for merchants hawking their wares, for others it was a symbol of excess and unhealthy consumerism, as well as a detrimental economic tie to Great Britain. For example, a measure to "prevent the Use of foreign Luxuries and Superfluities," publicly announced in the *Pennsylvania Gazette* of June 29, 1769, arose partly in response to the taxes levied on the colonies by London due to the Navigation Acts and partly to "promote, countenance, and encourage in others, a Habit of Temperance, Frugality, Oeconomy, and Industry." Among the items to be banished from the signatories' homesteads included "all Kind of Japan-ware." Certainly this sentiment would have found echoes in the spartan New England colonies, where a Puritan ethic still burned in the embers of its dying intensity. Exotic Japan for some was wasteful, a political and moral liability.

After American independence, political and social questions related to the survival of the new nation played a prominent role in national life. Among the most important debates in the early republic was whether to adopt a more centralized federal system. Some pamphleteers, championing their own version of natural law, stripped Japan of its exoticness and offered it as a symbol of the universality of certain principles across different cultures. Hence, "An Essay on the Means of promoting Federal Sentiments in the United States," printed in 1789, noted that "these principles of equity and benevolence are engraven on all human hearts by the same Almighty hand; known in Japan and America."[44]

In some eyes, then, Japan was part of a larger Orient, valuable largely for trade yet also "understandable" in moral terms as well. And, in the American geographic imagination, this conjoined Japan-Asia was but one part, the largest and most appealing perhaps, of a much wider and complex trading network stretching from the western coast of the American continent through the Alaska Peninsula, Siberia, Japan, and China on the northern circuit and directly across the Pacific to the Hawaiian Islands, Philippines, and central/southern China on the central circuit. In truth, of course, not one writer in ten who used the word "Japan" knew anything about the country. Rather, the word represented the ultimate malleable image, at least until American sailors ran up against the reality of Japan in their journeys across the Pacific.

The American Advance toward Japan

Although Japanese in the 1700s probably knew more about America (however limited that knowledge was) than vice versa, the maritime restriction edicts prevented any individual Japanese explorers from attempting to travel across the Pacific. It would instead be American ships that first appeared through the mists off Japan's shores, later giving rise to the legend that it was Americans who had "opened up" the isolated land. Given the American economic interest in Asia, it was perhaps inevitable that Americans would reach out to Japan, if in a hesitant way. Yet the initial impetus for the outreach came not from the Atlantic-based federal government but rather from private trading interests located on the West Coast. While these businessmen had little if any knowledge of true conditions in Japan, they believed that the land would prove crucial for their whaling or commercial prospects. As in the case of so much in early Japanese-American relations, however, the first contacts were as shadowy as the images in pamphlets and merchants' advertisements. Such encounters served only to whet appetites on both sides of the Pacific to finally break through to hard reality.

The first known American attempt to encounter Japan seems oddly anticlimactic, given the rigors of crossing the great ocean and the spine-tingling approach into a world of the unknown. This first "contact" occurred rather prosaically in 1791, when the sailing vessel the *Lady Washington,* out of the Pacific Northwest, approached the islands. Commanded by a John Kendrick, the ship traded in otter furs, as did so many harbored on America's Pacific coast. Appearing off the Kii peninsula to the southwest of the shogun's castle city of Edo, the *Lady Washington* did not land but darted in and out of a local bay almost as quickly as rumors about a giant sailing ship flashed through the peninsula. The men of the phantom vessel left an enigmatic message on the beach, stating, "This ship belongs to the Red Hairs from a Land called America," and listing their cargo.[45] Not only is it unclear if the American sailors even encountered any local fisherman during their hesitant excursion ashore, but the name of the first intrepid American to set foot on Japanese soil is likewise lost to history. By the time Tokugawa officials from the castle city of Nagoya reached the site, the ship was long gone, only its note—in Dutch and Chinese—remaining to announce that visitors from across the ocean had come.

American ships visited Japan irregularly in the decade after the *Lady Washington.* At least eight Yankee vessels returned to Japanese waters through 1801 or so, coming not as the emissaries of the American commercial class but as bit players in the first global conflict involving Asia. Half a world away from Japan, the Napoleonic Wars were raging during the last decade of the eighteenth century and first decade of the nineteenth. In the North Pacific, the Dutch East India Company feared capture of its ships by its enemy Great Britain. The Dutch hoped that neutral American ships would not be seized by the British and thus chartered them to carry vital trade up from Dutch ports in the East Indies. Once the American ships hove in sight of Nagasaki, they hoisted the Dutch flag, after ensuring no British privateers were lurking about.

It was the American sailors on these Dutch-flagged ships who were the first of their countrymen to be let into the secluded island country. Few recorded their visits, but the brothers William and George Cleveland of Salem, Massachusetts, visited separately in 1800 and 1801, both leaving brief recollections in their journals.[46] Although largely confined to the island of Dejima in Nagasaki Bay, like the Dutch in whose nominal employ they were, the Clevelands, like other American sailors, occasionally were able to travel throughout Nagasaki under the watchful eye of Japanese guards.

These visits yielded but ephemeral, kaleidoscopic images of a land almost no Westerners had ever visited, taking place on brief days ashore before the men embarked for more months at sea. None of the Americans visiting Japan on these ships could make any lasting contact with Japanese, let alone pick up any useful information about the country, except from their Dutch employers, who themselves were virtual prisoners. What survived from these brief encounters were trinkets, carefully carried back home across thousands of leagues of sea. What remains of these odds and ends today is reflected in the collection of the Peabody Essex Museum in Massachusetts. Here, ordinary items, such as combs purchased by sailors at brief stops in Nagasaki, vie with a few more ornate pieces of art. Combined with the goods brought out by the Dutch, an almost indistinguishably fine layering of Japanese goods settled on the American landscape in the first half of the nineteenth century.

Despite such an even and unpromising start, Japan was catching the attention of at least some observers in America. Three years after the *Lady Washington*'s voyage, the article "Advantages of Opening a Trade to Japan" appeared in the *Providence Gazette*. Arguing that Japan offered another "vent" for the American fur trade in the North Pacific, the article contained a compendium of contemporary images of Japan. The author gave a brief survey of Japan, noting that its "despotic government" ruled a people who were "ingenious, industrious, and commercial" yet at the same time "unenterprising" and who were the "grossest of all idolators." This, of course, was due to their being "totally irreconcilable to all who bear the name of Christians." Since, however, Americans were interested solely in trade, "prudence and integrity" would allow U.S. traders to avoid the political and theological pitfalls of the Europeans.[47]

Such facile reporting was the norm in an age before news bureaus and professional journalists. Most "news" was recycled information gathered from other sources or the occasional musings of sailors, merchants, and explorers who had been to far-off realms. Such was the case with the *Providence Gazette*'s article, which was based solely on the memoirs of a shady Hungarian adventurer, Count Benyowski, and had been published in London in 1790.[48] Despite this style of reporting, the average reader of these articles would no doubt assume he now had a good, if brief, grasp of Japan"s domestic conditions and foreign relations. These secondhand accounts in the American press were filled more with gossip than with facts, and we can only speculate the extent to which they stirred interest that later on resulted in bolder explorers and traders making their way across the ocean toward Japan.

In these decades, as whaling and trade were slowly bringing the two countries together, neither interest nor knowledge of Japan grew in the States in any appreciable way. Newspaper articles on Japan did occasionally appear, but these more often than not were limited to commercial items or brief mentions of Japan in relation to the China trade. Substantive articles were few and far between, but sometimes they did provide the glimmerings of what was happening inside the country. One such appeared in the *Farmers' Cabinet* in 1830, on the city of "Jeddo" (Edo), noting about this city of seven hundred thousand (a reasonably accurate estimate), "A man may live comfortably for three-pence a day." The article also reported that the wooden houses were "infinitely handsomer and more comfortable within" than American houses. The article gave a hint of the status system that rigidly separated social castes in Japan and noted how merchants were classed together, while the "noble and great men [inhabited] a distant part of the city," referring to the samurai areas, which were located around the castle and stretched toward the western precincts of Edo.[49] As in the case of most articles in early American newspapers, however, there is no indication of the source of the information, and the article itself is, like many from the era, merely a miscellany appearing out of context and with no follow-up.

For the most part, to the very few Americans who paid attention to foreign lands and to the even more select number that cared at all about Asia, Japan acted as the symbol of something both less concrete and larger than a single country. It remained a shadow on the wall of the American consciousness. The attention of Americans was clearly focused on Europe and their own backyard, the Caribbean. By the 1830s, though, a convergence of new conditions would reengage American attention with Japan, this time as a real entity with which it was necessary to deal.

While some of the early merchants may have looked to Japan and Asia as a market for American furs, it was, however, the growth of the whaling industry that really pushed the new country across the ocean by the 1830s. Driven by the need for oil and spermaceti in towns, like Boston, that hoped to introduce new creature comforts, American whaling ships regularly stalked the North Pacific. This brought them increasingly into contact with Asian lands, where crews bought provisions, stored up potable water, and sought shelter from the storms that ravaged the ironically named Pacific Ocean. Once a ship passed the Sandwich Islands (Hawaii), the first major landmass that the whalers encountered was Japan. Yet American ships were not allowed to port in Japan, due to the centuries-old maritime restrictions, even in order to provide shelter and treatment for shipwrecked mariners. That this was no idle proscription was shown by the capture of American sailors in the 1840s and the outraged American reaction to their confinement in Japan. At the same time, Americans had to figure out how to repatriate Japanese fishermen who occasionally washed up on American shores in the Pacific Northwest, as in the case of three castaways named Otokichi, Kyukichi, and Iwakichi, who landed in present-day Washington State in 1832. Legend and reality for the first time began to clash, and within a few decades both merchant and political circles began considering ways to formally open relations with the island nation.

Strategic concerns on the part of the growing nation provided yet another spur to American interest in Japan. As the U.S. Navy contemplated converting to coal-fired vessels in the mid-1800s, it recognized the need for stations in eastern Asia, Hawaii being too far eastward to provide coverage for the farthest voyages of American ships. This dovetailed with the interests of mail steamship–company owners, whose preferred route to

Shanghai, in China, passed right through Japan, which was believed to have significant coal stocks.[50] These beliefs led American naval leaders, politicians, and financiers to contemplate a more direct attempt to secure landing rights in Japan by the mid-1840s.

Well aware by this time of the Tokugawa maritime restrictions controlling trade, a group of New York financiers in 1837 sponsored a mission by the sailing ship *Morrison* to return a number of Japanese castaways picked up off the Philippines. Their real motive was to enter into negotiations with the government and gain landing and trading rights.[51] Once the *Morrison* made its first anchorage off Japan, the shogunate sensed a crisis and, for one of the few times in its history, acted upon a standing 1825 order to drive off foreign ships before they could make contact with Japanese. Antiquated land batteries fired upon the *Morrison* as it tried to enter Edo Bay. The civilian ship hastily turned around, its mission a failure. It was nearly a decade before Americans made another formal attempt.

Despite lacking direct contact, and perhaps being stimulated by the decidedly aggressive attempts by Japanese to keep their maritime restrictions intact, American interest in Japan continued to grow, though in comparison with other lands that interest was still minor. What interest there was and, equally important, what knowledge there was came from books, in an intriguing parallel with contemporary Japanese knowledge of America. For over a century in Europe as well as America, the main source on Japan was Englebert Kaempfer's three-volume *History of Japan,* first published in English in 1727.[52] Kaempfer was a German surgeon attached to the Dutch factory at Dejima from 1690 to 1692. Copies of this set of volumes existed in the United States in the early nineteenth century, one being held by the Library of Congress, and Commodore Matthew Perry consulted it before embarking on his voyage to Japan in 1852. Kaempfer's account was filled with geographical and scientific facts about Japan's flora and fauna, but it also contained colorful accounts of Japanese culture, politics, and daily life.

Equally influential in mid-nineteenth-century America was a slim volume, published in 1841, titled *Manners and Customs of the Japanese.* The putative author was Phillip Franz von Siebold, another German physician to the Dutch, who was resident in Nagasaki from 1823 to 1829. Siebold, who learned a fair amount of Japanese, made friends with some of the leading Western-studies scholars of the time, including the prolific Takano Choei. Siebold's scientific curiosity caused a minor crisis in Dutch-Japanese foreign relations, however, in 1828, when Siebold was discovered to have secreted away a number of maps of Japan, intending to carry them back to Europe. The bakufu had made it illegal for anyone to own a map without permission, and Siebold was imprisoned for a time and his maps confiscated. After being released, he penned an account of Japan, based on his travels and the records of a Dutch resident of Dejima in the late 1820s named Germaine Felix Meylan. Released in New York, the book became a best seller, being the only new information about Japan that had appeared since the early eighteenth century.[53] Although containing far less scientific material than Kaempfer's account, *Manners and Customs* described in detail the social, cultural, and political aspects of Tokugawa Japan. It was in part the realization that Japan had indeed isolated itself behind a seemingly impenetrable wall that suddenly heightened American interest in the hermit nation. What was lacking was direct contact of a sustained nature. That was soon to change.

The foreign, then, was experienced differently in Japan and the United States in the era of shadows and trinkets. In Japan, while Western objets d'art and other items of daily use, not American, found their way into the households and private collections of the samurai and merchant elite, the "foreign" was largely public, put on display in parades and festivals. It was thus made part of the Tokugawa-ordered public sphere, defanged but still exotic, employed to help define the power of both the shogunate and Japan vis-à-vis the outer world. In America, in contrast, the foreign was kept largely private, in the parlors of the wealthy and those who participated in the China trade. Japanese silks, porcelain, and other artifacts had no publicly defined role, no part in helping to create a shared American identity in the world. By the mid-1800s, however, all that was to change, as the two nations suddenly encountered each other in a way that destroyed old restraints and set both countries upon a new global path.

CHAPTER 2

Noble Adventurers

A S ASTONISHED JAPANESE fishermen watched the billowing sails of Commodore Matthew Perry's Black Ships approach the coast of central Japan in the hot summer of July 1853, the fishermen could not know that they and their country were about to be plunged into a new world. Over the centuries, the encounter between different cultures across the globe happened in many different ways, and Perry followed in a long line of maritime explorers charting new lands. While most of these global encounters were haphazard or accidental, Perry's government had sent him on an official mission to a specific land. Yet his own impact must be measured against that of those individual Japanese and Americans who came both before and after him, dramatically shaping American-Japanese relations.

Perry himself came near the end of the era of exploration that had propelled Westerners across the globe, their experiences forming the bulk of what was known about the "foreign." Some of these explorers were unwilling adventurers, such as castaways; others were soldiers of fortune seeking fabulous treasure or missionaries devoutly spreading the word of God. Many of the first explorers were drawn by images of far-off lands, some hoping to become rich and others being fascinated by the unknown.

The burst of cultural encounter really begins when images are replaced by living beings, when brave souls cross deserts or seas and begin to interact with other societies, changing those peoples and often being changed themselves. This period of the uncoordinated activities of individuals is shaped by those with a passion to create, who dream of serving as a bridge between two worlds and who are fired by a cosmopolitan impulse to expand their understanding of the world. Their tragedy is that they often help unwittingly to destroy that which they treasured. Such noble adventurers were found in both Japan and America in the middle of the nineteenth century and were in the vanguard of Japan's modernization, as the country self-consciously turned itself into a transition zone between its traditional Chinese-influenced culture and the new Western world. Yet even at this moment, cultural encounter took on varied shapes, its influence like the ripples of a pebble dropped in a pond. Let us begin with the pebbles.

First Contact

Within a few years of each other in the middle of the nineteenth century, an American and a Japanese were plunged into radically new worlds, one individual by choice, one not. The Japanese was a fourteen-year-old fisherman named Nakahama Manjirō, who was born in 1827. In June 1841, Manjirō and four companions were carried by the tides hundreds of miles away from Japan, coming to rest on an uninhabited volcanic isle in the Pacific. After six months, the small group was rescued by an American whaler out of New Bedford, Massachusetts, the *John Howland,* which was captained by a William Whitfield.[1] Whitfield dropped Manjirō's three fellow castaways off in Hawaii but took the teenager back with him to Fairhaven, Massachusetts. After completing a two-year journey to New England and after passing into another ocean almost entirely unknown to Japanese, Manjirō, nicknamed John, settled into Whitfield's modest captain's house near the sea. There, John lived for three years before embarking on a circuitous route home, finally arriving in 1851, a decade after leaving his shores.

Known by now as John Mung, Manjirō was versed in English and was a proficient ship's hand. Yet he had not served as a conduit of things Japanese to the New Englanders or sailors among whom he lived for nearly a decade. Manjirō's sojourn in America saw him attend the Fairhaven public school and attend church with the Whitfields, not to mention his working as a jack-of-all-trades on the Whitfield farm.[2] None of his recollections, which were mainly his testimony to shogunal officials on his return to Japan, indicate that his adopted family or American friends showed an interest in Manjirō's homeland, which we might consider surprising, seeing as how Manjirō was the first Japanese known to have lived in America. Seen in another light, this American reaction is an almost perfect reflection of the early years of the American-Japanese relationship, in which one side would be the teacher, the other the student.

Can we really believe that Manjirō never sat around the fire on a winter night, telling tales of his native Tosa domain (now Kōchi prefecture)? Of course he must have, but neither party thought it important to remember or write down what he said. Whatever he related was lost forever, making no ripple on the surface of American life. Rather, Manjirō was trained as a vessel of Western nautical and farming knowledge. His role, as understood by Whitfield and Manjirō himself, was to learn the skills necessary first to survive, then to return home, and finally perhaps to spread his new knowledge to his countrymen. In that sense, Manjirō was not unlike the Oriental fineries patronized by wealthy American elites: he was accepted and brought into their lives, but not to change them; rather, he was to be changed by them, Americanized and Christianized. He was a pebble without a ripple.

After working his way back across the Pacific as a boat steerer and a hand in charge of casks, important jobs by any standard, a new fate awaited Manjirō. Despite the traditional shogunate proscription on castaways returning to Japan, the Western encroachment of the past years had created a new sense of fear. Top policy makers—such as the young head of the Tokugawa shogunate, Abe Masahiro (1819–1857), and the lord of Manjirō's domain, Yamauchi Toyoshige (Yōdō; 1827–1872)—were hesitantly concluding that Japan had to respond in new ways to the world now pushing in at its boundaries.

Manjirō, therefore, not only was allowed back in but was not punished by the government. He was, however, ordered to undergo a full debriefing lasting over two months. This interrogation produced the first ripples

from his adventure. His home domain commissioned a profusely illustrated, detailed account of his travels abroad, *Hyōson kiryaku* (A Brief Account of Drifting Toward the Southeast, 1852). Although this account
contained information on the Ryukyus (Okinawa), Hawaii, and South
America, it was the account of America that most resonated among the
Japanese leadership who read copies of the book. Maps of the United
States, paintings and descriptions of the great city of Boston and its harbor, and accounts of New Bedford, all filled the four slim volumes. And
yet, it was mostly a dry, bare-bones account, including more detail on
nautical geography than on everyday life in America. Manjirō's recollections of New Bedford are drained of life; in them no individuals spring
forth, not even Captain Whitfield. Nothing is recorded of religion, children's games, or daily meals. It is a book designed solely to preserve the
unintended itinerary of the castaways.

Despite its circumscribed purview, the book nonetheless was blessed
with perfect timing. Within months of its circulation, Commodore Matthew C. Perry embarked on his first mission to Japan. Now in crisis mode,
the shogunate, being informed of Perry's approach, sent for Manjirō,
hoping to tap his unique knowledge. Soon afterward, he was enrolled as a
shogunal samurai, given a surname, Nakahama, and allowed to translate
English-language books and open a school. Manjirō was made public, so
to speak, in the same way inanimate Western cultural artifacts had been,
and was employed by the shogunate in the hopes of propping up its fal-
tering powers. In 1860, two years after the first American minister in Japan, Townsend Harris, had signed trade treaties with the Tokugawa
regime, the shogunate ordered Manjirō to accompany the first Japanese
mission abroad, in order to exchange ratified copies of the commercial
treaties. Sent to Washington, D.C., due to his knowledge of both sea-
faring and America, he briefly became a direct conduit between the two
nations.

Returning to Japan after the mission, Manjirō led a fairly quiet existence, but he never fully let go of his American experience, and later
pushed his son to become one of the early Western-style doctors in rapidly modernizing Meiji Japan. Manjirō, whose life spanned two cultures
and who played a unique role in introducing knowledge about America
to Japan, died in 1898, thirty years after the restoration overthrowing the

shogunate that had tried to use his knowledge to save itself and preserve Japan's traditions. Fittingly, in the very year of Manjirō's death, the first private group dedicated to cultural exchange between the United States and Japan, the American Friends' Association, was founded.

At almost the exact same time as Manjirō's last years in America, a castaway by choice became the first American to seek out Japan. American contact with Japan hitherto had been limited to passing ships and the knickknacks brought back home through indirect trade. In July 1848, however, Ranald MacDonald (1824–1894), a half-British, half-Chinook Indian born in the Oregon Territory, set himself adrift in a small boat from an American whaler off Japan's northern main island, Hokkaido. Mac-Donald was by his own admission pulled by the mystery of the secluded isles and impulsively decided to try and penetrate their veil.[3]

MacDonald was a fairly hapless adventurer. Shortly after casting himself away, he sighted a Japanese coastal boat and decided to swamp his whaleboat in the hopes of being picked up. The Japanese apparently didn't see him, and MacDonald had to climb back into his bark, having lost everything he brought with him. Managing to make landfall, he was promptly arrested by officials from the Matsumae domain, located at the very northern tip of the main Japanese island of Honshu. According to the maritime restrictions of the bakufu, Hokkaido was not the accepted foreign port of Nagasaki, nor was MacDonald a licensed Dutch trader; he thus had no justification for being in Japan. After journeying across the Pacific, MacDonald now encountered Japan from a variety of cells. Brought all the way to the southern end of Japan to Nagasaki for interrogation, he found that he was not even the first American to land on the fabled shores after all, for a group of fifteen mutineers from the whaler *Lagoda* were being held there as well.[4]

For seven months MacDonald languished inside a cell, though by his own account, he was well provisioned with pork and other Western-style foods derived from Dutch cooking. His most important relationship was with the government's interpreter, a samurai named Moriyama Einosuke, who was to play a critical role a decade later as the key translator between

Japanese officials and Western diplomats. MacDonald taught English to a select group of students, who were likely translators for the shogun's government, and endured hours of questioning on his background and conditions in America. Finally, in April 1849, bakufu officials transferred him to the Dutch factory at Dejima, in Nagasaki harbor, from which he was to be repatriated on the American frigate *Preble*. *Preble*, under the command of Lt. James Glynn, had come to rescue the mutineers of the *Lagoda*. To Glynn's surprise, the Japanese handed over another American, who had not been known to be stranded. His adventure over, MacDonald wrote that he happily embarked for "freer and more genial shores."[5]

Returning to America, MacDonald was silent about his experiences. His memoirs were published posthumously, and if he regaled his children or others in his orbit with tales of his time in Japan, we have no knowledge of it. Indeed, MacDonald's adventure, just like Manjirō's, played no role in creating a greater understanding of Japan in America. His adventure was not even mentioned in the brief press accounts of the *Preble*'s mission to Japan, and he was anonymously lumped in with the fifteen mutineers in a brief notice months later.[6] Not until the *New York Times* reviewed his memoirs in 1923 did MacDonald emerge from his anonymity, with the *Times* claiming, "Civilization is a debtor to Ranald MacDonald."[7] By then, of course, Japan and America had had over four decades of close interaction, and his account was of mere historical curiosity; there was nothing in it that could add to cross-cultural exchange.

However, MacDonald shared similar experiences with others in the small, unenviable group of foreigners to be imprisoned on Japan's shores during the waning days of official isolation. MacDonald most resembled perhaps the Russian Vasilii Golovnin, who was captured and held by the Japanese from 1811 to 1813 in response to Russian attempts to lay claim to Kunashiri, one of the Kurile Islands, which stretch north of Hokkaido up to the Kamchatka Peninsula. Although what we might term today a political prisoner, Golovnin forged a friendly relationship with his captors and, like MacDonald, added to Japan's knowledge of foreign countries, in this case, Russia. Golovnin also helped compile a Japanese-Russian dictionary and provided information on Western math, physics, and astronomy.[8] MacDonald does not seem to have provided nearly as useful information, but he did engage in long discussions with his captors and Moriyama, some of which must have helped prepare the bakufu for its encounter with American power just a few years hence.

At almost the same time that MacDonald was returning to his Pacific Northwest, Americans had another opportunity to encounter, or be encountered by, a Japanese in the twilight years of the Tokugawa era. Hamada Hikozo, born in 1837 in Harima, near present-day Kobe in central Japan, was another castaway who spent years in the United States. If Manjirō symbolized a Japanese encounter with America that initially had little impact on either party, Hamada, known as Joseph Heco, represented the fully internationalized life of late-nineteenth-century Japanese.

Heco was washed away while returning home from a coastal shipping voyage from Osaka to Edo in 1850.[9] Picked up by the *Auckland,* a bark destined for San Francisco, Hamada, only thirteen at the time of his rescue, and his companions were initially sent to China in 1851 to meet up with Commodore James Aulick's squadron, which was planning to try and open relations with Japan; Heco was a pawn in the proposed negotiations, and his return to Japan was intended to show American goodwill. As it turned out, Aulick was recalled and Heco returned with him to California. Languishing for another two years, he finally left for New York in July 1853, just as a new American squadron, under the command of Matthew Perry, reached Edo Bay.

"Adopted" by the San Francisco collector of customs, B. C. Sanders, Heco was brought to Baltimore and put in a Catholic school. Taken later to Washington, D.C., he was the first Japanese to meet American high officials, including President James Buchanan and Secretary of State Lewis Cass. More importantly, perhaps, Heco converted to Christianity, being the first Japanese to do so abroad. Christianity was at this time still strictly prohibited in Japan, and Heco's decision to convert, despite his desire ultimately to return home, suggests the magnitude of his transformation abroad. His changed identity was further revealed just before he left for Japan in 1858, when he became a naturalized American citizen, certainly the first Japanese on record to do so. This was in an era when Western nation-states were formalizing the very concept of citizenship and starting to employ passports, so perhaps the act was not as momentous then as it seems today. Nonetheless, as his memoirs attest, Heco saw himself as a new type of Japanese, one who identified as a global citizen yet at the same time remained connected to his national origins. Unlike Manjirō, who spent only a few years on American soil, Heco stayed for a six full years before joining an expedition, led by Lt. J. M. Brooke, to survey China and Japan.

And yet, in certain crucial ways, Heco and Manjirō painted strikingly similar pictures of their encounter with America. Although written four decades after the events it depicts, Heco's memoirs parallel Manjirō's account in the apparent absence of any American interest in Japan.[10] For all the rich detail in his book, Heco does not relate one instance when he shared information about Japan with his American counterparts, neither a story nor a description of daily life. Upon meeting him, American officials ask no questions and show no interest in who he is or what his homeland is like. Again, it strains credulity to believe that, in his six years in the United States, he kept silent about Japan, and yet that is how he (or his editor, James Murdoch) chose to portray his encounter with Americans. Although the first "accessible" representatives of a culture new to Americans, neither Manjirō nor Heco served as transmitters of new knowledge, at least as far as contemporary accounts attest. It would remain for an American, Commodore Perry to fill in that gap with his detailed account of his mission to Japan in 1853 and 1854.[11]

If, like Manjirō, Heco was the object of the apparent disinterest of Americans in his background, the two took very different routes after returning to Japan. Heco, in the eyes of the Americans now a countryman of theirs, enrolled as a translator in the service of the new consul general, Townsend Harris, who took up residence in Edo in 1858, two years after arriving in Japan. In this position, Heco met many of the main American and Japanese players responsible for creating the diplomatic relationship between the two countries. His later memoirs are spiced with reminiscences of Harris; Harris's secretary, Henry Heusken; the Japanese negotiator Mizuno Tadanori; and others. In yet another first, Heco joined the Western allied squadron that in July 1864 bombarded Shimonoseki, castle town of the Chōshū domain, in retaliation for Chōshū's firing on Western ships the previous year. From the deck of the USS *Wyoming*, Heco not only watched the attack but served as a political intelligence officer for the captain, relaying information about Chōshū, an anti-Tokugawa and anti-Western domain.[12]

After resigning from the U.S. Consular Service in 1861, Heco briefly turned to shipping and importing but soon returned to being a source of vital information to his native country. Even into the 1860s, knowledge in Japan about current events abroad was secondhand and minimal at best. The Tokugawa bakufu was so concerned about its lack of information on foreign events that it began a series of attempts to translate Western newspapers, locating the efforts in its Institute for the Study of Barbarian Books.[13] Some current foreign news was available, however, in the treaty ports of Yokohama and Nagasaki, which had been opened in 1859 and contained their own merchant newspapers, all in English.

Into this emerging community stepped Joseph Heco, who started in the spring of 1864 the first Japanese-language paper produced by and for private individuals.[14] Heco took as his sources the English-language newspapers available from mainly British ships docking in Yokohama. His biweekly publication was called initially *Shinbunshi*, later changed to *Kaigai Shinbun* (Overseas Newspaper).[15] While it lasted a mere twenty-four issues, the *Kaigai Shinbun* was the first hand-delivered paper aimed at a domestic audience. Unlike its domestic predecessor, the ubiquitous Japanese woodblock (a penny broadsheet known as *kawaraban*), Heco's paper avoided the gossip and inaccuracies prevalent in the age of shadows. His translated stories were from mainstream British papers and included maps, which themselves helped, if ephemerally, to increase Japanese geographic knowledge. Heco, the only one of Japan's press founders to have lived abroad, thus helped ignite the country's press tradition, which soon blossomed and cross-pollinated with the Western-language newspapers published in the treaty ports.

Perhaps Joseph Heco's final contribution to Pacific encounter was the publication of his memoirs, *The Narrative of a Japanese*, in 1894, the same year that Ranald MacDonald died at the age of sixty-nine. Undoubtedly substantially rewritten by editor James Murdoch, the autobiography was of course produced in a Japan radically different than the one Heco recounted. To some degree, Heco himself helped bring about the changes that made the Japan of his youth seem like a vanished dream. Whether as a young man living in the United States and becoming a naturalized American citizen and Christian or as a translator in the early days of Japanese-American treaty relations or as the publisher of the first private newspaper in Japan, Heco blazed a path along which Japanese internationalized themselves, created a new identity for themselves, and turned their energies back into reforming their own culture. And perhaps it is just as fitting that Heco's two-volume memoirs were published at the tail end of the period of the noble adventurer. In succeeding decades, the nature of cultural relations between Japan and the United States would permanently transform, as the first formal exchange organizations emerged and struggled to find their voice. All that, however, would be dependent on the two nations' finding common ground to open relations.

Enter Perry

Commodore Matthew C. Perry has been enshrined in history as the formidable soul that "opened Japan." Yet if his action was not sui generis, it was indeed epochal, for its effect was not limited like that of a pebble in a pond but instead spread ripples into every nook of Japanese life and a great deal of American life as well. The account of Perry's two visits to Japan, in July 1853 and March 1854, are too well known to repeat here. Indeed, they are one of the most enduring, if not indestructible, stories of American history: American warships, forever known to Japanese as the Black Ships, pry open an island kingdom closed for centuries to the West.

Few realize that when Perry first arrived in Japan in the summer of 1853, his "squadron" consisted of but four ships, only two of them steam powered. Moreover, Perry's officers had almost no contact with Japanese officials during the week the ships anchored in Edo Bay, and the commodore left Japanese waters a mere nine days after arriving, but not before handing over a letter from President Millard Fillmore. No doubt the only piece of paper from the Fillmore administration that is remembered today, the letter pledged friendship with the Japanese and requested the opening of relations. Perry's own naval instructions, which he also passed over to the Japanese, were to enter into negotiations with the Tokugawa government on a treaty of amity between the two nations.[16]

As Perry sailed away, Japanese were unsure of the import of his visit. On the face of it, there was every reason for them to suppose that Perry might not return the following spring as promised. After all, a previous U.S. attempt to open relations, in 1846, failed when Commodore James Biddle was shoved back into his gig by a mere Japanese sailor, and it had taken seven years for the Americans to return. Yet no matter the odds against seeing Perry again, the visit shattered Japanese complacency about their safety, which was the real impact of Perry's first landing. Japanese officials and commoners alike were in awe of the superiority of a people who could create such Black Ships and sail them across the ocean. For shogunal leaders, Perry's demands were a national security, and soon political, issue.

As for Americans, the literate public had been expecting news from the Far East for well over a year. The Japan Expedition's departure had been announced in the newspapers in March 1852, and starting in August the following year, Perry's dispatches back to Washington received prominent play.[17] Americans were more interested in the adventure of opening up a closed land than in the land itself. Few Americans had any material interest in the expedition, which was pushed by economic and security incentives, such as searching for coaling stations for whalers, mail ships, and of course the U.S. Navy. What captured the public imagination was the image of Americans flexing their maritime muscle, treading into lands surrendered decades ago by the Europeans, except for the irrelevant Dutch.

In Japan, of course, the level of interest was intense. The intervening eight months between Perry's departure and return were a time of tension, a sort of "phony war" in which the country could do nothing but wait. The Tokugawa government had compounded the weakness it had shown in failing to drive off Perry's ships, by polling the entire class of feudal lords in the country as to what it should do if he actually had the nerve to return. Polling had never been done before, since the Tokugawa shogunate's legitimacy was tied precisely to its supposedly absolute control of foreign affairs.[18] In response, the country's feudal lords ducked the issue, having little desire to risk their necks for the increasingly desperate Tokugawa, though some of the lords scented blood in the water.

The waiting did not last forever and, in mid-March 1854, the barbarians indeed returned. This was proof that the world had finally changed, and the shogun, the "barbarian-quelling generalissimo," once again proved powerless to protect the realm. This time, as Perry rounded the headland off Uraga on March 8, 1854, his flotilla had been doubled, to nine ships. With penny prints of American warships again circulating throughout Edo, the shogunate felt backed into a corner and was now ready to surrender centuries of authority and tradition in a vain hope of limiting the damage both internally and externally. Formal negotiations with the Americans commenced the following week, and by March 31 the imposing commodore had disembarked his flagship, rowing ashore to sign the Treaty of Amity and Friendship, also known as the Treaty of Kanagawa (as well as the Perry Treaty), with a number of low-ranking shogunal officials.

This first formal agreement between Japan and a foreign power was quickly followed by nearly identical pacts with Great Britain, Holland, Russia, and France, thereby seeming to mark the funeral of Japan's maritime restrictions policy. Yet the treaty was, in the end, a very limited agreement, concerned primarily with the provision of stores to U.S. ships and the succor of vessels in distress.[19] The only American allowed into the country under the provisions of the treaty was to be a consul, who was to be isolated a week's ride distant from the shogun's capital in Shimoda, a tiny fishing village at the southern tip of the Izu Peninsula. Encounter between the two cultures was unlikely to be promoted by this "opening" of maritime relations, which is exactly how the Japanese government wanted it.

Yet in its very existence, Perry's treaty nonetheless caused a tidal wave of reaction in Japan and a smaller surge in America. For Japanese, this seemed to be a moment of crisis, of life and death. The shogun's capital, Edo, was flooded with prints of the foreign intruders. The American commodore was portrayed as a devil, or a Japanese goblin known as a *tengu,* with an obscenely long, phallically inspired nose (the mark of the *tengu*).[20] His Black Ships belched brimstone and were decorated with equally ferocious animal faces on their bows and sterns. These popular images, passed by hand or sold in the numerous bookstores dotting Edo, helped stoke the hysteria that greeted Perry's return visit. To ordinary Japanese, the outside world could no longer be kept at bay by safely escorting it through the streets of the capital, like the shogun's white Vietnamese elephant of long ago or the Dutch on their occasional visits to Edo Castle. This encounter was unwanted, uncontrollable, and menacing.

Compounding this fear was the terror of technology never before seen, the steamships bristling with cannons larger than any in Japan. Just one of Perry's warships had more firepower than almost all of Japan's shore batteries combined. And since the commodore wisely chose not to approach the shogun's capital directly, no one would ever know whether the floating batteries in Edo Bay, batteries that had been constructed at breakneck speed between Perry's visits, could have repelled the barbarian. To the more foresighted bakufu officials, however, this terrifying American technology could also quite possibly become their savior instead of their executioner. Thus, bakufu draftsmen made careful drawings of almost every inch of Perry's ships, his armament, and the gifts brought by the barbarians. These last included the first telegraph and the now legendary one-quarter-size steam-engine and cars, which the delighted Japanese officials took turns riding. It is no stretch to say that Perry's visit ignited a technology boom in Japan, with the more perspicacious domains promoting gunnery and forge building, while hitherto ignored scholars of things Western now found themselves in demand at all levels of government.

There was of course no equivalent shock to the body politic of the United States in the wake of the Perry mission. Nonetheless, Perry's success brought forth a bumper crop of books and articles regarding Japan, foremost of which was the commodore's own three-volume history. His *Narrative of the Expedition of an American Squadron to the China Seas and Japan, Performed in the years 1852, 1853, and 1854* contained a minutely detailed recounting of the entire voyage, not merely the visit to Japan. Published by the U.S. Printing Office and lavishly illustrated, the book immediately became a best seller and the standard U.S. reference work on Japan. It finally supplanted Englebert Kaempfer's two-century-old account, as well as that of Phillip Franz von Siebold from the 1840s, *Manners and Customs of the Japanese*.

Yet Perry's account, for all its popularity, did not move much beyond the limitations of earlier books. After all, Siebold and Kaempfer had interpreted Japan through the lens of the Dutch confines at Nagasaki, garnering their information from less-than-forthcoming bakufu officials, while Perry's account was based on a similarly limited purview of Japan, seeing it from above, so to speak, from the line of sight of diplomatic negotiations conducted over a period of several weeks. But interest in that "double-bolted land," as Herman Melville so memorably described Japan *Moby-Dick*, was roused nonetheless, and popular press reports, along with unofficial accounts of Perry's mission, such as Bayard Taylor's *A Visit to India, China, and Japan in the Year 1853*, fed the public imagination.[21] In reality, the encounter between Japan and America was still little changed from the era of images and shadows before Perry, Heco, and Ranald MacDonald. It would require constant contact between Japanese and Americans for encounter truly to develop. Just such a world was created by the next diplomatic agreement between Edo and Washington.

Permanent Contact

Following the provisions of Perry's Treaty of Kanagawa, Washington dispatched a consul to Japan the year after the commodore's visit. Intensive lobbying of President Franklin Pierce and Secretary of State William Marcy had won for Townsend Harris this dubious honor. Harris, a failed New York businessman, hoped to make his name as the man who opened Japan to American trade. After nearly two years of effort, suffering illness both real and imagined, using bluster and scarcely veiled threats, and fighting off constant attempts by the shogunate to isolate him, Harris succeeded in forcing the Japanese to sign the first commercial treaty in their history, in late July 1858.[22]

The most important feature of the U.S.-Japan Treaty of Amity and Commerce (colloquially known as the Harris Treaty), at least from the vantage point of cultural relations, was an article allowing American merchants to reside in seven approved Japanese ports and cities. In the end, only the town of Yokohama became a significant site, at least until the port of Kobe opened in 1868, but despite the attempts of the shogunate to maintain a boundary between their subjects and Westerners, Americans and Japanese now came face to face in a way unimaginable just a few years earlier. In this respect, then, the opening of Yokohama to trade and foreign residence, on July 1, 1859, perhaps marks the dawn of a new era in Japan's cultural history.

What brought Japanese and Americans together at Yokohama, of course, was trade. None of the rather rough American traders or wary Japanese in the port thought much about learning from each other. Yet inevitably, mystery or, perhaps better said, ignorance resulted in curiosity. Even so, it was from the beginning an uneven and often misleading encounter. The Japanese were confronting just one minor segment of American society, mainly traders and sailors, while the Americans in Japan were constrained linguistically and geographically from experiencing anything representing the totality of Japan. Yokohama was not an "open" city, for the bakufu had not only attempted to seal off the foreigners from the rest of Japan but also dictated that only those merchants who were licensed by the government could actually live in the town. Moreover, the Americans were not the only foreigners in the treaty ports but were part of a larger group of outsiders, and Japanese came face to face with Americans as part of that larger pool.

Nonetheless, Japanese writers who attempted to interpret these interlopers focused a great deal on the Americans, no doubt since they were countrymen of the great Commodore Perry. One such writer was Hashimoto Sadahide, a prolific artist-writer whose three-volume *Record of Things Seen and Heard at the Open Port of Yokohama,* published in 1862, remains the best-known contemporary account of the treaty port. In the book he provides several pictures of Americans, along with descriptions of their way of life. For Sadahide, as for others, the Americans were always slightly set apart, since it was they who had first forced the shogun to relax the maritime restrictions. Perhaps Japanese really couldn't distinguish between Europeans and Americans in the flesh, but in the popular imagination of the Japanese, the few Americans in their country loomed large as the harbingers of a new world.

For Americans back across the Pacific, of course, Japan remained but a faraway image. However, within a year of the opening of Yokohama, ordinary Americans were presented with the chance to see in the flesh representatives of the land described in U.S. newspapers. A shogunal embassy, the first ever to be dispatched to a Western nation, set off for America to exchange ratified versions of the U.S.-Japan commercial treaty and ar-

rived in late April 1860. The embassy consisted of a group of senior foreign affairs officials plus a number of young students, including Fukuzawa
Yukichi, who was to go on to become one of the best-known intellectuals
in Japan. Landing in San Francisco, the large group took a three-week
transcontinental train trip to Washington, D.C., where they met President James Buchanan in the White House on May 20 and were hosted at
a gala ball.[23] Wherever the Japanese went in America, they were feted and
followed by large crowds, with women and children pushing forward to
try and shake hands with the dignitaries. One of the young clerks on the
mission, known as "Tommy" to readers of American newspapers, became
a favorite of society ladies and reporters alike, earning himself mentions
in various dispatches and even becoming the focus of a brief scandal over
the morals of the women crowding around the young Japanese.[24]

A steady stream of news reports throughout the spring followed the
Japanese journey to New York by way of Baltimore and Philadelphia.
On June 18, accompanied by a 650-man honor guard, the Japanese ambassadors paraded down Manhattan's Broadway for a reception by the
governor and mayor. The spectacle inspired Walt Whitman to pen the following lines:

> Over sea, hither from Niphon,
> Courteous princes of Asia, swart-cheek'd princes,
> First comers, guests, two-sworded princes,
> Lesson-giving princes. . . .
> This day they ride through Manhattan.[25]

For the first time, kimono-clad and sword-girded Japanese appeared
in city after major American city. To Americans high and low alike, it
was a cause for national pride to be the first Western nation to host an official embassy from a mysterious land that had been closed for over two
centuries, since before America was even settled by colonists, and that
now was forced into the world largely through American efforts. For the
Japanese, it must have seemed a bit like the world was turned upside
down, for now they, strangers in a strange land, were reenacting the very
role that they had long forced the Dutch to play—as objects of mob interest, paraded through city streets. Yet the tumultuous reception undoubt-

edly played into their beliefs that they had a special relationship with America.

Back home, the positive view that Japanese held of Americans was further influenced by the increasingly aggressive behavior of the British during the last decade of Tokugawa rule in the 1860s. Though it was Matthew Perry and Townsend Harris who had first engaged Japan in diplomacy, the British soon took the lead in treaty relations, having the largest presence in Asia, the most traders in Japan, the greatest amount of military force, and the most bombastic consuls, as well, in Rutherford Alcock and Harry Parkes. Anti-British feeling was exacerbated when British warships in 1863 bombed the capital of the renegade domain of Satsuma, in southern Kyushu, and later Shimonoseki, at the far western tip of the main island of Honshu, in response to attacks on British property and citizens. It was not lost on Japanese officials that the Americans in no way fully supported Britain's punitive policy, even when a U.S. naval vessel joined the mainly British flotilla attacking Shimonoseki. One reason for this was that Townsend Harris was dead set on protecting his own treaty, which had established the whole Japanese-Western trading relationship. Harris's support for the Tokugawa leaders was continued by his successor, Robert Pruyn, who seemed, if anything, more critical of British diplomats. And yet, in the end, the Tokugawa could not count too much on the Americans during the turbulent decade of the 1860s, since the Civil War was tearing apart the land of Perry and Harris.

In any case, American support of the shogunate was a losing proposition. Japan's political world was irrevocably changed by the arrival of the Westerners, and long-standing domestic grievances against the Tokugawa regime exploded during the 1860s into an antibakufu movement led by the great "outer" domains, primarily Satsuma, in southern Kyushu, and Chōshū, in western Honshu. These powerful domains had never been fully trusted by the Tokugawa, and while they had been allowed almost complete autonomy, officials from these domains were also prevented from holding any offices in the bakufu administration itself. Such restrictions stoked resentments that lingered for generations.

The general weakening of bakufu administrative authority in the mid-nineteenth century, combined with the appearance of weakness in the face of Perry, Harris, and other Westerners, gave the antibakufu great lords the opportunity to try and force changes in the centuries-old political equilibrium that marked Tokugawa domestic politics.[26] Internal leadership struggles between the senior councillors, who traditionally were the highest-level bureaucrats in the shogunate, and powerful Tokugawa family–related individuals further weakened bakufu decision making. Several attempts in the 1860s to forge an alliance between the bakufu and the imperial court also collapsed due to bureaucratic infighting and the inability of all parties to agree to a new set of political boundaries.

Further compounding the political uncertainty was the rise of a new breed of nationalist samurai, who called themselves *shishi,* or "men of high purpose." Given that they were steeped in proimperial ideology and led by disaffected middle- and lower-level samurai, it is unclear whether they were motivated more by their antiforeign views or their anti-Tokugawa stance. Chōshū samurai, in particular, took the lead in antishogunal activity, aided by such charismatic figures as Sakamoto Ryoma (1835–1867) of the isolated Tosa domain in southern Shikoku Island. After Chōshū broke all precedent and attempted to take control of the Imperial Palace in 1863, the bakufu launched a punitive campaign against that rebel domain the following year. Edo's success, and its evident willingness to use force against domains that considered themselves autonomous, soon led to an alliance between the outer domains of Satsuma and Chōshū, an alliance that made a pyrrhic victory out of the Tokugawa exertions.

Worrying about the new anti-Tokugawa coalition and feeling that Chōshū had not yet been tamed, the shogunate launched an ill-advised second war against the domain in 1866. This time, Chōshū's shrewd use of Western-style infantry decisively defeated the traditionally led samurai of the shogun. Withdrawing in disgrace, the Tokugawa left their centuries-old authority in tatters. Their enemies were emboldened, and dashing young samurai activists such as Satsuma's Okubo Toshimichi and Saigo Takamori now joined forces with Chōshū's Takasugi Shinsaku and Kido Koin and imperial courtiers such as Sanjo Sanetomi and Iwakura Tomomi. The new, young shogun, Tokugawa Yoshinobu, could not marshal the forces necessary to oppose this constellation of anti-Tokugawa groups. After giving up the shogunal position in November 1867, Yoshinobu and the Tokugawa were displaced by a Satsuma-Chōshū coup d'état in January 1868. The new leaders, samurai and aristocrats all, quickly proclaimed the formation of a new imperial government, which was headed by the sixteen-year-old Emperor Mutsuhito.

This "revolution" of the young samurai activists ushered in the Meiji (Enlightened Rule) period. Its first years were a highly uncertain time of negotiating a domestic political settlement and fighting straggling Tokugawa loyalists, particularly in the northern part of the country. At the same time, the new leadership was leery lest their weakness lead to further Western demands for concessions, even from their putative supporters. The fact that American representatives in Japan had stayed largely loyal to the Tokugawa did not endear them to the new imperial government, which found its staunchest Western sympathizers in the British.

The key political issue in Meiji Japan was at the same time a cultural one: what kind of country would Japan have to become in order to preserve its independence from the West? The "unequal treaties" signed back in 1858 maintained Japanese territorial integrity and political autonomy, though the country's foreign trade was highly regulated. Within just a few years, in fact, revision of the 1858 commercial treaties became the prime diplomatic goal of the government. In order to try and secure this goal, another major embassy to the West was dispatched, this one headed by the court noble Iwakura Tomomi and including top leaders Okubo Toshimichi and Kido Koin. The so-called Iwakura Mission spent the years 1872 and 1873 abroad, mostly in America, England, France, Germany, and Russia.[27] Once the ambassadors realized the depth of political opposition they faced in Western capitals, they quickly dropped their initial diplomatic goal of renegotiating the treaties and instead focused on investigating the sources of Western power. Unintentionally, then, the Iwakura Mission became an epochal event for the country that hastened its modernization.

The mission spent almost eight months in the United States, far longer than anywhere else, and its members investigated nearly every aspect of American life. Their encounter began the moment they landed at San Francisco, for after a citywide reception (similar to the welcome given to the 1860 embassy), they embarked on a transcontinental railroad journey, visiting the Great Salt Lake, getting snowbound in the Rockies, receiving the keys to the city of Chicago, and finally reaching the East Coast. When the embassy arrived in Boston, its members were hosted by Harvard University at a banquet presided over by university president Charles William Eliot and graced with a poem by Oliver Wendell Holmes Sr. and a speech by Ralph Waldo Emerson.[28] Months spent in Europe followed the American sojourn and, upon the diplomats' return to Japan, Okubo and the other leaders agreed that Japan would have to change radically its administrative, economic, and even social systems in order to achieve a position of equality with the West. Thus truly began the sweeping transformations of Meiji.

It is impossible to convey completely the magnitude of the cultural changes in Japan during the Meiji period. It is undoubtedly true that for most Japanese, especially those in rural areas, the rhythm of daily life changed little from what it had been for centuries. In cities and semiurban areas, however, the years after 1872 witnessed a dizzying kaleidoscope of importation and adaptation. Exposure to a critical mass of things Western, including the presence of foreigners in the trading ports and of repatriated Japanese students and businessmen, proved sufficient to permanently alter Japanese civilization.

During the Meiji period, Japanese were transfixed with the "West," and not just America, for inspiration and guidance. Not surprisingly, the wave of Westernization that began sweeping Japan in the 1870s had a distinctly English component. Socially at least, Great Britain and Japan would seem to have natural affinities, for both were status-based, hierarchically ordered polities run by hereditary aristocracies. And indeed, at elite levels, Japanese and British aristocrats formed natural bonds. The Meiji government, while eclectically borrowing bureaucratic and institutional forms from a variety of Western models, hewed closely to the British modes of royalty and aristocracy, including peerage ranks and modes of ceremonial dress. Whereas just a few years prior Japanese aristocrats filed into the imperial precincts garbed in ancient robes, now they lined up in military dress to be greeted by their young emperor, himself sporting ribbons, medals, and epaulets. Yet despite the Japanese propinquity to British social models, America continued to play an important role in the transformations of daily life in Meiji Japan. It is difficult to try and disentangle the strands of foreign importation, to try and unearth a specifically American flavor to some of these changes. Nonetheless, much of what the Japanese encountered and adopted that changed their lifestyle was brought, interpreted even, by Americans.

So much changed, so much was eagerly grabbed, used, and then discarded, that life in urban areas during Meiji seems like a fast-forwarded film. There was, for example, the first baby carriage in Japan. Purchased initially by the great intellectual Fukuzawa Yukichi during his 1860 mission to the United States, such carriages were imported to Japan starting in 1879.[29] Despite being a symbol of wealth for modernized, urban families, the baby carriage never supplanted the traditional Japanese manner of carrying infants, who usually remained securely swaddled to their mothers into the twenty-first century. Six decades after its first appearance, the writer Kurt Singer could all but overlook the carriage, celebrating instead the timeworn custom of a child "sharing in a half-drowsy state" the "warmth" of the mother "and her rhythm."[30]

Other American imports, however, fared better and were eagerly absorbed by a populace that was becoming deeply cosmopolitan in taste and outlook yet never lost its love for amusement. One such import was baseball, brought back home in 1871 by Hiraoka Hiroshi, a Japanese student who was sent to study America's railroads and who played on his company team. Organized by Hiraoka at Japan's first railway station in downtown Tokyo, the "Shinbashi Club" was the prototype not only for the professional and school teams that soon emerged but also for the semi-professional company leagues that still grace most Japanese businesses.[31]

Japan's material and food culture was deeply affected by the rage for things Western. As is well known, Japanese men in particular began wearing Western-style clothing to work, while women's hairstyles shifted from the highly stylized patterns of the Tokugawa era to much simpler, and easier to manage, cuts. Changes to the Japanese diet came more slowly, yet these became important symbols of modern, urban living, as Japanese began to eat meat and bread, drink milk and beer, and patronize upscale Western restaurants. The new trends perfectly encapsulated the globalized world into which Japan was entering. For example, it was a Swedish-born American, William Copeland, who opened with his German partner Japan's first beer factory in 1869. Within just a few decades, Japanese-produced beer would become the country's second-favorite alcoholic drink, after the indigenous rice wine called *sake*.

More soberly, perhaps, Japan's first coffeehouse opened in Tokyo in 1889, and its unique, if short, history perfectly captures the confluence of different cultures during Meiji. The coffeehouse's owner-operator was a Japanese of Chinese descent named Tei Eikei (Zheng Yongqing). Tei was uniquely suited to act as a cultural mediator in the mid-Meiji period. He was the descendant of Chinese interpreters in Nagasaki, those who had played a role throughout the Tokugawa centuries in maintaining trade between Japan and the outer world. After studying Buddhism in Kyoto, Tei traveled to America, where he enrolled at Yale University. Sickness cut short his studies, though, and after returning home, he worked in both the Japanese Foreign and Finance Ministries during the period of treaty revision in the 1880s. After fire destroyed his home, he rebuilt it and opened a coffeehouse like the ones he had seen in America. Despite its novelty, Kahi Cha Kan (Coffee and Tea House) did not fare well, perhaps due to the economic stringencies of the 1880s, when a government deflation plan caused widespread distress. It closed a mere two years after its opening, and in 1892 Tei returned to America, where he stayed until the end of his life.[32] This failure, though, did not end the experiment, and increasingly in the 1900s, Western-style food and drink establishments sprang up in urban areas.

America figured prominently in the growing Japanese wonder at Western technical devices. Japan, of course, had been largely cut off from the technological revolution that swept through the West starting in the 1600s. The Tokugawa had allowed into their realm a limited number of science books, but when Commodore Perry landed in 1853, there were no railroads, telegraphs, large-scale forges, street lighting, or the like in Japan. Japanese hunger for technology was amply supplied by American models. Newspapers, for example, offered their readers the latest in American ingenuity, such as a description of an 1872 prototype of a portable fire extinguisher, complete with illustration, explaining its mechanics in simple terms and noting that it came in two sizes, for thirty and fifty dollars, respectively.[33] It was the same with motion pictures, photographic slides, the pasteurization of milk, and the electric motor for Japan's first elevator, in the famous Twelve-Story Tower in Asakusa, which survived from 1890 until its spectacular collapse in the Great Kanto Earthquake of 1923.[34] Rightly or wrongly, all these devices were described as American inventions, thus solidifying the image of America as the pacesetter of modernity.

While we should not overestimate the Japanese relationship to the United States in the early and mid-Meiji period, given the importance of Europe to Japanese leaders, it is true that news of major events in America routinely filled Japanese newspapers. For example, the Great Chicago Fire of October 1871 received prominent play in the Japanese press, which was not surprising, given the tragic Japanese experience of major urban conflagrations.[35] In this case, an article on the devastation in Chicago went on to describe new building techniques, such as the use of marble and sandstone in construction, a novelty for Japan, which overwhelmingly built its structures out of wood and pottery shingles, but was soon to transform the face of its cities.

At times America stood out distinctly in the Japanese consciousness amid the flood of foreign influences. One such moment was in the mid-1870s with the publication of Kume Kunitake's *Bei-O kairan jikki*, the official record of the aforementioned Iwakura Mission, for which he had been a secretary.[36] Despite having to wade through Kume's difficult prose, Japanese readers made his account a best seller, and thus a whole new audience was introduced to detailed descriptions of American life and lists of vital statistics on the United States. While earlier reports on America had contained brief mentions of Washington, D.C. and New York, Japanese could now read Kume's descriptions of Chicago, the Rocky Mountains, the Great Salt Lake, and Boston, all areas where the mission had visited. Moreover, Kume's encyclopedic account dramatized for literate Japanese just what their country faced in dealing with powerful nations like America and in essence explained why their leaders were choosing the path Japan was now embarked upon.

Coincident to the appearance of Kume's diary was the publication of a three-volume work titled *Meriken-shi* (History of America) in 1873. This account provided even more information on the nearly century-old country and was one of a number of books on America for an audience hungry to encounter new ideas. By 1873, just five years after the Meiji Restoration, the scholar Obata Tokujirō translated portions of Alexis de Tocqueville's classic *Democracy in America* in his book *Jōboku jiyū ron*.[37] This was followed by translations of Ralph Waldo Emerson's philosophy, whose idea of transcendentalism was not entirely foreign to a Japanese audience raised on Buddhist concepts.

Providing a more pragmatic take on American life was a translation of a work by that quintessential American, Benjamin Franklin, whose *Autobiography* represented for Meiji elites the encyclopedic, can-do attitude they were adopting to change their own society. Franklin's *Autobiography* was influential enough to be read by the emperor himself and assigned as a sort of text at the court.[38] American literature, too, appeared in translation during the middle Meiji period, including the poetry of Walt Whitman and Henry Wadsworth Longfellow and the Midwestern stories of Mark Twain. All of these translations provided another, if indirect, way that Japanese encountered new concepts, such as independence, freedom, democracy, and equality.[39]

Translations of Emerson and his peers represented the first wave of literary and philosophical enthusiasm for America in modern Japan, a period when Westernization appealed to Japanese intellectuals intoxicated with the spectacle of a Japan free from feudal constraints.[40] During the late 1860s and early 1870s, writers such as Fukuzawa Yukichi and Mori Arinori popularized descriptions of American-style liberty, descriptions that perfectly reflected Japan's growing internationalization.[41] Fukuzawa (1835–1901) was perhaps the best-known intellectual in nineteenth-century Japan. He had been picked for two missions abroad to America, and his facility with English led him to write numerous best sellers about the West. In 1866, two years before the fall of the Tokugawa shogunate, Fukuzawa published *Seiyō jijō* (Conditions of the West), which detailed American political, economic, and military systems. Arguing that Western-style education was the prerequisite to creating a modern society that could maintain its independence, Fukuzawa established in the same year the Keio Academy, one of the first schools to break from the traditional *terakoya*, or Buddhist temple school, model that dominated Japan during the Tokugawa period. Fukuzawa's focus on the development of the individual was not solely American in inspiration but was part of his broader interpretation of Western society. Formulating one of the first modern Japanese expressions of democratic theory, he wrote in his pathbreaking *The Encouragement of Learning* (1872–1876), "Our Creator did not create men above men, nor set men below men." Fukuzawa was also one of the first advocates of female equality in Japan, taking a daring position in an overwhelmingly male-dominated society.

Mori Arinori (1847–1889), another of the era's great public intellectuals, hailed from the anti-Tokugawa domain of Satsuma, and after spending two years in Britain as a student, he arrived in America in 1867. There, he lived for a year with the Brotherhood of the New Life, a utopian colony in Brocton, New York. During his sojourn in America he was impressed most by the American education system, especially Horace Mann's advocacy of universal education. In 1871 Mori was appointed as Japan's first diplomatic envoy to Washington and, soon after arriving, published a study of American political and social life.[42] Like many Japanese of his era who were to live or study abroad, he translated into practice the lessons of his sojourns. Two years after his return to Japan, he founded Hitotsubashi University in Tokyo in 1875, and in the following year, he established the Meirokusha (the Meiji Six Society), a group of leading intellectuals who gathered to debate modernization and Japan's future; the group was the equivalent to America's salon culture, best represented by the Saturday Club of Boston.[43] In 1885, Mori became the first Meiji minister of education and argued for establishing secular education and for abandoning the Japanese language in favor of English. Like his fellow intellectual Fukuzawa, he was a firm advocate for the social emancipation of women. Yet, in a sign of the domestic tensions unleashed by the seemingly nonstop nature of modernization, Mori's radical views alienated tradition-revering nationalist fanatics, one of whom assassinated him on the day the Western-style Meiji Constitution was promulgated in 1889.

Indeed, part of the stresses caused by the reforms promoted by Mori and others came from the fact that formerly fixed boundaries between Japanese and foreigners crumbled like dust. Japanese now could encounter Westerners in the streets of Yokohama or the emperor's new capital city, itself renamed from Edo to Tokyo (often spelled "Tokio" by most Americans in the 1870s), as well as in a number of other port cities like Kobe and Hakodate. Most dramatically, however, Japanese, for the first time in centuries, could travel outside the boundary of their island nation and encounter the foreign while abroad.

Since a trip to America was far easier than a journey to Europe, most of the Japanese students and travelers in early Meiji went to the United States. In stark contrast to Tokugawa times, however, during the Meiji era it was the oligarchy that led the way in exporting its sons and daughters, if temporarily. This, of course, continued a tradition started by the domains of Chōshū and Satsuma during the last years of feudalism, when student groups were sent abroad, often surreptitiously, to Europe.[44] The practice also followed from one of the first statements of the new regime, in the 1868 Five Article Oath—"Knowledge shall be sought throughout the world"—a phrase already made good by the endeavors of the Iwakura Mission.

Many of modern Japan's leaders were educated in America during the last quarter of the nineteenth century, especially once the Japanese government provided funds for young scholars to study abroad, and in their travels we perhaps can see the growth of future educational exchange programs. The Japanese press, in its infancy in the 1870s, kept in the national spotlight those setting forth from Japan on officially sponsored voyages. The media treated these youngsters not merely as representatives of Japan but as the vanguard of Japan's attempt to absorb new knowledge from around the globe; for example, a series of articles featured two groups of students leaving for America in early 1872, five students to study mining and six to undertake farming studies.[45] But despite the press attention, those who traveled abroad in these early days were essentially free agents. They were neither watched over nor protected overseas by any established organization, nor did the Japanese government select or directly fund students in any type of formal program. In this sense, these first students were classic adventurers, being almost completely on their own after arriving in America.

One of the most interesting of the early foreign-trained students was Yamakawa Kenjirō, who became a proselytizer of modernization after 1868. Born in the year of Perry's treaty, 1854, he was the third son of the principal retainer of the feudal lord of Aizu domain. During the Meiji Restoration, Aizu was perhaps the most virulently pro-Tokugawa domain, and it fought a tenacious, though losing, civil war with the imperial forces. Yamakawa, just fourteen at the time of the war, joined the Byakkotai (White Tiger Brigade), a band of adolescent soldiers who became immortalized for committing group suicide during one of the key battles. Yamakawa was too young to take the battlefield, however, and escaped from the domain and the subsequent punishment visited on its samurai.

Yet just four years later, in 1872, when Yamakawa was eighteen, the new regime allowed him to travel to America for his education. He enrolled in the Sheffield Scientific School at Yale University, where he studied physics with the pioneering scholar Josiah Willard Gibbs, who derived the theoretical foundations of statistical mechanics. Returning from Yale as one of Japan's first Western-trained scientists, with a bachelor of philosophy degree, Yamakawa founded the Kyushu Institute of Technology in 1907 before serving as president of Tokyo Imperial University (now Tokyo University), Japan's premier educational institution, from 1913 to 1920.[46] Until his death in 1931, Yamakawa served as an elder statesman in Japan and a living symbol of its cosmopolitan educational and scientific communities.

Not surprisingly, many future members of Japan's political and social elite also attended prestigious American colleges. The same year that Yamakawa entered Yale, Kaneko Kentarō (1853–1942) enrolled at Harvard. There, the future confidant of rising political star Itō Hirobumi studied law with Oliver Wendell Holmes Jr. and became friends with a young New York patrician named Theodore Roosevelt. Kaneko would later study in Europe and help Itō draft Japan's Meiji Constitution, but it was toward America that he felt a lifelong connection. This affinity with the United States would make him the leading advocate of cultural exchange with America in the coming crucial years of early Japanese imperialism.

America's Ivy League played host to a number of Japanese during this era. Future diplomat Komura Jutarō (1855–1911) entered Harvard Law School in 1875. Graduating in 1877, Komura joined the Foreign Ministry in 1884 and became foreign minister in 1901. His Harvard connection held him in good stead when he joined President Theodore Roosevelt in Portsmouth, New Hampshire, to negotiate an end to the Russo-Japanese War. The groundwork for the peace settlement, however, had already been laid by fellow Harvard alumnus Kaneko, who had visited the United States the year previously and held at Yale a series of private meetings that served as the basis of the agreement. Another future politician to study in America was Hatoyama Kazuo (1856–1911), who attended both Yale and Columbia Universities. During the late Meiji period, he served as chairman of the Lower House in the Japanese Diet and was the patriarch of a political family that produced two prime ministers (his son and great-grandson) and a foreign minister (his grandson).

Budding politicians and scientists were not the only Japanese to study in America. The Meiji educational system grew from an urban and rural base long in the making. Japanese children in feudal times had traditionally been educated according to their social caste. Offspring of samurai were trained in private domainal schools, which emphasized Confucian ethics, martial arts, and administrative skills. Commoners also had various opportunities to become literate, mainly through temple schools, which stressed Buddhist teachings, although some merchant-only schools cropped up in major cities like Osaka. But the dawn of "civilization and enlightenment" in Japan was accompanied by a firm belief that Western-style education was vital to the modernization and survival of the country. Temple schools and domainal classrooms closed down in the gathering rush to implant a new educational template on the country. It was this belief in the superiority of Western education that pushed low-level samurai scholars such as Fukuzawa Yukichi and Mori Arinori to travel to America and return home to found colleges on the Western model.

Among these pioneers, several stand out due to the impact they had not only in Japan but also to a lesser degree in America. Among the most famous was Niijima Jo (1843–1890). In 1864, during the final years of the Tokugawa era, he risked a death sentence by fleeing Japan as a stowaway to America. Reaching Amherst College in 1865, he converted to Christianity and became the first Japanese to graduate with a degree from an American college, in 1870. He then went to Andover Theological Seminary, becoming the first Japanese to be ordained a minister.

Niijima, known by now in the United States as Joseph Hardy, returned to Japan in 1875 and founded Japan's first Christian-affiliated liberal arts college, Doshisha, in Kyoto. The school was begun with financial support from the Congregational Mission Board and reflected not only the religious mission of its founder but also his American-inspired liberal arts education. At a time when the national government was slowly coming to select the German-style university as the model for higher education, Doshisha offered an alternate path, one that focused on an American interpretation of the sources of Western culture and not just the scientific and practical forms of college learning. Throughout the following decades, Christian liberal arts schools like Doshisha played a major role in introducing classical Western thought into Japan and in providing a training ground in humanistic thinking for thousands of young Japanese.

Beyond pedagogy, one of the distinguishing aspects of Japan's modern educational system was its commitment to educating women. While there had always been specialized education for women of the samurai class in feudal Japan, the Meiji era opened up new vistas in learning for all women. As did the young men sent abroad soon after the Meiji Restoration, daughters of Japan's elite took advantage of the chance to study in the United States, thereby lending a different aspect to the question of cultural encounter and social modernization.[47] Most famously, the 1871–1873 Iwakura Mission brought to America not only diplomats and young male scholars but also five girls, aged seven to fifteen. The Meiji empress herself lauded the five—Nagai Shigeko, Tsuda Umeko, Ueda Teiko, Yamakawa Sutematsu, and Yoshimasu Ryoko—as models for Japanese women, giving a broad indication that the Meiji state planned on rethinking the social restrictions on women that had held firm throughout the Tokugawa period.

Each of the five young girls wound up playing a significant role in Meiji-era Japan, yet some already had a connection to America even before sailing in 1872. Yamakawa Sutematsu (1860–1919) was the eleven-year-old sister of Aizu samurai Yamakawa Kenjirō. Kenjirō was then at Yale and arranged for his sister to live with a Yale professor of theology and minister, Leonard Bacon, and his family.[48] After graduating from New Haven High School, Sutematsu enrolled at Vassar College, finishing in 1882 as the first Japanese woman to earn a BA in America, not to mention as the college's valedictorian. She married Japan's future minister of war, Ōyama Iwao, upon returning to Japan and remained committed to supporting and expanding women's education. In this endeavor, and due to her high social position, she was able to help her fellow Iwakura Mission traveler Tsuda Umeko (1864–1929).

Tsuda was the youngest of the five girls who studied in America in the 1870s, and she also stayed the longest, for eleven years.[49] She lived in Washington, D.C., with the family of Charles Lanman, who at that time was the American secretary at the Japanese Legation. During her sojourn, Tsuda converted to Christianity, following in the footsteps of fellow pioneer Joseph Heco, who had converted a decade earlier. Tsuda, however, returned to Japan during a period of cultural retrenchment against things Western, including English-language training. Yet she had been transformed during her adolescent years in America, coming to see the great inequalities in the social position of Japanese women compared with that of their American counterparts.[50]

Tsuda taught English for several years in the Peeress School, recently established by the Imperial Household Department, one of whose patrons was Yamakawa (now Ōyama) Sutematsu. In 1889, Tsuda returned to America and studied for three more years at Bryn Mawr College. There, she grew close to women in the American missionary community and with their help established a fund to bring young Japanese women to the United States for education. After graduating from Bryn Mawr, Tsuda remained in contact with American women in both the missionary and the educational fields and, finally, in 1900 started the Girls' Institute for English Studies (Joshi eigaku juku) in Tokyo, with the help of Ōyama. The institute later became Tsuda College for Women, one of the first and most famous of the dense network of women's colleges that thrive to this day in Japan. Five years later, Tsuda organized the Tokyo Young Women's Christian Association, which became the first in a community of Japan YWCAs.

Despite the ongoing activities of scholars such as Tsuda Umeko and Yamakawa Kenjirō, cultural trends in the middle of Meiji period adversely affected American-Japanese educational ties. A conservative swing away from America and the kind of freewheeling democracy it represented grew in strength during the late 1870s and throughout the 1880s. Inspired in part by a desire to emulate the more centrally organized European states, this movement was paralleled by a desire to "return" to bygone Japan on the part of many traditional intellectuals. In response to these trends, in 1887 the Meiji government stopped officially sponsoring students for study in the United States, urging instead that young Japanese go to Germany for training. This move helped ensure the growth of German-style faculty-oriented research universities, such as Tokyo Imperial and Kyoto Imperial, over the kind of liberal arts–oriented schools represented by American-inspired Doshisha.

Students, of course, represented just one segment of the movement of Japanese abroad after the loosening of travel restrictions. Not all of Japan's émigrés were privileged elites, nor did all go to American universities. A handful of Japanese who traveled to the United States decided to settle there, and when they did, they found themselves in the middle of a fight over Asian immigration, one that had overtones similar to the nationalistic arguments back home against mixing with foreigners, except that this time they were the objects of fear and resentment. On the whole, Japanese immigration into America was miniscule compared with that from China. Only 1,780 people of Japanese descent were listed as living in the United States by 1890, and until 1885, an average of only 20 Japanese per year immigrated to the United States.[51] In contrast, in 1870, just two years after Japanese first traveled to America, there already were 63,199 Chinese living in the United States. That number had nearly doubled to 107,488 persons of Chinese descent resident in 1890.[52]

After passage of the 1882 Chinese Exclusion Act, which shut off legal immigration of Chinese to America, impoverished Japanese peasants began moving to Hawaii and the West Coast, partly filling in the vacuum. Hawaii was the initial destination of large numbers of Japanese, especially since industrial concerns used large-scale contract immigration to fill menial jobs in sugar plantations or other agricultural businesses. The Japanese population of the islands grew from a handful in 1884 to thirty thousand by 1895.[53] From the beginning, in Hawaii in particular, the Japanese were sought as a counterweight to the Chinese laborers, who had often been ensconced for decades. Contract immigration in fact grew out of plantation owners' desire to weaken the potential influence of Chinese, who by the mid-1880s accounted for nearly a quarter of Hawaii's population.[54] The situation on the mainland was different. Here, the Japanese never accounted for more than a tiny number of immigrants. Their communities also grew slowly, remaining simple pockets among a dominant white population.

Ghettoized from the mainstream of American society, Japanese laborers both in the islands and on the mainland sent back to Japan for "picture brides" and slowly built socially and economically cohesive communities that spoke Japanese, lived a traditional lifestyle, and practiced the customs of the homeland across the Pacific. In economic activity, however, the Japanese mixed with the mainstream population, and a significant fraction of the immigrants ran simple American-style diners for laborers. By the turn of the century, there were 24,326 Japanese in the United States, of whom only a handful were nisei, or second-generation

Japanese-Americans. More important was the overwhelming gender imbalance, the census registering 23,341 males compared to a mere 985 females.[55]

Such Japanese workers occupied a liminal space between two countries, yet they played almost no role in mediating between two cultures. The Japanese-American community such as it was did not reach out and educate recent immigrants about their new homeland or bring into public view the customs that at least some Americans had read about in books and newspapers. Nor did visiting or resident Japanese become public commentators claiming a place in American public discourse, and it is not clear that any would have been given a forum to do so. The late nineteenth century was not an era in American society when multiracial intellectual fellowship flourished, beyond that advanced by a few black Americans, such as Frederick Douglass or W. E. B. DuBois. Advocates of racial minority viewpoints, and there were none in any case for the Japanese or broader Asian community, were almost invariably black, such as Booker T. Washington.

Added to this social marginalization was the fact that the Japanese settlers were haunted by the specter of anti-immigration movements almost from the day they arrived in America. In part this was due to the nature of the immigrants themselves. Mostly poor, from the margins of Japanese society, they were regarded as "undesirable" even by their own compatriots. Japanese political leaders, such as the minister to the United States, Mutsu Munemitsu, were concerned that the appearance and the activities of these denizens of the lower depths would harm Japan's image in America. The face of Japan that Tokyo wished to sell was that of the "legitimate" students in the Ivy League, sons and daughters of the elite.[56] This tension among nativist Americans, Japanese immigrants, and the U.S. and Japanese governments would simmer for decades before exploding in the 1920s.

Nor did the Japanese emigrants make a name for themselves back home. Though they lived among real Americans and saw aspects of society that the social elite could never understand, the "undesirables" played no role in educating their fellow Japanese about the United States. Perhaps their letters and infrequent return visits stirred occasional interest, but certainly nothing they experienced was publicized or added into the contemporary mix of public opinion. Their lack of a cultural voice, so to speak, paralleled their lack of a political voice. It was, not surprisingly, the poor emigrants' elite fellow travelers, those sent for study or business to the United States, who returned carrying the banner of civilization and enlightenment. It was former students, such as Niijima Jo or Tsuda Umeko, who founded Western-style liberal arts colleges, or writers, such as the Christian internationalist Nitobe Inazō, who served as heralds of a new vision of society and as the champions of U.S.-Japan relations.

The American Encounter with Japan at Home and Abroad

Japanese were of course but one side of this story of cultural encounter. Although Japan was far more profoundly changed by its relations with the United States than the other way round, the American encounter with Japan in the second half of the nineteenth century was inextricably tied to the country's growing consciousness of, interest in, and role in the Pacific Ocean world.[57]

Unlike Japanese, however, who sometimes saw the Americans as part of a larger, undifferentiated Western mass, Americans rarely seemed to lump the Japanese into one similarly undifferentiated group. This was not because the American mind possessed some greater ethnic or ethnographic sensitivity but rather because, to Americans, Japan was a unique land. Partly this image of Japan was due to its size and level of cultural sophistication, especially when compared with the numerous tiny Pacific islands that American whalers had encountered throughout the nineteenth century. Partly the image was due to the fact that Perry had "forced open" Japan, and Americans felt a corresponding paternalism and pride vis-à-vis the European powers who were otherwise dominant in Asia. And partly Americans saw Japan as a distinct culture because the Japanese were clearly not Chinese. As an *Atlantic Monthly* article in 1860 put it, "On close examination, [as] the imagined attractions of China disappear, those of Japan become only more definite and substantial. The old interest in China is transferred to its worthier neighbor."[58]

Such feelings only increased in the years after 1868, while Americans paid close attention to the progress of civilization, as many put it, in Japan. With the abolition of the feudal domains in 1871 and the consequent formation of a centralized government, Japan at a distance certainly seemed to Americans to represent the future in Asia. The feelings expressed by the *New York Times* on the return to Tokyo of the first minister to the United States, Mori Arinori, could have been extended to the society of Japan as a whole: "[His friends] regard him as not only a cultivated and very agreeable, but, in many respects, a truly remarkable man."[59] The Japanese had the stuff of civilization in them, and an American-style, forward-looking optimism, which the Chinese decidedly did not. This almost Herodotean interest in Japanese culture was often expressed in the American media. The *New York Times* and other papers occasionally ran long columns on daily life in late-Tokugawa and early Meiji Japan, introducing their readers to Japanese dining customs or scenes from village life, even if the writers of these columns were often more interested in color than facts. Periodicals too weighed in, often with longer, though not necessarily more substantial, articles on the political situation in Japan, along with cultural reporting.

It was the book, however, that served as the major American bridge to Japan in the nineteenth century, at least in terms of lasting influence. Unlike those written in the pre-Perry period, accounts by those who actually visited or lived in Japan blossomed in the United States, serving not only to create the major cultural template through which Americans viewed the Japanese but also to inspire more interest and more travelers—a type of cultural feedback loop.

For over twenty years after Perry's visit, his account reigned supreme as the definitive description of Japan, supplemented, of course, by books such as Bayard Taylor's *A Visit to India, China, and Japan.* But Japan was changing at an increasing pace, and contemporary observers began catching their fellow Americans up to the miracle in the Pacific. In 1876, just eight years after the Meiji Restoration, the most important book published by an American on Japan during the nineteenth century appeared. *The Mikado's Empire* by William Elliot Griffis set an endurance record unequaled by any book since and set the standard in Japan-related publications for nearly forty years.[60] Griffis was one of the first foreign employees of the new Meiji government and had initially arrived two days before the end of 1870 to start a scientific school run by the Dutch Reformed Church in New York, but he was soon tapped by the new government to establish a technical school. Although he lived in Japan only for three years, he maintained contact with Japanese students and leaders for another half century, until his death.

Griffis distilled his experiences and wide-ranging interest in Japan into *The Mikado's Empire*. Unlike previous books, which were an amalgam of travel reportage and the passing on of second- or thirdhand information, *The Mikado's Empire* was the first book on Japan to be published based on serious study of the country's history and culture. Yet it also was a celebration of the growth of Japanese-American relations and the dawning of a new era in world history. As Griffis put it in his preface, "Japan, once in the far-off Orient, is now our nearest Western neighbor. Her people walk our streets; . . . her art adorns our homes. . . . It is time that a writer treated Japan as something else than an Oriental puzzle."[61] Published in two volumes, the first was a detailed history of Japan from ancient times down to 1872, while the second volume contained Griffis's personal experiences and observations of his nearly four years in Japan. Of surpassing popularity, the book ultimately went through twelve revised editions through 1913, Griffis adding to each one a history of recent events in Japan. Through its long life span and evolution, the book itself became a kind of biography of the modernization of the country into a great power. More importantly, it gave Americans what most of the Japanese accounts of the United States did not, a comprehensive study of Japan's history and culture as experienced by a professional scholar.

Griffis's book would be followed by many others, but he had set the template in two ways. First, future books would have to treat Japanese civilization as something complex and evolving, each one attempting to understand the nature of the profound changes occurring in Japan. Many of these books were worthless, yet some, such as *Evolution of the Japanese: Social and Psychic* by the missionary Sidney L. Gulick, were comprehensive anthropological and sociological studies.[62] Second, though Griffis treated Japan seriously, he included such beguiling sections as "Children's Games and Sports" and "Folk-lore and Fireside Stories," thus fueling interest in the traditional aspects of Japanese culture, which were just starting to be highlighted by Japanese exhibitions abroad. As a result, however, much of the travel reporting on Japan after the appearance of *The Mikado's Empire* proffered to American readers a sentimental, romanticized view, such as that in Eliza Ruhamah Scidmore's *Jinrikisha Days in Japan,* published in 1891.[63]

The books played a role, as well, in balancing out the "ledgers" of U.S.-Japan relations during the last decades of the nineteenth century. The interest these books piqued may well have offset the fact that political and economic ties during these years were largely stagnant. Absent the reporting on Japan's exotic world, Americans might have lost interest completely in the islands, since few fortunes were being made there compared with those made in China, and the saving of Japanese souls by Christian missionaries seemed to be of more limited import compared to the great struggles going on in China. Despite the importance of such books, however, many of those that kept the embers of interest in Japan burning were, in the end, lifeless, devoid of color and vibrancy. What made up for their weaknesses was the opportunity for American citizens to encounter Japan at home, even if infrequently.

Embassies to America, such as those sent in 1860 and 1872, were but one way for ordinary Americans to view in living color what they read about in newspapers and journals. Another path was provided by Japanese participation in world's fairs. During the latter half of the nineteenth and first half of the twentieth century, world's fairs were a unique opportunity for ordinary citizens to encounter other cultures. Participation, of course, was dependent on a country's government and was often part of an official policy to expand commercial and political relations through a cultural forum.

Japan first participated in an American fair in 1876, at the Philadelphia Centennial Exposition. A mere eight years after the Meiji Restoration, the new government saw the fair as a way of bringing Japan onto the world stage, a very public demonstration that Japan was no longer shut off from the rest of world. Meiji leaders, however, chose not to stress the modernization just getting under way in their country but rather to highlight traditional art and craft work, such as lacquerware, inlaid utensils, and wood-carved pieces.[64] This approach set a template for much of Japan's subsequent cultural outreach. The fair was the first chance for many ordinary Americans to encounter products of Japan's culture, and what they saw reaffirmed the dominant cultural images of a land that seemed frozen in time, a land of exotic goods and preindustrial sensibility. The exhibit was wildly popular, and that helped convince the Meiji government that Japan would appeal to foreign lands as a cultural oddity, even as the country's leaders attempted to homogenize life in Japan with global trends.

Nearly two decades later, that tension was not yet resolved. Over 30 million Americans visited the 1893 Chicago Columbian Exposition, held on the shores of Lake Michigan and featuring the gleaming White City. By this time, Japan was a far more industrialized nation, one with a gross national product of roughly 1.2 billion yen.[65] It was more urbanized than in 1876 and boasted a modern army. Yet despite the handbooks, statistical compilations, and catalogs testifying to Japan's modernization, the biggest hit with visitors was precisely the traditional arts and crafts that signified a preindustrial age rapidly vanishing back home. Once again, the government chose to embrace this aspect of Japanese culture, thus giving official approval to the image of a Japan that remained "Oriental" and exotic.

Despite these fairs, as the nineteenth century drew to a close, the opportunities for Americans to encounter Japan in their own country were not much greater than when Nakahama Manjirō arrived in New Bedford a half century previously. Nonetheless, small steps brought the culture of Japan closer to ordinary Americans, helping to reinforce the by now accepted image of Japan as a country mired in traditional culture, despite its undeniable development.

One way of bringing the culture of Japan closer to Americans was through the first Japanese arts and antiquities galleries in the United States. New York was the location of choice for many of them, including that of Takayanagi Tōzō, who had a small shop at 160 Fifth Avenue in the early 1880s. Takayanagi sold to major collectors, such as Charles Lang Freer, who would bequeath his collection to the Smithsonian Institution in the 1920s. In January 1895, Yamanaka Sadajirō established the first store of what was to become an international company on West Twenty-seventh Street in Manhattan.[66] With support from notable Japan experts William Sturgis Bigelow, Edward S. Morse, and Ernest Fenollosa, Yamanaka was able to survive where a few Japanese arts dealers before him had not. Yamanaka and Company focused on traditional wares of the kind so popular in Chicago two years before. Moving within two decades to Fifth Avenue, Yamanaka helped define the canon of valued Japanese and East

Asian art. As the *New York Sun* put it in 1917, the company "had so much to do in times past with forming the tastes of New Yorkers in matters of Oriental art."[67] Yamanaka steadily expanded his business in the States, opening branches in Chicago and Boston, where he took advantage of the experts of the Boston Museum of Fine Arts, who themselves were building the West's greatest collection of Japanese art, under the direction of Fenollosa and expatriate Okakura Tenshin (Kakuzō; 1862–1913).

Okakura became perhaps the best-known Japanese in America in this period, aside from Nitobe Inazō. Born in Yokohama in the last years of the Tokugawa shogunate, he became the trusted partner of Ernest Fenollosa and first journeyed to America in 1886. If Nitobe translated into English the social ethos of Japan, through his writings on Bushido, Okakura translated Japan's aesthetic spirit. In 1904, he published *The Ideals of the East, with Special Reference to the Art of Japan,* a sweeping interpretation of the Buddhist impulse in Japanese art from the Asuka period of the sixth century to his times. Two years later followed his most famous work, *The Book of Tea,* which melded performance, architecture, social relations, and philosophy into an easily digestible brew for Americans. The success of these works helped move Japanese art into the mainstream and draw American patrons to shops like Yamanaka Sadajirō's.

Another type of artistic encounter between Japan and America came as Yamanaka was struggling to establish his business. In late 1899 and early 1900, Boston, New York, and Chicago hosted the first troupe of Japanese actors to appear in the West. Headed by Kawakami Otojirō, the group of nearly twenty actors presented a medley of plays that were a mix of recent Japanese drama and an adaptation of Shakespeare's *The Merchant of Venice*.[68] Again, it was the traditional features of the performances, from the kimono costumes of the female leads to the mock samurai battles, that appealed to spectator and reviewer alike. Meditations on Japan's modern experiences were not the point of the performances; rather, in pieces such as *The Geisha and the Samurai,* it was a dead and romanticized Japan that was being sold to American audiences. It was precisely that lost world that Americans were coming to expect, be it on stage or on the shelves of upscale antiquities shops or in the Japanese pavilions at world's fairs.

One group in America, though, did take great interest in the Japan of the day, and not in any romanticized image of what the country's culture was. Both before and after its emancipation, the black American community carefully watched Japan's attempts to maintain autonomy and independence in a world dominated by colonial powers. At the same time, America's outreach to Japan was used by black newspapers as a counterpoint to American lack of interest in Africa. For example, in mid-August 1852, as Perry was setting sail for Japan, *Frederick Douglass's Paper* reprinted a *Baltimore Sun* account of the "Free Colored People's Convention" held in that city. During a debate as to whether black Americans should emigrate to Liberia, one delegate, in setting up the preamble to his argument that the "redemption" of Africa was a matter of historical and world importance, first raised the example of how American Christian culture was transforming Asia and Japan.[69]

Christianity and the black American experience was a common theme in African American newspapers. Perhaps the paper that contained information on Japan the most frequently was the *Christian Recorder,* published in Philadelphia, whose religious grounding emphasized the universal connections among peoples. The *Recorder* was founded in 1852 as the official newspaper of the African Methodist Episcopal (AME) Church. Yet, as Gilbert Anthony Williams argues, the paper transcended its role as a religious weekly, becoming in effect the voice of black America in the Reconstruction and the post-Reconstruction eras.[70] Often reprinting items from large metropolitan newspapers, the *Christian Recorder* focused on the question of racial relations and challenged prevailing notions of what was "advanced." For example, at the height of the Civil War, in a comment on Japanese children, the *Recorder,* after reminding its readers that the Japanese were "heathen," reprinted an account by the American merchant Francis Hall, who painted an idyllic picture of happy, content, well-mannered youth in the feudal system. The *Recorder* then concluded, "We have nothing to teach them in this respect out of our abundant civilization."[71]

The greater goal of religious conversion, of course, was central to the mission of the black Christian newspapers. Reacting to the 1858 Harris Treaty with Japan, which granted Americans the right to practice their religion, the *Christian Recorder* misinterpreted the provisions of the treaty but proclaimed nonetheless, "The partial OPENING OF JAPAN to missionary labor is a matter which should excite the thankfulness of Christians everywhere."[72] Anticipation gave way to doubt, however, dur-

ing the early Meiji period, as centuries-old restrictions on the open practicing of Christianity remained. As the *Recorder* lamented in September
1873, "It would seem that the Japanese do not take to Christianity at least
with the avidity with which they take to the civilization that flows from it.
Railroads and telegraphs, steamboats, and mechanism in general, these
are accepted with all reasonable haste—some even think with a haste that
is unreasonable."[73]

Spurred in part by the sentiments reflected in newspapers like the
Christian Recorder, numerous Americans decided to experience Japan
directly, not just vicariously through newspapers and world's fairs in
America. The most vibrant moments of the encounter for Americans, of
course, took place in the country itself. If the half century from roughly
1850 to 1900 is best understood as the era of the noble adventurer, then
those Americans who saw Japan as a terra incognita to be explored and
experienced were in every way the equal of their Japanese counterparts
who came to the United States. Most of the Japanese who traveled to
America did so with an explicit mandate to return home and help change
their land. In the case of the Americans who came to Japan during the
Meiji period, it is hard to say who was more affected, the Japanese whom
they encountered or the travelers themselves.

Compared with other foreigners, the American presence in Meiji Japan was comparatively limited, not in the least due to formal restrictions
on residence. Until 1899, all foreigners had to live in specially designated
settlements or residential areas within cities. Established initially by the
1858 commercial treaties, the largest settlements were the treaty ports of
Yokohama and Kobe. Both Yokohama, which opened on July 1, 1859, and
Kobe, which opened on January 1, 1868, were dominated by British traders. Although Americans formed the second-largest group of foreigners
resident in Japan, they were still just a small percentage. The British minister Rutherford Alcock recorded that in 1861, only 38 Americans resided
in Yokohama, out of a total population of 126, which included 55 Brit-
ons.[74] Three decades later, out of 4,949 foreigners at Yokohama, there
were only 253 Americans, accounting for just 5.1 percent of the total. In
Kobe, the percentages were similar: in 1872, 43 Americans lived at the
port; in 1893, 102 Americans represented 5.8 percent of a total population
of 1,768 foreigners.[75]

Despite their small numbers, the Americans who journeyed to Japan did so largely in three distinguishable groups: employees, missionaries, and individual romantics. And yet, not surprisingly, those roles often blurred, with missionaries becoming key employees, and employees acting more like romantics. The employees' very presence was due to the modernization movement sweeping Japan. They were perhaps the most visible of the three groups and were hired by the Meiji government to assist in the project of civilization and enlightenment. They joined a much larger group of Westerners, known as the *oyatoi gaikokujin* ("employed foreigners" or, less charitably, "live machines"), including French military advisors, Scottish engineers, and Italian art scholars.[76] Modern descendants of the famed William Adams—shipwrecked pilot and advisor to shogun Tokugawa Ieyasu, and the first European samurai in Japan—these Westerners helped steer the Japanese ship of state toward modernity.

The dean of American *yatoi* was Guido F. Verbeck (1830–1898), a Dutch-born immigrant to the United States at the age of twenty-two.[77] Within two years he had enrolled in the seminary and was ordained. Verbeck might not even be considered an American, for just seven years after arriving in America, he was sent by the Dutch Reformed Church as one of three missionaries to open a Protestant mission in the southern domain of Saga, whose castle was located in Nagasaki, the traditional foreign port throughout the centuries of Tokugawa rule. Yet, shortly after taking up his duties in 1860, he was employed by the feudal lord of the domain to head up the official school that trained Saga's samurai. For the next four decades, Verbeck would live in Japan, witnessing the fall of the bakufu, the end of feudalism, and the development of a modern state.

Throughout the waning days of the shogunate, Verbeck taught in Nagasaki. In 1869, however, one year after the establishment of the Meiji government, he was asked by the new government to teach in the Kaisei Gakko in Tokyo, which the leadership was planning on turning into Japan's first public college. The Kaisei Gakko was the descendent of the Kaiseijo (Institute for Development), itself an offshoot of the legendary Bansho Shirabesho (Institute for the Study of Barbarian Books), which was the translation bureau and think tank of the Tokugawa bakufu, wherein Japan's first generation of foreign affairs "Wise Men" were trained. Verbeck was put in charge of educating a new crop of scholars, including the precocious Mori Arinori, who would soon be posted to Washington as Japan's first permanent representative.

Verbeck had a pervasive influence on the formation of Japan's educational system in the early Meiji period. He urged the use of German for modern medical studies and was sought out for advice on political issues, such as the establishment of the prefectural system in 1872, which ended seven centuries of samurai rule over semiautonomous domains. Yet Verbeck never left behind his missionary origins. Teaching at the predecessor of Meiji Gakuin University, he translated the Bible into Japanese, concentrating in particular on the Old Testament.[78] He transmitted Western and American ideas to the Japanese until his death in 1898, living to see the demise of feudalism and the rise of a world power. Yet unlike other Americans in Japan, Verbeck did not in turn educate the citizens of his first adopted country about Japan, neither writing a popular account of what he witnessed nor going on speaking tours back in America. That role, the interpreter of Japan to America, fell to another employee, William Elliot Griffis, author of *The Mikado's Empire* and biographer of Verbeck.

Americans also were brought over for agricultural and scientific-related work, yet they often as not became educators of a more traditional type. One of the best known was William S. Clark. Clark was a chemist, who as a professor at Amherst had taught Niijima Jo and who later became president of the Massachusetts Agricultural College. Lured by a government contract from Tokyo, he arrived in Japan in 1876 and was sent to the northernmost island of Hokkaido to set up a college. Smith thus was used to further the Meiji policy of colonizing Hokkaido, which was rich in natural resources but also was under threat from Russian and Chinese designs. He stayed barely a year, but in that time Clark established the Sapporo Agricultural College, which became a leading research school on modern farming methods. He thus helped import to Japan the idea of the American land-grant college at the very time it was spreading in America, into states such as Illinois, which set up its Agricultural College the same year Clark founded the Sapporo school.[79]

Another important American employee was General Charles LeGendre, a retired military officer and diplomat who became one of the first advisors to the new Foreign Office, along with his countryman Erasmus

Peshine Smith. Japan had never before had a formal diplomatic office, and American talent was particularly important for teaching how to blunt Western demands for greater trade concessions. As the Meiji foreign policy developed, LeGendre played a major role in the formative moments of Japanese imperialism. Although he came from a land that had not yet acquired an overseas empire, LeGendre was an ardent expansionist when it came to Japan. He was given the opportunity to put his ideas into practice in 1872, just four years after the Meiji Restoration, when a group of shipwrecked Ryukyuan sailors were massacred by Taiwanese aborigines. Taiwan claimed suzerainty over the Ryukyus, a policy that would lead to the annexation of the islands in 1879, and demanded restitution from China for the massacre.

Concurrent with the Taiwan crisis, the young government had split over whether to invade Korea to "chastise" the court for not recognizing the superiority of the Japanese emperor. Proponents of the invasion were samurai traditionalists anxious about what the increasing pace of modernization in Japan spelled for their caste. Meiji leader Ōkubo Toshimichi, who opposed the invasion of Korea, won out over his erstwhile ally and boyhood friend Saigō Takamori, in a victory that lead to Saigō's resignation from the government. In exchange for dropping the Korean invasion, Ōkubo accepted LeGendre's plan to send an expedition to Formosa (Taiwan) to claim revenge for the sailors' massacre. This became the first Japanese use of force outside the home islands since the invasion of Korea in the 1590s. LeGendre's policy was used by Tokyo to proclaim Japan as the upholder of law and order in East Asia and gave the country a foothold for asserting its interests in Taiwan in future years, which it did by annexing the island in 1895 after the Sino-Japanese War.

While most Americans played roles far less dramatic than General LeGendre's, each helped in setting up crucial parts of the Meiji administrative apparatus. George W. Williams, for example, was a financial expert who advised Itō Hirobumi on the organization of Japan's banks and currency system, while Horace Capron played a role similar to William Clark's in helping to settle Hokkaido. Nor were all the working Americans employed by Tokyo. Others came of their own accord, such as journalists, artists, and eventually scholars. The adventurers invariably found themselves changed by Japan, becoming cultural translators for Americans back home, some adventurers being more sober, almost academic, and others romantic, if not revolutionary. Some, such as Edward H. House, would meld their professional and personal lives, adopting Japanese children and arguing the case of Japan's equality before the court of public opinion.[80]

Without question, however, one of the largest and most important groups was the missionaries, most from the Congregational Church, or those employed in the denomination's enterprises in Japan. Yet the role of the missionaries is difficult to disentangle, for they soon acted as a major bridge between the cultures, though they did so only as a means of facilitating their proselytizing activities. As so often happens in history, it was the unanticipated "spill off" of their activities that often had the most lasting effects. Perhaps the best-known missionary, and the most important, was James Curtis Hepburn.[81] Born in Pennsylvania in 1813, he entered Princeton University in 1831 at the age of sixteen, graduating the following autumn and then earning a medical degree from the University of Pennsylvania in 1836. It was while in medical school that he committed himself to becoming a missionary. Hepburn's first posting was China, where he served from 1841 to 1846, with his wife, Clara Reed. After being forced to return to the United States due to Clara's illness, the couple returned to Asia in 1859 to become missionary teachers in the newly opened Japan.

Hepburn and his wife came to Yokohama, the key trading port under the new treaty system, and took up residence just outside the city, in the post town of Kanagawa. Living their first four years in the country in a small temple named Seifutsuji, they began their missionary activities in a land that still proscribed the teaching of Christianity. Watched constantly by shogunate spies, Hepburn concentrated initially on medicine, opening a clinic for local townspeople. Yet he soon realized that the success of transmitting the Bible to Japanese lay in translation, and for that a dictionary was necessary. Over the next eight years, from 1859 to 1867, Hepburn labored with Japanese accomplices to learn the language and compile entries. Published in Shanghai by the Presbyterian Mission Press as the *Japanese and English Dictionary,* not only was Hepburn's work the first English-Japanese reference volume, but also it introduced what became the standard system of transliteration of Japanese into English, which is still in use, despite certain modifications.[82] As a boon to the academic study of Japan, although not what Hepburn had intended, the dictionary also became one of the key tools of cultural exchange. It went through nine editions up to 1910, empowering a generation of individuals who could now interact with one another at a greater level of linguistic sophistication. Whereas the first edition contained 20,772 Japanese-English entries and 10,030 English-Japanese entries, by the third edition the numbers had increased to 35,618 and 15,697, respectively.[83]

For thirty-three years, until returning to America in 1892, the Hepburns sought to spread Christianity in Japan. By the mid-1870s the proscription on Christianity was lifted, and the couple could work openly. They soon founded the first of Japan's mission schools and, under Clara's guidance, opened their doors to Japanese girls as well as to boys. In addition, James Hepburn translated books of the Bible and oversaw the construction of churches in the Yokohama area. Yet it was for his dictionary and his medical work that Hepburn was most remembered, bringing, in the one case, the secular word to thousands and, in the other, the knowledge of science and healing to a nation eagerly embracing such worldly arts. Like their contemporary Verbeck, however, the Hepburns did not act consciously as cultural bridges, nor did they repackage their unique experiences into a homily for their compatriots on the culture, history, and changes of modern Japan. This lacuna detracted in no way from the missionaries' efforts across the Pacific, and indeed, any deviation from their calling might well have been considered an unacceptable price to pay for ephemeral fame and fortune back home.

One reason for the pervasive influence in Japan of some missionaries, such as the Hepburns and Guido Verbeck, was their longevity. The longest-serving of these missionary-scholars was likely Dwight Whitney Learned, who graduated from Yale in 1875 with a doctorate in Greek. Sent by the United Church of Christ to Japan, he took up a post at the newly formed Doshisha College, which had been started the year before by Niijima Jo. Learned remained at Doshisha for the next half century, living with his wife in a house across from the Imperial Palace, finally sailing home to California in 1928. In these five decades, during which he witnessed the transformation of Japan into a modern society and a great power, he translated books of the Old and New Testament into Japanese and almost single-handedly introduced the subject of political economy into Japan, through his lecture course on the subject.[84]

As Learned's life shows, the missionary endeavor was all but indistinguishable from the pedagogical. In the educational modernization of Japan, the various streams of Western employees and noble adventurers from both countries coalesced into a powerful current that transformed the Japanese landscape. Innovators such as Fukuzawa Yukichi and Mori Arinori have already been mentioned, as have pioneers such as Tsuda Umeko. Before the Meiji Restoration, Japan had a fairly high literacy rate, and temple schools *(terakoya)* dotted the landscape. As Mori Arinori and others in the new government attempted to craft a national educational system, they often found themselves in conflict with localities that had well-established school networks.[85] The missionaries, in contrast, were able to fit in between these two competing forces by offering an educational alternative, the Christian-based liberal arts schools, such as Doshisha.

One key element of the missionary-founded enterprises was the girls' school. Japan's traditional education had provided a few Confucian-based texts for the education of samurai women, primarily the *Onna daigaku* (The Women's Greater Learning), which sought to instill the ethic of obedience and hierarchy into girls' upbringing. The missionaries went far beyond this, however, creating full-fledged women's academic institutions. Mary E. Kidder (1834–1910) arrived in Japan at the beginning of the Meiji era, and with support from the Congregational Church and Clara Hepburn, founded Ferris Women's School in 1875. The Yokohama-based institution was situated in the exclusive foreigners' section known as the Bluff (*Yamate* in Japanese) and soon became the prototype for a host of women's mission schools that cropped up during the Meiji years. Along with other pioneers, such as Julia Carrothers and Mary Parke, Kidder and Japanese educators like Tsuda Umeko created one of the most extensive women's educational networks in the world. Not only did the schools bring ecclesiastical teachings to a large audience, they ensured that Japanese women would participate in some degree in the transformations sweeping through society. A literate, educated female population would soon contribute intellectuals, educators, internationalists, and women's rights activists to Meiji and Taisho civil society.

A final group of Americans for whom Meiji Japan formed a crucial part of their lives were the romantic adventurers. The romantics arrayed themselves in direct opposition to the missionaries and the employees, standing athwart history in Japan and demanding that it stop. For these men and women, Japan served as a kind of escape from the very modernity the Japanese themselves were increasingly embracing. Whether it was traditional art, religion, or social structure, the romantic adventurers celebrated the preindustrial, premodernized Japan that was often on display in the world's fairs. Their intellectual predispositions led them to search on the other side of the globe for what was missing in their own lives, by discerning, for example, the "Soul of the East," in Percival Lowell's understanding.[86] Lowell, like a large number of the romantics, was from a blue-blooded Boston family. Some of these sojourners had gathered at literary salons around Beacon Hill or patronized the Museum of Fine Arts, hobnobbing with Okakura Tenshin and others. Those among the romantics who were the most moved, or the most wealthy, traveled across the Pacific to directly encounter the culture that filled a gap inside themselves.

Yet not all these romantic adventurers were the equivalent of trust-fund babies. Perhaps the exemplar of them all was a wandering journalist of the lower class, Lafcadio Hearn, who arrived in Japan just as the period of the noble adventurer was about to close. Born on the Ionian island of Santa Maura of an Irish father and a Greek mother, Hearn was a restless, tormented idealist. Finding his way to Japan in 1891, he immediately became entranced with the land, its people, and its already transformed society. Indeed, it was with the vanishing traces of traditional Japan that Hearn was obsessed, watching them recede into the mists of history faster than he could learn of them. Hearn found his home in Japan, marrying a Japanese woman and taking Japanese citizenship. He changed his name to Koizumi Yakumo (his wife's family name, meaning "little spring," and the given name of "eight clouds") and began a prodigious outpouring of idealized, romanticized writing that, more than any other writer since Perry himself, brought Japan to the attention of the American public.

His books, such as *Glimpses of Unfamiliar Japan* (1894) or *Kokoro: Hints and Echoes of Japanese Inner Life* (1896), were masterful, sometimes too masterful, explorations of Japanese life. What made Hearn's writing so powerful was the palpable evanescence of the Japan he loved.

By the mid-1890s, the country was poised on the cusp of a modernity that would propel it into the ranks of the great powers and onto the road of imperialism. It was precisely that transformation that adventurers such as Hearn despised. What we now call "Orientalism," as applied to Japan, was born from these adventurers' pens. They served as the literary counterpart to the Japanese exhibitions at world's fairs, for the Japan they enshrined was one all but gone, in which the perceived virtues of a premodern, preindustrial life represented an innocence much like the halcyon image of Tom Sawyer's summer days. What Hearn sought to preserve, if not re-create, with his pen, men like Horace Capron and Charles LeGendre were destroying with their hands.

Regardless of the desires of adventurers like Hearn, modernity was just around the corner. A self-consciously rising power, Japan began to look outward in her orientation, to a role as a regional leader. It now found itself confronting an America equally committed to expanding its presence in Asia as a beacon of a particular style of civilization and wealth. This fertile mix of self-interest, fascination, and concern, nurtured by far-reaching changes in the nature of international society, provided the essential matrix for the birth of exchange after the period of initial encounter.

CHAPTER 3

The Birth of Exchange

NEAR THE ENTRANCE to Tokyo Bay, in Kurihama, stands a weath-
ered stone monument. Erected in 1902 on a cliff overlooking the
ocean, it commemorates the first landing of the American squadron led
by Commodore Matthew C. Perry in July 1853. The stela is unremark-
able, indistinguishable from the thousands of other stone monuments
around Japan, except for its origin. No government body, either local or
national, commissioned it. Nor did a religious group or business fund it.
Rather, a private group, the Beiyū kyōkai, or the American Friends' Association, raised the monument just a few years after the association came
into existence as the first organization in Japan dedicated to cultural ties
with the United States.

The Kurihama memorial and the American Friends' Association represent the first moments of organized cultural exchange between Japan
and the United States. They were part of a much larger change in the way
peoples around the globe interacted after centuries of unregulated encounter. Yet these kinds of exchange also posed a challenge to the traditional type of cultural engagement, for the more they partook of an
organized character, the more they threatened to make obsolete the noble
adventurers of the previous decades.

Yet the question of why the cultural relationship between Japan and the United States grew so rapidly remains unanswered. In part, bilateral ties changed because the nature of international cultural relations changed. Equally, the U.S.-Japan relationship deepened as both countries turned into world powers within the space of a few decades. In that respect, the story of U.S.-Japan relations is part of the story of global history in the modern era.

The Emergence of Global Community

Even as Commodore Perry steamed into a world that appeared unchanged for centuries, his own was transforming before spectators' eyes. The Industrial Revolution, now a century old, was producing spillover effects that went far beyond simple economic and even social change. Perry's whole mission, indeed, was to create a support network for a technological development, the steamship. Clipper ships and increasingly sophisticated marketing mechanisms were filling the increasing demand for foreign goods, as a growing American middle class in the second half of the nineteenth century created a large market for as many exotic knick-knacks as could be bought.[1] The world was shrinking, and new conceptions of nationalism and internationalism were being forged in the change.

The political-military system instituted by the European powers for the previous century faced new challengers at the end of the 1800s. The two key new players were the United States and Japan, both of whom were modernizing not only internally but externally as well. This meant extending their power in international relations and beginning to follow the example of European imperialist nations. Now that modernization was proceeding apace in Japan by the 1890s and America had largely recovered from the Civil War, the two states embarked upon a more interventionist path in east Asian international affairs.

The actions of the two nations had dramatic effects, and by 1900 the east Asian geopolitical situation was fundamentally different than it had been just a decade earlier. In 1894, the Meiji government finally succeeded in revising the four-decade-old "unequal treaties" with the leading Western nations, thus becoming the first non-European nation to negotiate its equality. In the years it had taken to rewrite the treaties, Japanese policy makers such as Yamagata Aritomo had developed clear strategic guidelines for the Meiji state. Of primary importance was keeping the Korean Peninsula free from foreign influence, particularly Chinese and Russian. Yet an aggressive Japanese policy was met by an equally resistant Chinese position on the peninsula. Barely two weeks after signing the treaty revision agreement with Great Britain, the Japanese launched a surprise attack on Chinese forces, inaugurating the Sino-Japanese War to determine mastery of Korea.

Within one year, the upstart state had defeated the venerable Qing Empire and radically altered the landscape of east Asia. The most powerful regional actor was now the still-modernizing Japan, while the long-held myth of Chinese hegemony, at least in political terms, had been shattered. The American public took notice. The *New York Times,* for example, called the war "one of the most glorious records in the annals of the Mikados."[2] Lafcadio Hearn, erstwhile champion of a bygone Japan, rejoiced at the news of the Japanese victories at Port Arthur and on the mainland. Some tried to link Japan's new strength to its American relationship, as the *New York Times* opined during the fighting: "There is a dot of pride in the fact that our American progression may have had something to do with [Japan's] determination to force civilized 'ways and means' upon China."[3] As the United States expanded its interests westward across the Pacific, the American public saw in Japan a harbinger of the future, which made the country that much more attractive to Americans.

By the late 1890s many in the United States perceived the Pacific Ocean as crucial to America's national interest. A paternalistic attitude toward what America's leaders now viewed as their "neighborhood" led to Washington's opposition to old-style European imperialism in the region, particularly in China and in the Philippines, which was then controlled by Spain.[4] A new foreign policy was emerging that combined elements of messianic Christianity, in the hopes of remaking the Pacific in the image of the "civilized" West, and the economic desire for expanded trade to fuel America's growing industrial society.

Spanish control over Cuba, just off the Florida shores, provided the pretext for the first real imperialist policy in American history. In 1898, the United States went to war over the island with Spain, and half a world away, in Manila Bay, Admiral George Dewey destroyed the Spanish fleet in the first stage of the American conquest of the Philippines. America had, almost overnight, become an imperial power in Asia, and in one fell swoop gained control of Hawaii, Guam, and the Philippines. While many in Washington questioned whether the republic could constitutionally possess colonies, newly found strategic concerns dictated a continued American presence in its new territories. Adding to the pressure to have a permanent American role in the Pacific region, trade interests in Asia had been steadily growing in the last decades of the nineteenth century, and Secretary of State John Hay made clear America's intention to maintain whatever economic presence it could in China through U.S. issuance of the Open Door notes. Two years later, the new order in Asia was underscored when both Japan and the United States sent troops to northern China to protect the foreign community from the Boxer Rebellion.

In short, both Japan and the United States became Asian powers at roughly the same time, not only sharing nationalistic feelings of pride and a desire to bring civilization and enlightenment to stagnant lands but also holding similar trading interests and a desire to play a political role on the global stage.

The Transformation of Global Society

What was happening in Asia mirrored to greater or lesser degree what was occurring all across the globe, as political and economic changes spelled the beginning of a new era of international relations. The last decades of the nineteenth century may well have been a fin de siècle foreshadowing of an end to European peace and prominence, yet these years also witnessed the development of an intellectual and cultural international community that paralleled the better-known economic and technological internationalization of the era. Like many international movements, this intellectual and cultural blossoming began at a national level. Among the most important developments was the emergence of the modern learned society. As the historian Joseph Kiger documented nearly half a century ago, the national and international growth of the learned society in the nineteenth century transformed academia and dramatically expanded the sphere of intellectual exchange. This resulted in a burst of activity comparable to that produced by the first wave of learned societies in the seventeenth and eighteenth centuries.[5] This second wave, however, was anchored by societies based largely in America.

Modern learned societies were intimately tied to the professionalization of academic disciplines and indeed helped create the modern university. Between 1869 and 1904, starting with the American Philological Association, practitioners of over a dozen academic subjects formed national societies in America. Built on the tradition of the American Academy of Arts and Sciences, founded by John Adams in the 1780s, these societies set professional standards, held regular meetings, and published the original work of their members. Starting in the 1880s, a constellation of societies formed, many of which would survive through to the present day, including the American Historical Association (1884), the American Economic Association (1885), the American Philosophical Association (1901), the American Anthropological Association (1902), the American Political Science Association (1903), and the Association of American Geographers (1904). These American groups reflected the growth of the United States during the nineteenth century, from an aggregation of largely agricultural states in the eastern half of the continent to a continental nation that was rapidly industrializing, thanks in part to its scientific, practical bent.[6]

These new societies emerged into an increasingly complex international intellectual network, in which Europe continued to play a central role. Technology, in fact, was the midwife of this network. Due in part to the spread of continental-wide rail systems and the growing ease of transatlantic travel, the late nineteenth century played host to a new form of gathering, the international congress. Cousin in spirit to the world's fairs, the international congress brought together scholars and specialists from around the globe, helping to spread cooperative academic endeavors across national boundaries. The first gatherings were devoted to science, during a period when that discipline internationalized itself and created transnational networks of practitioners. Brussels hosted the first international congress, on botany and horticulture, in 1864. This was followed by the Geneva congress on chemistry in 1892. And, in a logical marriage of fair and congress, the 1893 Chicago Columbian Exposition sponsored international congresses on math, history, and world religions.[7]

Despite the regularity of such international meetings, they were still ad hoc gatherings. Not until after World War I did permanent international organizations emerge. Coincident with the Paris Peace Conference of 1919, representatives of national science societies formed the International Research Council, while humanities associations established the International Academic Union.[8] National branches represented individual countries at the meetings of each of these umbrella organizations. In the United States, the American Council of Learned Societies was founded in 1919 and became the liaison to the International Academic Union, which focused largely on philology, archaeology, history, and the moral, political, and social sciences.

The turn of the twentieth century was thus a silver age of intellectual exploration, one that complemented an older cosmopolitan impulse to explore new lands and gather up far-flung facts. Even as the old political mechanisms that had held European power politics largely in check since the Napoleonic Wars began to shiver at their bases, scholars and scientists were driven closer together. Indeed, one can hardly doubt the causal connection between the end of the old political system and the rise of the new intellectual world. Colonialism and imperialism brought great swaths of the earth under the direct purview of professionals. New species to be gathered, new societies to be observed, new histories to learn and epics to read, all of this gave a second life to the old Enlightenment project of ordering, and ultimately perfecting, the world. The same steamships that had carried Lancers to Bengal now ferried bespectacled scientists to a London or Chicago gathering. The explosion of journals, travel accounts, and specialized books on all subjects attests to the globalization of knowledge—at least for Western explorers, though less so for the indigenous elites whose societies were often the object of study.

There were different kinds of "orderers of knowledge," however, and the permanence of their labors came in different ways. Intellectuals published on perishable paper, but wealthy collectors could bequeath to the public the fruits of their passion and travels. The founders of the Boston Museum of Fine Arts, men such as Ernest Fenollosa, were one such group, but as the twentieth century dawned, new institutions emerged that soon tied into an increasingly international comsopolitan network. The American millionaire and collector Charles Lang Freer was one who donated his vast collection of Japanese and Asian art to his fellow citizens, establishing in 1923 what became known as the Freer Gallery of Art, part of the "National Museum," which was later called the Smithsonian Institution. Freer, advised by Fenollosa, had been planning his gallery since 1904, a time coinciding with the rise of American interests and empire in Asia. The opening of a permanent home for his collection linked Washington, D.C., the capital of the new world power, with the cultural and intellectual currents to which European capitals were long accustomed, thanks to their global presence.[9] Freer's collection, parts of which had toured major American museums like the Art Institute of Chicago in 1917, became a nucleus of Asian art in America, bringing unknown masterpieces to a wide public and spurring both research and further acquisitions.

As important as cosmopolitan explorers like Freer were, the turn of the twentieth century was equally marked by the drawing together of the threads of global society in political and institutional ways, as the march toward "organization" became an ever-accepted part of social activity. As Akira Iriye pointed out in his study of global society, America was naturally poised to take a lead in this development, due largely to what Tocqueville saw as one of the principal characteristics of America democracy, the formation of "private associations." This American burst of activity helped foster a climate for the growth of the international nongovernmental organization, which throughout the twentieth century would pursue an increasingly complex set of cross-national activities, such as humanitarian relief, environmental protection, educational and cultural exchange, and human rights.[10] Such organizations, however, treated cultural relations as a means for a larger, political end and thus were animated by a spirit very different from a cosmopolitan attitude toward things foreign. Although America was a participant, even a leader, in this new world and Japan was not, the influence of intellectual discovery and of cultural exploration provided a powerful atmosphere in which the gestation of U.S.-Japan cultural exchange could begin, just as the two nations became political powers in Asia.

America's growing industrial might also gave birth to one final crucial element of modern international society, the philanthropic foundation. The vast sums of money at the disposal of industrial titans like John D. Rockefeller and Andrew Carnegie called forth a uniquely American response, grounded in a culture of mutual reciprocity and voluntary association. A firm believer in charity since his childhood, Rockefeller was persuaded by Frederick T. Gates, a minister, to create a foundation that would rationalize, in a scientific manner, the distribution of funds for worthy causes. As Gates described it, foundation reflect "an instinct of humanity, which cannot be fenced in by the boundaries of a merely national patriotism, a sympathy which transcends national boundaries and finds complete expression only when it identifies us with all humanity."[11] In many ways, this was a perfect summation of a modern cosmopolitan attitude, and tied to Rockefeller's money, it helped spread such beliefs into many lands.

Although both the Rockefeller and the Carnegie foundations were established after the first decade of the twentieth century, Rockefeller in 1913 and Carnegie in 1910, they represented the spirit of nineteenth-century global society and indeed soon became the central pillars in supporting the large network of nongovernmental organizations that developed in these years. Each foundation took its own path: Rockefeller focused increasingly on public health issues and education, funding the University of Chicago and building hospitals in China, while Carnegie took an approach that looked less toward solving discrete problems and more toward helping shape the nature of the global society itself. Indeed, the mandate of the Carnegie Endowment for International Peace was to "enhance international understanding at the level of . . . prominent individuals in different countries and between nations."[12]

Here, then, is the matrix in which cultural exchange emerged: an enduring intellectual impulse that now interacted with a fertile technological environment; the expansion of Western interests to hitherto unreachable cultures; the growth of voluntary academic societies, museums, and nongovernmental associations; and the rise of philanthropic foundations. The gaze of the American and European observer was extended to the far realms of the earth, fired by a curiosity to know, to understand, to order, and to perfect. Haphazard contact, now seen as an amateurish approach to knowledge, was no longer acceptable. The pools of talent and experience that were forming themselves could be harnessed to a project of rationalized outreach and formalized encounter. It is what the internationalist American statesman Elihu Root would later call the "revelation of the power of organization" to reshape global relations.[13]

The Birth of U.S.-Japanese Exchange, 1898–1924

By the dawn of the twentieth century, Japan and the United States had been in direct contact for nearly five decades and both were unrecognizable from the two nations that first encountered each other in the 1850s. It was, of course, those individuals who already had encountered the other culture who were the vanguard in the revolution of cultural exchange that was about to occur. After decades of sending young Japanese as students to the United States, Tokyo and other major cities had small yet influential contingents of returned travelers. It was no surprise that eventually some of them sought to form what we would now call alumni clubs. Their numbers did not allow for, say, a Harvard Club, at least not in the beginning, but they did allow for more regional gatherings.

In the autumn of 1896, nine young Japanese men gathered in Tokyo. Calling themselves the Brotherhood of Friends in America (Zaibei kyūyū shinboku kai), they doubled their number the following year. Recognizing that the majority of their members had studied on the West Coast of the United States, they soon began to call themselves the Western Club (Seibu ha).[14] While America was still recovering from the wounds of its North-South clash, in Japan it was traditionally an eastern (Tokyo) versus western (Osaka) identity that divided people. Thus, at the same time as the Western Club was formed, a group of five men who had studied on the East Coast of America organized their own group, called the American Travelers' Society (Yūbeijin kai), though of course they soon became known as the Eastern Club.[15]

With a few overlapping members, and after a few hesitant exploratory meetings, the two groups finally merged, holding their opening ceremony with thirty charter members on December 18, 1898, in the famous Kōyōkan (Autumn Leaf Hall) in downtown Tokyo's Shiba Park. The name of the new organization was the American Friends' Association (Beiyū kyōkai). Its aims seemed modest: to be an alumni club of no particular school, a support group for those who had spent time in America and who sought to create camaraderie with those having similar experiences. Soon they held a reception at the American consul's residence in Yokohama; the event was the first such U.S.-Japanese gathering of its kind. Within months, the new group had five directors and sixty-five members.[16]

This was a tiny group, of course, and its specific goals were singularly unfocused. Nevertheless, it set a crucial precedent: it gathered Japanese admirers of America together in their homeland, and it engaged with the American elite, diplomats primarily, who were resident in Japan. There was, as yet, no outreach to the hundreds of ordinary Americans living in Kobe or Yokohama or Nagasaki. But that, too, was not surprising, for this group of Japanese was largely upper class and counted members of the aristocracy among its members.

What could have remained an insignificant social club was transformed just two years after its founding when, on September 27, 1900, Kaneko Kentarō was elected president of the American Friends' Association. Kaneko was a major figure in Japanese society, already a baron at the age of forty-seven, and his life was tied to America from its start. He was born in 1853, the year Perry arrived in Japan, to a samurai family in Fukuoka, on Kyushu. For seven years after the Meiji Restoration he lived in the United States, entering Harvard, where he formed a Japan club and be-friended a New York patrician named Theodore Roosevelt. After return-ing to Japan, Kaneko found himself part of a large circle of transpacific cosmopolitans. He befriended William Sturgis Bigelow, a physician, art collector, and student of Buddhism, during the 1880s, and in 1889 Big-elow introduced Kaneko to Massachusetts senator Henry Cabot Lodge, thus keeping alive Kaneko's Boston connections.

In addition to his domestic and his foreign relationships, Kaneko be-came a disciple of the Meiji statesman Itō Hirobumi. Itō was the major figure in the government and in 1880 was beginning the process of draft-ing a constitution, one of the signal accomplishments of the Meiji era. Kaneko served as one of Itō's key assistants during the drafting process, earning the sobriquet "Guard of the Constitution." He would later serve in the Ministries of Agriculture and Industry and the Justice Ministry be-fore becoming a special advisor to Japanese leaders, including his old mentor, who served four times as prime minister.[17]

Under Kaneko's leadership, the American Friends' Association ex-panded its activities, while staying largely in the channel of elite relations. It now regularly hosted leading American visitors to Japan, such as Wil-liam Jennings Bryan and William Howard Taft, both of whom came in 1905. It feted each American ambassador and welcomed leading admirals when American warships called on Japanese ports; indeed, the association took the lead in organizing the welcome for the American Great White Fleet during its visit in July of 1908. Over a period of two years, soon after the group's formation, one of its major activities was raising the monument at the site of Perry's first landing in Japan, at Kurihama. Building the monument required raising funds, commissioning a design, and hiring craftsmen to shape and engrave the marble and stone. In a ceremony attended by Commodore Rogers of the U.S. Navy, who had been a midshipman on Perry's flagship back in 1853, the memorial was unveiled on July 14, 1901.[18]

Yet social activities were not the limit of the role that the American Friends' Association played in Japanese-American relations. With this very first group devoted to nascent cultural exchange, there occurred a blurring of the lines between public and private diplomacy, between state policy and private activity. Because Kaneko Kentarō was a member of the aristocracy, and because he remained on friendly terms with Theodore Roosevelt, who had become U.S. president in 1900, Kaneko was chosen by the Meiji government to travel to America in early 1904. Leaving on February 24, he did not return to Japan until October of the following year. His objective was to win American support for Japan in the just-commenced Russo-Japanese War.[19]

This conflict was the first truly great war of the new century. More importantly, it was the first war fought between an industrialized Asian country and a European great power and was being fought to determine the future of mastery in Asia. Kaneko, however, was not sent as an official representative of the government of Japan but as the president of the American Friends' Association. He was a goodwill ambassador, yet he was also tasked while in the United States with beginning informal negotiations to end the war. He inaugurated what we now call "public diplomacy," giving interviews to nearly a dozen U.S. newspapers and periodicals, including *Collier's* and the *Chicago Daily News*. In November, he penned an article in the prestigious *North American Review,* an article designed to counter the hysteria in some quarters of a "Yellow Peril" that would threaten Western interests in Asia if Japan defeated Russia. He not only linked Japan's policies in Asia with America's Monroe Doctrine but transcended mere power considerations by asserting that

Japan's aim, "as shown by the whole course of [its] modern history, [was] to introduce to the distant and long-neglected East the blessings of Western civilization."[20] And that Western civilization was increasingly an American one, in Kaneko's eyes.

His connection to the government was understood, for his bylines noted that Kaneko was a member of the House of Peers. This made clear that his private group had now been enrolled in official service. It raised the question of how groups like Kaneko's, composed of elites who interacted with American high society, would define themselves in the future. When does a private, voluntary association act on behalf of a particular government, and if it does so, how does that influence the organization's identity and activities?[21] These were not yet consciously formulated questions, but as a private organization, it was forming a template for the future, and Kaneko brought the association into new territory, with the full support of the Japanese government.

The activities of the Beiyū kyōkai contained the germ of cultural exchange. Not only did its members have a personal interest in America, but they understood the importance of maintaining friendly relations with the United States as part of the modernization, the internationalization, of Japan. The association's ultimate goal, even if not fully articulated, was to promote good relations with America through members' activities. It had come a long way from being simply an alumni association.

As these actors groped toward a new type of relationship with the United States, a group in America was similarly rethinking its approach to Asia. It must be remembered that for every William Elliot Griffis or Lafcadio Hearn, there were tens of nameless missionaries and entrepreneurs who saw America's future as linked to China rather than to Japan. Empire in the Pacific was only feeding the appetite of those who saw in China either one hundred million souls to be saved or one hundred million customers to reach. Though the missionaries already had the organizations that supported their cause, namely their churches, the businessmen required something new. The result was, again, a peculiarly Western response: the formation of a trade association devoted at first to China and then to east Asia more broadly.

On January 6, 1898, nearly a year before the American Friends' Association held its first banquet in Tokyo, a group of New York businessmen organized the American Asiatic Association (AAA). The aim of the AAA, as written in its charter, was to determine the "methods to be adopted to conserve the rights of citizens of the United States in the Chinese Empire."[22] Nearly half a century of trade relations with China had not solved such vexing problems as hidden tariffs, bribery, graft, legal ambiguities, and numerous economic inefficiencies. In addition, the European nations were carving up spheres of influence in China that largely excluded merchants from competing Western countries. This would lead, in September 1899, to U.S. Secretary of State John Hay's issuance of the first Open Door note, in an effort to establish equal trading opportunities for all Western business concerns.

Yet if trade was the raison d'être of the AAA, its founders clearly understood that at some basic level, all relations among peoples were interlinked, economic as well as cultural and intellectual. As this realization was acted out, the path toward cultural exchange was cleared even for a group devoted to commercial relations. The American Asiatic Association's constitution outlined the goal of the AAA's activities: "To contribute to a satisfactory adjustment of the relations between Asiatic countries and the rest of the world by the removal of sources of misunderstanding and the dissipation of ignorant prejudices; and to cooperate with all other agencies, religious, educational and philanthropic, designed to remove existing obstacles to the peaceful progress and well being of the peoples of these countries."[23] Here was the recipe for cultural exchange: increasing mutual understanding, dispelling ignorance, and seeking mutual action with other voluntary organizations to bring peoples together. Creating goodwill and increasing understanding would be achieved through activities that introduced cultures and societies to one another, even if eschewing immediate political or economic goals.

The AAA made good on its ambitious words. The year following its founding, it established a subcommittee for "Education and Promotion of Knowledge of Far Eastern Affairs among the American Public."[24] Here was a clear distinction from the path pursued by the Japanese American Friends' Association, for the American group immediately recognized the importance of reaching out to a wider audience and educating them, if not actually involving them in the AAA's activities. The main instruments of this outreach were the publication from 1900 of its journal, and after 1917 the association's sponsorship of the glossy general affairs magazine called *Asia*. The direction of interaction between the AAA and the American public was a one-way street, perhaps, but it laid the groundwork for making this group and future ones far more public players.

Though the AAA was most concerned with China, on June 26, 1899, a branch of the association opened in Tokyo, with subbranches in Yokohama, Kobe, and Nagasaki quickly following. Headed by prominent American business leaders in Japan, such as E. W. Frazar, its only regular event was an annual dinner, which put the number AAA activities at half that of the American Friends' Association, which hosted two annual meetings. However, the AAA of Japan was more inclusive than its Japanese counterpart, welcoming Japanese as guests at its gatherings in addition to American consular and business leaders.[25] Its activities slowly broadened, and by 1905 it was hosting U.S. Independence Day celebrations at Yokohama, events that drew large crowds of Japanese to view horse races, a baseball match, and fireworks.[26] The journal of the home-based AAA regularly published reports on the economic and political state of Japan, reprinted major news stories, and printed the texts of important diplomatic agreements. This made the *Journal of the American Asiatic Association* one of the more comprehensive sources of information about Japan for American readers, who, it should be stressed, were largely business professionals. Trade could be promoted by various means, of course, and the AAA served in its early years as the sole American group maintaining unofficial ties between the two countries' elites. Thus, in December 1904, it hosted a banquet in New York in honor of Prince Fushimi, brother of the emperor, who had arrived to visit the Saint Louis World's Fair.

As the world of twentieth-century international relations was being knit closer and closer together through nongovernment groups such as the AAA, the group's economic internationalism soon broadened into a more general internationalism. It was one of the first and foremost American voices against the growing anti-Asian immigration movement, publishing articles critical of anti-immigration legislation and exposing the activities of groups such as the California Japanese and Corean League, which sought to extend the Chinese Exclusion Act to all Asian immigrants.[27] At its annual dinner on April 25, 1911, the Japanese ambassador to the United States, Baron Uchida Kōsai, the U.S. secretary of state, Philander C. Knox, and William Sulzer, the chairman of the House of Representatives Foreign Affairs Committee listened to addresses condemning anti-Japanese feelings in the United States.[28] To some degree, the goal of all the AAA's endeavors was to ease tensions that directly threatened the economic internationalism it embodied and promoted.

In addition, the organization soon moved beyond these activities and began various charity works in Japan. Paradoxically, however, the AAA's first charity venture was in partisan support for Tokyo's imperialist military policies, which were making Japan a great power and which were clearly opposite to the very internationalism the group championed. The Russo-Japanese War, which began in 1904, was not simply a military victory for Japan. It was also a devastatingly costly war, in terms of casualties on both sides. It was in many ways the forerunner to the First World War, witnessing trench warfare, the intensive use of automatic weapons, artillery, months-long stalemates, and amphibious operations. Japan suffered at least 85,000 casualties, and the Russians in excess of 125,000. In response to the carnage, the AAA of Japan formed the Perry Memorial Relief Fund, which soon was renamed the Japanese Relief Fund. Chaired by former Columbia University president Seth Low, the fund gave aid to "families of soldiers and sailors in Japan left destitute by death or disablement" in the Russo-Japanese War. By June 1905, it had raised $26,000 and already disbursed over $7,000 to needy families.[29] There were few, if any, qualms reflected in the AAA's published material about supporting an aggressive Japanese war to control the Korean Peninsula; rather, the association focused on showing support for the innocent Japanese families whose lives had been shattered by the conflict. It would become harder to suspend criticism of Japanese imperial aggression in coming decades.

Aside from such potentially problematic initiatives, the American Asiatic Association's less controversial charitable activities continued, including earthquake relief and urban renewal, particularly in Tokyo. Further modernization took place in Japanese health care, the very field in which philanthropists like John D. Rockefeller Sr. were helping out in China and one in which both Japan and China were continuing to move away from traditional medical practices and toward Western-style allopathic medicine. Western-modeled clinics had been founded in Japan since the beginning of the Meiji period, often by Protestant missionaries, but none had developed facilities to become true hospitals. In 1916, the AAA of Japan endorsed a campaign for the endowment of Saint Luke's Hospital in Tokyo. Saint Luke's, founded in 1902 by the missionary doctor Rudolf Bolling Teusler, was the main international hospital in Tokyo, and the AAA led in the effort to raise funds for the construction of a modern, Western-style hospital building, with full knowledge that at least a portion of Saint Luke's patients would be from the foreign community. Yet Saint Luke's also served as a model for modernized health care throughout Japan, spurring innovation outside Tokyo and not incidentally showing up further differences between that country and its less developed Asian neighbors.

Despite the activities of the largely China-oriented American Asiatic Association, there still was no group in the United States devoted solely to Japanese-American relations after the turn of the twentieth century. The Russo-Japanese War of 1904–1905 would prove to be a catalyst in bringing about just such an organization. Through its victory over tsarist Russia, Japan had now vaulted onto the world stage and was a recognized great power. President Theodore Roosevelt himself, with help from his old friend Kaneko Kentarō and Yale University professor Asakawa Kan'ichi, had mediated the peace talks between the belligerents at Portsmouth, New Hampshire. American interest in Japan, combining equal parts admiration and concern, was never higher, creating an atmosphere conducive to the formation of cultural societies. A sign of things to come was an informal discussion group in Boston that met irregularly during the Russo-Japanese War, although it would take a decade and a half for it to formally organize itself as the Japan Society of Boston. Indeed, the first steps to formal exchange would be taken not by Americans but by Japanese living in the United States.

By 1900, there were over twenty-four thousand Japanese residents of the United States.[30] Most were laborers and shopkeepers, but the major U.S. cities boasted a small population of businesspeople and professionals. New York, not surprisingly, was home to a contingent of successful Japanese, who were unofficially led by a small circle known as the Oceanic Group. The leaders of the group were Satō Momotarō, the first successful Japanese retailer in the States; Morimura Yutaka, head of the

Noritake china company in America; and New York's leading silk merchant, Arai Rioichirō, who had moved to America to expand his family's silk exporting business.[31]

On May 13, 1905, the Oceanic Group invited seventy-five of the most prominent Japanese business leaders in the area to a meeting to form the Nippon Club, the first social organization for Japanese in America. Its members were bankers and merchants, government officials, and professionals. Heading up the club as its first president was cofounder Takamine Jōkichi, who worked closely with Arai and Morimura. Born a half year after the signing of the 1854 Perry Treaty, Takamine was a trained scientist, who immigrated permanently to America in 1890 and became best known for isolating the chemical adrenaline. Originally sent as the official Japanese representative to the 1884 World's Industrial and Cotton Exposition held in New Orleans, he became one of the first Japanese to marry an American, a New Orleans native named Caroline Field Hitch, and the two created a hybrid Japanese-American lifestyle until his death in 1922.[32]

While described as a "social club" by the *New York Times,* the Nippon Club held a loftier goal. Takamine openly noted that fostering cultural exchange was the motivating spirit behind the group, claiming at the club's inaugural dinner, "The desire of our people [is] to become better acquainted socially with the American people."[33] To do this, the Nippon Club instituted another innovation that soon set a pattern for cultural exchange groups: its clubhouse contained not only Japanese artwork and furniture but also one whole room in traditional Japanese style, with tatami matting, a tokonoma for displaying hanging scrolls, shoji paper–paneled doors, and sliding *fusuma* doors decorated with Japanese art motifs. Here special events, such as tea ceremonies, were held and club visitors could experience some of the style of Japanese living. In addition, Japanese meals were served in the club, with the *Times* reporting that most of the cooking ingredients were imported from Japan. While such accoutrements may have seemed insignificant window dressing, a slice of Japan now existed in the heart of America's biggest city, one that announced itself prominently with a giant Rising Sun flag flown above the entrance on West Ninety-third Street.

As the Nippon Club formed, the overriding issue of the day was the Russo-Japanese War, and the Japanese were keenly focused on their country's success on the battlefield. The early formal events of the Nippon Club celebrated the first victory of an Asian nation against a major European power, with grand banquets featuring Japan's naval heroes (though the true architect of success, Admiral Tōgō, was not among them) and diplomats such as Foreign Minister Komura Jutarō. The American Friends' Association's Kaneko Kentarō, in America to help with Tokyo's public relations efforts, also joined the Nippon Club's celebrations on at least two occasions, thus bringing together the first two transpacific organizations devoted to Japanese-American relations.[34] Japanese newspapers, as well, followed the activities of the Nippon Club and printed Takamine's thoughts on the U.S.-Japan friendship, thereby making him the unofficial spokesman of Japanese in America.[35]

Coincidently with the Russo-Japanese War, the pace of interaction between Japan and the United States increased, and within a decade the contours of cultural exchange would become clear and recognizable to future generations. In 1905, the same year that the Nippon Club was founded the Japan Society of San Francisco, known for nearly three decades as the Japan Society of America, first met.[36] But, like the Boston circle, the San Francisco group was informally organized and lacked a clear agenda. Not until the early 1930s did the group reorganize itself, regularizing its activities and hosting prominent Japanese visitors. By that time, it had been joined by the Japan Society in Los Angeles (later the Japan America Society of Southern California), founded in 1909; the Trans-Pacific Society, also organized in Los Angeles, in 1916; the Japan America Society of Washington State, founded in 1920; and the Japan America Society of Chicago, which held its first meeting in 1930.

The pattern was almost always the same: several American businessmen, perhaps with the leading Japanese merchant in town, would form the core of the group. Henry Bowie, an avid collector of Japanese painting, for example, founded the Japan Society of America (in San Francisco).[37] The groups would host visiting Japanese dignitaries and have an annual dinner. For most of those involved in founding such groups, it appeared that the rise of Japan as a commercial and military power was a central, but not the sole, reason for forming such a society. Japan's traditional culture, as showcased at the world's fairs and at the Nippon Club itself, also was gaining popularity and thus became a powerful impetus in the formation of exchange societies. Added to that was the pull of an expanding internationalist community, which appealed to the sentiments of many who led the various Japan-U.S. groups Perhaps this is best illustrated by looking at the history of the largest and most important of the associations, the Japan Society of New York.

The Japan Society of New York

In April 1907, a circle of New York business leaders formed their own Japan society, timed to coincide with the visit of Admiral Ijūin Gorō and his warships, *Tsukuba* and *Chitose,* to the city. Feeling there needed to be an official "nonofficial" reception, the group arranged a lavish banquet for the admiral, with General Tamesada Kuroki acting as the official Japanese host. The leading figures in the nascent club were Lindsay Russell, who served as president from 1910 to 1919; lawyer Henry W. Taft, brother of President William Howard Taft; banker August Belmont, who was married to Commodore Perry's daughter; and the financier Jacob H. Schiff, who had provided massive loans to Japan in the war against Russia. Arai Rioichirō, cofounder of the Nippon Club, also joined as one of the directors of the new Japan Society of New York.

Like the earlier binational associations, the new group began modestly, meeting semiregularly for formal dinners. Perhaps this lack of innovation led to an initially lackluster public reaction, expressed by the *New York Times* of May 21, 1907, which opined that there was "no possible use for such an organization, and no work for it to do."[38] Despite such barbs, the Japan Society of New York's location at the epicenter of the American financial community provided both a level of publicity and a correspondingly greater activist outlook among its founders. Within months, the group had moved beyond merely hosting dinners and began to pursue two paths: the first was to integrate itself into the growing internationalist community; the second was to sponsor a regular round of activities that would reach a wide audience of ordinary Americans.

Internationalism was a growing movement during these years, and much of its strength came from the forging of transnational links among like-minded groups that held political goals of creating some type of global government or at least establishing global institutions that could work to limit states from pursuing their own narrow interests. The Japan Society of New York quickly followed suit in embracing the global internationalist movement. After rejecting a proposal to associate with the Japan Society of London, the new group agreed in October 1908 to become an affiliate of the New York Peace Society, itself part of the larger American Peace Society, which had been founded in 1828 by amalgamating several older local peace chapters.[39] On the suggestion of E. W. Frazar, leader of the American Asiatic Association of Japan and concurrently head of the American Peace Society of Japan, the new Japan Society sent three members as delegates to the Third National Peace Conference in May 1911.[40] Five years later, the society agreed to work with the international Committee on Friendly Relations among Students in aiding Japanese studying in the United States.[41]

That same year, the Japan Society took the lead for the first time in trying to expand the network of which it was a part. In late 1911, it acted as an advisory council to committees in Tokyo and San Francisco that were interested in promoting friendly relations between Japan and the United States.[42] In Tokyo, the Japan Society of New York worked on this project with Baron Shibusawa Eiichi, Japan's premier industrialist and philanthropist, about whom more will be said later. By 1919, the society sponsored the Pan Pacific Forum, thus moving to integrate itself with broader-based Asian movements. Nor was the Japan Society solely Asiacentric, as it helped organize the Italy-America Society in early 1918, using its own offices and facilities.[43] Through its various efforts, the Japan Society of New York brought the U.S.-Japan relationship into the center of the internationalist movement that would help define the Wilsonian world order. As impressive as these internationalist activities were, though, it soon became clear that the real strength of the society lay in promoting cultural exchange between Japan and the United States. Accordingly, the society decided in 1911 to increase the number of lectures by experts it hosted, sponsor more exhibitions, and schedule more meetings on Japan and U.S.-Japan relations.[44] Its goal was now to promote better relations between the two countries and to increase mutual understanding, insofar as possible in nonpolitical ways. The society thus consciously straddled the worlds of cosmopolitanism and internationalism, and not always successfully.

The leaders of the Japan Society of New York considered the diffusion of knowledge and the promotion of education perhaps the most powerful vehicle in inculcating an appreciation of Japan among Americans. Such an inclination had been apparent even earlier, for in 1909 there had been a motion made to publish a "brief, reliable history of Japan," thereby reaching an audience not willing to wade through the thick tomes of William Elliot Griffis or the lyrical prose of Lafcadio Hearn, who had been dead for five years.[45] In late 1909 and early 1910, the society took the first steps toward public outreach by distributing nearly four hundred copies of a travel book on Japan published by the Welcome Committee, a group formed in Tokyo in 1893 to help foreign travelers.

Starting in 1911, however, the Japan Society embarked on a new approach, which required a far more demanding commitment of financial and intellectual resources. Throughout April and May, it sponsored an exhibition of Japanese prints in New York, complete with catalogs and lectures. Held at the Aldine Club, the exhibit was the first major showing in America of Tokugawa-era ukiyo-e woodblock prints and in particular those of the genre's masters, Harunobu, Utamaro, Hiroshige, and Kiyonaga. No one was quite sure if the market existed for a professionally produced exhibition or if the society would even follow up with similar events. The society need not have worried, however, for a full-page article in the *New York Times* noted that the show was "remarkable," praising especially the "dignity of the art employed and the noble restraint and healthy taste of the artist."[46] Buoyed by this success, the society instituted a regular schedule of major exhibitions, which helped fuel the fashion for pre-Meiji art of the type sold by art dealer Yamanaka Sadajirō in his New York gallery.

Student education formed another key element of the Japan Society's cultural exchange program, which blossomed in these early years. In the first decades of the twentieth century there were, for all practical purposes, no Japanese-studies programs in America's colleges and universities. Interested students could study with Asakawa Kan'ichi at Yale or, more likely, with teachers of Chinese civilization who knew a bit about Japan, but few students could take any classes on Japan's institutional, economic, or social structures. In order to foster greater attention on the country, the society promoted the "development and direction of the study of Japan and Japanese subjects" in selected colleges and universities. It hoped to spark interest in Japan by donating $100 for student prizes at Columbia University and the Universities of Michigan and Kentucky; the following year, the donations were extended to Yale, Cornell, and Harvard, and in 1913 to Amherst College and Iowa State University.[47] It appears the funds were raised by subscription directly from among members of the group, as the society's records indicate that the Nippon Club president, Takamine Jōkichi, personally provided the monies for the Yale prize.

Despite such advances, the opportunities for an educated American public to more directly and personally engage with individuals from Japan were still far and few between. In 1911, however, the Japan Society helped run the first privately sponsored intellectual exchange program between the two countries. From New York, the Japan Society sent member Hamilton Holt to Tokyo on a lecture tour; at the same time it welcomed the famous writer and Christian Nitobe Inazō (1862–1933) to America. The society followed on its commitment to higher education by making arrangements for Nitobe to lecture at American universities from August to December. He spoke on U.S.-Japan relations at schools ranging from Johns Hopkins to the University of Illinois, and was almost certainly the first famous Japanese to directly address American university students.

In picking Nitobe, the society had selected the one Japanese superstar of the day. Nitobe was well known to Americans primarily as the author of the best seller, *Bushido* (The Way of the Warrior), which soon defined the samurai genre for curious Americans. But he was also a well-known Christian pacifist, and the Japan Society's sponsorship of his tour was in line with its participation in the American Peace Society's activities during the same period. The Nitobe tour therefore created yet another link between the Japan Society and the larger internationalist community. The funding for Nitobe's trip, and quite likely the initiative as well, came from the Carnegie Endowment for International Peace, which had been organized only the year before; the trip thus linked together at least two, and by extension three, internationalist organizations. It set the standard for future lecture tours, which became a staple of the society's activities.

The Publication of Exchange

Intellectual exchanges and art exhibits, however popular, were ephemeral, the echoes of their resonance limited by time. Surprisingly, the written word continued its dominance in the world of cultural exchange long after the age of noble adventurers had passed. What had changed from earlier decades was the regularity of printing, the support of an organization, and the growth in the number and types of publications. No longer was the impetus for writing tied to the haphazard whims of those who had sojourned in Japan. Now there was increasing demand, partly from those who participated in the activities of the exchange groups, and an organizational support system that provided funds, commissioned professional works, and then distributed them to a targeted audience.

Again, the Japan Society of New York took a lead in forming the contours of exchange through the publishing industry. It established a regular publication schedule, printing or subsidizing the production of various books, reports, and tracts on Japanese history, society, immigration issues, and the like. One of its first major publications, in 1912, was Nitobe's book *The Japanese Nation,* which focused largely on the Japan-America relationship and which derived from his speaking visit sponsored by the society the year previously.[48] By 1918, the society had distributed over two thousand copies of *The Japanese Nation* to libraries and universities, along with journalist K. K. Kawakami's *Japan in World Politics.* For many institutions these were the first books on Japan they had ever added to their collection.[49]

In these early years, the society also sponsored the writing of one of the first academic histories of Japan for a general audience. In 1918, while American doughboys fought their first major foreign war, *The Development of Japan* was published by the well-known Yale historian of Christianity, Kenneth Scott Latourette. Originally known as the "Japan Society Syllabus," it served as one of the primary texts on the country for nearly four decades, much as William Elliot Griffis's work had in the late nineteenth and early twentieth centuries. Latourette's volume went through three editions in the pre–World War II years before being succeeded in 1955 by Columbia University historian Herschel Webb's *An Introduction to Japan,* which also was sponsored by the Japan Society. By the middle of the second decade of the twentieth century, the society was the major distributor of books on Japan, including its 1915 mailing to libraries, subscribers, and universities of over forty-two hundred copies of a collection of essays, *Japan to America,* and three thousand editions of the companion book, *America to Japan,* all entries being written by distinguished public figures from each country.[50]

By this time, the society had over fifteen hundred members, far beyond what its founders thought would be reached, and in 1920 it approached the major Japanese businesses in New York to permanently support its publishing activities.[51] Led by Mitsui and its American head, Kobayashi Masanao, Japanese firms donated approximately $74,000 worth of securities to the Japan Society. The society then established the Townsend Harris Permanent Endowment Fund, which was to focus on "educational work along the broadest lines among Americans to disseminate a knowledge of Japan and the Japanese."[52] The monies were employed almost immediately to distribute over ten thousand copies of Latourette's syllabus to members and libraries. In addition, the society now had a secure source of money to publish some of the more noteworthy lectures given at meetings. The first beneficiary of this largesse was the venerable William Elliot Griffis, author of the famous *Mikado's Empire.* A January 1919 talk of his was published in the early 1920s as *Some of Japan's Contributions to Civilization,* a brisk forty-four-page outline of Japanese society and cultural achievements, which particularly focused on material conditions and the arts.[53]

This otherwise forgettable pamphlet, however, was symbolic of the way in which formal cultural exchange had altered the atmosphere of U.S.-Japan relations. We last saw Griffis as one of the exemplars of the age of the nineteenth-century noble adventurer, a foreign employee reaching Japan's interior in the last moments of feudalism. His four years in Japan translated into the best-selling American book on the history and culture of the country. Now, half a century after he first rode into Fukui, Griffis was speaking before the members of a association that was established in America's leading city and that was providing numerous talks, exhibitions, and publications on the country that he had helped define for his fellow Americans. And out of that talk came yet another publication, paid for by an endowment set up by Japanese business firms and distributed as far away as Kobe, Japan, where it wound up in the library of Kobe University.

The continuing importance of the printed word to U.S.-Japan relations suggests limitations to the era of direct contact. Though technology was bringing the world together and transnational social organizations of various types were forming, cross-Pacific travel would still be time consuming and expensive until the advent of the commercial jetliner after World War II. Thus the interests and desires of a large, heterogeneous audience were served on both sides of the Pacific by a steady diet of reporting and editorializing. Interestingly, most of the journals on Japan that were published in English were done so in Tokyo. Perhaps the best known was the glossy, lavishly produced *Japan Magazine,* which appeared from 1910 to 1941. In its pages, American (and of course British Imperial) readers could peruse articles on Japan's traditional arts and festivals, read tales of old Japan, and see beautifully reproduced images, both photographic and painted. While stories of Japan's modernization also received prominent play, much of the effect of coffee-table journals like *Japan Magazine* was to reify the image of Japan that had been presented at world's fairs—the image of a still semi-isolated fairyland, except that now travelers could come and visit, if they could afford the passage.

Such periodicals promoted cultural exchange, particularly since their messages dovetailed with private and official publications that urged tourism. Nonetheless, tourism was increasingly a commodified experience in the early twentieth century. The same forces that allowed for international congresses made possible the creation of comprehensive travel packages. It was a far cry from the age of the noble adventurers. In the case of Japan, such tourism was being sold as an adventure to a land of the past, but one with a complex message. One could see ancient temples and beautifully dressed geisha, but one would cross the ocean on the most modern steamers and ride a world-class rail system while in the country. There of course had been travel books printed prior to 1900, but only after the turn of the century was there a particular push to bring Americans and other English-speaking tourists to Japan. Some of these efforts were private, such as those of the Nippon Yusen Kaisha (Japan Mail Steamship Company), which put out a typically lyrical, and superficial, pamphlet titled *The Charm of the East* in 1919.[54]

Starting in 1913, however, the Imperial Japanese Government Railways and later the Japanese Tourist Board published extensive, detailed guides to Japan. These competed on an equal level with long-established guidebooks such as *Murray's Handbook for Japan,* which was authored in large part by the famous Japanologist Basil Hall Chamberlain. The Imperial Railways collection was particularly impressive, not to mention particularly political. The four-volume set was called *An Official Guide to Eastern Asia*. Volumes 2 and 3 handled southwestern and northeastern Japan, respectively, but volume 1 covered Manchuria and Chosen (Korea), and volume 4 was devoted to China proper.[55] Reissued and updated in 1920, the guide contained not only finely drawn maps but also a wealth of material on Japanese customs, history, culture, and current affairs. Anyone who read through the books would be nearly as well informed as most professionals of the time on Japan, especially in regards to history and society. Yet at the same time, the books sent a very clear message regarding Japan's regional power, special interests in China and Manchuria, and control over formerly independent nations such as Korea. The vast majority of Americans who owned the set probably never traveled to Japan or east Asia, but for them as much as for those who did take the journey, the books, while promoting cultural exchange, contained an unambiguous official message about contemporary Japan's place in the world.

Cultural exchange between Japan and America was not a one-way street, however. As much as Americans were waking up to their various interests in Japan, the rapidly modernizing Japanese public retained its fascination with the land that had played such a large role in propelling Japan along the road to world power. Recognizing that interest, the Japanese vernacular press during these decades contained numerous, regular stories on American life. For many in the press, what moved them to write was fascination, sometimes horror, at what their country was becoming, often reflected through the prism of American daily life and national power. The famous novelist Nagai Kafū, for example, compared life in America (and Europe) with that in Japan in a 1909 issue of the leading journal *Shinchō*. Nagai, known for his elegiac stories of the disappearance of traditional Japan, used America as a foil for his critique of late-Meiji society, noting, for example, that life in the new Japan was hurried and without *yoyū*, or ease, leeway, something that had made the Japanese special and correspondingly aware of the world around them.[56]

Yet most of the coverage in the regular press celebrated America for Japanese readers. It was not necessarily the thought-provoking ruminations of literary figures such as Nagai that most interested late-Meiji Japanese. Rather, it was articles that spoke directly to their experiences of a changing daily life, changes that increasingly came to be seen as American in origin. For example, the April 1914 issue of *Shukujo gahō,* a monthly women's magazine, printed a detailed article on the technological innovations in American kitchens. Written by an author identified only as "Hanako," the article related the growing ease of domestic chores in the United States. Hanako had encountered these new innovations while studying at an unnamed women's college in America and noted with approbation everything from the icebox ("the most excellent thing inside kitchens") to recipes for new dressings such as mayonnaise. For Hanako, such developments were not simply technological but also cultural. The new "kitchen life" was linked to the deeper streams of American history, which from its origins as a colonized land had emerged into a "magnificent country," due in no small part to its focus on domestic life.[57]

In 1911, the Japanese periodical *Shin Nippon* (New Japan) devoted an entire issue to America. The special issue itself had political overtones, as it was sponsored by the People's Education Association, which was run by the liberal politician Ōkuma Shigenobu, a steadfast proponent of greater civil liberties and voting rights in Japan. The issue's cover was emblazoned with the Stars and Stripes, and its three-hundred-plus pages were filled with articles on nearly every aspect of life in the United States, from the American spirit to agricultural techniques, from adoring reports on the latest American theatrical stars to the state of women's education.[58] At the same time, however, contrasting views of the uniqueness of American culture and the U.S.-Japan relationship were revealed in this special issue.

Ōkuma himself penned the lead article, using it as a springboard for his political program. In his view, Japanese-American relations were neither a historical accident nor the result of crass commercial opportunism. Rather, they were unique in world history, for they grew out of the spread of freedom, first on the American continent, then through the Western hemisphere, and finally across the Pacific. Allying himself with American populist figures such as William Jennings Bryan, Ōkuma identified the expansion of self-government and liberty as the future for Japan and the motivating spirit in relations between the two countries. The exchange of culture between them would serve not only to bring Japan into line with American practice but indeed to make it one of the world's leading democracies, along with America.[59]

The second article in the issue belonged to Kaneko Kentarō, president of the American Friends' Association. Kaneko, a baron and member of the House of Peers, struck a different note from that of the populist Ōkuma. Kaneko's interest in what made American culture and society great was more pragmatic than Ōkuma's and, in that way, more American as well. It was, he argued, the American fascination with having the "most"—be it the largest, smallest, or rarest—that was the engine that raised the country to the first rank of nations. The American experience was one of optimism and a can-do attitude that recreated the world around it. It was this trait that was responsible for American urban life and material culture. This was the lesson Japanese had to learn: that they could remake their world, that with their heritage they could become a leading power and partner naturally with America.[60] Not all popular publications went as far as *Shin Nippon,* but in the aggregate they celebrated and embraced the new world that Japan was entering as the first among Asian nations.

Not all observers cheered the spread of cultural exchange, and an alternative view of the Japan-American connection emerged contemporaneously with the paeans to progress. Belief that exchange was but a cynical ploy to further the goals of the state seeped into American media, just as the exchange organizations were beginning to play a more public role advocating for closer relations and better understanding. Perhaps the most direct attack came from American author Carl Crow, who had published several volumes critical of Japan. In an article titled "The Two Japans: The Land of Facts v. the Land of Press Agents," in the March 1916 issue of *McBride's Magazine,* he attacked each of the shibboleths paraded by those in favor of Japan, from the politeness of the people to its public sanitation. His strongest barbs were reserved for his compatriots who surrendered to the wiles of the publicity agents of the government: "It is a remarkable fact, probably nothing more than a curious coincidence, that among the many prominent Americans who have been entertained in this way and converted to Japanese propaganda within the past few years are to be found some of those who are most prominent in their agitation to keep down the armaments of the United States, and have been most outspoken in their assurances of Japan's good will.... These Americans who have been decorated by the Japanese Emperor are serving Japan much more faithfully than they are serving their own country."[61]

This was a serious charge and one that would intensify in later decades. There is little doubt that such critical views helped to provide a more balanced picture of conditions in Japan. Yet those disposed toward cultural exchange then (as now) asserted that it was natural for those fascinated by a particular land, or those who were committed to breaking down boundaries between peoples, to look for and celebrate the positive in cultural relations. But Crow was unyielding, for he was in essence arguing that cultural exchange, a variant of internationalism, had already by 1916 been enlisted in the service of the state. He was among those that charged that the goodwill and immense efforts of many on both sides of the Pacific were being distorted by the Japanese government into propaganda that would be spread in America, not by Japanese, but by Americans themselves.

Crow's critique is not easily dismissed, even today, for cultural exchange of course is not free from the values its participants hold, and is used by many to achieve different goals. Nagai Kafū used America to attack the superficiality and haste of Meiji Japan. The Nippon Yusen Kaisha painted an idyllic portrait of Japan to lure paying customers. The Japanese Foreign Ministry clearly aimed to support the state's foreign policies (as will be discussed in Chapter 4). So was it simplistic for the Japan Society or the American Friends' Association to desire better relations between the peoples of Japan and the United States and to increase knowledge of the other in their countries? This, too, was advocacy, if of a benign kind.

This struggle to define Japan for Americans was played out, among other places, in the pages of the glossy, general circulation journal *Asia*. It was founded in 1918 by the American Asiatic Association, which was now struggling to balance Tokyo's political and military dominance in the region with the organization's two-decade-old interest in expanding trade and relations with Asia. Some of the numerous articles on Japan were moderately sympathetic to the Meiji state, such as Walter Weyl's October 1917 piece, "Japan's Diplomacy of Necessity," which explained how Tokyo viewed its national interests in China and why Japan desired a predominant role over the former hegemon of Asia. Other articles were openly critical, such as "Japan and World Order." Written by Jackson

Fleming, it claimed, "The essence of our present problem lies not in the Japanese people, but in the Japanese as a nation. It is the conception of Japanese destiny held by Japan's present leaders."[62] Both of these articles, of course, were responding to Japan's 1915 Twenty-one Demands to the Chinese government and which would have given Tokyo a predominant say in China's foreign and economic policies. Other articles in the magazine were more negative toward Japanese society as a whole. For example, a grim picture was provided by Gertrude Emerson, who criticized the vaunted Japanese modern schooling system, saying this about a typical student who had gone through the system: "He has been given few tools to carve his own destiny; and with scarcely a murmur he quietly steps into line."[63] From such early criticisms more blatant stereotyping of modern Japanese would develop in later decades.

Other articles in *Asia,* perhaps the premier magazine devoted to Asian affairs in America at the time, were more positive or at least sought to avoid contentious political issues, much like the exchange societies themselves. Thus there was "Vignettes of Old Kyoto," by the same Gertrude Emerson (June 1918), a picture essay on "The Children of Japan" (February 1918), and "Japan's Greatest Store" (February 1918), which explored the famous Mitsukoshi. Stories such as these serve to familiarize, even to normalize, the Japanese for American readers: the charming streets of Japan were of interest to American travelers, while Japanese housewives shopped in stores little different from what a reader in Chicago or Kansas City would visit. Yet the tinge of the fairyland, of exoticism, never lay far from the surface. In the end, though, each stab at revealing Japan was an honest attempt to explain the country—as honest as was the writer's own understanding. Advocacy was often placed in the service of higher goals: development, understanding, interested critique. Whether in intellectual or artistic expression, formal dinners or world's fairs exhibits, there was, not surprisingly, a multiplicity of cultural exchange—numerous avenues, numerous views, and numerous activities.

The Variety of Exchange

As they grew, the cultural exchange organizations and their publications provided a larger institutional context in which the various forms of cultural contact that already existed between Japan and the United States continued to occur. Some of those activities appeared to be remnants of the era of informal cultural encounter, but in the twentieth century they took on larger and more impressive proportions, fueled perhaps by the growing contact provided by the exchange organizations. A good example was the continued importance of the world's exposition.

The Japanese government had participated in over two dozen world's fairs by the early 1900s, including the 1876 Philadelphia Centennial Exposition and the 1893 Columbian Exposition in Chicago. But Japan's display at the 1904 Louisiana Purchase Exposition, as the Saint Louis World's Fair formally was called, exceeded all previous ones in size and grandeur.[64] Costing over $800,000 dollars, the Japanese exhibit covered more than 150,000 square feet in various buildings, many of which were devoted to advanced industrial processes and, of course, the fine arts. An imperial Japanese garden was set up, with a replica of the Kinkakuji, the Golden Pavilion in Kyoto, and an unofficial Japanese village sprang up, complete with teahouse, theater, and various gateways. Over the six months of the exhibit, various Japanese and American dignitaries visited, such as Prince Fushimi, cousin of the emperor, who was hosted by the American Asiatic Association in New York on his way to Saint Louis, and Alice Roosevelt, then-President Theodore Roosevelt's daughter.

Politics played a major role at the St. Louis World's Fair, as Japan was in the middle of the Russo-Japanese War. Tokyo deliberately used the fair as a means of announcing Japan's new international status as a colonial power. Its victories in the 1894–95 Sino-Japanese War and its ongoing success in the Russo-Japanese War were recounted, and its control over Formosa (Taiwan) was symbolized by the erection of a bamboo teahouse. The display also showed how cultural relations could reveal an inhuman face of the modern, imperialist state. As part of the government's attempt to highlight the home islands' modernization, the Japanese set up an exhibit on Hokkaido's indigenous Ainu society in the fair's anthropology pavilion. As visitors approached a faux village of traditional thatched straw houses, they were undoubtedly surprised to encounter a group of Ainu families, on display like specimens in a zoo, who had been brought over to be part of this unique testimonial to Japan's power. Yet, in that era, there were no public expressions of outrage at the Ainu exhibit, or at least none that registered enough to be recorded in the media. No records exist to highlight the fate of the living exhibits who so poignantly impressed their American viewers.

All told, more than eighty thousand Japanese exhibits in Saint Louis testified to the military, industrial, and cultural power of the country—in short, to its modernity. Tens of thousands of Americans visited the Japanese pavilion, whose main draw was its central building, featured prominently in photographs, which was built entirely in traditional Japanese style and whose construction by skilled Japanese craftsmen was recorded in the local newspapers. After the fair ended, Tokyo gave the building to famed scientist Takamine Jōkichi, who moved the structure to upstate New York (where it remains to this day), renamed it the Shofu-den, and used it to host American and Japanese visitors in his capacity as president of the Nippon Club and as an elder statesman of U.S.-Japan exchange.

The magnificent Japanese exhibit at the St. Louis World's Fair soon was dismantled, along with all other national pavilions. Other expression of U.S.-Japan relations, however, would be longer lasting. In 1909, author Elizah Ruhamah Scidmore and U.S. First Lady Helen Taft came up with a plan to beautify the new Tidal Basin in Washington, D.C., with the flowering Japanese cherry tree. Nippon Club president Takamine Jōkichi soon heard about the idea and offered to donate two thousand trees. These, along with another two thousand trees given by Ozaki Yukio, the famous liberal politician and then mayor of Tokyo, soon arrived, but were destroyed upon inspection, as they were found to be carrying various insects and diseases. Takamine, though, continued to support the plan, along with the First Lady and Scidmore, and in 1912 successfully reimported and planted the trees, which quickly became an enduring symbol of the binational relationship between Japan and the United States, as well as a highlight for spring visitors to the American capital.[65]

It is tempting to ascribe to the ethereal cherry tree the impetus for greater intercourse between Japan and America, but the process was of course well under way by the time Helen Taft and Viscountess Chinda, wife of the Japanese ambassador, planted the first of the Tidal Basin trees on March 27, 1912. A century later, the annual Cherry Blossom Festival in Washington, D.C., is a highlight of U.S.-Japan cultural exchange and a major spring event in the capital. The success of the cherry blossoms in Washington may have helped spur the creation of public Japanese gardens in the United States, including the famous Japanese-Hill-and-Pond Garden in the Brooklyn Botanic Garden. Planned by Shiota Takeo (1881–1943), it became in 1915 the first Japanese garden to open to the general public.[66] Some, such as the Seattle Japanese Garden, were planned in the 1930s, but not completed until after the war and even into the 1960s. By the twenty-first century, there were nearly 300 public Japanese gardens in the United States, drawing thousands of visitors every year for both horticultural and cultural events.

As the twentieth century deepened, Americans interested in Japan could participate in an ever-widening circle of activities, some of which were made possible by a number of exchange organizations working in tandem. One such event was held in January 1914 on the campus of Harvard University. A Japanese-American conference was hosted by three groups: the sporadically active Japan Society of Boston, the Japan Club of Harvard, and the Naniwa Club of Boston, about which no information has survived but which likely was a group for Japanese businessmen in the city. The conference attracted a number of high-level speakers, including Edward S. Morse, the famous scientist and archaeologist, who gave a talk titled "Japan's Contributions to Science"; Charles W. Eliot, the president of Harvard, who discussed ancestor veneration; and the religious scholar Anesaki Masaharu, who gave a talk titled "The Problems of Modern Japan." Invitations were sent to sister organizations, such as the Japan Society of New York.[67] While no information on the number of attendees exists, the conference was a step forward in uniting the intellectual resources of a major university with the enthusiasm of a private group and the all-but-certain funding of a businessmen's organization.

Much of the exchange in U.S.-Japan relations appeared to be occurring in America, as the above discussion shows. Yet during the first decades of the twentieth century, a few Americans attempted to provide a more focused Japanese engagement with America, analogous to what was happening in the United States. One such endeavor came in 1918, when Alonzo Barton Hepburn, chairman of Chase National Bank and one of America's most powerful financiers, donated $60,000 dollars to Tokyo Imperial University for a chair in the study of the Constitution, history, and diplomacy of the United States.[68] The endowment provided funds for Nitobe Inazō and Japan's foremost constitutional scholar, Minobe

Tatsukichi, to lecture on American law and history, while the first holder of the chair was scholar of American political history Takagi Yasaka. Though American history had of course been taught in Japan before this, the endowment of a permanent chair in many ways marked the beginning of formalized American studies in Japan.

Japanese benefactors were no less committed to the cause. While Takamine Jōkichi acted as a bridge between his native and adopted countries from his base in New York, other Japanese took the lead from Japan and added to the growing community of U.S.-Japan cultural organizations and their activities. One of the most important was Japan's premier industrialist, entrepreneur, and philanthropist, Shibusawa Eiichi.[69] Shibusawa was born in 1840 as the son of a farmer in modern-day Saitama prefecture. Raised on the Confucian classics and Japanese history, Shibusawa joined the antibakufu movement in the early 1860s. After a brief fling with political activism, he enrolled as a retainer to the future shogun, Tokugawa Yoshinobu, then known as Hitotsubashi Keiki, son of one of the most progressive feudal leaders in Japan.

Shibusawa was thus fortuitously placed at the center of Japanese politics. His position got him appointed to the Japanese embassy to the Paris Universal Exposition of 1867, where he saw for the first time modern Western technologies and industrial products. After the fall of the Tokugawa shogunate the following year, his talent was recognized, and despite his continuing loyalty to the erstwhile shogun Yoshinobu, Shibusawa was employed by the new Meiji government in a variety of financial positions, including as the head of the Tax Bureau and the Reform Committee. In 1870, at the age of thirty, he was put in charge of the state-owned Tomioka Silk Mill, in the current Gunma prefecture. As silk and tea were Japan's most important exports, Shibusawa was placed in a crucial position to help the new government develop foreign trade.

Bureaucracy was not in Shibusawa's blood, however, and in 1873 he resigned his government positions. His official connections served him well, nevertheless, and got him appointed as the head of Japan's first financial and industrial concerns, including the Dai-Ichi Ginkō (First National Bank) and the Oji Paper Manufacturing Company. From here, he began an unparalleled career of founding or being the director of major businesses in mid-Meiji Japan, including the Osaka Spinning Company, the Japan Railway Company, the Japan Mail Steamship Company, the Imperial Hotel, the Sapporo Brewery Company, the Tokyo Ishikawajima Shipyard Company, the Tokyo Savings Bank, and the Tokyo Gas Company. In all, Shibusawa founded or directed approximately five hundred companies in his lifetime, essentially creating the modern Japanese industrial state.

Shibusawa shared another trait with the American industrialists whom he surpassed in achievements. Like John D. Rockefeller and Andrew Carnegie, he was committed to bettering society through volunteerism and philanthropy. In 1876 he became secretary general of Tokyo Yoiku-in, a welfare institution for orphan and handicapped people that was managed by the Tokyo prefecture; in 1880, he was a founding member of the Japanese Red Cross; and later he became president of both the Tokyo Jogakkan School for Young Ladies and Japan Women's College. At the age of seventy-three, in 1913, he founded the Japan Tuberculosis Prevention Association, and at the age of eighty-nine, just two years before his death, he established the Central Association for the Welfare of the Blind.

While the modernization of Japan was Shibusawa's focus and passion, he was not restricted by the boundaries of the islands. After a lifetime of economic accomplishment, his strength being poured into making his country the economic and social equal of any other, Shibusawa became a committed internationalist. It was natural for him to focus on America, as it was perhaps the leading industrial country in the world at the turn of the twentieth century, next to Germany. In 1902, he took his first trip to the United States. The journey could not be easy for the sixty-two-year-old, but he traveled across the continent, crowning his visit with a personal interview with President Theodore Roosevelt, who was rapidly becoming America's leading booster of Japan. After all this, Shibusawa then moved on to Europe, spending several more months there.

Seven years later, in 1909, he traveled again to the United States. This time, however, it was as head of an official delegation from the Japan Chambers of Commerce. Shibusawa, of course, had founded the Tokyo chamber, Japan's first, back in 1878. This journey was a grueling eight-month tour of fifty-three American cities. It was also one of Japan's first full-scale attempts at "people's diplomacy."[70] And while Shibusawa was representing the combined economic interests of his country, these of course were closely tied to the Meiji government. It was therefore hard to draw a precise line between official and nonofficial roles during this visit, as it was increasingly hard to do with some aspects of cultural exchange practiced by groups such as the American Friends' Association.

The Honorary Commercial Commissioners, as Shibusawa's group was called, were received by President William Howard Taft and interacted with ordinary Americans and elite business leaders, as well as with the network of exchange societies that already existed. The Nippon Club of New York hosted the commissioners during an evening of relaxation and dinner, and it was as a result of this visit that Shibusawa would found the Supporting Association of the Japan Society of New York a few years later in Tokyo. The New York Chamber of Commerce also hosted them at a formal lunch. During his translated remarks at the chamber, Shibusawa laid out the philosophy guiding his visit and his broader international activities, stating, "We bring no official message, but a message of good-will and peace from the people of Japan to the people of America. The two nations facing each other across the Pacific should be friendly and act in union and understanding."[71] While both he and his hosts were frank about growing economic competition between the two countries, they were united in the entrepreneurial belief that healthy, fair competition would benefit both countries and both peoples, an unabashed support of laissez-faire policies.

Upon returning to Japan, Shibusawa deepened his internationalist activities and created a broad spectrum of groups; he founded the Japanese Association for the League of Nations in 1920 and became chairman of the Japan Institute of Pacific Relations in 1926. Through it all, however, he maintained his special relationship to America, ultimately making four extended trips across the Pacific. In 1913, he organized the Nichibei Dō shikai (the Japanese-American Friendship Society), whose goal was to strengthen relations and counter the rising anti-immigration movement on the West Coast. This was an ad hoc organization, however, and after a third visit to the United States in 1915, when he visited President Woodrow Wilson and celebrated the opening of the Panama Canal, Shibusawa established a more formal group, the Nichibei Kankei Iinkai (the Japanese-American Relations Committee, or JARC).

The JARC, however, was not a true cultural exchange organization, for Shibusawa formed it largely as a private diplomacy venture. In its activities, the JARC more closely resembled what the Council on Foreign Relations in America would become in the 1920s and later. Yet the ethos of the JARC reflected the explosion in international nongovernmental organizations during the first decades of the twentieth century. Even a partial list does not begin to illuminate the structure of this web of groups, or their overlapping nature. Japan-U.S. groups formed a minor part of this network, although many of the individuals connected to the binational organizations found themselves involved with numerous other groups, as did many in the internationalist community. There is still no comprehensive study on the history, roles, and effects on international history of this kaleidoscope of organizations, and perhaps there never can be, for their reach and interests were nearly universal.

One cannot class the Japanese-American Relations Committee in with the pacifist, sometimes Christian, sometimes socialist-leaning, internationalist groups in terms of its membership or activities. But, as part of a global movement, the history of the JARC raises the question of how cultural exchange, broadly defined, fit into the larger network of internationalist activity. Some groups, like the Japan Society of New York, participated equally in both the world of cultural exchange and the larger network of international organizations; others, like the JARC, were more narrowly defined. For example, membership in the JARC was strictly limited to thirty Japanese handpicked by Shibusawa. Those tapped included leaders of cultural exchange with the United States, such as Kaneko Kentarō and Nitobe Inazō, as well as prominent figures such as Admiral Uryū and Baron Kondō Renpei of the Japan Mail Steamship Company.

The JARC's main activities took place in the 1910s and 1920s, when the organization hosted a series of unofficial bilateral meetings with leaders of American groups, such as Frank Vanderlip and George W. Wickersham of the Japan Society of New York, and the missionary and author Sidney L. Gulick, who headed the New York–based National Committee on American-Japanese Relations. Unlike most of the global peace groups, however, the JARC was untouched by World War I and postwar reconstruction concerns; in this sense, the JARC and similar U.S.-Japan groups were incidental to the major thrust of internationalist activity in the early twentieth century.

But within their own sphere of interest, the Japanese-American Relations Committee and its American counterparts engaged in what is now called Track II diplomacy, forming an interest lobby that primarily pressured American leaders to improve Japanese-American relations and to respond to the anti-Japanese legislation that was passed in California in 1913 and now proposed on a national scale.[72] These activities, and all the activities of the JARC, were private and aimed directly at policy makers in both countries. The JARC did not publish any formal records of its activities and never engaged in the type of public education and outreach practiced by the Japan Society of New York. Nonetheless, the JARC survived Baron Shibusawa's death at the age of ninety-one, in 1931, and continued its behind-the-scenes activities until 1939, when U.S.-Japan relations were all but ruptured by tension in the Pacific.

Formalizing Exchange in Japan: The America-Japan Society of Tokyo

On May 11, 1917, Shibusawa Eiichi was one of the honored guests at a lavish banquet in Tokyo. The banquet announced the merger of Kaneko Kentarō's American Friends' Association with the American Asiatic Association of Japan. That evening, Shibusawa became the vice president emeritus of the new group committed to U.S.-Japan relations. The host of the event, and the president of the new organization, was Kaneko. The group was to be called the Nichibei kyōkai, or the America-Japan Society of Tokyo (AJS).[73] The banquet undoubtedly passed unnoticed by almost all Americans, whose attention was focused on the great battlefields of Europe, to which they were just sending their first soldiers to fight in the Great War. Yet inside the small world of Japan-U.S. exchange, the AJS would soon become the Japanese equivalent of the Japan Society of New York, with Kaneko as the driving force, and take its place as the most important Japan-based society devoted to binational exchange.

From its beginning, the America-Japan Society included Japan's political and social elite among its members. Other guests at the opening dinner included Prime Minister Terauchi Masatake, Foreign Minister Motono Ichirō, and President of the House of Peers Tokugawa Iesato, head of the former shogunal family. The society's 438 members counted 129 Americans and included honorary members Tokugawa, Shibusawa, Takamine Jōkichi, and future finance minister Takahashi Korekiyo. The original Executive Committee included the industrialist Dan Takuma, educator and scholar of English language Kanda Naibu, future foreign minister Shidehara Kijūrō, and Nitobe Inazō.[74]

The AJS had a clear mission statement, as rewritten in the 1927 articles of incorporation, one that encapsulated the prevailing goal of cultural exchange by the end of the 1910s: "to promote friendly relations between the peoples of Japan and the United States of America, and to study the aims of the national life of the people of the United States, their ideals, learning, arts, industries, and economic condition, and a more general dissemination of such knowledge among the people of Japan."[75] With its offices in the heart of Tokyo, in the Mitsubishi Building in Marunouchi, the AJS symbolically occupied a spot overlooking the Imperial Palace, and yet the AJS's gaze was firmly focused across the Pacific. One of the group's first acts was to link past and present U.S.-Japan relations when, on July 5, 1918, former foreign minister Viscount Ishii Kikujirō presented a sword on behalf of the society to Fairhaven, Massachusetts, in memory of Captain William H. Whitfield, rescuer of Nakahama Manjirō back in 1841. The ceremony served as a symbolic testament to the modern nature of cultural exchange, as a formal binational organization celebrated the first Japanese to come to America.[76]

The AJS aimed at educating Japanese through its meetings, Tokyo-based activities, and personal networks. It mirrored the actions of the U.S.-based Japan Society and other groups, in serving largely as a venue for Japanese elites and Americans in Japan to maintain relations. Early events included a banquet to celebrate the armistice in Europe in November 1918 and, on December 4 that year, a reception for the commander of the American Asiatic Squadron, Admiral Austin M. Knight.[77] The AJS also became the main facilitator in Japan of joint activities with the network of U.S.-Japan exchange groups. During May and June 1920, for example, it hosted Frank Vanderlip, president of the Japan Society of New York, arranging his speaking events and institutional visits throughout the country.

The Vanderlip visit, in particular, helped define the internationalist stance within the cultural exchange community on increasingly troublesome questions of colonialism and great power politics. Japan had come out of the 1919 Paris Peace Conference controlling the former Asian colonial territories of Germany, including the Shantung (Shandong) Peninsula and Tsingtao (Qingdao) on the Chinese mainland. Yet Tokyo was losing the public relations war, for Chinese public diplomacy had cast Japan as a territorial aggressor and revived memories of the infamous Twenty-one Demands of 1915.[78] Vanderlip's public speeches directly tackled the question of Japan's current problems and ambitions in the Asian region. In a speech, given to an audience of eight thousand, sponsored by the *Osaka Mainichi* newspaper, Vanderlip spoke as a self-identified advocate of the "New Diplomacy" popular after World War I and addressed the choices available to Japan to deal with its rapid population growth. It could pursue industrial development, like Great Britain, or export its peoples, like Italy, Vanderlip noted. But if Tokyo chose the path taken by Germany in 1914, that of territorial expansion, it "would be a policy directly against the highest moral standards, [and] would result in ruin to Japan." Conveniently ignoring Great Britain's worldwide colonial expansion, Vanderlip was moved to such ruminations because he recognized the danger of the Japanese military gaining "an unduly potent voice in shaping events."[79] This, undoubtedly, was a reference to the formation of cabinets by military leaders such as Katsura Tarō starting in 1901.

The AJS's response to Vanderlip's speech reveals the lack of consensus within the cultural exchange community when it came to issues of foreign policy and thus highlights the tensions that would worsen over time. Despite the warnings given by Vanderlip and others about the dangers of an aggressive policy in China, the AJS supported Japan's "rightful position" in Shantung, though Tokyo returned the peninsula to China in 1922.[80] Against their will, the exchange groups were being drawn into the politics of the 1920s, and contentious issues would threaten to derail not only still-tender internationalist visions but the deeper nonpolitical sentiments long identified with a more cosmopolitan outlook.

Even as political issues began intruding on the consciousness of the AJS, it continued to identify its mission as improving Japanese understanding of America; this approach soon broadened to educating Americans about Japan. Taking a clue from the Japan Society of New York, the AJS began publishing various journals, including the English-language *Transactions of the America-Japan Society,* the *America-Japan Society Bulletin,* and a magazine titled *America-Japan,* which lasted only two years but during which time translated major Japanese periodical writings and essays for a foreign audience. The topics covered by *America-Japan* reflected mainstream internationalist thought combined with a type of indirect championing of Japanese culture and values.

Japanese Premier Hara Takashi, the first popular politician to be elected prime minister, provided a good example of this type of writing in *America-Japan.* In an article titled "Fusion of Oriental and Occidental Cultures: A Basis of Permanent Peace," Hara attempted to show how Japanese civic loyalty was not different from that of other countries and yet at the same time was a unique cultural characteristic of his compatriots. Patriotism, he wrote, is "not an external rule . . . but rather the racial intuitions springing from the inmost deeps of national consciousness." Repeating current ideas of the indissolubility of the ethnic and political components of society, Hara went on to argue, "The State is the nation, and the nation the State." In his conclusion, he tied this ethnic nationalism to a traditional internationalist vision: "Permanent world peace will be impossible unless the nations seek by mutual contract and mutual respect to combine the cultures of all races so as to enrich life."[81] Nationalism was a shadow beginning to cloud the worldview of Japanese.

Increasingly, in the second and third decades of the twentieth century, the particular and the universal, namely, nationalism and internationalism, were coming into conflict. In the case of the U.S.-Japan relationship, a number of bilateral problems were coming to the fore that would ultimately prove to be irreconcilable. Foremost among them was Japan's interests in Manchuria and mainland China, the growth of the Imperial Japanese Navy, and American security interests in the Philippines.[82] Each of these reverberated in the cultural relationship between the two countries, eventually forcing those involved with exchange to choose sides between nationalism and internationalism.

Yet one crisis in U.S.-Japan relations united the exchange community during these decades: the anti-Japanese immigration movement in the United States. This would prove the greatest challenge to both internationalist and cosmopolitan visions of cultural relations. Anti-Asian immigration had been part of the American political landscape since 1882 and the passing of the Chinese Exclusion Act. As a result of this first closure of U.S. borders, Japanese immigration to the United States jumped in the following decades, leading to another round of tensions and calls for legislation to ban immigrants coming from Japan. The state most affected by this grassroots movement was California, which boasted the largest population of Japanese in the country, even though they were statistically insignificant as a proportion of landowners. As a result of growing tension, the Japanese and American governments concluded the Gentlemen's Agreement of 1907, by which Japan voluntarily agreed to limit the number of immigrants to the United States.[83]

By 1913, there had been forty anti-Japanese bills introduced into the California legislature, including proposals for a poll tax and the segregation of schoolchildren. In fact, Japanese schoolchildren had already been segregated in San Francisco, in 1906, despite an uproar in Japan. The key issue soon became landholding, and the bill that passed the California legislature in 1913 prevented Japanese in California, who were not eligible for citizenship, from holding land.[84] Over the next decade, the calls for national legislation to stop Japanese immigration entirely grew in volume.

The exchange societies realized that this was a direct threat not only to U.S.-Japan relations but also to the societies' own vision of what the future should look like. From the beginning of the crisis, then, the exchange organizations mobilized against the anti-Japanese immigration movement, although each did so in different ways. The Japan Society of New York for the first time became involved in public advocacy, sending to President Woodrow Wilson a telegram that condemned the legislation and vowing to continue the society's "campaign of education" through publishing and speaking events.[85] In late 1913, after the passage of the California anti-Japanese act, the society published and widely distributed two pamphlets that had grown out of Hamilton Holt's speaking tour of Japan in 1911. Holt was becoming one of the main publicists against the anti-immigration movement, and his talks were printed as "International Conciliation" and "Wanted—A Final Solution of the Japanese Problem."[86]

It was clear that the major battle over Japanese immigration would be fought at the national level, however, and the Japan Society of New York was finding that its influence was limited. In June 1918 it urged the U.S. government to send a mission to Japan to discuss problems in bilateral relations, but Secretary of State Lansing, who was focused on the war in Europe, refused the entreaty.[87] The society continued to insist that it saw itself as a "factor for good in international relations" but soon adjusted to the reality that it was having little impact for good on U.S. policy.[88] Never having played a major internationalist role before now, the Japan Society soon retrenched in favor of its traditional nonpolitical leanings. In early 1920, the leadership of the society made a public surrender, claiming that the group "had carefully avoided taking any part in political discussions." A statement read at its annual meeting noted that, "Its work is along educational, cultural, social, and business lines. . . . creating and stimulating interest in and diffusion among the American people a more accurate knowledge of the people of Japan, their aims, arts, sciences, industries, and economic conditions."[89] An excuse for political inactivity was expressed in an executive committee decision that, since the society was a New York–based group, it would be interfering in California's affairs if it made any "campaign in regard to the anti-Japanese Land Legislation in California."[90] By the time of the final fight against national anti-immigration legislation, in 1924, the Japan Society refused to take any role in defeating the proposals. Instead, it urged the New York–based National Committee on American-Japanese Relations to send to society members a pro-immigration pamphlet written by its head, Sidney Gulick.[91]

If the Japan Society of New York had decided that it would focus on education as a way of garnering public support to defeat the anti-Japanese bills, other groups on both sides of the Pacific moved to take up the advocacy role. Gulick's group, the National Committee on American-Japanese Relations was one, as was Shibusawa Eiichi's Japanese-American Friendship Society, founded back in 1913. These groups often coordinated their activities, particularly between Gulick's committee and Shibusawa's Japanese-American Relations Committee (JARC), which the viscount set up expressly to deal with the political problems in the bilateral relationship.

Perhaps no group became as involved in the fight, however, as the America-Japan Society of Tokyo. AJS president Kaneko Kentarō's two-plus decades of efforts in cultural exchange were threatened by the anti-

Japanese movement sweeping the United States. Prodded perhaps by his connections in government, Kaneko took the lead in attempting to find a political solution to the crisis, for example, by proposing in May 1921 the establishment of the "Joint High Commission on the Japanese-American Problem," which was never formed. [92] He also loosed the publications of the AJS on the issue. Indeed, the October 1920 number of *America-Japan* was devoted almost solely to the issue of race relations, condemning the already existing California immigration restrictions and discussing racial tensions from a global context. Yet this special issue, perhaps acknowledging the intensity of American opinion, presented a variety of positions, some in direct opposition to others. An article by the editor, J. T. Swift, for example, covering the history of the problem, shied away from a traditional internationalist view and resorted to a parochial bilateral frame of reference, pleading the case of the Japanese by noting, "[They] are the only Oriental people who organize on their own initiative and build constructively in all phases of society, industry, and military enterprise."[93] However, Hugh Byas, longtime newspaper editor in Tokyo, took a more internationalist approach in an article titled "Race Contact: A Worldwide Problem." Byas argued in his piece that, "Civilization is a unity, and its frontiers are not marked by race or complexion, but by moral and intellectual qualities. It is as equals in the comity of civilized nations that Japanese and Americans approach [this problem]."[94]

The "comity of civilized nations," however, had no vote in the United States Congress. There, debate over the Immigration Act of 1924 opened in the House of Representatives on April 5, 1924. Japanese newspapers covered the proceedings regularly and reprinted the statements of Japanese officials, such as Ambassador to the United States Hanihara Masanao's denunciation of the bill as unnecessary in light of the 1907 Gentlemen's Agreement, which voluntarily limited immigration.[95] Advocacy on both sides of the Pacific had little effect. Within a week of its introduction, the bill passed the House and moved on to the Senate, where it was passed in just two days with a special anti-Japanese provision barring entry into the United States of any person who was ineligible for citizenship, now defined by a 1922 Supreme Court decision as those not eligible for naturalization: in other words, nonwhites.

The blow was devastating, not just for the Japanese-American community, but also for those who had devoted their lives to better relations between the two nations. Foreign Minister Matsui Keishirō called it of "major concern to Japanese-American friendship," an understatement necessary for diplomacy and one soon overshadowed by Ambassador Hanihara's statement that the law "magnified the problems" between Japan and the United States.[96] Public anger in Japan grew over the spring and summer, and by early July anti-U.S. demonstrations took place in Tokyo, Osaka, and other major cities.[97] To the proponents of cultural exchange, their energies and interests had been steamrolled by a nativist movement in America that smashed their cosmopolitan dreams and violated their belief in a special relationship between Japan and the United States.

In shock, feeling that he had no other honorable option, Kaneko Kentarō, founding spirit of U.S.-Japan cultural exchange and its most impassioned advocate for nearly three decades, resigned from the presidency of the organization he had founded. In his farewell letter to the America-Japan Society he wrote,

> Ever since the outbreak of the anti-Japanese movement on the Pacific Coast, we were persuaded by America to be patient . . . but our patience was betrayed and our expectation disappointed. Thus for more than forty years have I endeavored to contribute whatever lay in my humble power to cultivate a felicitous and cordial feeling between our two countries; therefore, when I learned the Immigration Bill was passed in so drastic a manner and with such an overwhelming majority, I felt as if the hope of my life were destroyed. It was the 'unkindest cut of all," and the wounds will not be healed so long as the racial discrimination clause remains in the law.[98]

A quarter century of organized cultural exchange—the printing of untold books and pamphlets, the hosting of hundreds of dinners, the staging of numerous exhibitions, and the exchange of hundreds of persons—had amounted to little, if anything, during the greatest crisis yet between Japan and the United States. Cultural exchange had evolved from encounter and had matured since the turn of the century but suddenly found its very foundations questioned. A retrenchment and accounting would have to take place. This would occur in a very changed environment in U.S.-Japan relations, one in which traditional cosmopolitan impulses would be challenged by nationalist and internationalist fervor alike.

CHAPTER 4

Storm on the Horizon

A S CULTURAL EXCHANGE develops, it often becomes more complex, embracing more ambitious goals and divergent views. Indeed, the history of exchange lays bare the interplay of social, intellectual, and national development, and the fact that a simple cosmopolitan impulse is often no match for more powerful global currents, such as nationalism or internationalism. History also shows that nationalism intimately and always coexists with internationalism and that cultural exchange can be used for narrow purposes that have more to do with state policies than an increase in mutual understanding.

These complexities grew acute during the third and fourth decades of the twentieth century. This is nowhere better shown than in the history of U.S.-Japan relations from 1924 through 1941. These years reveal how cultural exchange evolved in response to global conditions. This period also points out the limits of classical exchange in a world dominated by military and economic concerns and yet paradoxically shows the strength of such exchange, as it becomes clear that only the crisis of war can fully disrupt cultural interaction, and even then only for the duration of the conflict.

The quarter century of cultural exchange after 1898 was marked on the whole by positive relations between Japan and the United States. Yet beneath the surface bubbled questions on both sides about national interests and immigration, perhaps the most elemental form of cultural encounter.[1] The 1924 anti-immigration act proved a turning point in U.S.-Japan relations, unleashing outrage in Japan over the American insult. The cultural exchange organizations were well aware of their impotence during the anti-immigration debate, and in response, they began to rethink their activities, though they never surrendered their ultimate goal of bettering relations between the two countries.

In the years after 1924, many activities of the organizations seemed unchanged on the surface, as they continued to host white-tie dinners and publish various newsletters and pamphlets. But they had learned a lesson from the inability even of elite private diplomacy groups such as Shibusawa Eiichi's Japanese-American Relations Committee to influence American leaders. Groups like the Japan Society of New York and the America-Japan Society of Tokyo now began to reach out to a wider public audience and to support programs aimed increasingly at ordinary citizens and especially students, perhaps in the hope of mobilizing the public to influence elites and state policy. Yet even as such organizations did so, national governments had begun to utilize public diplomacy as a key element of foreign policy, thus putting pressure on the exchange groups to follow the government lead and abandon their internationalist allies.

Internationalism and State Policies

The framework for much internationalist activity in this period came from the loose network of groups arranged around the League of Nations. In 1922, the league had created the International Committee on Intellectual Cooperation (ICII). Supported by a cluster of national committees, the ICII focused on creating transnational links among teachers, scholars, scientists, and those in the arts. The ICII included some of the most prestigious intellectuals in the world, including Marie Curie, Albert Einstein, Béla Bartók, and Thomas Mann.[2] Yet perhaps as an indication of the relatively low esteem in which such efforts were held, the League Assembly refused adequate funds for the ICII. In 1926, it was reestablished as the International Institute of Intellectual Cooperation (IIIC), headed by the French philosopher Henri Bergson. Housed in Paris, the IIIC maintained links with over forty intermediary organizations that kept it in touch with the hundreds of cultural and scientific societies around the world. This umbrella organization, underfunded as it was, attempted to globalize intellectual activity and continued its activities through the 1930s, until the beginning of World War II.

The world of transnational societies was not limited to the League of Nations and its subsidiaries, of course. Indeed, the growth in international nongovernmental organizations (INGOs) was most pronounced after World War I, as private citizens banded together to try and repair the bonds of civil society that had been destroyed in the Great War. Working at times with established philanthropic foundations, these organizations ran the gamut from the 1919 League of Red Cross Societies and its later 1928 reorganization as the International Red Cross, to the International Research Council, a pet idea of Woodrow Wilson's for international scientific cooperation.[3] These professional groups were joined by a host of internationalist societies, such as the Women's International League for Peace and Freedom, which had been formed in 1915. Many of these groups played a publicly prominent role during the 1930s, attempting to influence public opinion, and conducting research and organizing programs on global problems.[4] Yet their ultimate success in preventing conflict and increasing global understanding was less impressive than their presence might indicate and indeed had little effect on the growing international tensions of the 1930s.

Even as these private and quasi-public groups bonded intellectuals together around the globe, they were being chased by the cultural activities of official governmental organizations sponsoring cultural exchange activities. The Japanese government, unlike many of its European counterparts, had long focused on public diplomacy, in part as a means to offset its limited formal diplomatic influence. Tokyo, for example, had dispatched Kaneko Kentarō to the United States back in 1904 to serve as a goodwill ambassador in the beginning days of the war with Russia. Direct propaganda efforts were also begun during this period. In April 1914, the Foreign Ministry provided funds to help start two Japanese news organizations, the International News Agency (Kokusai Tsushinsha), which soon became a subsidiary of Reuters, and the Eastern News Agency (Tōhō

Tsushinsha), a semiofficial organ responsible for providing news on Japan in China.[5]

What Tokyo desired to create was a centralized operation that could link the various public information activities spread among independent government agencies. In 1920, the Foreign Ministry moved to formalize such activities by creating the Information Bureau (the Jōhōbu) to coordinate the dissemination of public information abroad. The main force behind the bureau was Ijuin Hikokichi (1864–1924), a career diplomat who was serving at the Paris Peace Conference and who was the first to propose a central-government information body. Later in the decade, the Foreign Ministry expanded its public outreach by opening the Cultural Affairs Bureau (Bunka jigyōbu), which also began issuing reports and sending information abroad to embassies and consulates for dissemination in their host countries' media outlets.

Both these departments were ahead of their time and made Japan a front-runner among governments that were beginning to discover the importance of public diplomacy. Both gained in importance as information—and its disreputable cousins, intelligence and propaganda—played an increasingly vital role in the operations of the modern nation-state. Resistance in other countries to the role of information and intelligence was evident, as in America, where Secretary of State Henry Stimson closed down America's first permanent intelligence gathering operation with the remark "Gentlemen do not read each other's mail." That blindness to the importance of the systematic gathering of information was to haunt the United States in 1941. Similarly, neither Great Britain nor the United States undertook serious public diplomacy initiatives until after World War II, though the U.S. Department of State opened a small office focused on Latin American affairs in 1938.[6]

Continuity and Change in the Japan-U.S. Societies

Japan's Information Bureau was as ineffective in heading off the 1924 Immigration Act as were the private exchange organizations. Nonetheless, it continued its activities, and in doing so, further muddied the waters of cultural relations, for now a state actor competed with the independent organizations in reaching out to foreign audiences. For the imperial government, education of overseas audiences was a central prop in its attempts to gain favorable coverage of Japan in America and to build a body of public opinion supportive of Japanese policies, especially in China and Manchuria. Some contemporary observers, like American journalist Carl Crow, however, sought to lump private and public organizations together, seeing their activities as all in the service of the state.

Yet, if anything, the old societies followed a confused path during these years, vainly attempting to preserve a "pure" cosmopolitan stance along with their usually ineffective internationalist activities, all the while being buffeted by growing nationalist forces. To an observer decades later, it almost seems as though there was a rush to assure each side of the Pacific of the continued support and good intentions of the other, that their old nonpolitical cosmopolitan attitude had not been shaken by the Immigration Act. Thus, for example, the Japan Society of New York continued to raise funds to help Tokyo recover from the massive Great Kanto Earthquake; indeed, the society's first donation had been at the height of the immigration controversy, when, in late 1923, it sent over $117,000 to the Japanese government for disaster relief.[7] Moreover, the year the anti-immigration bill passed, Japan Society registered 1,332 members, its highest level yet.[8] Yet under the leadership of George W. Wickersham, the Society reaffirmed its nonpolitical stance and declined to attend the 1924 Pan-Pacific Union conference at Honolulu.[9]

New groups also reached out to the old societies in their efforts to increase cross-Pacific understanding. In late 1925, the Japanese Brotherhood Scholarship Committee approached the Japan Society of New York for administrative help. The brotherhood was a circle of Japanese students in New York who had raised funds for sending an American student to Japan.[10] Most of the Japanese members of this group were connected with the International House in New York, itself a new innovation. The International House (I-House) of New York was established in 1924 by Harry Edmonds, a YMCA official. In 1909, after meeting a Chinese student at Columbia University, Edmonds realized that a community-oriented living and study center for foreign students could be a crucial ingredient in promoting cultural understanding and mitigating the loneliness often experienced by overseas students. Funding for the I-House of

New York came from John D. Rockefeller Jr. and the Cleveland H. Dodge family, and a building at 500 Riverside Drive on the Upper West Side of Manhattan was purchased to house the community. That the Japanese students connected with I-House would turn to the Japan Society was not surprising, for the chairman of the house's board was the society's president, George W. Wickersham. Over the succeeding years, the Japan Society provided office space and modest personnel help for the Japanese Brotherhood Scholarship Committee.

It was, however, the America-Japan Society of Tokyo (AJS) that was among the most active of all exchange groups during this period and the one that seemed most to champion the old cosmopolitan outlook. Its activities clearly show an evolution in exchange toward a more grassroots orientation, aimed at ordinary Americans and Japanese alike. The organization, however, first had to recover from the sudden departure of Kaneko Kentarō, whose resignation in protest of the Immigration Act was as symbolic a gesture as could be made. Kaneko, however, was in good company, for Nitobe Inazō, despite his Quaker beliefs, swore he would never set foot again in the homeland of his wife until the act was repealed, and Shibusawa Eiichi, who had devoted so many years of his life to U.S.-Japan relations, stated that he would never rest peacefully while the restrictions remained on the books.

The AJS quickly moved to fill the vacancy created by Kaneko's absence, and it chose for its president Prince Tokugawa Iesato, the most distinguished Japanese to serve in any of the exchange groups. Iesato was the head of the main branch of the ex-shogunal Tokugawa family. Born in 1863 as the heir to the Tayasu house, one of the blood-related branches to the shogunal line, he was installed by the new Meiji government as the head of the family after the last shogun, Tokugawa Yoshinobu, was forced to relinquish his familial role in 1868. In 1869, while still just a child, Iesato was made "governor" of Shizuoka, the home domain of the Tokugawa family. From 1877 to 1882, he studied in Britain, and then in 1903 he became president of the House of Peers, the second-most prestigious position in the civilian government after the prime ministership.

Iesato headed the House of Peers for nearly three decades, until 1930, and maintained a high profile in a variety of positions. In one of the great ironies in Japanese history, on March 29, 1914, he was summoned to the

Imperial Palace in the midst of one of Japan's early political crises. Admiral Yamamoto Gonnohyoe, the prime minister, had been forced to resign the premiership due to a naval procurement scandal, and the Taisho emperor turned to Tokugawa Iesato to replace him. Despite the imperial command, the "sixteenth shogun" declined to become Japan's seventeenth prime minister, though he remained at the center of government. Seven years later, Iesato was named as a delegate with full power to the Washington Naval Conference, and in 1929 he became president of the Japan Red Cross.

Yet it was to the America-Japan Society that Iesato devoted nearly all of his nonofficial time. In doing so, he thus potentially if, unintentionally, blurred the line between official state policy and the activities of the cultural exchange organizations. From the beginning, of course, the AJS had been run by elites, and Tokugawa was even better known than Kaneko Kentarō, so it was not considered controversial for him to take the position. Indeed, he was precisely the type of leader expected for such an organization. Nonetheless, Iesato's role as one of the government's leaders must have given a semiofficial cast to the activities of the AJS. This was highlighted during Iesato's visit to America in November 1930, when news reports referred to him as both the president of the House of Peers and the president of the America-Japan Society. He visited as a private citizen, but he gave speeches in New York and was hosted by the Japan Society of New York at a luncheon for four hundred invited guests, most of whom assumed that his comments reflected government policy.[11]

Yet, even when led by the most blue-blooded of Japanese, the AJS continued to shift its focus toward a broader, nonelite audience at home and abroad. A few years before Iesato's visit, in June 1925, during the immediate aftermath of the Immigration Act, the AJS opened an information department for American tourists in Japan.[12] This made the AJS the successor in Japan to the old Welcome Society, which no longer existed, and the parallel to the Japan Society of New York, which in 1914 had opened its own travel bureau and served as the American representative of the Japan Tourist Bureau. In conjunction with the Japan Society of New York and the Japan Tourist Bureau, the AJS sought to enhance the experience of Americans visiting Japan. The more tourists, the better the chance for improving Japan's image back in America, which could have positive effects on American immigration policy. The AJS assumed that a support system in Japan would help to stimulate tourism and thus bring more Americans over, although no reliable records exist for the total number of Americans visiting Japan in the latter 1920s.

In other ventures, the AJS deepened its cooperation with Japan Society of New York. Though no position statements reflected a conscious turn toward sister societies, the AJS downplayed its earlier internationalist focus, such as participating in the international Peace Society network, after the passage of the Immigration Act. Instead, it redoubled its activities to focus on purely U.S.-Japan relations or on Asia in a regional context. The AJS–Japan Society cooperation, however, shied away from political concerns and concentrated on traditional cultural issues. In August 1925, for example, the two groups established a fund-raising committee to help repair the Gyokusenji Temple in Shimoda, the site of Townsend Harris's first American Consulate back in 1856.[13] The following year, the AJS provided to the New York group sets of colored lantern slides covering Japanese life and customs.[14]

And yet such traditional activities seemed small beer during times of growing international tension. Perhaps even the societies realized they could not continue with business as usual, and one of the first signs of their groping toward a new type of activist orientation came on February 14, 1927, when the AJS held a luncheon banquet celebrating the anniversary of Abraham Lincoln's birth. The centerpiece of the luncheon was the attendance of sixty Japanese youngsters, dressed in the naval-style school uniforms of the day, with brass-buttoned coat and cap for the boys and blouse and blazer–skirt combinations for the girls. Indeed, the society made a special effort to invite representatives from Tokyo's many girls' schools. The students were present to participate in the first "Lincoln Essay Contest in Japan." In cooperation with the Lincoln Centennial Association of Springfield, Illinois, which ran its own contest, the AJS established the competition as a means "to encourage the study of the life and character of Lincoln as an incentive to better government."[15] To hold up an American as a moral model for Japanese was unquestionably something new in society.

There were two levels of competition in the Lincoln essay contest, one for college- and university-aged students, and one for middle-school children. The upper division was won by Okuyama Takato of the Peers' College, while the lower division crowned Tsuruta Eiko of the Japan's Women's College Girls' High School the champion. In her speech, Tsuruta summed up precisely the modern liberal, internationalist spirit that the AJS was looking for in the contest, declaiming, "[Lincoln] taught us that liberty, humanity, justice, and love are eternal. So our daily life must come from the firm belief about these; and that we could in that way gain the true peace."[16] Both winners received bronze medallions emblazoned with Lincoln's silhouette. The contest was so popular that it would be held five more times, from 1928 to 1931 and in 1934, each time garnering national press coverage and highlighting the role, in particular, of the schoolgirls who participated. In 1929, for example, the *Yomiuri Shinbun* devoted nearly an entire page to Tokuda Junko, an upper-school student and that year's winner.[17]

Such activities, designed to actively engage the young Japanese elite in the transpacific relationship, coexisted with more traditional approaches that were being offered to ever-larger groups. That same spring, in April 1927, the National Memorial Foundation in Washington, D.C., held the first annual Cherry Blossom Festival at the Tidal Basin. Representatives from the major Japan cultural groups were present, and the AJS sent a message from Tokyo that was read in the shadow of the Jefferson Memorial.[18] The Cherry Blossom Festival became an annual event and one of the highlights of Washington's seasonal rites.

Both the Lincoln essay contest and the Cherry Blossom Festival represented the broadening of organized Japan-U.S. events and an attempt to shift the cultural zeitgeist in favor of U.S-Japan ties, by holding them annually and targeting general audiences. Of signal importance was the essay contest's focus on the younger generation. The pictures of Japan Society of New York events from this period are replete with graying coiffures and ample stomachs. Indeed, the attendees of a Nippon Club event were nearly indistinguishable from those of an AJS gathering. No average age can be calculated for exchange groups' members, but it was clearly in the fifties and sixties, at best. What the AJS inaugurated in 1927 was a policy of educating members of the next generation, to try and grab their interest at a formative age and to have an influence on the future leaders of society. The Japan Society, of course, had already tried this back in 1911, with its gifts for U.S. student prizes on Japanese subjects, but after the debacle of 1924 there was a renewed desire to reach out to younger members of society. The growing student population in both the United States and Japan provided a nearly limitless pool in which to try and deepen interest in U.S.-Japan relations.

By the time that Tsuruta Eiko received her Lincoln medal in 1927, the need to increase interest in bilateral relations was becoming critical. The central geopolitical problem in Asia was China and, specifically, Japan's growing sphere of influence in Manchuria, which had been largely under the control of the warlord Chang Tso-lin since 1922. Having given up control over the Shantung Peninsula in February 1922, the Imperial Army focused on expanding its influence in Manchuria and the vital South Manchurian Railway, first by supporting Chang, and then by murdering him in 1928 when he resisted becoming the army's puppet. This act was undertaken without the knowledge or approval of Tokyo and marked the beginning of the loss of central control over the Kwantung Army.

Ultranationalists now began to wreak havoc on Japan, whether inside the military or out. After Japan was forced to accept further reductions in its navy at the 1930 London Naval Conference, Prime Minister Hamaguchi Osachi was shot in November by a fanatical member of a nationalist group while waiting for a train at Tokyo Station. Although Hamaguchi survived for a year, the attack on him marked the end of civilian supremacy over the military and the end of party cabinet rule by professional politicians.[19] On September 18, 1931, two weeks after Hamaguchi succumbed to his wounds, the Kwantung Army used the pretext of an explosion along the South Manchurian Railway at Mukden as the excuse for the military to occupy the city and expand their control over Manchuria and parts of northern Korea.

Ultranationalists in the Kwantung Army had detonated the explosion themselves and on their own authority moved over ten thousand troops into Manchuria. The Kwantung forces were no longer under either civilian or central military control. Within days, the Manchuria issue had reached the League of Nations, and despite Tokyo's agreeing with a league resolution that Japanese troops be withdrawn, the military refused to comply. By February 1932, the puppet state of Manchukuo had been set up, with the last Chinese Ching emperor, Pu-yi, as its titular head.

That same month, extremists in Japan began assassinating prominent civilians. This culminated in an attempted coup against the government on May 15, 1932, in which Prime Minister Inukai Tsuyoshi was assassinated. International opprobrium was severe, and after a League of Nations report criticized Japan for extending its campaign to Inner Mongolia, delegate Matsuoka Yōsuke walked out of the proceedings and Japan quit the league.

These events, collectively, seemed to spell the end of internationalism in Japan. In hindsight, historians have assumed that the road to Pearl Harbor had now been surveyed and cleared. As the geopolitical crisis intensified, the list of Japanese aggressions at home and abroad not only mocked the pretensions of cultural exchange but also seemed to render such activities irrelevant to the reality of a world spinning out of control. The presumption by many that cultural relations played no role in stopping the eventual war overshadows any discussion of the actual role of exchange organizations at the time. Yet not only did cultural exchange continue, but it in fact deepened as crisis loomed and politics seemed to fail as a means of ensuring peace.

Cultural activities actually picked up pace as Japanese aggression in Manchuria unfolded during the early 1930s. To be sure, Tokyo sponsored exchange as a means to repair its image abroad, especially in America. Among the more ironic moments, at least in hindsight, was the visit of the Japanese Naval Training Squadron to New York in late September 1927. The Japanese government apparently hoped to carry a big stick and use the most visible means of Japanese power to influence American views. The young cadets and their officers were followed by avid American journalists, who made detailed newspaper reports on the visitors' activities. After cheering on Babe Ruth and the New York Yankees along with twenty-five junior officers, Rear Admiral Nagano Osami, head of the squadron, gave a series of talks, one at the Lawyers' Club and another at the Japan Society, where he expressed his pro-American feelings.[20] Fourteen years later, as chief of the Japanese Naval General Staff, Nagano would give the approval to attack Pearl Harbor.

In addition to such state-sponsored activities, private individuals also continued to try and steady U.S.-Japan relations. Some, such as the scholar Tsunoda Ryūsaku, held to the belief that education offered the best way to increase understanding and prevent crisis. In March 1928, he organized the Japanese Culture Center in America, collecting more than thirty thousand books, manuscripts, and other documents related to Japan and Japanese-American relations. He soon reached an agreement with Columbia University to house the center on campus, where it formed the seed for the Institute of Japanese Studies.[21] At the same time, Tsunoda became a lecturer in Japanese history and the curator of the Japanese collection at Columbia, a post he would occupy until his retirement in 1955, thereby educating generations of students and utilizing his extensive archive of sources from the Japanese Culture Center.

Tsunoda had few colleagues in academic positions, however, as the growth in Japanese courses at American universities lagged next to that in Chinese studies.[22] On the West Coast, the diplomatic historian Payson J. Treat taught Japanese-American relations at Stanford, and at the University of Washington, Henry S. Tatsumi taught Japanese studies, while Yoshio Kuno served as a language and history teacher at the University of California at Berkeley. In New England, Asakawa Kan'ichi continued to build up the Japanese collection at Yale. Concurrent with his administrative duties, Asakawa taught and conducted research and was about to publish his pathbreaking 1929 work on Japanese feudalism, *The Documents of Iriki*, but despite his decades of administrative and scholarly work, the university had so far declined to make him a full professor. The paucity of talent in Japanese studies began to change in 1932, when Serge Elisseeff arrived from Paris to head up the Harvard-Yenching Institute. Joining Langdon Warner, pioneer of Japanese art history, Elisseeff soon began training the core of the next generation of scholars, particularly in history, political science, and anthropology, thereby making Harvard the center of Japanese studies in the United States.

Not all institutional development, limited though it was, went on at universities. Independent scholars also responded to the tensions in the U.S.-Japan relationship by creating new venues for cultural exchange. Nearly contemporary with the efforts of Tsunoda, Asakawa, and Elisseeff were those of Louis V. Ledoux (1880–1948), who was a major collector and scholar of Japanese woodblock prints on the East Coast. After authoring *The Art of Japan* in 1927 for the Japan Society of New York, he formed the Society for Japanese Studies around 1933. A specialist group, it had about sixty members, who were mainly interested in art, and under its auspices, Ledoux, along with Harold G. Henderson, published in 1939 a major volume titled *The Surviving Works of Sharaku,* on one of Tokugawa Japan's most enigmatic artists.[23]

In Japan, in contrast to America, there was not as great an emphasis on building new organizations during the late 1920s. Rather, existing groups sought to come up with more effective activities, which would be guided by an internationalist orientation. In the first week of October 1928, for example, the Rotary Club of Tokyo hosted the Second Pacific Conference of Rotary International. The Tokyo chapter had been started in October 1920 by Yoneyama Umekichi, who first encountered the Rotary Club in Dallas, after being invited to a meeting by a Japanese member named Fukushima Kisanji. Other than organizing Rotary International relief for the 1923 earthquake, the club's activities were limited, even though by 1928 six other branch groups had been set up in Japan. Hosting the Pacific Conference, however, moved the Tokyo club into the first rank of Rotary groups. Over five hundred participants joined the conference, four-fifths of whom were Japanese. They were hosted at a reception by Prime Minister Tanaka, the architect of the hard line in Manchuria that five months previously had resulted in the murder of warlord Chang Tso-lin. The America-Japan Society joined in the events by throwing a formal dinner for the American participants.

Perhaps it was the sense of foreboding that moved even those still wounded by the 1924 anti-immigration bill to try and maintain good relations. In 1929, Shibusawa Eiichi, for example, funded a memorial plaque in Tokyo's Ueno Park to commemorate the fiftieth anniversary of the former U.S. president Ulysses S. Grant's visit to Japan. The octogenarian Shibusawa had been head of the official delegation welcoming Grant to Tokyo and had accompanied him to Ueno on August 26, 1879, when the general and his wife planted two trees as symbols of harmonious relations. Half a century later, the trees still stood, the general's a pine, Mrs. Grant's a white magnolia. Just off to the side of the trees, Shibusawa had a large stone memorial with a bronze plaque erected, which described the general's visit. In a clear reference to the troubles of the time, Shibusawa had included on the plaque Grant's statement while in Japan: "Let us have peace."[24]

These American and Japanese efforts, some of which were jointly pursued but most of which were independent of direct contact with other groups, were not the only attempts to cement better ties between the two nations. One of the more prominent, and ultimately controversial, venues for such internationalist activity was the Institute for Pacific Relations (IPR).[25] The IPR was founded in 1925 by leading private citizens from the Pacific Rim countries, with a goal to "facilitate the scientific study of the peoples of the Pacific Area." Results from IPR's sponsored investigations appeared in two journals it published, *Pacific Affairs* and *Pacific Survey*. National councils from each of the member nations conducted studies and published reports, while the IPR held biennial conferences throughout the 1920s and 1930s.

The Institute of Pacific Relations served an important function in bringing together Americans and Japanese who otherwise might not have had direct contact with each other in the years before World War II. The most important meeting for the future of U.S.-Japan cultural exchange was the third biennial conference, held in Kyoto in the summer of 1929. There, a young scion of America's wealthiest family, John D. Rockefeller 3rd, formed a fast friendship with a young Japanese delegate named Matsumoto Shigehara. The two would maintain their relationship and in the postwar years collaborate on some of the most important exchange projects undertaken between Japan and the United States. Other Japanese who were exposed to America through the IPR included the scholar Takaki (Takagi) Yasaka, who conducted a major review of Japanese studies in American universities for the IPR in 1935, and Matsukata Saburō, a leading collector of Western art. Beyond facilitating these personal experiences, however, the IPR was as ineffective in damping down geopolitical tensions as other internationalist groups.

Within the more traditional cultural exchange community, the older organizations conducted much of the activity while struggling to remain relevant amidst the swirl of political tensions clouding U.S.-Japan relations. On February 22, 1932, for example, the America-Japan Society of Tokyo threw a gala celebration in honor of the bicentennial of George Washington's birth. Over two thousand Japanese and American guests were invited to a Tokyo hotel, where they were treated to a movie about Washington's life; plays, in both Japanese and English, about the first president; and a lavish dinner.[26] Turning back to the past, however, was no escape from the grim reality of the day. The Washington birthday celebration was bracketed by another ultranationalist outburst in Japan, including the first killings of prominent Japanese civilians, such as former foreign minister Inoue Junnosuke, known in particular for his pro-U.S. views, who was murdered on February 9, and the industrialist Dan Takuma, husband of the younger sister of Kaneko Kentarō, who was killed on March 5.

After the Japanese walkout from the League of Nations in early 1933, the international isolation of Japan began to pick up pace. Internationalist societies began to pressure the Japanese government to renounce its aggression, and the Women's International League for Peace and Freedom, the War Resisters League, and the Fellowship of Reconciliation all condemned Japan's Manchurian invasion and called for sanctions and a boycott of Japanese goods.[27] Tokyo's response was to try and use people's diplomacy as it had three decades earlier, during the Russo-Japanese War, relying now on the large network of private organizations as outlets for its attempts to shape public opinion. Yet with private groups acquiescing to the government's bidding, they came perilously close to abandoning their independence and led many observers to question whether they were abetting official propaganda by the Foreign Ministry.

One of the first such people's diplomacy visits was also one of the most contentious. Former delegate to the League of Nations Matsuoka Yōsuke arrived in New York on March 24, 1933, for a two-week tour as a "private citizen." His steamer was met by jeering crowds of Chinese waving placards, and a Chinese immigrant in the crowd carrying a pistol was arrested by New York police.[28] Matsuoka's message was simple: the Japanese colony of Manchukuo was a legitimate state, and the 1922 Nine-Power Treaty that guided great power relations in China was mistakenly based on the fiction that China was a nation. This blunt assertion of Japan's interests, as anti-internationalist as any message delivered by a Japanese in America, was repeated at a private dinner at the Japan Society of New York that evening, the following day at Yale University, and the next Monday at the Council on Foreign Relations back in Manhattan.[29] Matsuoka then traveled to Boston, where at the Boston Japan Society he gave an address proclaiming an "Asian Monroe Doctrine" for Japan, according to Japanese newspapers.[30] He next traveled to Washington, D.C., and Chicago before heading to California, repeating the same message.

Matsuoka's words may have been particularly defiant, but not all visits by Japanese to America were as contentious as his, nor were all statements from Japanese officials in the mid-1930s simply anti-internationalist in tone. These pronouncements, too, were delivered to the cultural exchange groups and show the complex character of relations between state representatives and the private associations. On May 30, two months later after Matsuoka's trip, Viscount Ishii Kikujirō stopped in Washington, New York, and Boston on his way to the World Economic Summit. After a meeting with the new American president, Franklin Roosevelt, Ishii traveled to New York, where he accused the Chinese of violating the covenants of the League of Nations and the Kellogg-Briand Pact by using economic aggression in the form of anti-Japanese boycotts to violate treaties with Japan. Here, before New York's elite, the message delivered was a subtle one that stressed the defense of international conventions and interpreted Japan's role as that of maintaining international order in east Asia. That evening, Ishii spoke at a public dinner hosted by the Japan Society of New York at the Waldorf-Astoria, where he claimed before an audience of six hundred guests that rumors of war between Japan and America were "ridiculously absurd." In response, George W. Wickersham, president of the Japan Society, stated that America was in "no position to assume a 'pharisaical [sic] attitude' toward Japan," as the *New York Times* reported the next day.[31] Ishii then traveled to Boston, where he repeated the same sentiments on U.S.-Japan relations at a dinner hosted by the Japan Society of Boston and former U.S. ambassador to Japan W. Cameron Forbes.

Regardless of the tensions brewing, public interest in Japan-U.S. relations remained high throughout the 1930s in both countries. The Japan Society of New York celebrated its twenty-fifth anniversary in the year that both Matsuoka and Ishii spoke before its members, although its rolls had declined by nearly 400 persons, to 937 registered members.[32] While Ishii was in America, moreover, two new units of Saint Luke's International Medical Center in Tokyo were opened on June 4, 1933, with funds coming from the Rockefeller Foundation for the College of Nursing, while subscriptions in America provided most of the money for the seven-story central unit.[33] Despite such evidence of goodwill, Tokyo's walkout from the League of Nations overshadowed most of the cultural activities between the two countries.

The America-Japan Society of Tokyo was particularly affected by the downturn in cross-Pacific ties and responded by revamping its structure to provide what it hoped would be a more rationalized approach to cultural exchange. In February 1934, under the leadership of Prince Tokugawa Iesato, the AJS created an advisory committee for the "formal outreach for non-official cultural relations" between Japan and the United States. The committee was to help the AJS implement a plan that included greater services for American visitors to Japan; facilities and help to "investigators or students on things Japanese and the facts and culture of Japan"; greater cooperation with sister organizations in America; a library of books on Japan, Japanese culture, and U.S.-Japan relations; and occasional publications to assist American visitors in promoting the understanding of Japan.[34] As if to symbolically start its mission anew, the AJS reincorporated itself and elevated Count Kabayama Aisuke to the position of director and vice president.

Kabayama, who was to prove one of the most important cultural exchange leaders during the worst decades in U.S.-Japan relations, was born on May 10, 1865, to a samurai family in Kagoshima on the southern island of Kyushu. He studied abroad at Wesleyan and Amherst colleges in New England, and also in Bonn, Germany. In 1914, he was one of the founders of the International News Agency, which was set up partly with Foreign Ministry money. Maintaining his ties to America, he became the chairman of the Bancroft Scholarship in 1928, named for Ambassador Edgar A. Bancroft, who died while serving in Japan; this was one of the first American scholarships providing funds for Japanese to study in the United States. Because the AJS president, Tokugawa Iesato, was in declining health in the last years of the 1930s, much of the leadership role actually fell on Kabayama. He would take the helm of the AJS in 1941 and serve as its president until 1950.[35]

Despite Kabayama's efforts, the reorganized AJS did not succeed in reaching all of the goals set by its Advisory Committee. Some of those aims, of course, represented merely an intensification of the activities already undertaken by the society, such as cooperation with American organizations and publication of booklets for visitors. One plan left unfulfilled was the proposal to provide facilities, such as hostel rooms in Tokyo, for investigators and students. This became one of Kabayama's key goals, and it would absorb his energy in later years, as he turned this AJS proposal into the International House of Japan in 1952.

The AJS did undertake one innovation, however, that was both obvious in hindsight and yet perfectly representative of its new focus on outreach and grassroots activities: the hosting of numerous gatherings for young Japanese who had been born in America and returned to Japan. There are no precise records of the numbers of such Japanese, but the U.S. census noted that in 1930 there were over 138,000 persons of Japanese descent living in the United States, though only 70,477 of them had been born in Japan.[36] Though this of course does not include the number of deaths of those born in the United States, the figures reveal that approximately half of the Japanese-American population was born in America. There was thus a large pool of potential returnees, and the AJS identified them as likely sympathizers with the cause of U.S.-Japan relations.

In February 1935 the America-Japan Society held the first of a series of activities devoted to bringing these binational individuals into the cultural exchange community. At a park in Tokyo, several hundred of the returnees were hosted at a country fair held in honor of Abraham Lincoln's birthday.[37] This was followed later in the year, on November 28, by a Thanksgiving Day party for young Japanese Americans living in the Tokyo-Yokohama region. The next year, the AJS hosted a series of four informal social gatherings at the YMCA in Tokyo, from March through May 1936, for the American-born Japanese community.[38] Around this same period, the society created the Young People's Committee and in 1938 organized an umbrella group called the Japanese-American Young Peoples' Federation. The federation was designed to bring together for social events American-born Japanese and American citizens living in Tokyo.[39] Before it could really get organized, however, the war shut down all AJS activities.

Tokugawa Iesato and Kabayama Aisuke's efforts both were making headway and yet swimming against the tide of U.S.-Japan relations. If numbers count, then interest in U.S.-Japan relations increased even as

crisis deepened. In the second half of the 1930s, the AJS saw its membership rise almost every year, if modestly. In 1936 the organization had 726
enrolled, 329 of whom were Americans, while in 1937 it listed 768 members. Ironically, the greatest level of membership was reached in 1941,
when the society boasted 778 members, 344 of them from the United
States.[40] Moreover, the AJS now was participating in a vastly broader
Japan-America Society network in both countries, although not all of the
branch societies had active programming. In 1936, the society listed the
following fellow organizations: the Japan-America Society of Kansai (centered in the industrial city of Osaka); the Japan Societies of New York,
Boston, Seattle, Portland, and New Orleans; and the Japan America Societies of Chicago, Santa Barbara (California), and Los Angeles.[41]

The AJS focus on the younger generation was part of a larger movement to incorporate youth into exchange activities. At the same time that
the AJS was beginning its outreach, an independent student exchange
developed that was run by Japanese students themselves. In the spring of
1933, representatives of various English-speaking societies on the cam-
puses of Tokyo's universities gathered to propose a new venture with
their American peers.[42] The students soon formed a group called the Japan Student English Association and began planning for a conference to
be held the next year. A delegation was sent to the United States to dis-
cern American student interest in the idea, and the association's members
were enthusiastically received at leading institutions, including the University of Washington, Princeton, and Columbia. With interest levels as-
sured, the Japanese organizers returned to begin fund-raising.

After a two-week Pacific crossing by the American delegation, the first
Japan-America Student Conference (JASC; initially called the America-
Japan Student Conference) began on July 14, 1934. It was held at Tokyo's
Aoyama Gakuin University, where American Ambassador Joseph C.
Grew and AJS President Tokugawa Iesato attended the opening ceremonies, which were broadcast on radio. Far exceeding the organizers' hopes,
seventy-nine American students, along with twenty faculty and spouses
as chaperones, joined seventy Japanese counterparts for several days of
talks on current affairs, Japanese society and history, and issues in American life. The Foreign Ministry recognized the public affairs potential of the
conference and allowed the delegations to travel to Japanese-controlled

Manchukuo and Korea after a visit to the ancient Japanese capitals of Kyoto and Nara. The binational group of students was unresponsive, however, to the official interest shown in their venture and continued their independent planning for subsequent gatherings.

The JASC's basic structure was established at this first gathering. The conferences were entirely planned and run by the students themselves. The funds for the meetings came from the private sector, despite the Japanese government's later desire to fold the program into the activities of the Ministry of Education. All discussions were held in English, and the formal session lasted approximately a week, followed by travel through Japan or the West Coast of the United States. The conference also aimed for gender equality among its participants, which set JASC off from many other exchange events. The second conference took place during July and August 1935 at Reed College in Portland, Oregon, and thereafter the conference sites alternated between the two countries. The American hosts included Stanford in 1937 and the University of Southern California in 1939. The conference attracted the cream of Japanese students, including future prime minister Miyazawa Kiichi, who often called it one of the formative events of his lifetime.

The student conferences continued through 1940, each time garnering major media attention in Japan, partly due to government interest in showing the continuing good relations between Japan and America and the peaceful intentions of Japanese society as represented by its youth. Nonetheless, deteriorating political conditions soon halted the gatherings, as the eighth conference, scheduled for the summer of 1941, was canceled amidst the breakdown in diplomatic relations between Washington and Tokyo. What remained, however, was the memory of a viable private student enterprise and the continuing level of interest on the part of students of both countries, despite increasing political and military tensions. Along with the youth programs of the America-Japan Society, the JASC foreshadowed the greater attention that would be paid to student exchanges in the postwar era.

While much of what constituted cultural relations between Japan and America fell under the auspices of formal cultural exchange organizations, shared popular culture was becoming increasingly important in the relationship during the 1930s, and was seemingly unaffected by the seriousness of the political crisis. One aspect of this popular exchange that caught the public's eye in both countries was the meeting of Japanese and American baseball teams. Collegiate teams, such as the University of Chicago team, and clubs consisting of Japanese Americans had been occasionally touring Japan since 1906, but major leaguers had not visited before the 1930s. During that decade, however, baseball was in its golden era in America and catching on fast in Japan, although there the game was still limited to amateur and university clubs. Private interests now laid plans to bring together the best players from both countries in head-to-head matchups purely for the sport's sake and not for political relations, as became common in later decades.

Just two months after the expansion of Japanese military control over Manchuria, a team of American major league players managed by the legendary Connie Mack arrived in Tokyo in November 1931 to take on the Waseda University team. The series received full-page treatment in the national newspapers in Japan, with minute descriptions of the plays.[43] Three years later, fan hysteria erupted, with the arrival of a team of eighteen American All-Stars led by Babe Ruth and Lou Gehrig. A full month before the players' arrival in November 1934, newspapers began their coverage, and stories followed the Americans' arrival in Japan literally down to the minute.[44] One of the most famous images from the tour showed the Babe playing outfield in a rainstorm, covering himself with a traditional Japanese folding paper umbrella—the juxtaposition of the hulking player with the delicately lacquered handicraft titillated American audiences.

The All-Star tour, though, wound up as much a cultural event as a sporting one. Babe Ruth's daughter, Julia, for example, was given space in the *Yomiuri Shinbun* to write an exhortatory letter to Japan's schoolgirls, one that critiqued the social limitations on Japanese women, but registered the author's appreciation for Japanese culture.[45] For Japanese, it was a point of pride that no American All-Star team had traveled so far, or had traveled to any other Asian country, and the national coverage portrayed the encounter as a meeting of equal societies, even if the American team overpowered its counterpart by winning every game. As a sidelight to Japanese baseball history, the 1934 series spurred the development of Japan's first professional team, the Yomiuri Giants.[46]

Despite the vibrancy of activities like the All-Star tour, cultural exchange organizations could not avoid the political tensions that steadily mounted throughout the 1930s. The national security policies of Japan and the United States were becoming irreconcilable, though no one as yet really believed the two countries would go to war. Nonetheless, the atmosphere, even at events sponsored by the mainstream exchange groups, slowly but surely reflected the underlying tensions in the relationship.

Of all the annual gatherings, the dinner of the Japan Society of New York was possibly the most important. The keynote address at the dinner traditionally was given by the Japanese ambassador, and just as traditionally it extolled the strength and friendship of the U.S.-Japan relationship. By the mid-1930s, however, that tone had begun to change. At the annual dinner in January 1936, for example, Ambassador Saitō Hiroshi addressed a crowd of eight hundred invited guests. He began by defending Japan's recent expansion in Manchuria and China and argued that Japan would not be bound by the naval armament limitations of the 1930 London agreement after they expired that same year. In justifying Japan's call for parity among the three leading naval powers (the others being Great Britain and the United States), Saito cloaked his comments with assurances that no one contemplated war and the rhetorical device of proclaiming that Tokyo was interested only in a just peace. Ominously, however, according to the *New York Herald Tribune,* Saito went so far as to "applaud European dictators for 'patriotism and sincere purpose.'"[47]

The Japan Society, like other groups, was caught in a triple bind. One problem was its traditional role as the leading forum where Japanese and American elites met and exchanged semiofficial statements. As relations worsened, the exchange groups could not contemplate giving up their special role, but they found themselves increasingly serving as a vehicle for the more extreme claims of the Japanese government. The second bind was connected to the first, namely, that society members saw their unique role as being facilitators of conversation between the two countries. If members were to shut off that debate in order not to deny a venue for anti-internationalist comments, no matter how sugarcoated, then the society's major reason for holding public events would cease to exist. Thirdly, the organizations were trapped by the protocol of polite society, whereby unpleasant truths were rarely uttered. Thus it was that in rising in response to Ambassador Saitō's blunt speech to the Japan Society in

1936, Harry Woodburn Chase, chancellor of New York University, could somehow make himself claim it helped "to promote better understanding between Japan and the United States."[48] Polite words could not paper over the reality of a Japan spinning out of control, however, and less than a month after Saitō's talk, on February 26, 1936, over fourteen hundred ultranationalist junior army officers mounted a coup against the civilian government. It took the personal intervention of Emperor Hirohito to defeat the rebels, who in the process assassinated Finance Minister Takahashi Korekiyo, an honorary vice president of the America-Japan Society of Tokyo.

Being boxed in by events, the Japan Society of New York's new president, Henry W. Taft, officially maintained the policy of not becoming involved in political issues. Yet the speeches of major figures inevitably dragged the society into the political debate. As if in response, the Japan Society attempted to redouble its efforts to offer Americans a nonpolitical engagement with Japanese culture. In addition to maintaining its publication schedule, the society heavily stressed traditional Japanese art during the late 1930s. In 1936 alone the society published three pamphlets for members and for distribution to libraries; these were an *Illustrated History of Japanese Art, Craft of the Japanese Sculptor,* and *Japanese Flower Arrangement for Modern Homes.* The Japan Society also held a special event related to flower arranging in April 1937. It was as though the society's administrators believed that shifting the focus of Japan-American relations to cultural issues would somehow defuse the tensions steadily building. Not only were they wrong, but also they were soon challenged by quasi-governmental exchange organizations that pursued similar activities for directly political goals.

The Emergence of National Cultural Exchange Organizations

From one perspective, 1933 seemed to mark the end of an era in Japan's international history. For exactly eight decades since Commodore Perry's arrival, many of Japan's leaders and leading citizens had consciously sought to internationalize their country, whether through official policy or the transformation of Japanese society. The goal, of course, had always been to defend Japan from real or perceived threats. Cultural exchange was but one part of internationalization, and it was viewed as a double-edged sword—necessary for the importation of useful knowledge, dangerous for carrying seeds of ideas that could threaten the position of the state or its elites. But the pace of change was impossible to stop, and, from the brick buildings in Ginza to a modern military, Japanese life was changed almost beyond recognition from what it had been just a few decades previously.

Internationalization had also meant Japan's participation in transnational organizations and forums, as well as multilateral military activities. This was first evident in 1900, when Tokyo sent the largest contingent of foreign troops to Beijing to protect the foreign community from the Boxer Rebellion. Similarly, in 1918, Tokyo again dispatched the most Allied troops to Siberia after the Russian Revolution, in an attempt to support the White rebels in the Civil War. In 1919, of course, Japan was admitted to the table of the great powers at the Paris Peace Conference, and the country became a charter member of the League of Nations. Two years later, in 1921, Japan was at the center of the first true arms-limitation treaty, which was hammered out at the Washington Naval Conference. This was in addition to Japan's membership in international NGOs such as the International Red Cross and the Institute for Intellectual Cooperation.

Yet all careful observers understood that a major, if not the only, reason Japan was admitted to the high councils of multilateralism and internationalism was due to its very aggressive unilateralism. The 1894–95 Sino-Japanese and 1904–05 Russo-Japanese wars had catapulted the nation to the ranks of regional and global power, respectively. Such was the standing of Japan in 1918 that even so meticulous a student of international relations as Walter Lippmann automatically included it in the list of true world powers that would shape the post–World War I environment, when he handwrote the first draft of the organization of the League of Nations.[49] Tokyo's colonization of Formosa in 1874, Korea in 1910, and Manchuria in 1932 had put Japan on the level of all but a few of the great imperial powers in the twentieth century.

These successes revealed the great tensions animating Japan's internationalization after 1868 and especially in the twentieth century. These were the tensions between unilateralism and multilateralism, between internationalism and nationalism (and empire). Japan was not the only great power facing such dilemmas, for these tensions existed at the heart of the international system in the late nineteenth and early twentieth centuries. During these decades the growth of transnational bodies was accompanied by the carving of the globe into colonial territories, and the interests of states faced organized resistance by a multitude of internationalist groups.

At one level, then, Tokyo's walkout from the League of Nations in 1933 was a triumph of unilateralism. Nor was Japan alone in this course, for a total of fifteen nations resigned during the league's history, including Germany in the same year as Japan, as well as Italy and Brazil.[50] Regardless of the double standard involved in the major European imperialist powers condemning Japan for expanding its own empire, Tokyo's walkout seemed to signal that the Japanese government considered the cost of multilateralism too high and that at the level of intergovernmental organizations it would act independently of the international community. This was a profound policy change for a government that had been trying for decades precisely to join that international community at the highest levels.

The rise of fascist regimes in Europe in the 1920s and 1930s proved to be a turning point in cultural relations as well as in military, economic, and social ties between nations. With Mussolini's exhortation of the Roman spirit and Hitler's invocation of a Romantic Aryan supremacy, the forces of antimodernism began to cause ripple effects in countries far and wide. Internationalism, as we have seen, was a direct offspring of modernity and the Enlightenment project. But buried within internationalism was always the germ of its great opposite, parochialism. With the emergence of a fascist critique of modernity, a parochial or particularistic critique of internationalism was also unleashed. In response, the Western democracies turned to promoting national aims and buttressing their own claims of superiority, providing an alternate vision of an internationalist order centered on the Anglo-Saxon heritage or French civilization.

The institutional innovation arising from the ideological competition between fascist and democratic states was the national cultural exchange organization. Unlike previous, private voluntary associations, the national cultural exchange organizations were nominally independent yet funded with government money and designed clearly to educate a foreign audience about the culture of the sponsoring nation as a means to influence public opinion and create a sympathetic community of supporters abroad. "Exchange," therefore, took on quite a different meaning from what it had meant to people like Kaneko Kentarō or Lindsay Russell. The line between advocacy and propaganda was dangerously painted over, and the imprimatur of the state worked to make the new groups far more powerful than their private cousins.

To some degree, of course, all modern governments had practiced cultural diplomacy, though not on a very organized scale. Archibald MacLeish noted just after World War II that governments traditionally used "certain aspects" of their national cultures for the purpose of foreign relations.[51] As longtime British Council official John Mitchell pointed out, particularly in the 1930s, states used cultural relations to gain political and economic ascendancy over other nations.[52] Foreign ministries in various countries had spread positive images for decades, and propaganda organs such as the Japanese Foreign Ministry's Information Bureau had developed more sophisticated means of reaching foreign publics.

Prior to the twentieth century, however, the organizational component of these state policies lagged behind bureaucratic thinking. Indeed, during the nineteenth century, only France established a semiofficial organization to promote French culture abroad, the Alliance Française, in 1883. Over four decades later, in 1925, France's neighbors began to catch up, with Berlin opening the Deutsche Akademie, which soon was renamed the Goethe-Institut. Both of these organizations were narrowly oriented in their early years and limited their activities largely to teaching their respective national languages to children of expatriots and to interested parties, along with sponsoring a few cultural events, such as celebrations for national holidays, and the shipping of basic information on their countries to their branch offices.

With the spread of nationalist and ultranationalist politics during the 1920s and 1930s, however, the governments of most of the great powers moved to set up quasi-official organizations to promote their national cultures in other countries. Both France and Germany greatly increased the budgets of the Goethe-Institut and the Alliance Française. In 1934, London created the British Committee for Relations with Other Countries, inspired by Sir Reginald ("Rex") Leeper's championing of "cultural propaganda" for foreign policy purposes. The outfit was soon renamed the British Council and, with part of its budget coming from Whitehall, it taught English classes around the world and shipped books and films about Britain to selected libraries and embassies abroad. In this, it did not differ so much from the Japan Society of New York, which had done the same for decades. The United States did not set up a semi-independent organization but rather created the Division of Cultural Relations in 1938; this, along with Nelson A. Rockefeller's Office of Inter-American Affairs, initially focused on cultural contacts with nations in Latin America, but soon was active also in Europe and Africa.[53] By the late 1930s, cultural propaganda was part and parcel of the international activities of leading states, and the old internationalist community found itself in competition with a new set of actors, who viewed cultural exchange as a one-way street: disseminated by bureaucrats and received by a largely passive audience.

Tokyo acted simultaneously with this outbreak of institutional cultural particularism. In January 1933, the Foreign Ministry formed a steering committee of prominent Japanese to draw up plans for a national cultural exchange organization. The six-man committee included Marquis Tokugawa Yorisada, member of the House of Peers, and Kabayama Aisuke, vice president of the America-Japan Society.[54] The participation of Kabayama, who had proven his commitment to internationalist activities, showed the complex nature of the connection between the state and the exchange organization in the 1930s. The expansion of the committee to eleven members in December of that year did nothing to change the complexity of its character, for it added, among others, scholar of Japanese religion Anesaki Masaharu, who had lectured at Harvard in the second decade of the twentieth century. The December expansion also revealed the name of the new organization: the Society for the Promotion of International Culture (Kokusai Bunka Shinkōkai, or KBS).

On April 1, 1934, the Foreign Ministry announced the board of the new organization. The president of the KBS was to be Prince Konoe Fumimaro, current president of the House of Peers, future prime minister, and one of Japan's most elite aristocrats. Vice president was Marquis Tokugawa, while Anesaki, Kabayama, and fifteen others were named directors. Honorary board members included the venerable Kaneko Kentarō and the heads of the Mitsui, Sumitomo, and Iwasaki families, directors of the country's greatest *zaibatsu* (industrial-commercial combines).[55] On April 11, the Society for the Promotion of International Culture opened its headquarters in Tokyo's Kojimachi ward, an event covered by major newspapers.[56]

From the beginning, the KBS seemed infused with a cosmopolitan spirit, as had earlier groups promoting Japanese culture abroad, despite its government ties. That the KBS intended itself to be more than simply a vehicle for state propaganda was revealed in its organizational state-ment. The goal of the society, the document stated, was "to contribute to the development of world culture and the enrichment of human society through the exchange of international culture, especially in making known to foreign countries Japanese and Asian culture."[57] Here lay the organiza-tion's complex make-up, for its goal may have appeared cosmopolitan, but it was yoked to very particularist aims. The KBS genuinely sought to expose Japanese to foreign culture and "promote" international exchange, while championing positive views of Japan abroad.

The KBS took an inclusive view of its promotion of culture and di-vided its activities into ten main divisions. The first division, on which the society placed a major emphasis, was publication, compilation, and translation. The KBS listed history, language, literature, religion, ethics, education, law, politics, economics, art, and song as the areas in which it would commission and publish works in both Japanese and foreign lan-guages. It would also support Japanese scholars' research on Japanese and Asian culture and translate such work into foreign languages. At the same time, however, the KBS also stated its intention to translate into Japanese important works in foreign languages.[58] Its multilateral focus was stressed in the remaining nine areas of activity. In addition to publica-tion activities, the society would support the development of Japanese culture and language courses at major foreign universities; exchange speakers with foreign countries and support exhibits of Japanese culture abroad and foreign culture inside Japan; exchange cultural artifacts with foreign museums and libraries; introduce eminent foreigners to their counterparts in Japan; support foreigners' research in Japanese culture; promote student exchanges and study-abroad opportunities; promote connections between cultural organizations; support the production of films on Japan and their export abroad; and establish a meeting hall, library, and study center.[59]

Since the KBS was charged with promoting Japan abroad, it also required a foreign presence. It soon opened branch offices in Paris, New York, Berlin, and Buenos Aires, which were followed by offices in Rome, Geneva, and Melbourne. Despite its outreach to various countries, however, from the beginning a large proportion of the society's energies were focused on America. In May 1934, just one month after the founding of KBS, President Konoe traveled to the United States, introducing the society and its goals to American leaders in Washington and New York. He was followed in June by Anesaki Masaharu and in August 1935 by Kabayama Aisuke, who met more than two thousand Americans at over one hundred meetings during a two-and-a-half-month visit.[60]

As the KBS's programming activities developed, the society attempted to balance a wide range of events in various countries. With government funding, the KBS was able to ship large volumes of material abroad. By 1938, American and European universities, libraries, cultural centers, and museums had received nearly thirty thousand books, twelve thousand photographs, twelve thousand lantern slides, and two hundred motion pictures on Japanese subjects.[61] All of these were used in Japanese festivals held abroad, in order to educate schoolchildren, and at general cultural institutions.

While the KBS sponsored numerous programs in Europe and brought Europeans to Japan, the importance of the U.S.-Japan relationship, especially in a time of growing tension, led the society to host numerous American-related programs. Needing a central office in the United States to deal with the amount of work required, Kabayama Aisuke returned to New York in the spring of 1938 to establish the Japanese Cultural Hall (JCH). In November of that year the JCH opened offices on the thirty-sixth floor of the Rockefeller Center International Building, at 630 Fifth Avenue, directly across the street from Saint Patrick's Cathedral. The JCH was headed by KBS administrator Maeda Tamon and comprised a meeting space and a library with over seven thousand Japanese and English-language books. The JCH acted as a mini-information center on Japan and provided American newspapers, magazines, and radio shows with Japanese photographs, lantern slides, motion pictures, and informational books.[62]

Clearly, the goal of the KBS was to spread positive images of Japan abroad. It was not, however, a direct arm of the Foreign Ministry, though the society's funds came from the ministry. In this, the KBS did not differ from the British Council or the Alliance Française, both of which were also autonomous yet supported at least in part by government monies. The questions raised by the links to the government, and by the very fact that the KBS was conceived in an era of nationalist sentiments and quasi-official exchange organizations, is whether its activities were simply propaganda and whether its programs or works were not reliable and balanced. This would be a particularly important critique in relation to the KBS's publishing activities, on which it placed a great emphasis and expended large sums of money.

A glance at the English-language publications of the KBS dispels the simplistic idea that all that was being produced was propaganda. In the seven years before war erupted between Japan and the United States, the KBS published approximately fifty books, booklets, and pamphlets in English, along with its journal, the *KBS Quarterly*. All of the publications dealt with traditional or modern culture or Japanese studies. None addressed political, military, or economic problems; and the only one to touch on current issues was a 1935 booklet by Yamada Waka, *The Social Status of Japanese Women*. Yamada's book, it must be noted, took a positive view of the role of Japanese women, implicitly contrasting their position to women in other, less industrialized Asian countries, who were less educated and not able to join the workforce. In contrast to Yamada's book, the other KBS publications covered various aspects of Japanese culture, including the titles *Dolls of Japan* (1934), *Art of the Landscape Garden in Japan* (1935), *Masks of Japan: The Gigaku, Bugaku, and No Masks* (1935), *Buddhist Philosophy and Its Effect on the Life and Thought of the Japanese People* (1936) by the famous philosopher D. T. Suzuki, *An Introduction to Japanese Art* (1936), *An Outline of the Japanese Dance* (1937), *Religious Life of the Japanese People: Its Present Status and Historical Background* (1938) by the KBS director and scholar Anesaki Masaharu, and *Introduction to Contemporary Japanese Literature* (1939), as well as volumes on architecture, industrial arts, and gardens. The books were in some cases just brief introductions; others were extended treatments by world-class scholars such as Suzuki and Anesaki. The KBS also sponsored in part and published the work of Northwestern University scholar John Henry Wigmore (1863–1943), who edited a pathbreaking study and translation of Tokugawa legal codes from the seventeenth through the nineteenth centuries.[63] Given the paucity of publications in America on Japanese subjects, one would have to conclude that the KBS volumes formed an important corpus of writings for students and laypersons alike.

Similarly, the KBS helped map the terrain of contemporary Japanese studies by compiling surveys on existing publications and organizations. Such titles as *A Short Bibliography of English Books on Japan* (1936), *A Handbook of International Cultural Organizations in Japan* (1934, 1936), *Catalogue of Periodicals Written in European Languages and Published in Japan* (1936), and the annual *K.B.S. Bibliographic Register of Important Works Written in Japanese on Japan and the Far East* provided the first comprehensive bibliographical collection for the use of scholars undertaking research or American libraries intending to build their holdings in Japanese studies.

If the KBS's publishing activities far outstripped anything achieved up to that time, so did its individual and group exchanges. Until the KBS was established, intellectual and artist exchanges were relatively rare, partly due to limited funds and partly due to the technical difficulties of the transpacific crossing. The KBS was a pioneer in sponsoring individual and large-scale exchanges and in particular brought Americans over to Japan. From the beginning of its existence, this proved to be one of the KBS's most important activities. Starting in 1934, the KBS focused heavily on programs for students and academics. In July of that year, just three months after formally beginning its operations, the KBS brought over seventy American university students (and a group of professors) to Japan for the first Japan-America Student Conference.[64]

Perhaps at the suggestion of Kabayama Aisuke, whose America-Japan Society was making links to young Japanese born in the United States, the KBS also undertook a major survey of the state of Japanese studies on the West Coast of the United States. Recognizing not only that Japan's closest ties to America were with states on the Pacific coast, but also that the greatest number of second-generation Japanese Americans (nisei) lived in that region, the KBS sent Mimiya Miyako, a teacher at the Tokyo YWCA, to undertake a comprehensive study of the state of U.S. knowledge of Japan.[65] Arriving in Seattle on October 24, 1934, she traveled the entire length of the coast, visiting all major cities down to San Diego, through the middle of January 1935. Mimiya concentrated on seven main areas: the number and level of "Pacific Rim" courses in high schools, Japanese research organizations, women's circles devoted to Japanese art, nonprofit voluntary organizations such as the Rotary Club and Kiwanis Club, high school Japanese-studies courses, Japanese immigrant life, and something called the "Junior Institute of Pacific Relations." She concluded that, despite an interest in Japan, the level of knowledge among Americans and the number of opportunities to study about Japan were not high. Moreover, reflecting contemporary concerns, most Americans were suspicious of anyone with a Japanese government connection who spoke about Japan. She recommended focusing in particular on the nisei community as a target group for sponsored visits to Japan that would educate them about contemporary Japanese society.

As revealed by Mimiya's trip, the KBS was very interested in women's issues. Indeed, a good number of the early exchanges focused on women. In 1935, the KBS funded a trip to Japan for 115 members of the Women's Committee of the Garden Club of America, who spent a month visiting famous gardens in Kyoto, Tokyo, and Osaka. Their visits to Kinkakuji (the Golden Pavilion) in Kyoto and other spots were recorded in the press, and the visitors later published a KBS-sponsored book on their trip.[66] In July of the same year, following up on Mimiya Miyako's survey of Japanese studies, the KBS sponsored eight female professors from West Coast colleges and high schools, on a monthlong visit to Japan for discussions on the state of Japanese studies and women's education in the two countries.[67] In 1936, the KBS hosted a visit by playwright Zona Gale, who in 1921 had become the first woman to win the Pulitzer Prize for Drama.

The list of publications, studies, exchange, and other activities of the KBS do not settle the argument over the nature of national cultural exchange organizations. But that debate is one that erupted years after the actual work of the KBS. Some scholars now object to these outfits even being called exchange organizations. In the view of such critics, these groups did little more than try to indoctrinate uneducated persons or further claim the loyalties of those interested in or supportive of Japan.[68] There was no exchange, only a thinly disguised attempt to whitewash Japan's aggressive policies in east Asia, or so goes the critique.

How, the critique continues, could a truly internationalist encounter, a true exchange of cultures, occur if the underlying tensions and political problems, indeed the immorality of government policy, was not challenged head on? Cultural exchange is politicized, in this view, by the very act of drawing attention away from politics. Focusing on culture implies a nonjudgmental stance toward militarist aggression or diplomatic bullying. We have seen the Japan Society of New York struggle with this very question when the dinner speeches of Japanese diplomats served to justify Tokyo's China policies in the 1930s.

And it is true that the activities of the KBS in no way addressed the politics of the day. Yet what the KBS did in the prewar years seems on the surface no different from earlier programs of the Japan Society of New York or the America-Japan Society; indeed, the KBS seems to have taken their template and intensified the level of activity. In 1907 and 1937, a focus on culture was justifiable from an educational point of view, but in both eras such a focus ignored questions of politics and eschewed criticisms of Tokyo's policies (or Washington's, for that matter). The KBS's publication and exchange programs cannot be dismissed or considered as simple propaganda, and not merely because they were not directly produced by the Foreign Ministry. Did the books published by the KBS present a positive view of Japan because of an unspoken agenda, or did they do so because they addressed Japan's impressive cultural achievements? Because there was no KBS booklet critiquing Japan's Manchuria policy, should Wigmore's translation of Tokugawa legal codes or Anesaki's ruminations on Japanese religion be dismissed? Does the fact that the KBS never held a conference on ultranationalism in Japan mean that it was a waste of time to send an American playwright to Japan or to give the director of the Seattle Civic Theater historical materials that helped him stage a production of the *Forty-seven Ronin*, or *Chūshingura*?[69]

The complex nature of the KBS's activities meant that a desire to promote a positive image of Japan coincided with an active cosmopolitan agenda of exchange and publication; in other words, the KBS was an organization of "cosmopolitan patriots," to use Kwame Anthony Appiah's phrase.[70] In another time, perhaps, patriotism and internationalist activities might have been reconciled; given the tragic history of the 1930s and 1940s, such cosmopolitan views are given less credence. The sincerity of men like Kabayama cannot be doubted, however, and in the global conditions of the 1930s, their continued commitment to the vestiges of cosmopolitanism or internationalism, even if in a tortured sense, required no little bravery, given the assassinations of those who dared to slow down the Japanese militarist juggernaut. The irony of the KBS is that it was born in a time of nationalism but was the most developed expression of cosmopolitanism yet conceived by Japan.

The Eclipse of Exchange and the Coming of War

The manifold activities of the KBS, along with those of the other exchange organizations, were soon buffeted by the winds of war. In mid-1937, Japanese Imperial Army forces had crossed into northern China and soon were fighting Chinese Nationalist troops outside Beijing. Within months, the conflict had spread southward along China's coast and relations between Tokyo and Washington deteriorated rapidly. Caught in the buildup to confrontation, the exchange societies attempted to meliorate U.S.-Japan relations. Yet even as the KBS was planning on opening the Japanese Cultural Hall in New York, a crisis erupted. On December 12, 1937, the U.S. gunboat *Panay* was bombed by Japanese forces while evacuating Americans from Nanking during the Japanese attack on the city.[71] In just a few years, the attack would seem like something from another era, with Japanese canvas-winged biplanes dive-bombing the old two-stack steamer. The results were real enough, however, as three American sailors were killed and dozens injured, and the ship itself sunk in the Yangtze River, along with two of the three Standard Oil Company tankers it was escorting.

The attack was carried out by renegade units of the Imperial Navy that were not acting under orders. Tokyo immediately apologized for the attack, which also targeted two British gunboats, and promised a full investigation. Yet in a sign of how the nature of cultural exchange organizations had changed during the 1930s, the Foreign Ministry asked the America-Japan Society to head up a public subscription campaign for the American casualties. Former president of the House of Peers, Prince Tokugawa Iesato, led the drive as head of the AJS, raising over ¥16 million for the families of the victims and survivors.[72] Iesato personally delivered the funds and a message of regret to U.S. Ambassador Joseph C. Grew in February 1938, calming American opinion. It undoubtedly helped that the two men already knew each other well, for Grew was an honorary vice president of the AJS, as all U.S. ambassadors had been since the society's inception in 1917. Tokyo did not hesitate to use an ostensibly private association for crisis diplomacy, and Iesato's links to the American ambassador in Japan almost certainly explain why the Foreign Ministry chose him and the AJS for the task.

Despite the diplomatic solution to the crisis, the sinking of the *Panay* ushered in the final act leading up to Pearl Harbor. Shortly after the attack, Japanese Imperial Army troops entered Chinese Nationalist leader Chiang Kai-shek's capital and commenced a brutal occupation soon known as the Rape of Nanking, in which hundreds of thousands of Chinese were killed and wounded. In March 1938, just a month after Tokugawa Iesato handed over the donation for the victims of the *Panay*, the Japanese Diet passed Prime Minister Konoe Fumimaro's National General Mobilization Bill, drafting all human and material resources in Japan and giving Tokyo the tools for putting the country on a general war footing. While remembered today as a war leader, Konoe also was a past president of the KBS, thus giving ammunition to those who claimed that the organization was little more than a propaganda organ for Japan's ultranationalists. In November, Konoe proclaimed the New Order in East Asia, which linked Japan, Manchukuo, and China together for the "defense" of east Asia and which was designed to create a political and economic bloc integrating the Japanese empire; this was followed in August 1940 by the first mention of the Greater East Asia Co-Prosperity Sphere.

On September 27, 1940, Tokyo tied itself to the European conflict that had started the year before, by joining Nazi Germany and Fascist Italy in the Tripartite Pact. The following month, Prime Minister Konoe inaugurated the Imperial Rule Assistance Association (IRAA). The clearest expression of what can be labeled Japanese fascism, the IRAA was designed to be a single national party that linked the Cabinet, the Diet, financial and industrial interests, and the nationalist societies. the IRAA marked the end of prewar democracy in Japan and soon came under the control of Imperial Army leaders.

The final steps to war were driven by the military's need for oil. Throughout 1940, the army moved closer to French Indochina and Dutch Indonesia, and by July 1941 the Cabinet had decided on a policy of advancing southward, which almost certainly would bring about conflict with Great Britain and the United States. The United States responded to the first insertions of Japanese soldiers into French Indochina by freezing Japanese assets abroad and imposing an embargo on crucially needed oil, of which the United States supplied nearly 60 percent of Japan's total. Throughout the year, Secretary of State Cordell Hull had been trading notes and holding talks with Ambassador Nomura Kichisaburō, but the talks had all but broken down by midsummer, and last-ditch attempts to set up a summit between Prime Minister Konoe and President Franklin Roosevelt fell by the wayside.

Despite the seemingly inevitable slide to war, cultural exchange continued throughout these final years. No one involved in such activities was unaware of the crisis brewing between the two countries, nor were they so unrealistic as to think that all could be settled by a few dinners or exhibitions. And yet they were not fatalistic, for the web of cultural exchange had been tightly woven and their various programs continued apace. To the historian, there is an almost inconceivable divergence of two streams, the political and the cultural, and yet on reflection it is inconceivable only if one accepts that the political is always predominant in daily life. The continued operation of the cultural exchange groups challenges that assumption, even in the face of crisis and its looming shadow.

There was no doubt that diplomatic problems influenced those activities that touched on current events or political issues. In the summer of 1940, for example, the Japan-America Student Conference held its seventh conclave. Over one hundred participants from both countries gathered in Japan, where the Japanese student delegation had just rejected a proposal by the Ministries of Foreign Affairs and Education that they sponsor the conference, which of course would have brought it under government supervision. Nevertheless, the conference discussions focused on Japan's aggression in China, and police watched the young debaters clash over the future of Japan-U.S. relations. By the time of the eighth conference in 1941, diplomatic relations between the two countries had broken down, and the gathering was canceled, not to be revived until 1947.

Portents of doom abounded in these last, uneasy years before war. As if to mark the end of an era, Tokugawa Iesato, longtime president of the America-Japan Society of Tokyo, former head of the League of Nations Association of Japan, and president of the Japanese Olympic Committee, died on June 5, 1940. With his passing, a major figure in Japanese internationalism left the scene just at the moment when voices of moderation were most needed. This tireless advocate of U.S.-Japan relations was succeeded by his protégé, Count Kabayama Aisuke. Yet by now, even the AJS could not avoid questions of war. Foreign Minister Matsuoka Yō suke, a leading nationalist, exposed the divergence between the exchange groups and the state at an AJS lunch on December 19, 1940. In his prepared remarks, Matsuoka defended Tokyo's policy in China, claiming, "Japan is engaged in a moral crusade . . . fighting not for destruction but for construction. We are endeavoring to initiate an era of enduring peace and unlimited prosperity, based on justice, equity, and mutuality in Great East Asia."[73] There were no more attempts at bridging differences or in coming to a mutual understanding. Words were empty rhetoric, designed to convince, not engage. AJS president Kabayama himself continued to hold out hope for a peaceful solution and planned a trip to the United States in 1941. Although reported in the press, the trip was canceled, symbolically marking the end of direct attempts by the AJS to stand athwart the tide of events.[74]

Politics did not dominate all, however, and a surprising amount of cultural activity continued even through 1941. Educational institutions remained at the forefront of nonofficial relations. In 1939, two years after Japanese planes bombed the USS *Panay,* Rikkyo University founded the Institute for American Studies, one of the oldest such specialized programs in Japan, while Doshisha University in Kyoto maintained its exchange programs with Amherst College throughout the 1930s.[75] Meanwhile, in late 1939 through mid-1940, an exhibit of works by the

Tokugawa-era woodblock artist Sharaku toured the United States. The organizer of the exhibit was Louis Ledoux and his Society for Japanese Studies, and the show followed the well-received publication of his book on Sharaku that year. The Boston Museum of Fine Arts described the prints as "masterly" and an "extraordinary type of pictorial representation."[76] The exhibit traveled to the Art Institute of Chicago before ending at the Museum of Modern Art in New York. Whatever the strategic disputes between Tokyo and Washington, they failed to dissuade American observers of Japanese art from appreciating and celebrating its value.

Perhaps quixotically, the Japanese Tourist Board continued to believe in the viability of its attempts to bring Americans over to Japan. Reorganized in 1930 as the Board of Tourist Industry, it continued to sell Japan abroad by focusing on those interested in art, architecture, and religion. Even as late as 1941, the board published its main English-language guidebook, *Japan, The Official Guide,* which ignored the years of fighting between Japan and China and instead gave potential visitors a brief introduction to Japanese history, society, and culture. The guide did, of course, cover Korea and Taiwan as parts of the empire but, unlike earlier official guides, did not include Manchukuo or China. No reliable records of the number of American tourists to Japan in 1941 exist, however, and *Japan, The Official Guide* would soon seem a relic of a past era of misplaced hope.

The KBS, too, continued its activities in the face of adversity. In May 1941, it donated seven valuable volumes on Japanese culture to the William Lyon Phelps Collection of Bates College in Maine.[77] And even after Pearl Harbor, as the Japanese extended their empire throughout the western Pacific, the KBS commenced with the printing of John Henry Wigmore's translation of Tokugawa legal documents, although it is lost to history whether anyone considered it ironic that a study of law should be published by an enemy combatant in a relationship that no longer had any legal restraints.

In the very last moments of peace, the shadow of catastrophe brought forth a last effort by the father of U.S.-Japan cultural relations. On December 6, 1941, Kaneko Kentarō, who had largely stayed out of the world of exchange since 1924, broke his silence to urge the appointment of a special commission to peacefully solve the U.S.-Japan crisis. His plea fell on deaf ears, and as he spoke, the pilots on the mission to destroy the U.S. Pacific Fleet were climbing into their cockpits. In an instant all now changed, and within weeks of Pearl Harbor, the Japan Society of New York stopped its operations, an action soon followed by that of the America-Japan Society in Tokyo. Six months later, just weeks after the Battle of Midway marked a turning point in the war, Kaneko Kentarō died in Tokyo at the age of eighty-nine.[78]

Few either at the time or later ever seriously entertained the idea that cultural exchange could have prevented war. Yet the endeavors of those on both sides of the Pacific did not cease until their two countries were engaged in a death struggle. Long before the first bombs fell on Pearl Harbor, advocates of internationalism had found themselves marginalized by a rise in nationalist ideologies and a complete divergence between Washington's political goals and Tokyo's. Yet the older strain of nonpolitical cosmopolitanism continued to struggle with those destructive ideologies until December 1941. To modern observers, the cosmopolitans were naive, unworldly, and ineffectual at best. Yet the pull of cultural engagement was not vanquished so easily. It took slaughter to stop it, but once the guns fell silent, the sprouts of a new era of exchange pushed up through the ashes of war.

Joseph Heco, 1837–1897, the first Japanese to become a naturalized American citizen. Joseph Heco Papers, Special Collections Research Center, Syracuse University Library.

Photo of Commodore Matthew C. Perry at the time of the Japan Expedition, ca. 1853. Library of Congress.

Japanese ukiyoe illustration of Commodore Perry, ca. 1854. Library of Congress.

Modernization in Ginza in Tokyo during the Meiji period. A print by Utagawa Hiroshige III. Courtesy of Waseda University Library.

Kaneko Kentarō, founder of the Japan America Society of Tokyo, ca. 1900. Library of Congress.

Gateway to Fair Japan Bazaar at the St. Louis World's Fair, 1904. St. Louis Public Library.

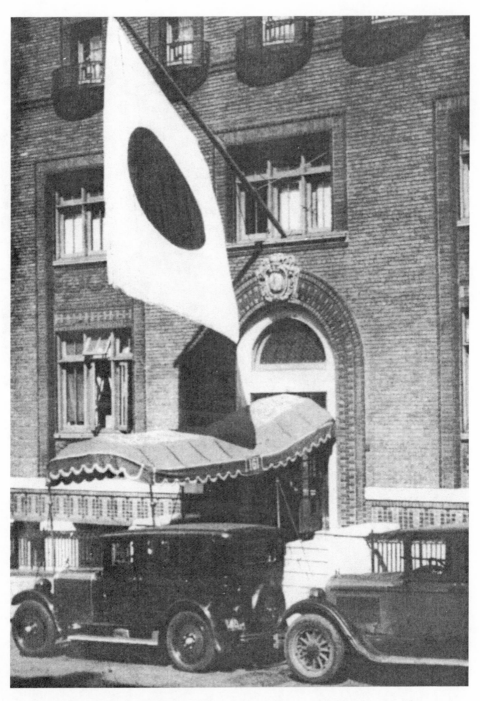

Entrance to Nippon Club in Manhattan on West Ninety-Third Street, 1915. The Nippon Club, Inc. (New York).

Birthday celebration at Maneki Restaurant, Seattle's oldest sushi restaurant, January 27, 1941. Courtesy of Maneki Restaurant.

Crown Prince Akihito addressing Japan Society of New York dinner at the Waldorf Astoria, September 1953. Second from left, front row, Crown Prince Akihito; third from left, Japan Society President John D. Rockefeller 3rd; fourth from left, Secretary of State John Foster Dulles. Japan Society, New York.

Premiere of "Ugetsu" at New York's Plaza Theater, 1955. Japan Society, New York.

I-House: Aerial view of International House of Japan shortly after completion in 1955. Courtesy of International House of Japan, Inc.

Sony TR-55 transistor radio, 1955. Sony Corporation.

Toyota Corolla, 1968 model, soon to be Japan's most popular auto export to the United States. Courtesy of Toyota Motor Sales U.S.A. Inc. Archive.

Exterior of Japan House, home of Japan Society of New York, after completion in
1971. Japan Society, New York.

I-House: Banquet in honor of I-House's 30th anniversary, 1982. Left to right: John W. Hall (Yale), Marius Jansen (Princeton), Edwin Reischauer (Harvard), Matsumoto Shigeharu. Courtesy of International House of Japan, Inc.

Advertisement for Grand Sumo Tournament, held at Madison Square Garden in June 1985. Japan Society, New York.

Out of the Ashes

T HE ATOMIC FURIES that ended the war in the Pacific culminated four years of some of the most savage fighting ever between two peoples. The intensity of the war, and its totality, led many observers to assume that, even with the fighting over, Japanese and Americans would remain implacable enemies for years to come. Yet, just as for Americans, World War II would be known as "the good war," for Japanese the post-war years would soon be memorialized as "the good recovery," a difficult period that nonetheless set the stage for the country's rise to global prominence in the postwar era. During those years, there were numerous attempts to create a particular narrative about the rebirth of Japan and its revivied, intimate relationship with America.

That such a positive story could triumph was due, in large part, not only to the American Occupation policies but also to the reemergence of cultural exchange and its role in renormalizing relations between the two former enemies. The basis for this rebirth lay in the survival of the long-standing ties and cosmopolitan feelings that had driven both countries together since the nineteenth century. Yet such renormalization was not a simple affair, for nearly two decades after the end of the Occupation witnessed a de facto, if unacknowledged, three-way competition over the meaning and practice of cultural exchange. The participants in this cultural jousting were the prewar traditional societies that sought to recapture their leading role, new organizations that attempted to broaden the base of intellectual and grassroots contact, and the unregulated "free market" of popular cultural importation in both countries.

The Silence of War

The postwar reconstitution of U.S.-Japan cultural relations started from the silence of the years of conflict. The ferocity of the fighting between American and Japanese troops, the bombing of civilian targets in Japan, and the inhumanity of the Japanese Imperial Army toward captured American soldiers quickly erased decades of positive, even warm, feelings between the two combatants. Images of Japanese as subhuman animals, usually apes, proliferated in American propaganda, while Japanese propaganda portrayed GIs as bloodthirsty monsters raping Japan.[1] All the volumes on Japanese art and architecture in American libraries, all the fascination with American technology and achievements were impotent in the face of total war.

The decades of cultural exchange before 1941 had been dedicated to the deepening of human relations, personal ties, between Japan and the United States. Yet the war destroyed precisely those relations so that it was not merely a terrible conflict far away from home but also a daily assault on the very beliefs of those who once thought that these two nations had a unique relationship. The U.S. firebombing of Japanese cities by war's end brought to Japanese soil the full horror of modern war. The internment of Japanese-Americans living on the West Coast of the United States depersonalized and criminalized tens of thousands of innocent U.S. citizens solely due to their race. Whereas a few years previously, the culture of Japanese Americans might have been admired and celebrated, now it was seen as an imminent threat that could cause entire families to become a fifth column against their own country. Japan's new image was sealed in wartime films portraying the brutality of the Imperial Army. Some, indeed, served to remind American audiences of how long-lived Japanese militarism was, such as *Blood on the Sun,* released in April 1945, in which James Cagney played a 1930s newspaper reporter in Tokyo trying to convince his superiors about the threat of war. No greater turn away from the cosmopolitanism of cultural exchange could be imagined, and no harder task might have been envisaged than seeking to find common ground once the guns fell silent.

While the overwhelming majority of American books published on Japan in the war years were about its evil government or fanatical society, a few serious works came out. These, less hysterical in tone and more objective, were done for government planning purposes. One such was a study by famed anthropologist John Embree undertaken for the Smithsonian Institution's *War Background Studies* series, in which Embree eschewed demonizing the Japanese.[2] One of the more incongruous was a booklet titled *Guide to the Western Pacific: For the Use of the Army, Navy, and Marine Corps of the United States,* commissioned by the public affairs section of the commander in chief of the Pacific, Admiral Chester W. Nimitz.[3] This guide, presumably to be carried by U.S. Marines as they hit the beaches under withering enemy fire, listed information one would more likely expect in a tourist leaflet, including temperature ranges, basic physical descriptions, and the like.

For civilians, however, nearly half a century of organized cultural exchange disappeared within weeks of Pearl Harbor. To no one's surprise, Japan-America societies large and small, from New York and Tokyo to Seattle and Osaka, shut their doors. Most went into a legal limbo, with their assets frozen and their boards of directors in abeyance. For the first time in decades, there were no Japanese festivals in America or celebrations of America's Independence Day in Japan, and no museum exhibitions of Japanese art or visits by American professional baseball players. In Washington, D.C., the famous cherry blossoms continued to bloom each spring, oblivious to the carnage across the Pacific, but they were now officially labeled "Chinese cherry blossoms." Four times they flowered while Japanese and Americans slaughtered each other, and few could have expected to see the old celebrations return to the American capital in their lifetimes.

Reshaping Japan: The Occupation

On August 15, 1945, normalcy and pacific relations between Japan and the United States were impossible to foresee. An exhausted Japanese citizenry heard the voice of their emperor for the first time, as he issued the surrender proclamation on the radio, amidst the devastation of their country. Over 4 million Japanese had been killed in the war, either as combatants or as civilian casualties of American bombs and the invasion of southern islands like Okinawa and Saipan. Every major Japanese city, save Kyoto, had been all but destroyed by American bombing attacks, and two of them, Hiroshima and Nagasaki, had been obliterated by a new and terrible atomic weapon. The Tokyo air raid of March 9–10, 1945, killed over one hundred thousand civilians, as many as did the Nagasaki bomb, and burned sixteen square miles of the heart of the city. Three-fourths of Japan's industrial infrastructure had been wiped out. Near starvation was common, and no organized type of municipal services existed. Once Americans landed on the home islands of Japan, they expected the Japanese to fight a guerilla war against the occupying troops and waited for counterattacks by remobilized military units.

It was shocking to many, then, that relations between Japanese and Americans did not descend into a tribal bloodbath. Despite continuing problems with food supply and medical services, not to mention the rise of a pervasive black market and the difficult repatriation of millions of Japanese soldiers and civilians from overseas, observers were amazed at how quickly the emblematic images of the war years were replaced by pictures of Japanese children crowding around American GIs handing out gum and chocolate.[4] General Douglas MacArthur's descent onto the Atsugi airfield on August 30, 1945, may have marked the military end of the war, perhaps even more so than the surrender ceremony in Tokyo Bay several days later, but the pictures of Japanese and GIs peacefully coexisting ended the cultural aspect of the conflict.

Such pictures, of course, did not change the reality of American control over Japan, but they did point to the beginnings of a new era in U.S.-Japan cultural contact. The Occupation was a unique moment in U.S.-Japan relations. The goal of the Occupation was not merely the demilitarization of Japan, nor was it the oppression of Japan in revenge for the war. It was, rather, the attempted remaking of Japanese society along liberal, democratic lines as interpreted by U.S. policy makers and the Occupation authorities on the ground. Prior to 1945, the exchange of cultures had been driven by the "market," so to speak, and Japanese had determined the pace of their encounter with America. Now, with the establishment of the general headquarters of the supreme commander for the Allied powers (SCAP), there was to be a direct effort to impose a particularly American vision of society on Japan. Nearly five hundred thousand U.S. troops were stationed on the islands to ensure the success of the Occupation.

President Truman appointed General Douglas MacArthur as SCAP to deal with the key political, military, and economic questions related to demilitarization and recovery.[5] MacArthur was ostensibly responsible to all the Allied powers through a body called the Far East Commission, but as is well known, he ran SCAP headquarters independently of any foreign input, defining "foreign" in a way that seemed to include Washington, D.C.. And whether openly expressed or not, the fundamental concern of SCAP headquarters in the immediate postwar period was to reorient Japanese culture toward a liberal, democratic path.

SCAP's vision for Japan was breathtaking. Demobilizing the Imperial Army and Navy and imprisoning its leaders for future trial was a necessary step in exorcising militarism. The virus of ultranationalism was to be extirpated by purging right-wing politicians, destroying the semidivine mystique of the emperor, and scrapping the Meiji Constitution. A democratic political system was to be strengthened by providing a new constitution, one that located sovereignty in the Japanese people by extending the franchise to women and by holding free elections. Economic freedom was to take root through the abolishment of the *zaibatsu* financial-industrial-commercial combines and through a thorough land reform that would end tenantry in the countryside. And finally, a culture of liberalism was to be created by revising the education system and by supporting civil society.

The magnitude of the task facing SCAP officials, brought on in large part by their ambitious designs, meant that illiberal means would be used at times to bring about liberal ends. The constitution became a classic case in point. After rejecting a Japanese commission's draft proposal because it was considered insufficiently liberal (in maintaining, for example, the emperor's supreme political position), SCAP bureaucrats crafted a constitution from scratch in the space of a week. The most noteworthy article in the document was the ninth, which permanently renounced war as a means of national policy and forbade Japan from possessing armed forces. After a hasty translation, the emperor promulgated the constitution without presenting it to the people, from whom it supposedly arose.[6]

The reach of SCAP's bureaucrats also extended into amorphous realms, such as that of popular culture. The Civil Information and Education (CIE) Section and the Civil Censorship Detachment (CCD), part of the Press, Pictorial, and Broadcast Division, were responsible for vetting all manner of publication in Japan. All references to feudalism, the divinity of the emperor, and the glorification of Japan's military were excised by the censors' pens. The literal mandate to scratch out such references can still be seen in school texts blacked out by the students themselves—though one must assume the young pupils had to read the offensive passages in order to actually blot them out. The extent of the censorship was preserved by Professor Gordon W. Prange, of the University of Maryland, who collected over six hundred thousand pages of material censored from 1945 to 1949.[7] Similarly, SCAP censors rewrote magazine articles, often to portray positive images of American domestic life. Motion pictures, of course, came under particular scrutiny. Japan's national film industry had been a central component of Tokyo's propaganda during the Pacific War, glorifying the Japanese military as a liberating force and portraying the Japanese and their colonial subjects as mutual allies. SCAP headquarters destroyed 236 films made between 1931 and 1945 that censors considered "militarist" or ultra-nationalist."[8]

Yet such a remolding of Japanese society was doomed to be uncompleted. As early as 1947, America's strategic interest in Japan shifted from controlling to rebuilding. As U.S. relations with the Soviet Union deteriorated and as Chinese Nationalist leader Chiang Kai-shek proved increasingly unable to control mainland China, Washington planners began to conceive of their erstwhile enemy as the linchpin to America's hard-won position in the Pacific. Japan would have to be remade into a dependable, stable ally, the "unsinkable aircraft carrier of the Pacific," as a future prime minister would put it.[9] Economic and political stability were paramount, and SCAP officials received orders to shift resources to those two goals.[10]

The initial American emphasis on purging suspected war criminals and on liberalizing Japan's educational, political, and economic systems was now put on hold. This so-called "reverse course" included the freeing of large numbers of Class B and C war criminals and, starting in 1949, the imposition of a strict anti-inflation and balanced budget policy drawn up by U.S. banker Joseph Dodge.[11] Further economic recovery for Japan came in unexpected ways. In 1950, when North Korean forces attacked south of the thirty-eighth parallel on the divided peninsula, the U.S. Army turned to Japan's nascent light industries to fill orders for the UN-sponsored forces being sent to repel the Communists. This jump-started the Japanese economy and helped focus it on export-driven consumer goods.

Concurrent with this economic resurgence was Japan's political rehabilitation. The Cold War was now in full swing, and China had fallen to Mao Zedong's Communist forces. Washington believed Japan was needed as an ally to hold the line in the Pacific, in the same way that West Germany was now the front line against the Soviet bloc. This new stance drove American leaders to end the Occupation, and not incidentally free up thousands of U.S. soldiers for combat in Korea. On September 4, 1951, President Harry S. Truman opened the San Francisco Peace Conference and a peace treaty between Japan and the Western allies was signed four days later. At the same time, Japan and the United States signed the Mutual Security Treaty, which mandated American aid for Japan in the case of an attack on that country. Tokyo joined the United Nations and, despite Article Nine of the new Constitution, started rebuilding its army and navy. The military, maintaining the spirit if not the letter of MacArthur's intentions, were known as the Self-Defense Forces. The U.S. Occupation ended in February 1952, after seven turbulent but productive years, and Japan rejoined the community of nations at the same time that the country took its place within the Cold War U.S. alliance structure.

The Rise of Popular Culture in the Postwar Period

The end of the Occupation did not end American influence over Japan. In fact, in certain ways, it freed up Japanese to adopt American ways of life on their own. During the Korean War, nearly a quarter of a million U.S. troops remained in Japan, and half that number remained after the armistice was signed in 1953. Culturally, America cast a large shadow over Japan, just as in prewar years. Significantly, the semipermanent stationing of U.S. military forces insured continued daily contact between Japanese and young Americans. Much as in the prewar period, Japan's urban centers became the focus of a vibrant mixture of Western and Japanese cultures, though in this period, except that now "Western" was largely synonymous with "American." What marked this movement was its undirected nature, in some ways reminiscent of pre-twentieth-century cultural encounter, in which personal tastes and fashions determined popularity and influence.

Despite the desperate desire of Japanese to recreate a normal life after the grueling years of conflict, the development of postwar consumer culture had to wait for at least a moderate level of economic recovery. As cities such as Tokyo slowly rebuilt themselves, erecting new concrete buildings from the smoldering ruins of bombed-out areas, young Japanese began crowding into entertainment areas. Jazz clubs, like the Blue Note in Tokyo, which often brought over top American talent, were particularly popular. Indeed, American music became an enduring fad in postwar Japan. Louis Armstrong, for example, toured Japan three times during the 1950s alone, in 1953, 1954, and 1956, and fans mobbed him wherever he went.[12] A decade later, in the summer of 1964, Duke Ellington visited Japan as a goodwill ambassador for the U.S. Department of State. His visit was filmed for a documentary, *Duke Ellington Swings through Japan,* and the tour inspired the piece "Ad Lib on Nippon," which appeared on his 1966 album *Far East Suite,* produced with pianist Billy Strayhorn. The film director Akira Kurosawa captured this musically fervid cultural mix in a scene in his 1963 film *High and Low (Tengoku to Jigoku),* itself inspired by the Ed McBain detective novel *King's Ransom.* In the film, as the police close in on a kidnapper (played by future superstar Nakadai Tatsuya) in a crowded club, Kurosawa pans around the dance floor, which is filled with young Japanese couples and wildly gyrating black and white Americans, while an insistent calypso beat permeates the scene.

Kurosawa's film reflected the freedom of the post-Occupation cultural scene and was part of the flood of books, magazines, and films flooding the Japanese marketplace after the end of censorship. But the censors of the CIE section had done their job, for the image of "the foreign" in 1950s and 1960s Japanese popular culture was decidedly pro-American. American models and sense profoundly influenced material culture, this at the very time when the postwar boom in America was celebrating suburbanization and the return to "normalcy" under President Dwight D. Eisenhower. In Japan, the carefully selected images of American life provided a goal to strive toward. Even the Buddhist scholar D. T. Suzuki approvingly noted in a 1952 article that the first thing that strikes a Japanese upon entering America was its "abundance" *(juntaku),* not necessarily the take one might expect from an advocate of a religion devoted to ending one's ties to material desires.[13]

Much of the desire for American goods lay with Japan's middle-class families. Early on in the postwar period, the American domestic experience regularly was drawn upon to highlight the path that Japanese society should be following. A June 1949 edition of *Shūkan Asahi,* for example, deconstructed a recent Sunday *New York Times,* identifying how many ads appeared in its five sections and 160 pages and proclaiming that, based on the number of sales advertised, America was in an "Age of Widespread Price Reduction" on household goods. From major appliances like phonographs and televisions to women's bags, consumer desires were believed to be easily satisfied in America, thereby steadily influencing the conception of a domestic normalcy desired by Japanese.[14] A decade later, during the 1960s, the dream for these urban dwellers was to purchase the "three treasures," a play on Japan's traditional symbols of imperial authority.[15] The modern treasures were a television, a refrigerator, and a washing machine. Sales of these items jumped in the 1960s, thereby narrowing the gap between Japanese and their American counterparts, who inspired Japanese desires in the first place. Central to the endurance of such dreams was the portrayal of these items not as luxuries but as affordable necessities.

Of the "three treasures," the television became the most ubiquitous, although its popularity was due to the unlikely confluence of two diametrically opposed influences. In April 1959, Emperor Hirohito's son, Crown Prince Akihito, married a commoner, Shōda Michiko. The fairytale wedding had its origins on a tennis court, and the country was enraptured by the first marriage of an heir to the throne in over four decades. Much like Elizabeth II's coronation in England six years previously, the public ceremonies were broadcast live, and in Japan hundreds of thousands of orders for television sets came in during the weeks before the imperial wedding. With the modernizing of the world's oldest monarchy, no one thought it ironic that ancient ceremonies resulted in the popularization of the newest of technologies.

Concurrent with the refined imperial wedding was a draw of another sort. Professional wrestling, an American import, became a national craze during the 1950s and 1960s, precisely at the same time that Americans were captivated by the sport and its heroes, such as "Gorgeous George" Wagner. In Japan, *puro-resu,* as it was known, went beyond simply sport and took on political connotations. Matches in Japan often pitted large Americans against smaller, quicker Japanese, who invariably won, thereby vicariously redeeming Japan from its ignominious military defeat of a decade previously. The biggest star of the time was Rikidozan (Momota Mitsuhiro), whose increasingly bizarre behavior led to his murder by a Japanese gangster in a Tokyo nightclub in 1963.[16] Yet, in another symbol of Japan's tenuous domestic racial relations, not until years after his death was it revealed that Rikidozan was actually a North Korean who had been raised in Japan. As the fever from pro wrestling died down, television found its savior in Japanese professional baseball, and televised games soon dominated the weekly broadcasting schedules during the season. The cultural mystique of the television was the central conceit in director Ozu Yasujirō's 1959 film *Ohayō* (Good Morning), in which two youngsters from a working class Tokyo neighborhood eagerly await the arrival of their own TV set.

These changes in Japanese popular culture continued even though consumer spending was dampened by the government's export-led growth policy. In 1952, at the end of the Occupation, Japan's per capita consumption was merely one-fifth that of the United States. But the gross national product grew at an average of 8 percent over the next two decades, ultimately leading to a significant rise in the standard of living. In December 1960, Prime Minister Ikeda Hayato unveiled a plan to double household income by 1970, basing his estimates on the previous decade's growth levels. By 1968, national income had in fact doubled, even though the emphasis remained on expanding the export sector. Despite this, most Japanese urban households had become more consumerist in nature, coming closer to the standards of their freewheeling American counterparts.

For most Japanese, these profound changes in society simply were the rhythm of their lives, unremarked upon and largely unanalyzed, as is daily life in all countries. Yet such changes engendered a variety of responses among intellectuals and social observers. The meaning of the Americanization sweeping through postwar Japan was a highly contested subject, for it cut to the heart of Japan's encounter with modernity. If colonialism and the war had shown the dangers of the Western-run international system, the economic recovery raised similar questions about how Japan was to reinvent itself for a second time in a century.

Simple celebration of America was rare, even for those who held a generally positive attitude toward Japan's erstwhile occupier. D. T. Suzuki, for example, in the 1952 article mentioned above took a complex view of the United States' strengths and weaknesses. In this article, "American Life and Culture," Suzuki was above all concerned with the question of individual and religious freedom. As a preacher, popularizer of faith, and prophet, he championed American liberties in comparison with the lack of religious rights then permitted in the Soviet Union. In this sense, Suzuki's article fit neatly into a larger Cold War social discourse in Japan and the United States. Suzuki, however, was not blind to the various problems in American society, writing, for example, that "although Americans talk about democracy and humanity, their treatment of [American] Indians is full of failures."[17] On the one hand, this was an ironic criticism coming from Japan, which continued to discriminate against the Koreans in the country, either those who had lived there for generations or the laborers forcibly brought in during the war; on the other hand, as the spokesman for a universal religion, Suzuki could point out the failings precisely of those countries that held themselves up as universal exemplars of human rights.

For most critics, the issue of course was the nature of Japanese society, not American. Yet few needed to be reminded that the contours of modern Japan were in crucial ways shaped by Americans. Intellectuals in particular stood aloof from the country's general cosmopolitanism and consumerism. Over two decades after the war, in 1968, the writer Yukio Mishima, probably the best-known Japanese author in the United States, penned a wide-ranging critique of contemporary Japan titled "An Argument in Defense of Culture" *(Bunka bōei ron)*. Mishima, as is well known, was a vociferous critic of postwar Japanese society, and just two years after this article appeared in *Chuō Koron,* Japan's leading intellectual journal, he would commit suicide after a failed attempt to raise a revolt among Japan's military as the first step to restoring traditional, imperial values.

Castigating the postwar Japanese desire to embrace a "gentle culture" *(kokoro yasashii bunka)* of flower arrangement and the tea ceremony, Mishima laid the blame on policies of the Occupation period, which banned martial expressions of Japanese culture, such as samurai movies and the feudal themes from Kabuki plays. In relation to foreign countries, he argued, current Japanese culture was a form of penance for past sins.[18] Yet, as Mishima knew, it was precisely this emasculated Japanese culture that was most celebrated in the United States, one that could trace its origins back to Americans' first images of Japan and to the first exhibitions of Japanese products in America.

Mainstreaming Japan in Postwar American Culture

It is tempting to reflect on how, after the brutality of the war, a general acceptance of, if not fascination with, Japanese culture could regain a toehold in American society. One answer, undoubtedly, is that not only is it easier for the victor to pick and choose what is acceptable about the defeated, but it is also more psychologically comfortable. Americans were not faced with the tensions besetting the Japanese in their postwar cultural encounter with the United States, namely, recognition of the at least militarily superior nature of the adversary, as well as the necessity to change one's system to adopt the other's strengths. Moreover, the reconstruction of Japan and its peaceful reentry into the community of nations was a postwar success story for the United States, unlike the war's aftermath in China, Eastern Europe, or the Middle East. A general feeling of goodwill developed toward Japan as it became clear that Tokyo would be a key ally in the Cold War and, more importantly, not a resurgent challenger to Washington.

After a war that had severed all normal contacts between the two nations, the role of nonofficial actors would prove to be crucial in restarting cultural relations. Some efforts, however, seemed premature at best. Just months after the surrender, for example, the renamed Japan Travel Bureau reissued its main handbook, *Japan: A Pocket Guide.* This 1946 imprint, appearing on wartime pulp paper, was unchanged from prewar editions, providing a capsule overview of Japanese history and customs and highlighting major tourist spots. With no apparent irony it invited tourists to the ravaged land, noting that there might be some inconveniences due to reconstruction in major urban areas. Despite the fact that there was no tourism in the immediate postwar years, other than very restricted traveling by GIs on leave, the fact that the guide was printed in English and distributed in the United States made it in a sense the government's announcement that it desired to resume people-to-people ties. Another such effort was a tour book aimed at the American forces in the country. Published in October 1947 by a group called the Society for Japanese Cultural Information, *Japan Today* was "intended as a picture album of colorful memories to those who . . . spent their days" in the war-shattered country. Unlike the official guide, *Japan Today*, traditionally bound with string, perhaps due to postwar shortages, confronted the recently concluded war head-on, celebrating the fact that for two years the country had been peacefully recovering thanks to the guidance of Americans.

Such indeed would be the main trope of postwar relations. The war, it appeared, had only buried, not destroyed, the interest each country felt for the other, though the relationship was forever altered by the brutality of the fighting. For Americans, the spectacle of a Japan reinventing, recovering, and resuming its position as one of the world's leading powers would engender a professional fascination with its culture that far outstripped any prewar interest. This was not evident, however, in the first years of peace. Japan's early postwar image in U.S. popular culture was a dismissive one, deriving from Japanese production of cheap, mass-produced consumer goods, such as toys and knickknacks. "Made in Japan" became a slogan for shoddy craftsmanship and vulgar items.[19] Yet as companies such as Sony and Toyota expanded their presence in the United States during the 1960s, Japan slowly became identified with quality, high-end consumer products, such as cameras, tape recorders, and automobiles.

Nor was it surprising that the immediate postwar cultural image of the defeated enemy was not particularly charitable. In the days when no one knew if the recently fanatical enemy could be successfully demilitarized, Hollywood productions were little changed from wartime propaganda films and were full of suspicion of the defeated country. Historically interesting, if not cinematically worthwhile, in this respect was 1949's *Tokyo Joe*. This film reportedly was the first to be filmed partly in Occupied Japan, thus making it somewhat the Japanese equivalent to Roberto Rossellini's *Open City*, which was filmed even while German troops were withdrawing from Rome. In *Tokyo Joe*, Humphrey Bogart plays an American who ran a bar in prewar Tokyo and returns after the war to search for his European wife. Its political message is clear, as Bogart tangles with crime lords and revanchist Japanese militarists, until his climactic death as he defeats their plans to sabotage the Occupation.

Yet as American fears of Japanese remilitarization dimmed, such images soon receded before a different set of interests. Visual media helped promote this trend, swiftly breaking down wartime images of the fanatical Japanese. American moviegoers began a love affair with Japanese films even while the Occupation still limited what could be made by Japanese directors. Akira Kurosawa's *Rashomon* was the breakthrough production. The 1950 film won the Venice Film Festival's Golden Lion award and in 1953 received a special honorary Academy Award for most outstanding foreign-language film released in the United States in 1951. The picture also gave a boost to translations of Japanese literature, as the short tale that inspired the film appeared in a collection of Akutagawa Ryūnosuke's stories in American bookstores in late 1952, with praise from the *New York Times* over the writer's "muscular morality."[20] With the success of *Rashomon*, films from leading directors like Kurosawa, Mizoguchi Kenji, and Ozu Yasujiro began to have a major impact on American audiences, and a fascination with Japanese settings spread in American society. Many films were straightforward heroic or morality tales, such as Kurosawa's iconic *Seven Samurai*, and the popularity of samurai films indicated that Americans were returning to their earlier obsession with the image of premilitarist, premodern Japan.

Not all Japanese films, however, received an unquestioned reception by American audiences or elicited a perfect understanding of the point of the stories. In September 1954, *Ugetsu*, Mizoguchi Kenji's ghost story set in sixteenth-century Japan, premiered in New York at an opening attended by the Japanese ambassador, Iguchi Sadao, and sponsored by the newly restarted Japan Society of New York, which was under the leadership of John D. Rockefeller 3rd. *Ugetsu* had won the Silver Lion at the 1953 Venice Film Festival, yet its sparse set decorations and haunting symbolism were far different from *Rashomon*'s multiple-perspective approach. The *New York Times* was not quite sure what to make of the film, commenting on its "strangely obscure, inferential, almost studiedly perplexing quality."[21] In a follow-up article a few days later, the same critic, Bosley Crowther, attempted to explain his confusion by writing that "the very Japanese culture from which these pictures spring is one that evolves in symbolisms, innuendos and subtle moods quite unlike the forms of factual expression that are native to American thinking and films." Seeking perhaps to extricate himself from this extended commentary on Japanese culture, Crowther plaintively ended his review by stating, "We have no way of knowing what was in the producer's and director's minds."[22] Despite such reviews, *Ugetsu* soon became widely regarded as a masterpiece of postwar Japanese film.

Yet it was also a symbol of the wide cultural acceptance of such "art films" that *Ugetsu* also could be parodied on *Caesar's Hour,* one of the most popular comedy shows on the newly expanding medium of television. A February 1956 skit, featuring the show's stars, Sid Caesar and Carl Reiner and titled "U-Bet-U," had no relation to the actual film, being instead an off-kilter combination of *Madame Butterfly* and Chinese opera. Yet it was notable that Caesar assumed his largely urban audience would recognize the source and be willing to sit through the extended "Japanese" doubletalk that satirized the imported production.[23]

During this period, American films, too, began to comment on the U.S.-Japan relationship from a variety of perspectives. One was 1956's *Teahouse of the August Moon,* which originally was a novel and then a Broadway play. Showing that nothing was sacred, this comedy about the recently concluded Occupation told a subversive story of Japanese villagers led by Sakini (Marlon Brando), wreaking havoc on the Americans sent to control their hamlet under the command of Captain Fisby (Glenn Ford). On the other end of the spectrum was a film based on James Michener's *Sayonara,* a lavish 1957 production again starring Brando and Kyō Machiko, one of Japan's leading actresses, who was known to American audiences not only from *Teahouse* but also *Rashomon* and *Ugetsu*. A dramatic love story between Americans serving in Korea and Japanese civilians, it costarred James Garner and Red Buttons and took aim at the U.S. law preventing servicemen from bringing home their Japanese brides. Yet in true Hollywood fashion, the dark and natural ending of Michener's novel was changed to an upbeat celebration of individualism in the face of bureaucratic oppression.

Equally pervasive during these years was a move in film to incorporate Japan not as a subject but as a statement of fashion sense. Appealing to the young American urban consumer, a number of films played off the current interest in Japanese interior design, eschewing true Japanese themes but subtly celebrating Japanese style. One memorable image came from the 1959 Doris Day–Rock Hudson hit film *Pillow Talk,* in which traditional Japanese paper shoji doors serve to frame the title sequence. Similarly, in the 1961 repairing of Day and Hudson, *Lover Come Back,* Hudson's ultramodern New York bachelor apartment is graced by a large Japanese print above, of course, his bed. The image of Japanese aesthetic as hip was undeniable and quite a change from prewar reverence for Japan's traditional arts.

This interest in Japanese design led to a subtler and more pervasive change in American images of Japan, as a form of "Japan chic" evolved in urban areas. Japanese aesthetics and popular art forms became not merely accepted or prized by a small group of collectors but valued by status-conscious American consumers and artistic producers. Japanese interior design and decorative arts were perhaps the most visible in American society. Pottery, scrolls, and paintings all came to adorn urban, sophisticated living spaces in a mirror reflection of the Japanese craze to Westernize their everyday consumer culture. Within a few years, this consumer-driven interest was recognized by professionals and scholars; in 1962, for example, the Rochester Institute of Technology held a special exhibit, Graphic Design/Japan, highlighting an exotic mix of American and Japanese styles that could enrich upscale urban and newly built suburban homes throughout the United States.

Even in popular American music, Japan was present, if far more tenuously. In contrast to Japan, where American jazz was triumphing, at the height of the rock-and-roll craze Japanese influence was much fainter in the United States. Yet in a parallel to the Japanese stylistic influence in American movies, Japanese themes and "Oriental pop" songs were ubiquitous during the 1950s and 1960s. Recordings by Elvis Presley, Artie Banks, and the Four Tops provided exotic images and lonely hearts ballads of love lost between American boys and Japanese (more often, Asian) girls.[24] Such numbers had little, if anything, to do with the real Japan, but they helped maintain the hip cachet of the country among American youth. One Japanese song, however, did burst through in America to become a symbol of a bouncy, recovering Japan. In 1961, the singer Sakamoto Kyū released "Ue o muite arukō" (Let's Walk with Our Heads Up"), which soon appeared in the United States as "Sukiyaki." Despite the completely nonsensical title translation—the song might as well have been called "Karate"—its upbeat melody propelled it to number one on the American charts on June 15, 1963. The success of "Sukiyaki" helped to spur further pop songs with Japanese and Asian themes, such as the forgettable "Yoshiko" and "Yoko-Hoko-Hama," both by minor artists.

Americans were fascinated not only with Japanese art and film but also with aspects of its culture that only a few years before had been blamed for Japan's militarism. A craze for Japanese martial arts began in the 1950s and never died down. The interest grew at least in part out of the experiences of thousands of GIs who first were taught karate, judo, or aikido by Japanese instructors on their bases. As the servicemen returned home, they brought with them a desire to keep practicing these skills in America and soon found a homegrown audience. Movies such as Spencer Tracy's *Bad Day at Black Rock* (1955) featured short karate sequences, while Japanese teachers, such as the aikido master Koichi Tohei, who first reached Hawaii in 1953, toured American cities, performing their art for eager spectators and growing numbers of practitioners. Part of what gave the martial arts craze its traction was its supposed connection to the deeper philosophical and social sources of Japanese civilization. In a period of growing consumerism in America, a consumer-led reincarnation of the "warrior ethic," Bushidō, and a focus on the self-discipline in Zen Buddhism served as the harbingers of a later countercultural movement emphasizing philosophy and inner harmony.

No discussion of Japan's cultural influence in America would be complete without mentioning Buddhism, and its most popular variant in

the States, Zen. This school of Buddhism caught the fancy of disillu-
sioned Americans as a reaction to the perceived cultural conformity of the
Eisenhower era and even more as part of the counterculture revolution of
the 1960s. Popularized by writers such as D. T. Suzuki and Alan Watts, a
writer associated with the Beat poets, Zen became a touchstone for an
entire generation professing the desire to seek the transcendental and re-
ject what they perceived as the rampant materialism, corruption, and aggression of the Cold War and Vietnam-era American society. What in
Japan was a strict discipline practiced by a relative few became in the
United States a do-it-yourself mélange of meditation, exercise, and cultural exploration. Yet Zen offered a true counterculture, one that could
include everything from physical exercise to food to spartan interior design. It bespoke of a want to look for the deeper sources of satisfaction
in life, those that, though foreign, were universal and therefore cosmopolitan.

Zen, not surprisingly, appealed to a select demographic in the United
States, as did most Japanese imports. For the most part, Japanese cultural
influence in America was limited to middle-class, educated urbanites.
Japanese food, for example, became popular during this period as a
healthier alternative to the high-fat American diet, but it found niches
only in East and West Coast cities, and a few interior locations, such as
Chicago, that had decent-sized Japanese-American populations. Unlike
Chinese food, whose popularity came in part due to its being inexpensive
and ubiquitous in large cities, Japanese cuisine was considered elite, as
much a visual presentation as a meal. Japanese cuisine also came with
correspondingly higher prices, which made it unaffordable on a regular
basis and thereby even more valued. Part of its appeal, indeed, lay in its
turning the unfamiliar into the newly discovered. For some, the sense of
discovery was the experience of eating raw fish; for others, it was in first
seeing a Japanese beer bottle, which was twice as big as American ones
and boasted white labels with bold red stars in the middle.[25]

In both Japan and America, the three decades after World War II saw a
steadily increasing engagement with the other, driven in part by government policy and in part by the mechanics of a consumer market fed by
images as enticing as they were often misleading. In this process, the traditional cultural exchange organizations would have to redefine their

roles, even as the nature of exchange was changing. The older, elite groups would soon awake from their slumber, but by that time the focus on grass-roots contact would give a very different cast to cultural relations. If it took the cataclysm of World War I to bring about the rise of "people's diplomacy" and grassroots internationalism in Europe, it took the Pacific conflict in World War II to supplant the essentially elite nature of contacts between Japan and the United States.

The Silver Age of International Exchange

Despite the unexpected and widespread growth of interest in things American and Japanese among consumers in both countries, elites would continue to play a crucial role in post–World War II global cultural exchange. The major difference from the prewar era, however, would be the final success of meritocracy in the conduct of international relations. Indeed, the period from 1945 to 1965 soon would come to be regarded as a "silver era" of international exchange, especially in the Atlantic relationship between the United States and Western Europe. In that global process, the role of private institutions would prove crucial and highly influential in reorienting the U.S.-Japan relationship as well.

If the potent triad of learned society, nongovernmental organization, and philanthropic foundation represented the mix of ingredients required to engender cultural exchange at the turn of the twentieth century, then the linking of philanthropy, state interests, and private institutions would transform and rationalize global society after 1945. Central to this process was a sense of shared interests among these three groups. Not only was there the overwhelming need to rebuild Europe and much of Asia after 1945, but there was also a keen understanding that the entire system of global governance forged after 1918 had failed and that a new set of institutions and structures would have to be built.

At the level of international organizations, hopes were placed in the new United Nations, and a host of supporting multilateral institutions, from the World Bank to the United Nations Educational, Scientific, and Cultural Organization (UNESCO), which replaced the old International Institute of Intellectual Cooperation. With financial aid from the United States' Marshall Plan and cooperation through the Organisation for European Economic Co-operation and the Council of Europe, the road to officially sponsored recovery was well under way by 1952. At the same time, though, a separate set of nonstate actors began to play an increasingly important role. The problems faced by the Western governments in recovery after World War II were so daunting that they clearly could not undertake all the work by themselves, or even collectively. The need for expertise and support from the private sector was also necessary.

In the postwar years, a great deal of such support came from the large American philanthropic foundations, especially the Ford Foundation. This foundation had been established several decades before but was a minor player in the philanthropic field compared with its elder cousins Rockefeller and Carnegie. All that changed dramatically a decade after the war. Largely to avoid crippling inheritance taxes on the death of company founder Henry Ford, the foundation sold its family-held Class A stock to the public in January 1956, stunning observers by immediately raising nearly $700 million in capital to be put to use in charitable programs. Other private American foundations quickly joined in the rush to fund reconstruction, development, and exchange programs across the globe. The various Rockefeller organizations, including the flagship foundation and the Rockefeller Brothers Fund, and the Carnegie Corporation also played major roles in postwar philanthropy, as did the Eli Lilly, Kettering, Sloan, and Kellogg foundations.[26] Whereas many of these outfits had worked independently of Washington, D.C., in the interwar period, after World War II they operated more as active partners and collaborators with the American government, especially once the Cold War began with the Soviet blockade of West Berlin in 1947.[27]

With the support of Western governments and philanthropic foundations, a number of high-profile groups and meetings began that helped cement a community of interests among the NATO allies and even began to reach out to Soviet bloc states. Among the more important groups was the Council on Foreign Relations, which had been founded in the wake of the 1919 Paris Peace Conference. Due in part to its wartime collaboration with the State Department through its War and Peace Studies program, the postwar council became simultaneously a venue for leading American policy makers to present speeches, a repository of talent on which the government could draw for bureaucratic appointments, and a think tank that continued to run large-scale, long-term research projects on international problems and issues. Headed in the postwar years by John J. Mc-Cloy, former U.S. high commissioner for Germany, and directed by such luminaries as David Rockefeller, Allen W. Dulles, W. Averell Harriman, and Hamilton Fish Armstrong, the Council on Foreign Relations was both lauded and derided as the place where the "wise men of foreign affairs" gathered and helped plan the postwar world.[28]

Like the Council on Foreign Relations, many private institutions and groups served to create networks among political, educational, and business leaders as a way of finding common ground and forging enduring transnational links.[29] Other important nonstate venues included Harvard University's Salzburg Seminar, first run in 1947, which especially focused on young leaders and midcareer professionals among Americans and Europeans; the Aspen Institute (1950); the Bilderberg meetings, which began in 1954; the International Institute for Strategic Studies (1958); the Ditchley Foundation (1958); the Atlantic Council of the United States (1961); and the Atlantic Institute for International Affairs (1961). While these groups reflected the quintessence of elite networking, they also served as a central mediator of cultural exchange, through the fostering of dialogue and the transmission of various ideas regarding postwar development and reconstruction. They not only complemented the official work of Western governments but also provided another form of transnational relations not covered by the traditional internationalist groups, though clearly the goals of the two communities could often be at odds. Over time, however, and particularly after the 1960s, the efforts of both the large philanthropic foundations and the private institutions merged more and more with revived internationalist groups dedicated to peace, economic development, and human rights issues, along with increasing criticism of Western capitalism and military power.

Official Efforts to Stimulate U.S.-Japan Exchange

The revival of cultural relations between Japan and the United States thus took place within a context of reshaping the global community. The great concern was whether the exchange organizations had learned from their prewar experience of political impotence or de facto co-optation by state interests. In short, the question was whether a more traditional cosmopolitanism could reassert itself amid the newly repackaged forms of national interest represented by the community of semiprivate international institutions.

It was an evolutionary moment in cultural exchange, and the U.S.-Japan relationship did not simply mirror those trends but actively helped create them. In addition to the prewar exchange organizations, new types of institutions emerged, and, at the same time, a greater emphasis on studying each country was made by leading academic institutions. Compared with the desperate days of the 1930s, when the focus of cultural exchange began to move toward the younger generation, the postwar period saw intellectual exchange move to the fore. In these early postwar years, the American government played an important role in reviving exchange, particularly through the Fulbright and International Visitor programs.

Fulbright was the eponymous brainchild of U.S. Senator J. William Fulbright, a Democrat from Arkansas. In 1946, the then junior senator tacked onto the reorganization of a 1944 relief bill a provision that foreign credits from the sale of U.S. surplus war properties abroad could be used for international educational activities.[30] Designed to increase mutual understanding among future leaders and those who taught the young, the program sought to bring foreign students, teachers, and scholars to the United States and send Americans abroad. Within half a century, it would dispatch nearly 100,000 Americans to foreign countries and bring close to 160,000 foreigners to the United States to study. As part of U.S. attempts to shape the postwar world, the program aimed at broadening the cultural horizons of foreigners by allowing them to participate directly in American society and to bring back to their homelands American visions of social organization.

Due to its status as a defeated country, Japan was not initially allowed to participate directly in Fulbright exchanges. It was, however, enrolled into the program under the auspices of the Government Aid and Relief in Occupied Areas (GARIOA) program. The first Japanese grantees left for the United States in 1949, and through 1951 nearly one thousand students studied at U.S. institutions of higher education. GARIOA selected students from top Japanese universities, "seeding" them throughout the

United States. It thus aimed at Japan's young elite, much in the same way that the Meiji leadership had selected their own children to study abroad back in the nineteenth century. Due in part to this early success, in August 1951, Japanese Prime Minister Yoshida Shigeru and U.S. Ambassador William Siebold signed an agreement formally opening the doors of Fulbright Program to Japanese.

With the end of the Occupation in 1952, GARIOA was folded into the Fulbright Program. The program in Japan was funded entirely by the United States government until 1979, when an independent, binational body, the Japan–United States Educational Commission, was established to run it and raise funds for the scholarships. Through the turn of the twenty-first century, over five thousand Japanese and twenty-one hundred Americans were sent as students, lecturers, and speakers to each country.[31] The Japanese, in particular, formed an impressive alumni cohort, including Japanese Supreme Court Justice Chikusa Hideo, University of East Asia President Yamazaki Masakazu, heads of major corporations, and leaders in the Japanese media. A particularly large contingent of grantees came from Okinawa, which remained under U.S. control until 1972. A Fulbright alumni network operated not only to sponsor future scholarships but also to create connections between Japanese and American grantees.

The focus of Fulbright Japan, as with all the Fulbright programs, remained on university-level education, but it slowly expanded the range and types of scholarships it granted, thereby eventually reaching a broader sector of Japanese society. The majority of grants went to those pursuing doctoral dissertation research in America or graduate study leading to the receipt of a master's degree. A second set of grants was designed to allow university faculty or professionals of nonprofit organizations to conduct research in American universities and in collaboration with U.S. scholars. Eventually, grants for Japanese journalists to study for shorter terms in American universities, with the stipulation that these journalists would write articles based on their experience, also was established.

Fulbright also recruited Americans for study and research in Japan. As with the program for Japanese grantees, the largest component of Americans was those pursuing graduate research, particularly for the doctoral dissertation. Yet as the overall mandate for the Fulbright Program was the increase of mutual understanding, Fulbright Japan also recruited American faculty specializing in U.S. history or American studies as lecturers, placing them in Japanese universities and colleges for an entire academic year, where they would directly teach Japanese students. The Fulbright office in Tokyo also acted as a clearinghouse of information for Japanese students interested in studying in America, whether as Fulbright Scholars or not. Throughout the 1950s and 1960s, the number of Japanese exchange students grew slowly, given the expense of a year abroad, yet just two years after the end of the Occupation, in 1954, there already were more than fifteen hundred Japanese studying in the United States. This number grew to just over four thousand by 1970. With the emergence of Japan as an economic power in the 1980s, the number of students exploded, reaching over forty thousand each year throughout the 1990s, before dropping nearly by half in the first decade of the twenty-first century.[32]

Fulbright was not the only U.S. government effort to forge cultural links. More limited in scope, but important nonetheless, was the International Visitor Program (IVP) run by the U.S. Department of State. The IVP had its origins in the 1948 Smith-Mundt Act. Best known as the enabling legislation for the United States Information Agency (USIA) and the Voice of America, the act was broadly conceived to promote better understanding of the United States through the "broadest possible" sharing of information with foreign publics and would become controversial for barring the domestic dissemination of official information aimed at foreign audiences.[33] Yet the Smith-Mundt Act also created exchange-of-persons programs that built on wartime visits of Latin American and Chinese leaders.

In 1953, Japanese were allowed for the first time to participate in the IVP, and forty invitees traveled to America between 1953 and 1954. Unlike the Fulbright, which placed students and researchers in home institutions for a year, the IVP was a short-term program. Japanese participants could travel anywhere in the United States for approximately a month. Moreover, despite the IVP's government funding, the actual running of the IVP was largely delegated to local affiliated councils made up of private citizens scattered throughout the country. In the decades since its inception, over twenty-three hundred Japanese have participated in the IVP, rivaling the numbers hosted by the Fulbright Program. And similarly to the Fulbright Program, the IVP aimed largely at young Japanese or those in the early stages of their careers. The IVP alumni list is impressive, including former Prime Minister Kaifu Toshiki and the heads of most of Japan's major newspapers, in addition to well-known writers such as Ōe Kenzaburo and Murakami Haruki.[34] Those running the IVP vociferously defended their programs as activities presenting America "warts and all" to foreign audiences, facilitating the exposure even of the underbelly of American society to those who sought to see such parts of the United States.

The Smith-Mundt Act was of course most responsible for the setting up of USIA. As the public diplomacy arm of the U.S. government abroad, USIA ran American Centers in cities throughout the world. The centers were separate from U.S. embassies and consulates and largely concerned themselves with organizing speakers programs and maintaining English-language libraries for the use of Japanese citizens. In the 1960s sixteen American Centers in Japan employed approximately 350 people as programmers and public affairs specialists.[35] Throughout the 1950s and 1960s, USIA produced programs about America to be put on Japanese television and radio, and the American Centers acted as foreign "community centers," showing U.S. films and running libraries as a resource for the local communities.

At their height in the 1980s, the American Centers in Japan hosted five hundred speakers a year, averaging two per day. These speakers addressed audiences of students, academics, business and government officials, and ordinary citizens on all aspects of American life. The American Centers shied away from supporting commercially viable programs, assuming those would find their way to Japan in any case; rather, those in charge of the centers sought to bring events to Japan that would not otherwise have sponsorship, such as the Boys Choir of Harlem.

In the Cold War era, such public diplomacy was a central part of U.S. global strategy, and the resources devoted to this diplomacy dramatically expanded the range of cultural exchange. Few were concerned that Washington bureaucrats attempted to ensure the dissemination of positive images of America through the various programs, especially when popular artists like Duke Ellington were the face of such activities. Given Tokyo's position on the front lines of the struggle against Communism in Asia,

Japan remained the focus of much official effort throughout the postwar decades, even though it was already a strong ally of the United States.

Ironically, one of Washington's greatest successes in fostering cultural exchange between Japan and the United States was due to a political appointment. In 1961, the new president, John F. Kennedy, turned to his alma mater to help stabilize U.S.-Japan relations. The previous year, the renewal of the U.S.-Japan Mutual Security Treaty had resulted in the largest postwar protests in Japanese history. Over one hundred thousand anti-U.S. protesters ringed the National Diet Building in downtown Tokyo, and the ruling Liberal Democratic Party, under Prime Minister Kishi Nobusuke, resorted to illegal parliamentary tactics to force through the treaty. Kishi not only had to resign, but Dwight D. Eisenhower's planned trip to Japan, the first by a sitting American President, was canceled. The antitreaty protests showed the other, and equally powerful, side of the U.S.-Japan relationship, one that comprised a variety of left-wing student and labor groups, as well as pacifist Japanese. Their opposition proved that the postwar encounter with America was not a mindless acceptance by all Japanese of American economic, political, and cultural dominance. In response, the new U.S. administration turned not to a politician or a diplomat but to an academic to try and smooth over relations.

In March 1961, Edwin O. Reischauer, professor of history at Harvard, became the U.S. ambassador to Japan. Born in 1910 and raised in Japan by missionary parents, Reischauer spoke fluent Japanese and was an expert on the country's history. His wife was Haru Matsukata, granddaughter of Arai Rioichirō, cofounder of the Nippon Club in New York, and Matsumoto Shigeharu, the founder of International House of Japan, was a cousin of hers (see below in this chapter). Japanese considered Reischauer's appointment a coup, and he and his wife became media celebrities. The announcement of his appointment took up half the front page of the *Asahi Shinbun,* which declared it a "180 degree turn in U.S. policy toward Japan" and a "new direction in U.S.-Japan relations."[36] *Life Magazine* profiled the ambassadorial couple in its June 1, 1962 issue, and Japanese coverage of the ambassador and his wife throughout his tenure was ubiquitous.

Reischauer clearly served largely as a cultural ambassador, visiting thirty-nine of Japan's (then) forty-six prefectures and interacting regularly with young Japanese, especially students. As focused as he was on political issues, like the deepening of U.S.-Japan security cooperation at the height of the Cold War, Reischauer could not get education out of his blood, and while in Tokyo he worked to establish the United Nations University in Japan, an institution dedicated to an internationalist vision of knowledge and educational opportunity. Japanese goodwill for Reischauer only intensified after a mentally unstable young Japanese seriously wounded him in an assassination attempt in 1964. Ending with his return to Harvard in 1966, Reischauer's ambassadorship was a unique experiment in people-to-people diplomacy and showed how nonbureaucrats steeped in traditional cultural exchange professions could collaborate with the government in promoting the U.S.-Japan relationship. Soon enough, Reischauer would be attacked by academic critics precisely for his role in supporting state policies that upheld American hegemony in Asia and around the world.

A New Life for Old Organizations

Just as much as cementing political relations with Japan was an objective for Washington, the desire to revive binational cultural exchange was a deeply cherished goal of the old exchange organizations. These groups had gone into hiatus with the attack on Pearl Harbor, but their assets, records, and membership lists had been carefully preserved during the hostilities. During the Occupation they remained moribund, due in no small part to still-fresh memories of the brutal fighting as well as the uncertainty about the fate of Japan–United States relations. As the Occupation wound down in the early 1950s the major exchange groups began reorganizing themselves. And yet, as they did so, they had to balance rebuilding their old links and restarting their traditional activities with the new varieties of official programs and the unregulated vibrant popular culture exchange that was radiating throughout both countries. In seeking to return to their position as the focal point of cultural exchange, these organizations were thus forced as well to search for a new role.

In Japan, Kabayama Aisuke officially had been president of the America-Japan Society (AJS) throughout the war years and up to 1950. He then resigned to focus on another cultural project, and the presidency passed to Komatsu Takashi, who slowly restarted AJS activities in the waning days of the Occupation. Komatsu was the chairman and founder of Komatsu Ltd., which became one of Japan's largest manufacturers of construction equipment. In 1910, he had studied at Monmouth College, a small Presbyterian institution in Illinois, and then at Harvard Law School, and he soon became a leading member of Tokyo's Rotary Club. In the decade before Pearl Harbor, Komatsu had been one of the few Japanese who sought to carve out an internationalist path. He toured the United States along with Kabayama in January 1932, and returned alone the next year as the special commissioner of the Japan Economic Federation to the Chicago World's Fair.

As president of the AJS from 1950, Komatsu used his prewar contacts with American officials to host leading U.S. statesmen for luncheon talks in Tokyo, thereby paving the way for resuming social contacts between high-level Japanese and Americans. During 1950 and 1951, SCAP General Matthew B. Ridgway (who had replaced Douglas MacArthur), California Governor Earl Warren, and Chairman of the Rockefeller Foundation John Foster Dulles all spoke before the society. In July 1951, Komatsu hosted New York Governor Thomas E. Dewey, whose visit to Japan included a speech, given at the AJS urging a strengthening of U.S. military power in the Pacific and later visits to Kamakura, Kurihama, and Yokohama.[37] The following February, presidential envoy Dean Rusk gave a major policy speech before the AJS, confirming that U.S. troops would stay in Japan after the Occupation, under the auspices of the Mutual Security Treaty.

In late 1951, Komatsu traveled to the United States to offer a proposal that would symbolically mark the beginning of a new era in cultural exchange. On October 11, he addressed the first postwar luncheon of the revived Japan Society of New York. There, Komatsu announced plans to begin preparations to celebrate, two years hence, the centennial of Commodore Perry's arrival in Japan. The celebration would, he asserted, commemorate the "tremendous contributions Americans have made to the people of Japan."[38] Given that American MPs patrolled Japanese streets and that most cities in Japan were still covered in rubble from American firebombing during the war, Komatsu's plan was an almost irrational attempt to put the recent bloody past behind the two countries. It also was a subtle effort to portray the war as an historical deviation from the democratic development of Japan. That this might not be a feeling shared by his audience or his fellow Japanese seemed not to intrude on Komatsu's thoughts, focused as they were on an idealistic, prewar conception of the U.S.-Japan relationship.

Komatsu's speech was notable mostly, perhaps, for marking the reopening of the Japan Society of New York. By the end of 1951, the board of directors of the society had begun meeting regularly again and started planning for restarting their programs. The real launch of the Japan Society's second era, though, began on March 25, 1952, with the election of John D. Rockefeller 3rd as its president and John Foster Dulles as chairman of the Board of Directors. Though Dulles would soon resign in order to become secretary of state under newly elected President Dwight D. Eisenhower, Rockefeller would remain the principal benefactor of the society and of U.S.-Japan cultural exchange for the next two and a half decades, until his death in a car accident in 1978.

Rockefeller, born in 1906, was the eldest son of John D. Rockefeller Jr., the heir to the founder of Standard Oil, John D. Rockefeller Sr.[39] In 1929, newly graduated from Princeton, JDR 3rd, as he was called by associates, traveled to Kyoto, Japan, as the secretary to the U.S. delegation at the Third Conference of the Institute of Pacific Relations. There, the young Rockefeller met fellow internationalist Matsumoto Shigeharu, with whom he was to form a lifelong relationship. Rockefeller also became entranced by traditional Japanese art, especially Buddhist statuary; he and his family would amass one of the largest private collections of Asian art in the world over the succeeding decades. Rockefeller did not return to Japan for two decades, but in 1951 he was asked to accompany John Foster Dulles as the cultural consultant to the diplomatic mission to discuss the upcoming peace treaty and conference in San Francisco.

As a committed collector of Japanese and Asian art, Rockefeller considered the Japan Society of New York to be one of the primary venues where the two cultures could interact and a place that could provide the administrative support for serious exchanges of art and intellectuals. In 1951, he provided the bulk of the funds to reopen the Japan Society, and on becoming president, he summed up his views of its importance: the society's objective was "to help bring the people of the United States and of Japan closer together in their appreciation and understanding of each other and each other's way of life."[40] With this goal in mind, Rockefeller worked closely with new Executive Director Douglas W. Overton to move the Japan Society again to the center of U.S.-Japan cultural exchange.

As in the prewar years, Japan Society returned to its focus on speeches, exhibits, and educational activities. Within months of resuming its activities, the society became the main venue for speeches by major figures involved in U.S.-Japan relations. While maintaining its nonofficial character, it nonetheless entered frequently into political issues, all the while taking no organizational stance other than as a supporter of firm bilateral relations. This was made clear at its first important postwar gathering, on June 17, 1952. Just two months after Japan regained its sovereignty, Araki Eikichi, Tokyo's first ambassador to the United States since 1941, gave a speech before 750 guests at the Hotel Plaza, urging for more foreign trade and industrialization for Japan. Rockefeller, acting as host, seconded the ambassador's request, arguing for a more liberal American trade policy, which would help Japan recover quickly.[41] While the topic may have been related to sober policy issues, the speech was a very public affirmation that Japan was once again a member of the community of nations, that the postwar period was well under way, and that Japan Society was a leader in rebuilding U.S.-Japan ties.

Not all speeches, however, assumed a perfect complementarity between American and Japanese positions. In September 1953, former society chairman John Foster Dulles, speaking as U.S. secretary of state, addressed a Japan Society dinner of fifteen hundred persons gathered to welcome Crown Prince Akihito to New York. In his remarks, Dulles chastised the government of Prime Minister Yoshida Shigeru for not allocating enough resources to Japan's defense, a sticking point between the two countries that would bedevil relations for decades. For his part, the nineteen-year-old prince made reference to Japan's failure to gain admission to the United Nations, though he refrained from pointing out that it was Soviet objections that had so far frustrated Tokyo's attempts to join the world body.[42] Again, however, the substance of the speeches was less important than the symbolism provided by elites of both nations reengaging in public and private diplomacy.

Political speeches were not the bulk of the society's activities, though, as Rockefeller's vision of a vibrant cultural program was soon realized and expanded upon. Continuing its prewar tradition, the Japan Society helped sponsor a major exhibit of Japanese art treasures at the Metropolitan Museum of Art in March 1953. The show, which included seventy-seven sculptures and fourteen statues, toured Washington, D.C., Seattle, Chicago, and Boston in addition to New York. Not only was it the largest showing of art from Japan mounted in the United States up to that time, but also it was the first major exhibit since World War II, and the preview itself was attended by six thousand people.[43]

Japan Society also had been one of the first private groups to support academic study of Japan, starting back in 1911. In August 1953, the society resumed its role in the academic community by providing $14,000 for grants-in-aid to twenty-five Japanese postgraduate students in the United States whose funds had run out and who would soon be forced to suspend their studies at some of America's top universities, including Harvard, Illinois, Indiana, Johns Hopkins, Michigan, and Yale. As fifteen of the students had originally come to the United States on Fulbright scholarships, the society's financial aid showed that Japan Society could play a role even among the major new government programs designed to expand intellectual exchange.[44] The society followed on this academic endeavor by giving the City College of New York approximately $1,000 in October 1954 for a course on Japanese civilization and by sponsoring in 1955 the publication of *Introduction to Japan,* a new history by a young scholar named Herschel Webb, who went on to teach Japanese history for several decades at Columbia University.

The success of the revived Japan Society convinced John D. Rockefeller 3rd of the viability of and need for such cultural exchange organizations. While he remained a key benefactor of the Japan Society and retained his intense personal interest in Japan, he also sought to more broadly engage Americans in Pacific Rim issues. In 1956, he founded the Asia Society, designed to educate Americans about China, Korea, Thailand, and the other leading Pacific nations, as well as to bring about better mutual understanding between those peoples and the citizens of the United States. The new society also centralized Rockefeller's efforts to collect Asian art, including Japanese, and to provide a suitable permanent exhibition space for public viewing. With headquarters in midtown Manhattan, the Asia Society often worked closely with Japan Society, especially on large exhibitions, but most observers believed that the unique ties between Japan and the United States provided a rationale for continuing the existence of a separate organization devoted to the reborn bilateral relationship.

A New Paradigm: International House

The activities of the revamped Japan Society and America-Japan Society showed the continued viability of prewar styles of cultural exchange programming in a new social environment. The organizations' events and publications contributed to the contact that was being fueled by tens of thousands of GIs in Japan and an increasing consumer interest on both sides of the Pacific. Even within this mix, however, the 1950s would witness yet another evolutionary step in U.S.-Japan cultural exchange.

As active as the main organizations were, they could not provide a physical community that could serve as a permanent place for meetings, research activities, and social gatherings. Back in the mid-1930s, the America-Japan Society, under Kabayama Aisuke's prodding, had proposed extending physical facilities to students and researchers on temporary stay in Tokyo, but the war had put any such ventures on hold. With the end of hostilities and the Occupation, Kabayama returned to his idea of building a permanent institutional base for intellectual exchange.

To help with the ambitious project, Kabayama turned to Matsumoto Shigeharu. Born in 1899 to a prestigious Osaka family, Matsumoto was one of the best traveled and most cosmopolitan Japanese of his generation. He had studied at Yale from 1924 to 1925 and then spent another year at the University of Wisconsin. In 1929, he had served as the Japanese delegation's secretary to the Third Pacific Council of the Institute of Pacific Relations, where he met John D. Rockefeller 3rd, becoming Rockefeller's closest Japanese friend. Immediately prior to the war, Matsumoto worked on U.S.-Japan relations in the cabinet of Prime Minister Konoe Fumimaro, a posting that resulted in Matsumoto's purge under the Occupation, from 1946 through 1950. In 1954, however, he was appointed to the National Commission of Japan for UNESCO, and later in that decade he was named president of the Japan Association for American Studies.[45]

He continued to serve on numerous bodies connected to international cultural exchange, until his death in 1989.

Kabayama and Matsumoto together began preparations for what they planned to call the International Cultural Center. Unlike all previous private exchange organizations, the center would be a permanent facility that contained meeting spaces, study-bedrooms for short- and long-term stays, and a library for researchers. The venture received the support of the Society for the Promotion of International Culture (KBS), which remained the main Japanese organ for cultural exchange, and of its chairman, Kano Hisaakira. Matsumoto soon turned to his old friend Rockefeller for help, and the philanthropist met with Kano and the famed Japanese novelist Kawabata Yasunari to discuss the plans while on Rockefeller's 1951 mission with Dulles. After the meeting, Rockefeller noted that the proposed center would be "rendering a useful service in furthering international understanding."[46]

With Rockefeller's tacit approval, Matsumoto and Kabayama established the Cultural Center Preparation Committee, which worked with Dean Rusk and Donald H. McLean of the Rockefeller Foundation. In late May 1952, Matsumoto wrote a proposal to the Rockefeller Foundation for funding to build the center. In his proposal, he emphasized the centrality of America to his cosmopolitan thinking, noting that the goal of the center was the "promotion of international understanding and the development of cultural and intellectual interchange between Japan and other countries, particularly the United States."[47] The center would work closely with the Japanese Committee for Intellectual Interchange, chaired by Takagi Yasaka, who had compiled reports on Japanese studies in the United States for the KBS during the 1930s, as well as with the Committee for Intellectual Interchange, located at Columbia University and headed by two historians of Japan, George Sansom and Hugh Borton. With no monies available from still-impoverished Japanese sources, American funds were necessary for the project. The Rockefeller Foundation responded with an initial grant of $676,121 (¥243,400,000), and the center was brought into being on August 27, 1952, as the International House of Japan Inc.[48]

I-House, as it soon came to be known, was to be a purely nongovernmental, nonprofit organization. In its 1952 articles of endowment, I-House explained that its mission "shall be to promote cultural exchange and co-operation between the people of Japan and the peoples of America and other countries, and thereby to contribute to the cultivation of international friendship and understanding."[49] The key to the project, as Kabayama and Matsumoto understood it, would be the house itself, and intensive planning went into its construction. The organization secured part of an estate that had been owned by feudal lords, Japanese aristocrats, and industrial chieftains in Tokyo's Roppongi district, near Azabu Jūban. Graced by an extensive traditional Japanese garden, I-House opened on June 11, 1955. The building contained sixty study-bedrooms, a two-hundred-person lecture hall, and a five-thousand-volume library on Japan. The design, meant to provide a home away from home for visiting scholars and researchers, won the Japan Institute of Architecture Award for 1956. Fired by a cosmopolitan vision, Kabayama and Matsumoto conceived of I-House as a "model international community."[50] Kabayama, the guiding spirit of I-House, did not live to see the fruition of his efforts, however, for he died on October 21, 1953, just after the incorporation of the I-House foundation.

After Kabayama's death, Matsumoto became the chief force at the new institution. He was appointed managing director in 1952 and remained in that position until he became chairman of the foundation in 1965 (which he held until his death in 1989). Reflecting the American influence at I-House, the first associate managing director was the American Gordon T. Bowles, who served until 1958, and fully two-thirds of I-House's foreign members were Americans. The directors of I-House, moreover, represented the cream of Japan's cultural and intellectual elite. In 1957, they included Yanaihara Tadao, president of the University of Tokyo; Jodai Tano, president of the Japanese Women's International League for Peace and Freedom; Fujiyama Aiichirō, the foreign minister; and Ishikawa Ichirō, commissioner of the Atomic Energy Commission. The councillors, an outside advisory group, included the future Nobel Prize–winning novelist Kawabata Yasunari and Komatsu Takashi, president of the America-Japan Society.[51] I-House's membership grew steadily, from 1,041 persons (226 of whom were foreign) in 1956 to 2,143 by the end of its first decade.[52]

I-House served as a vehicle for the reinternationalization of Japan among intellectual elites. The organization did not run traditional cultural exchange events itself, but it did serve as a venue for other groups' activities and began to provide administrative expertise for a wide variety of events. Yet its main focus was on creating links between academics and other intellectuals. In its first decade, from 1952 to 1962, one of I-House's main efforts was the Intellectual Interchange Program (IIP), which brought some of the West's most prestigious thinkers to Japan. The IIP was crucial in exposing postwar Japan to Western intellectuals, primarily Americans, and allowing those individuals to witness the country's recovery and its reengagement with the community of nations. The program also sent eminent Japanese, mainly academics, to America, allowing them to interact with American counterparts under conditions that otherwise would have been difficult, given how few resources like the Fulbright Scholarship Program existed. The IIP, with its dual focus, consistently reflected the cosmopolitan leanings of Matsumoto and I-House.

For the Japanese participants, the IIP often marked their most intense encounters with America. Nagai Michio (1923–2000), for example, spent his time visiting American universities and returned to become one of Japan's key advocates for liberal arts education, writing books on the subject in both Japanese and English. He directed the U.S. government-sponsored East-West Center in Hawaii from 1972 to 1973 and then served as Japan's minister of education from 1974 to 1976. In the last decade of his life, Nagai returned to the organization that had sponsored his visit to America and served as chairman of the Board of Trustees of I-House before his death in 2000.

In May 1953, even before its permanent facilities opened, I-House brought Eleanor Roosevelt, then sixty-eight years old, to Japan as the first of the IIP visitors. The former First Lady, who had just finished chairing the United Nations Commission on Human Rights, stayed for two months, giving numerous talks and visiting key cities. To underline the importance of both the program and the visitor, Takagi Yasaka, head of the Japanese Committee for Intellectual Interchange, Matsumoto Shigeharu, and other Japanese and American dignitaries met Roosevelt at the airport. As a symbol of the overcoming of wartime enmities, the widow of Franklin D. Roosevelt was also welcomed at Haneda Airport by Nomura Kichisaburō, special envoy to Washington in 1941, whose mission to prevent war had ended in failure with the attack on Pearl Harbor. The *Asahi Shinbun* noted that Eleanor Roosevelt's visit would include meetings with leaders of cultural, labor, agricultural, and women's movements, as a way of furthering U.S.-Japan relations.[53]

Those with internationalist leanings were particularly favored by the heads of the IIP program. Roosevelt was followed in September 1953 by Norman Cousins, editor of the *Saturday Review* and one of America's key advocates of world federalism. Cousins had a particular interest in Japan, for it was the atomic bombings of Hiroshima and Nagasaki that particularly spurred his internationalist activities. It was Cousins who arranged for the *Saturday Review* to fund the medical treatment in America of twenty-four young women suffering from radiation sickness; they became known nationally as the "Hiroshima Maidens," and Cousins and his wife eventually adopted one of them. His magazine's readers also supported the medical care in Japan of four hundred children orphaned by the bomb. Following in Cousins's pacifist footsteps, the theologian and peace advocate Paul Tillich made a three-month stay from May to July 1960 under IIP auspices, promoting an end to Cold War rivalries.

Perhaps the most ironic, and most moving, visit arranged by the IIP was that of J. Robert Oppenheimer, who arrived in September 1960. The father of the atomic bomb, the scientist-administrator most responsible for making possible the horrors of Hiroshima and Nagasaki, was of course by that time a confirmed opponent of the use of atomic weapons or the development of more powerful devices, such as the hydrogen bomb. So outspoken was Oppenheimer that he had his security clearance stripped by the U.S. government in 1954. At a packed press conference at I-House immediately after his arrival, Oppenheimer stressed that his visit was to strengthen the bonds between international scientists, and that he planned to meet the physicists Yukawa Hideki, winner of the 1949 Nobel Prize, and Asanaga Shin'ichirō, who would share the Nobel in 1965 with Richard P. Feynman.[54] For some, Oppenheimer's visit could have been an outrage; for those committed to U.S.-Japan intellectual exchange, it was a powerful symbol of the laying aside of old enmities in the quest for global cooperation.

A second, parallel I-House venture was the Distinguished Visitors Program, which brought preeminent Westerners to Japan for extended visits. Unlike the IIP, which focused mainly on Americans, the Distinguished Visitors Program reached out largely to Europeans. The architect Walter Gropius, for example, visited from May through August 1954, while the English historian Arnold Toynbee was in residence during October and November 1956. Each met with Japanese academics and students, gave public lectures, and participated in various I-House programs, making I-House for a time an intellectual center on a par with some of Japan's best universities.

Intellectual exchange remained at the heart of I-House's mission over the decades. Whereas the early efforts of the institution focused on young or established scholars, I-House eventually began to concentrate on students as well. In 1970, it took over the administration of two of the oldest U.S.-Japan scholarship programs, the Bancroft Educational Aid Fund, which had been established in 1928 to honor the memory of U.S. Ambassador Edgar A. Bancroft, and the Grew Foundation. The latter was founded in 1950 as a testament to the long-serving prewar ambassador Joseph C. Grew. The expressed goal of the Grew Foundation was the "cultivation of understanding between the peoples of Japan and the United States," to which end it sponsored Japanese youth to study at four-year undergraduate institutions in America. One of the first recipients was a student named Akira Iriye, who enrolled in Haverford College in 1953 before doing graduate work at Harvard. Iriye would become one of the leading historians of Japan-U.S. relations and chair of the History Department at Harvard University as well as president of the American Historical Association.

As Japanese and American academics began the rapid buildup of binational studies, I-House participated by sponsoring several initiatives. One of the key issues for postwar Japan was the institutionalization of foreign-language study. The main government emphasis was on English, mastery of which by students, scientists, and professionals was considered essential for Japan's internationalization and economic recovery. In 1956, I-House contributed to this effort by running the English Language Exploratory Program, which looked at means of increasing English-language education in schools and of continuing learning through venues such as community centers.[55]

The United States was the focus of much of the scholarly research on foreign countries that was conducted in Japan during the 1950s and 1960s. Not only did Tokyo have its closest economic and political relationship with Washington, but also the very definition of the goals of postwar recovery and modernity was provided by America. As a center for U.S.-Japan academic exchange, I-House was ideally situated to address these themes in a binational way. In 1959, it inaugurated a research seminar on problems of American civilization and, in the early 1960s, ran a research project on Japan-U.S. Relations. The latter resulted in the publication in 1968 of a two-volume study titled *Nichi-Bei kankei no kenkyū* (Research in U.S.-Japan Relations). In 1958 I-House began the annual publication of *Kaihō—Bulletin of the International House of Japan, Inc.,* which presented general information as well as reports and summaries from the various research projects under way at I-House.

Yet despite all this impressive activity in bringing together intellectuals and sponsoring research, I-House was not a formal research institute, let alone an academic organization. It would soon find itself eclipsed by the growth in Japanese and American professional research on each country. The professionalization of academic disciplines had its own negative effects on the more traditional type of cultural and intellectual exchange.

Studying the Other: The Intellectual Aspect of Cultural Exchange

As the focus and activities of the International House indicate, the postwar U.S.-Japan cultural relationship saw a distinct shift in priorities arising from social changes in both America and Japan. Prior to the war, cultural exchange had been largely the world of elite social gatherings, such as exhibitions and dinners. There had, of course, been an intellectual component to these activities, a component represented by the publications of groups like the KBS or the Japan Society of New York. Yet the pool of professional academics had been small, and for every Hugh Borton or Anesaki Masaharu, there were several amateur art specialists or literature scholars.

After the war, the round of social events, white-tie dinners, and museum openings did not disappear. That type of social glue was necessary, in a practical sense, not only because much of the funding that fueled private cultural exchange was provided at such events but also because those with the leisure or means to enjoy such cultural activities were used to doing so in a particular style. What changed during the 1950s and 1960s was the adding of another layer to cultural exchange, one that challenged and expanded the definition of "exchange" itself. This was the rise of the professional study of Japan in the United States and, to a lesser extent, of America in Japan. Much of this change was due to new currents in American society, but the shift also represented an evolution in the intellectual engagement with the world begun centuries before by the original European learned societies.

The profound social and political transformations sweeping postwar Japan had no analogue in the United States. The victor of World War II, however, was attempting uneasily to reconcile its desire to return to normalcy with the growing realization that it had entered yet another global struggle, this one against international Communism. The reorientation of the United States to a Cold War footing had deep and lasting cultural effects in addition to political, military, and economic alterations to American society. Within this larger process, study of the world that Washington was attempting to remake became of central importance. The nexus of government, think tanks, and private institutions took an early lead in conducting various studies and compiling extensive reports. Groups such as the Council on Foreign Relations began regularly to publish the results of their working groups and special studies. And while the focus was largely on Communism, the need to better understand America's allies pushed countries like Japan into the spotlight. Japan and Germany, in particular, seemed important test cases of democratization, economic recovery, and liberalization.

The Council on Foreign Relations conducted one of the earliest but also most in-depth postwar projects on Japanese culture and its relations with the United States. Under the direction of John D. Rockefeller 3rd, the council ran a study group on U.S.-Japan cultural relations from 1952 to 1954. The group included of some of the council's leading figures, among them, Joseph W. Ballantine, former U.S. consul in Tokyo; Percy W. Bidwell, director of the council's Studies Program; William Diebold Jr., a senior fellow at the council; Douglas W. Overton, Japan Society executive director; and Shepard Stone, a director of the Council. It also attracted a number of leading scholars of Japan, including Hugh Borton and Harold G. Henderson of Columbia University, and Yale's Kenneth Scott Latourette.

The lasting result of the study group was produced by Robert S. Schwantes, a young scholar in residence at the council as a Carnegie Research Fellow. Schwantes used the group's discussions as the springboard for a comprehensive study titled *Japanese and Americans: A Century of Cultural Relations,* which was published in 1955 by Harper and Brothers. Schwantes's book was an exhaustive cataloging of the U.S.-Japan relationship, a book that operated from a wide definition of culture to include economic, political, and social issues, as well as a more traditional treatment of artistic, educational, and intellectual exchange. It was the first book of its kind to attempt to sum up the influence of the encounter with America on the development of modern Japan, and the book's comprehensiveness would remain unsurpassed in English for over half a century.

Although groups like the Council on Foreign Relations and Ford Foundation sponsored various projects on Japan, by far the largest growth in the cross-Pacific intellectual encounter occurred in U.S. universities. The origins of this growth were twofold, both having to do with military conflict. One of the unintended consequences of World War II was the creation of a large corps of highly trained specialists, most with excellent linguistic skills. Before the war, of course, Japanese studies were a highly rarified field, with programs at only a handful of top universities, including Harvard, Yale, Stanford, and Columbia. The wartime need for translators, interpreters, and specialists, however, pushed the armed forces and civilian departments into creating language-training centers during the years of conflict. Some of these centers produced many of those who became professional Japanologists after the war.

Perhaps the leading program was the U.S. Navy's Japanese/Oriental Language School at Boulder, Colorado. From 1942 through 1946, thousands of young men and women passed through the school and into a variety of military or government positions. At Boulder alone, future scholars included the historians Delmer Brown of Berkeley, Sidney DeVere Brown of the University of Oklahoma, and F. Hilary Conroy at the University of Pennsylvania; literature professors and translators Donald Keene of Columbia, Donald Shively of Berkeley, and Edward Seidensticker; William Theodore De Bary, scholar of Confucianism and provost of Columbia; Otis Cary, longtime teacher at Doshisha University in Kyoto; political scientists Robert Scalapino of Berkeley and Nobutaka Ike of Stanford; as well as nonacademic specialists such as Robert Schwantes, journalist and author Frank Gibney, and the military scholar Roger Pineau.[56] The need to understand and to communicate with the enemy meant that postwar America was filled with a corps of highly trained, intelligent men and women who could continue their role as interpreters of Japanese culture.

The second military influence on the development of Japanese studies was the exigencies of the Cold War. Washington's new role as organizer and protector of the liberal, democratic capitalist system required specialized knowledge of entire geographical regions, and particularly of the languages, history, economics, and politics of areas that were perceived as strategically important. U.S. government funding in the 1950s created such multidisciplinary area-studies programs, which were centered on a traditionally defined continental or subcontinental scheme. Of cardinal importance was Russian studies, and large, federally funded centers developed for this field at Columbia, Michigan, and Indiana, among other universities. Viewing the origin of area studies from this perspective, the programs were tied into the larger network of government-affiliated exchange programs symbolized by the Fulbright Centers and USIA American Centers across the globe.[57] This government-inspired effort in fact preceded the crash buildup of science programs in the United States resulting from the 1957 launching of Sputnik by the Soviet Union.

Two equally important processes, however, drove the dynamism animating the development of Asian-area studies: the triumph of Communism in China and the rebirth of Japan as an economic success story. The victory of Mao Tse-tung over Chiang Kai-shek's Nationalists in 1949 sent political shock waves through America, not in the least among China scholars, many of whom had been children of missionaries or missionaries themselves. What did it mean that the world's most populous nation, the oldest continuous culture in the world, and the traditional hegemon of east Asia was now controlled by Communists and a vital part of the worldwide Communist movement centered in Moscow? Such were the questions driving the growth of Chinese studies after 1949, a field populated with academic powerhouses such as John King Fairbank at Harvard, Arthur Wright and Mary Clabaugh Wright at Yale, and Derk Bodde at Pennsylvania.

Yet Chinese studies were almost completely consumed with the question of how China could have been "lost" and what the Moscow-Peking axis meant for American policy in east Asia. Over a decade would pass before the inevitable Sino-Soviet split would allow China scholars to return to a focus on "indigenous" Chinese Communism and thence to a reconsideration of China's historical development. Before that occurrence, however, the field would be dragged into American domestic politics and the rooting out of suspected Communists in government and academic posts during the 1950s. Scholars with old or transient ties to socialist or communist movements were hauled before the House Un-American Activities Committee, and China specialist Owen Lattimore was charged with perjury while being investigated for being a Communist agent (the charges were later dropped). The Institute of Pacific Relations also was accused of hosting those who were sympathetic to or who were members of Communist movements; its reputation never recovered and it shut its doors in 1960.

The story for Japanese studies was far different, one that some would see as a misguided triumphalism over Japan's adoption of policies aligned toward Washington or over Japan's capitalist recovery. Japan had become one of America's key global allies during the 1950s, and successive leaders of the Liberal Democratic Party, which held power nearly continuously between 1955 and 2009, hewed closely to Prime Minister Yoshida Shigeru's policy of economic recovery and security dependence on the United States. The questions for American scholars were, what accounted for this remarkable turnaround, and how could it be transferred to other Asian countries struggling to shed colonial legacies and develop modern economic and political systems that were non-Communist?

The result was an explosion in Japanese studies and the emergence of what was known later as the "modernization school," which sought clues for modern Japan's developmental trajectory in indigenous changes in economy and society during the two-and-a-half-century Tokugawa era. By 1950, major Japan-studies programs were located at Far Eastern Studies at Yale (founded in 1945), the University of Washington's Far Eastern and Russian Institute (1946), the Center for Japanese Studies at Michigan (1947), Harvard's East Asia Regional Studies Program (1947), Columbia's East Asian Institute (1948), and the Institute of East Asiatic Studies at the University of California at Berkeley (1949). Government funding at these and other programs was estimated to total $19 million between 1958 and 1970.[58] To these funds were added those of private institutions, such as the Ford Foundation, which supported advanced individual research, especially fieldwork; the Carnegie Corporation, which aided area studies centers; and the Social Science Research Council, through its Committee on World Area Research.[59]

From these programs came the first group of professionally trained Japanologists, many of whom had already received language training before or during World War II: John Whitney Hall of Michigan and Yale, Thomas C. Smith of Berkeley, Marius B. Jansen of Princeton, William Theodore De Bary of Columbia, Robert Scalapino of Berkeley, and Howard Hibbett of Columbia, among others. These scholars would soon begin training the second and third generation of Japan specialists, who would then seed universities throughout the United States. The advanced training now available resulted in growing numbers of those with professional credentials; for example, as Marius Jansen pointed out, the number of PhDs granted in Japanese history alone quadrupled between the period 1945 to 1955 (twenty-five PhDs awarded) and the period 1966 to 1975 (ninety-six awarded).[60] By the end of the 1960s, a survey for the American Council of Learned Societies (ACLS) and the Social Science Research Council (SSRC) found approximately five hundred faculty and advanced graduate students in Japanese studies at 135 colleges and universities.[61]

Yet can this impressive growth in Japanese studies be considered part of the larger experience of cultural exchange between the two countries? If so, how did it change the practice of cultural relations? What the increase in PhDs, faculty, and graduate students meant, of course, was a jump in the number of courses offered to undergraduate students at a variety of institutions, not only Ivy League ones, and in the number of books published on Japan. If learning the language, history, and literature of another country is part of exchange, and indeed it was the primary form of encounter prior to the twentieth century, then Japanese studies in the United States resulted in the greatest amount of exchange yet in the

U.S.-Japan relationship. More students also meant the growth of language study abroad, and hundreds of American students a year traveled to Japan for varying lengths of time, thus experiencing a direct encounter with the culture. Specialist programs also developed, such as the Inter-University Center for Japanese Language Studies in Yokohama, which in 1963 began training a large percentage of the corps of American graduate students pursuing Japanese studies. Funding from Fulbright Program, Ford Foundation, SSRC, and other institutions helped ensure a regular flow of Americans heading to Japan for language study and research.

This increase in human exchange resulted in the publication of literally thousands of books on every aspect of Japan. An entire class of academic works, increasingly specialized, was now overlaid on the existing stratum of generalist histories, journalistic accounts, loose translations of literature, and memoirs that had dominated so much of the writing in English on Japan. Any type of list can only scratch the surface, but publishing milestones included Hugh Borton's *Japan's Modern Century* (1955), Robert Bellah's *Tokugawa Religion* (1957), Sir George Sansom's three-volume *A History of Japan* (1958–1963), Thomas C. Smith's *The Agrarian Origins of Modern Japan* (1959), Howard Hibbett's *The Floating World in Japanese Fiction* (1959), Donald Keene's *Major Plays of Chikamatsu* (1961), and John Whitney Hall's *Government and Local Power in Japan* (1966). These, and hundreds of other important titles, set new standards of scholarship and the use of primary sources.

There was no question that the professionalization of Japanese studies in the United States meant increasing specialization and in many cases a narrowness of approach. Indeed, as Japanese programs were established at various universities, the once-close ties between leading scholars and such traditional exchange groups as the Japan Society of New York began to weaken. In their stead, the scholars developed professional organizations, such as the Association for Asian Studies, that more directly addressed scholars' interests. These new academic associations supplanted the old learned societies, and not only hosted regular conferences where the most advanced research could be presented and discussed but also provided administrative support for academic collaborations and the funding of individual research projects.

These professional groups soon sponsored major research endeavors.

For example, in 1960, the Association for Asian Studies (which had been formed as the Association for Far Eastern Studies in 1941) received Ford Foundation support to begin a conference on modern Japan. The conference was a binational meeting of American and Japanese scholars and was held at the resort of Hakone, near Mount Fuji. A total of six conferences were held, resulting in the publication of six major volumes in the Princeton University Press series Studies on the Modernization of Japan, which Marius Jansen argued "set the agenda" for history and social science studies in the 1960s.[62] In 1968, the ACLS and SSRC established a joint committee on Japanese studies, which reviewed the state of each discipline and partially administered the Foreign Area Fellowship Program funded by Ford. By the end of the 1960s, professional Japanese-studies programs not only were an established presence in the American academic environment but also served as the primary vehicle of cultural exchange for students, teachers, and researchers.

Nothing like the depth of the American system existed in Japan. Despite the intense interest in American culture, as well as the need to confront more fundamental questions about the nature of Japan's postwar society and the effect of America's influence, Japanese universities lagged far behind their U.S. counterparts. At first it appeared that things might turn out differently, for just two years after the end of the war, on September 27, 1947, approximately twenty-five scholars gathered in Tokyo to inaugurate the Amerika Gakkai (America Institute). After a few years, the circle was disbanded due to lack of funds. Over a decade passed before a second attempt was made to create a formal institution, and in 1966 the revived Amerika Gakkai (renamed in English as the Japanese Association for American Studies, or JAAS) started activities with about two hundred members. The main events of the JAAS were an annual two-day conference and the publication of two journals, *Amerika kenkyū* (American Review) and the quarterly *Amerika gakkai kaih ō* (American Studies Newsletter).[63]

During the the 1950s and 1960s, Japanese focus on American studies was limited, and students who could manage it went to America for graduate education, such as Asado Sadao, who received his doctorate in American diplomatic history from Yale in 1963. Prewar programs, such as Rikkyō University's Institute for American Studies, slowly revived their activities, increasing the number of majors in American studies and eventually publishing research journals. An important development, however, came in 1951, when Doshisha University started the Kyoto American Studies Seminar. This became a key academic gathering and ran for over thirty-five years, until 1987, under Doshisha auspices. During that time, more than 150 leading American-studies scholars from the United States joined over 3,000 Japanese teachers and students for courses relating to America and for presentation of research.

Funding for Japanese programs on the United States, however, was minimal despite the importance of the bilateral relationship. There was no comparable system of government support, even for the national universities, and no network of private philanthropic groups to fund such programs. Thus, in contrast to America, where the Ford Foundation, Carnegie Corporation, SSRC, and other bodies fueled the increase in Japanese studies, Japan could only cobble together a few college and university programs. What funding there was often came from American sources, such as the Asia Foundation, the Rockefeller Foundation, and the Ford Foundation.[64] For some colleges with long-standing ties to America, the process of promoting American studies was a bit easier, especially when foreign funding could be secured. In 1958, Doshisha became one of the first Japanese institutions to open a postwar program, when it established the Center for American Studies with a $60,000 grant from the Rockefeller Foundation. A decade later this program was followed by one created by the flagship Japanese educational institution, the University of Tokyo, which opened its own Center for American Studies (CAS) in 1967.

The University of Tokyo center was especially important, for it had as one of its key goals not only the offering of courses on American culture and history but also the development of a first-class research library. The CAS became the leading institution at a national university to focus on collecting primary and secondary source documents related to American politics, culture, and economics. The CAS library became a backbone for research on contemporary America and was opened to all qualified researchers in Japan. At the same time, smaller colleges, including women's colleges, started receiving minimal funds to offer American-studies courses, run international seminars, or send their professors to American academic meetings.

Throughout the 1960s, in particular, the San Francisco-based Asia Foundation promoted American studies at a number of leading Japanese institutions. As a result, though not comparable to the numbers of Asian-studies experts in America, Japanese universities began producing distinguished scholars of American studies, including Saitō Makoto, and attracting attention to more serious treatments of America. The internationalization of Japan's intellectual centers was complete by the end of the 1960s, and its scholars and students, while smaller in number, became as engaged in the social and political debates of the day as their American counterparts were. Specialized knowledge of America led some to celebrate the transpacific relationship and others to decry it, especially during the Vietnam War. Both groups, however, shared in the growing discussion of the future of U.S.-Japan ties as the postwar era wound down.

By the beginning of the 1970s, the U.S.-Japan cultural relationship was dramatically different than it had been just three decades before. In the first place, World War II had forever altered the ties between the two countries. That loss of innocence, so to speak, would haunt the relationship, and tens of millions of Japanese and American citizens would always hold in their hearts the memories of one of the most brutal clashes in history, one that had ended with the atomic incineration of hundreds of thousands of civilians.

Beyond the remnants of battle, however, a new and more complex relationship had developed. Japan and America were tied closer together than ever after 1945, indeed to a degree that could only be dreamed about by prewar Pacific internationalists such as Nitobe Inazō or Yone Noguchi. Tokyo became Washington's most important ally in Asia and perhaps even America's second-most important ally in the world, after Great Britain. Moreover, Japan's rapid economic recovery from wartime devastation was due in large part to its political-economic alliance with the United States. By the 1970s, Japanese corporations were beginning to make major inroads on the American domestic market, particularly in automobiles, high-end consumer electronics, steel production, and shipbuilding. The health of both economies was slowly being tied ever more to the trade relationship between them.

Finally, the lives of citizens in both countries were affected by the popular culture of the other, more so in the case of Japan, of course, but not negligibly in America. Japan's social and economic recovery had witnessed a combination of Occupation-era reforms that liberalized key components of Japanese society, such as land ownership, education, and universal suffrage, and the triumph of an American-inspired ideal for standards of living that drove consumer spending. Sporting events, entertainment, and dietary habits all became increasingly "Americanized," especially as the standard of living in Japan's major cities inched upward. In America, Japanese high culture, such as art and cuisine, held increasing cachet for status-conscious consumers, while popular cultural forms, from Kurosawa movies to karate, spread throughout the burgeoning middle class.

In many ways, though, the most important change in the cultural relationship was in the growth of Japanese studies in the United States. With the introduction of Japanese language, history, literature, and cultural courses in hundreds of American colleges and universities, a far larger population than ever before could be exposed to aspects of Japanese civilization. Thousands of American students were sent abroad for language study, and hundreds of researchers could travel to Japan for extended periods. Japanese and American scholars met regularly, collaborating on long-term research projects and setting up academic organizations that established professional norms. The library of professional-level books on Japan multiplied exponentially, reaching a potentially even larger audience.

All this was a new variant of cultural exchange, one that was at the same time far more meritocratic than that traditionally practiced by the exchange organizations and yet also far more rigorous. It would not be erroneous to claim that the prewar exchange groups were "amateur" or that those who participated in their activities lacked a sophisticated understanding of Japan. Yet such groups were not professional in the way that the Japan-studies community came to be. Most members of the Japan Society, for example, spoke no Japanese despite their deep interest in the country; one could not, however, become a professor of Japanese studies without the requisite language skills and bona fides of having undertaken in-depth research.

What the two communities did have in common, however, was an unquestioned commitment to the U.S.-Japan relationship, one that was largely defined as cultural and animated by a cosmopolitan impulse. Neither group was overtly political, nor did they have any pecuniary interest deriving from their exchange activities. They shared a general belief in the compatibility of interests of Japan and America and worked together to spread awareness of America among Japanese and of Japan among Americans. If the two communities were boosters of the binational relationship, that was no surprise, for they had powerful personal or professional interests that guided their actions. Nor was it a surprise that most of those who had devoted their lives to understanding the other country did so because of their approbation of aspects of the other. This is not to say that there was no criticism but rather that an interest in facilitating relations and working to solve differences motivated those at I-House, in the major Japan-studies programs, and in the Japan America societies.

In the early 1970s, however, that broad consensus would break down, concurrent with a change in the political and economic relationship between the two countries. As a result, new institutions would be created to foster exchange, and exchange itself would become ever more tied to political and economic issues, just at the moment when popular culture in both countries turned decidedly against the positive visions of the first postwar decades. Cosmopolitans on both sides of the Pacific again would find themselves struggling directly with the question of politics and state interests.

CHAPTER 6

New Challenges, New Hopes

B Y THE DAWN of the 1970s, Japan had largely emerged from the shadows of World War II. It was an increasingly important industrial power in the world and was soon to become the world's second-largest economy, something few would have predicted in the early postwar years. Its orderly society and technological prowess were the envy of developing countries across the globe. Moreover, its apparent ability to easily withstand the strains of rapid modernization confirmed its status as a stable, mature, industrial society. Japanese consumer goods were flooding the globe, raising the country's image even further.

As Japan's role in the world grew, its cultural products, those both traditional and radically new, became correspondingly attractive and even a major source of trade revenue once they were commoditized and sold around the world. The next several decades saw Japan rise to the heights of economic power and international acclaim, which were followed by a stunning collapse and protracted recession at the end of the twentieth century that mirrored long-simmering domestic political stagnation and social uncertainty. America's fascination with Japan and its culture swung dramatically during the last decades of the twentieth century, from near worship to dismissal, and the world of cultural exchange found itself buffeted by the dying off of old trends and the rise of new fads.

Despite its impressive postwar recovery, Japan's development was not without bumps, some severe, which began to drag on the country by the 1970s. A political and social failure to fully address questions of war responsibility hampered, and sometimes poisoned, Japan's relations with its neighbors and former enemies, leading to questions about the dark side of Japanese culture. Further, despite the touting of the postwar economic miracle in Japan, domestic dissatisfaction with the costs of Japanese industrialization gave rise to citizens' movements demanding a cleaner environment. The country's stability also was shaken as home-grown terrorists, the Marxist-inspired Red Army, conducted attacks inside the Japanese homeland and abroad in the 1970s and 1980s. Moreover, beginning in the 1970s, the postwar pattern of U.S.-Japan bilateral relations was disrupted, which lead Japanese intellectuals and policy makers to consider new policies to win friends and increase Japan's influence around the world. Over the succeeding two decades, the U.S.-Japan relationship would be strained by tensions over bilateral and global trends. In response, both governments would seek to use cultural exchange more directly as a tool of public diplomacy, thereby raising questions again about the nature and role of cultural exchange and its relation to state policies.

A New Political Relationship

The postwar political arrangements that shaped U.S.-Japan cultural exchange from the 1950s on stayed relatively stable for two decades. Although tension remained over issues such as the continued basing of nearly forty thousand U.S. troops in Japan and the "don't ask, don't tell" policy regarding American deployment of nuclear weapons in and around Japanese waters, both sides had come to see the alliance as a quasi-permanent foundation of their Asia policies. By the late 1960s, however, U.S. foreign policy was undergoing a period of upheaval, and its political effects would spill over into the realm of cultural relations. The Cold War was heating up due to the expansion of the nuclear arms race, U.S. involvement in Vietnam, the Sino-Soviet split, and the 1968 Soviet invasion of Czechoslovakia. High expenditures on both war and domestic programs like the so-called War on Poverty began to take their toll on the

U.S. economy during the 1960s. After 1969, the new administration of President Richard M. Nixon sought a strategic departure from many of the policies of the decade. Several of these moves, known as the "Nixon shocks," would directly affect the U.S.-Japan relationship, leading to the end of the "postwar era" for Japan.

The signature policy of Nixon and his national security advisor, former Harvard professor Henry A. Kissinger, was détente with the Soviet Union. Desiring a way to reduce both tensions and military expenditures, Nixon and Kissinger sought to engage the Soviets—led by Leonid Brezhnev, who had recently led a putsch to overthrow Nikita Khrushchev—in a wide range of political, military, and cultural agreements.[1] A central element of this plan was what came to be known as the "China card": that is, using the possibility of an improved Sino-American relationship to pressure the Soviets into dealing with Washington, especially in terms of nuclear arms control. Such proxy gamesmanship was by no means limited to Washington planners, of course. Beijing, ever wary of the U.S. position in Asia and desirous of using the military quagmire in southeast Asia against America, threw its support behind the North Vietnamese, as did Moscow, as a means to both wound the U.S. and force it into global retreat.

The United States had not diplomatically recognized China after Mao Zedong's Communists took power in 1949. Moreover, Washington had put pressure on its major Asian ally, Japan, not to normalize its relations with Beijing after the war, despite Tokyo's long-standing desire to do so. The shock to the Japanese government was thus palpable when Nixon made a surprise visit to China in 1972, following on the heels of Kissinger's secret mission the year before. It appeared to Tokyo that, far from being protected by its special relationship with America, Japan was a cog in the United States' larger geopolitical wheel and was at risk of being taken for granted.[2]

Japan's prime minister at the time of Nixon's opening U.S. relations with China was Tanaka Kakuei, who, thanks to a well-developed domestic power base, was perhaps Japan's most powerful postwar politician.[3] During World War II, Tanaka had been deeply involved in economic activities in occupied Manchuria, and he remained a key proponent of closer relations between Japan and China in the years after the war.

Tanaka saw Nixon's new China policy as both a challenge and an opportunity. He rushed to normalize relations with the mainland and in September 1972 made his own trip to Beijing, where he held talks with Chinese Premier Chou En-lai, following on discussions both Tanaka and his predecessor, Sato Eisaku, had made with Nixon regarding normalization.[4] This rapprochement raised serious strategic questions for Tokyo regarding the future of the U.S.-Japan alliance, specifically about the extent that Japan could act as a free agent in its dealings with China.

The second of the so-called Nixon shocks was Washington's decision to take the U.S. dollar off the gold standard and to impose domestic wage and price controls. The goal of these economic moves was to control inflation and trim the U.S. balance of payments deficit, then running at $29 billion, of which $3.2 billion was owed to Japan, by letting the dollar float against other currencies, including the Japanese yen. This would make Japanese exports more expensive and in theory cut down on American consumption of foreign goods. Combined with the 1973–1974 OPEC oil shock, the macroeconomic policies of the Nixon administration caused a sharp slowdown in Japan's economic growth (not to mention a U.S. recession in the same years); in fact, Japan entered its steepest recession since the World War II itself. As the yen depreciated nearly 20 percent relative to the dollar, consumer prices in Japan in the same period increased by 25 percent. The result was a contraction in the gross national product of nearly 1.25 percent in 1974.[5] Japanese rushed to hoard suddenly scarce daily commodities, such as toilet paper, leading to fears over the sustainability of the economic system responsible for recovery after the war.

The effect of the Nixon shocks threatened to destabilize the U.S.-Japan relationship, which might well have encouraged China to put further pressure on Washington to restrict the scope of America's alliance with Japan. In part as a sop to Tokyo and partly out of a desire to reduce American responsibilities, Washington decided to end its quarter-century occupation of Okinawa and return control of the island to Japan.[6] This move was not accompanied by a military retreat from the region, however, for Okinawa remained the main American military base in northeast Asia for the U.S. Marine Corps, in addition to hosting key Air Force units. Yet even this move was balanced by Washington's diplomatic watering down of its support for Japanese control of the Senkaku (Diaoyu) Islands, located between Taiwan and Okinawa, which were in strategically important waterways and contained potentially important oil reserves.

Nixon's policies deeply shook the foundations of the U.S.-Japan relationship. Of particular concern to policy makers on both sides was the slowly growing economic tension between the two countries. Americans questioned why they should shoulder the burden of unfair trade when their own economy was slowing down and when Japan had access to all U.S. markets, though Americans were frozen out of many Japanese economic sectors. For Japanese, there was the uncertainty of whether their special relationship with their most important ally was as secure as it had been since the end of the Occupation. Due in large part to these trends, Tokyo sought both to realign its relations with Washington and to reach out in a more sustained way to Asia. Cultural relations would play a role in expanding economic and political contacts in Japan's backyard, as Tokyo explored the possibility of wielding its own "Asia card" against the United States.

Expanding Public Diplomacy, Deepening Cultural Exchange

Primarily, however, the Nixon shocks resulted in Tokyo's desire to solidify, if not deepen, Japan's relationship with America, a desire that itself led to conflicting feelings of dependence and entanglement. Recognizing that the unique nature of nonofficial contact between the two countries had played a role in influencing official relations in the past, bureaucrats in the Ministry of Foreign Affairs embraced an aggressive policy of bolstering the country's official public diplomacy while also searching for new "private" organizations to promote positive images of Japan.

At the same time, the traditional private network of exchange groups, such as the America-Japan Society, continued the role they had played for over half a century in the shadow of official or quasi-official organs. The commingling of official messages with independent outreach led the government to seek an ostensibly nonpolitical outlet through which to strengthen U.S.-Japan ties. The sometimes conflicting goals of government ministries and private groups would give rise to public misunderstanding and suspicion of the roles and aims of the cultural exchange organizations.

By the early 1970s the government considered the old Society for the Promotion of International Culture (KBS) no longer appropriate for the task of acting as an independent exchange organization. On the one hand, Tokyo recognized that support from the United States was largely responsible for funding most KBS activities.[7] This meant that Japan had a correspondingly smaller role in determining the types of activities that were funded and the general direction of exchange activities. On the other hand, Tokyo was also increasingly interested in expanding its cultural relations with Asia, which was one indication of a more globalized Japanese perspective that would challenge the dominant assumptions regarding the centrality of the U.S.-Japan relationship. In response, in March 1972 the decision was made to form a new body for cultural exchange, an organization that would be independent yet have semiofficial status and official funding. On October 2, 1972, the new organization, named the Japan Foundation (Kokusai kōryū kikin; literally, the International Exchange Foundation) was opened. As an indication of its importance, the Japanese government funded it with 5 billion yen, equivalent at the time to approximately 150 million U.S. dollars.[8]

The Japan Foundation and America's Fascination with Japanese Success

In taking over the activities of the now-disbanded KBS, the Japan Foundation was indeed international in scope; it intended to become the "single national organization with independent resources having overall concern for various kinds of international cultural exchange."[9] Yet the Japan Foundation articulated its mission much in the way that the KBS had; its first president, literary critic Kon Hidemi, wrote that the new organization was designed to "contribute to mutual understanding and the enhancement of world culture through the expansion of cultural exchange."[10] This would be achieved through five targeted goals, which included fostering exchange of individuals between Japan and foreign countries; assisting the development of Japanese studies and language programs abroad; participating in activities that promoted international cultural exchange; preparing, collecting, and distributing materials necessary to introduce Japanese culture abroad; and conducting research necessary to carry out international cultural exchange activities.[11] From its own perspective, the Japan Foundation would be nonpolitical, despite being funded by government money, and it would act as had the KBS in conducting research, educating, and publishing.

The Japan Foundation was administratively organized to focus on the five goals enumerated in its founding document, and administrators established initial departments for exchange of persons, Japanese studies, arts, cultural materials, and audio-visuals. Furthermore, the foundation expanded the KBS's global presence by opening small offices in Bangkok, Jakarta, and America and by taking over the old Japanese Cultural Institutes in Rome and Cologne. To lend weight to the Japan Foundation's activities, an advisory council was established that included eminent scholars such as the sociologist Nakane Chie, leading cultural figures like Sen Soshitsu, head of the Urasenke tea school, and national administrators such as Umesao Tadao, then director of the National Museum of Ethnology.[12]

Yet, also like the KBS, the Japan Foundation focused a great amount of its effort on the United States, thereby underlining a continuation of promoting positive relations with Japan's key ally. As an indication of the importance of ties with America, the foundation opened two U.S. offices, in New York and Washington, D.C. Moreover, an American advisory committee was established, which included such prominent names as McGeorge Bundy, head of the Ford Foundation; Blanche Rockefeller, wife of John D. Rockefeller 3rd; and former ambassador to Japan, Edwin Reischauer. Leading American scholars of Japan also sat on the committee, including John Whitney Hall of Yale, Marius Jansen of Princeton, Richard Beardsley of the University of Michigan, Robert Ward of Stanford, Donald Shively of the University of California, Berkeley, and James Morley of Columbia.

The Japan Foundation thus sought from its beginning to move beyond the traditional focus on private groups, by engaging the increasingly well-developed and active Japan-studies community in the United States. Such an approach had not been an option in the years before World War II, when Japan studies barely existed in America. The Japan Foundation did not see itself as independent of the network of professionals that had emerged in the 1960s, and indeed it considered its role to be one of facilitating their efforts through grant making, programming, and general support. This approach would be a major departure from that of the KBS and other prewar groups, which had undertaken the bulk of their intellectual activity on their own. The postwar form of the cultural exchange organization, represented by the Japan Foundation and International House of Japan, would seek to leverage the expertise of others and provide the resources necessary for them to do their work.

With such an emphasis, the Japan Foundation quickly became the major U.S.-Japan cultural exchange organ, providing funding for scholars, artists, and grassroots activities. The Fellowship Program was designed as the key individual exchange component of the foundation. In its first year, the program sent sixty scholars, researchers, and specialists from Japan abroad, thirty-five of them to the United States. In addition to these thirty-five individuals, five specialists in Japanese studies were sent to top American universities to teach and research for the year.[13] The Fellowship Program thus provided an institutional mechanism whereby Japanese scholars could have a semipermanent presence abroad and interact with the major overseas Japan-studies communities. These specialists, both Japanese and later American, were of course professionals with their own views of U.S.-Japan relations, and they neither considered themselves nor were considered de facto agents of their respective governments. In time, however, such assumptions of neutrality would be challenged by others within the U.S.-Japan relationship.

Similar to its support of Japanese scholars, and perhaps even more important, was the role the Japan Foundation now played, along with the Fulbright Scholarship Program, as the most important funder of advanced academic research on Japan by Americans. Japan Foundation fellowships helped train generations of American scholars, and in its first year alone, the foundation provided research funds to leading young academics, such as Harumi Befu, John Dower, G. Cameron Hurst, Richard Chang, Mikiso Hane, and Gordon Berger, many of whose books were supported with Japan Foundation funding and became standards in the field. Intellectual independence was the hallmark of these young scholars, and the American academic community was particularly sensitive to any hint of political restrictions on the funding it received. In doling out funds to these scholars, the Japan Foundation burnished its nonpolitical bona fides, even as it hewed to its overarching goal of spreading information about Japan abroad and promoting a positive picture of the country.

The funding activity of the Japan Foundation increased its connection with the Japan-studies field in America, and this funding came at a crucial time. The field was growing in the 1970s, as Americans began taking more and more notice of Japan's economic prowess and became correspondingly interested in understanding the country's successes. Both scholarly and popular treatments in America were highlighting Japan's supposedly unique industrial, political, and social strengths and giving rise to both envy and very nascent stirrings of concern.

In March 1970, *Time* magazine put Japan's Expo '70 on its cover, and an interior story titled "Toward the Japanese Century" breathlessly declared, "No country has a stronger franchise on the future than Japan." The story quoted renowned management guru Peter Drucker, who said that Japan was "the most extraordinary success story in all economic history."[14] In the same year, Herman Kahn, a famed futurist and the inspiration for the movie character Dr. Strangelove, wrote that the "emerging Japanese superstate" would transform its role in the world in the 1970s and 1980s, much as Prussia did exactly a century previously. Kahn asserted that with Japan's rise, the pole of world power would slip irresistibly to the East.[15] Although Tokyo was today an ally of Washington, Kahn believed the growing power of Japan would inevitably lead it to adopt new national goals of increasing its political and military prominence in the world.

Over the succeeding decade, American authors sought to explain the durability of Japan's growth, even as it appeared that there were clear limits to how much Japan would become a traditional political and military power. Herman Kahn's radical view of the early 1970s was countered a dozen years later by Chalmers Johnson's detailed academic study of Japan's economic policy making in the twentieth century. Johnson was not a flamboyant futurist but a sober economic historian, who explored the role of Japan's economic bureaucracy, specifically the Ministry of International Trade and Industry (today called the Ministry of Economy, Trade, and Industry). In his well-received *MITI and the Japanese Miracle*, Johnson argued that Japan's growth during the twentieth century could largely be located at the nexus of government institutions and industrial policy, a link that resulted in the adoption of successfully targeted industrial growth and export policies. This rather classically rational approach to state power was not due, in Johnson's view, to any particular uniqueness of Japanese society but nonetheless had produced economic growth rarely seen in the industrialized world, and therefore it was one leading example of how best to achieve such results.[16]

The success of books such as those by Kahn and Johnson, and even the very disagreements between them, furthered American interest in Japan during the 1970s and 1980s. Although the bulk of study on the country was being conducted in universities across the United States, resources were increasingly scarce at the very time that demand was increasing for PhDs to fill academic positions in newly created Japanese studies programs. For these increasing numbers of dissertation writers, there needed to be an increase in graduate-level scholarship funds beyond those available through the Fulbright Program. The Japan Foundation stepped in to fill this gap and thus helped to ensure the continued growth of professional Japan studies at the moment when such support was most needed. And in classic supply-and-demand fashion, more interest led to more professorships, which led to more classes for undergraduates and thus a wider pool of prospective participants in cultural exchange programs. In a sense, a tight institutional circle was being created, yet it was one that was vital for a field far larger and more complex than that of the 1950s and 1960s.

The Japan Foundation did not merely focus on individual researchers, however, for one of its major goals was to build up full-fledged programs in Japanese studies overseas. Such funding would include monies for libraries and research materials, professorships (that is, classes), and relevant staff positions. This was undoubtedly a key aim share by Tokyo in its attempts to develop Japan's cultural and intellectual relations abroad. The Japan Foundation met this goal by serving as the distributor of Japanese government grants that provided large-scale institutional support for Japanese studies in the United States. It thus acted directly in conjunction with the Japanese government, and wound up disbursing as much as ¥4.8 billion to ten leading U.S. universities in 1973, including Harvard, Yale, Stanford, Chicago, Berkeley, Columbia, Hawai'i, Michigan, Princeton, and Washington.[17] This funding was given in addition to nearly four hundred textbooks, over six hundred reference books, and twenty-two sets of audio-visual materials that were shipped to selected universities and libraries in the same inaugural year.[18]

The growth in Japan studies at the higher education level in the United States was impressive, but it was not, of course, the only arena in which cultural exchange occurred between Japan and America. One of the Japan Foundation's key directives was to increase the presence of Japanese artistic activities abroad, thereby continuing the tradition of the prewar exchange organizations such as the Japan Society of New York. One of the major problems for the Japan Society network in the prewar days had been the relatively limited funding available for art exhibits and artistic performances. The result was that most of the important exhibitions or performances of the Japanese arts were limited to a few major cities in America. Now, however, the Japan Foundation dramatically expanded the reach of Japanese artists by providing generous funding on an ongoing basis. The foundation's support resulted in thousands more Americans being exposed to Japan's traditional arts than in previous decades.

The foundation's Arts Department was the key division responsible for such activities. It began by sponsoring various touring performances, traditionally the activity most difficult to host in America yet also the most popular, due to its scale and uniqueness. In 1972–1973 alone the Arts Department sent an Osaka-based Bunraku, or puppet theater troupe, to six U.S. cities and one from Awaji Island to sixteen more locations. For the first time, ordinary Americans could enjoy one of Japan's most revered art forms, watching puppets, two-thirds human size, being operated by a three-person team on nearly life-size sets. The Japan Foundation also sponsored extremely popular Kabuki theater performances in New York and Washington, D.C., in the same year and arranged the visit of Kabuki master Kuroemon Onoe II to the University of Wisconsin at Madison, where he taught and performed.[19] A mixture of comedy and pathos, along with gaudy costumes and explosive music, Kabuki became an instant hit in America and drew comparisons to Italian opera.

This array of activities set the basic pattern for Japan Foundation programs during the 1970s and 1980s. The question for the foundation's directors, and indirectly for Tokyo, was, what effect would the new organization have on U.S.-Japan relations in general and on cultural relations more specifically? With its links to the American academic community, its various outreach programs, and its large funding base and organizational structure, the Japan Foundation seemed to have carved out for itself a central role in a short period of time. The Foreign Ministry considered the experiment a success and moved to expand the role the Foundation would play. Given an initial ¥5 billion grant from the government, the foundation saw its budget increased six times just three years later, in 1975, to a total of ¥30 billion; by its tenth anniversary, in 1983, the Japan Foundation had an annual budget of ¥48.5 billion.[20] Program-specific increases were no less impressive. For example, the Exchange of Persons Department budget grew nearly ten times in just five years, from ¥98 million in 1972 to ¥890 million in 1977, while funding for Japanese studies abroad went from ¥90 million in 1972 to ¥847 million in 1976.[21] By 1982, the Exchange of Persons budget had increased to ¥1.2 billion, and Japanese-studies funding skyrocketed to ¥1.67 billion.[22]

By the late 1970s, the Japan Foundation was increasingly becoming the public face of Japanese philanthropy in the United States. It now played a role that the older organizations could not match, and in the process the foundation became identified as a major supporter of Japanese high culture in the States. The Japan Foundation helped its image through some highly visible donations in these years, including $1.4 million to the Boston Museum of Fine Arts in 1978 for a Japanese arts exhibit hall, $1 million to the Asia Society of New York to build its headquarters in 1979, and $1 million to the Smithsonian Institution in the same year for to support the Freer gallery of Asian art.[23] The institutional network created by the foundation's funds thus ensured a more visible role for Japanese arts in American cultural life, thereby stimulating even more interest and complementing the activities of Japan-studies specialists.

Given the scale of these activities, Japan Foundation's first president, Kon Hidemi, was not exaggerating merely three years after the organization's birth when he claimed that it was the "nucleus of Japan's international cultural exchanges."[24] With its large funding base, the Japan Foundation immediately outstripped all other sources of funds for U.S.-Japan–related cultural activities. Though an independent organization, the foundation was of course funded by the Japanese government, which clearly focused on expanding U.S.-Japan links as a means of promoting good will between the two countries. It soon would be joined by other state-sponsored exchange institutions, all of which would tread the line between responding to government interests and serving the larger cultural exchange community.

Expanding Government Support for Cultural Exchange

Government programs such as Fulbright Scholarship Program had been crucial in the 1950s and after as a means of expanding intellectual exchange between America and Japan, but public diplomacy as practiced by Washington during the Cold War focused largely on Eastern Europe and Latin America. Tokyo, in contrast, concentrated on maintaining the alliance arrangements that ensured Japan's national security and relieved the country of having to field a large and expensive defense establishment. But as relations wobbled in the 1970s due to economic and political pressure alike, both Washington and Tokyo realized the important role that cultural relations could play in successfully implementing foreign policy, particularly in influencing public opinion.[25] Traditional private diplomacy and cultural exchange did not cease, of course, but government funding was playing an increasing role in helping to foster and sponsor such activities. What gave credence to the entire enterprise was the neutrality of the actual programs, especially those connected with American and Japanese scholars, who tended to be increasingly critical of both governments through the 1970s and 1980s. Nonetheless, Washington and Tokyo were firmly committed to supporting this new type of hybrid activity by independent scholars and organizations.

After the founding of the Fulbright Program in the 1940s and the International Visitor Program a decade later, the United States had established no new official initiatives in cultural exchange with Japan until the 1970s. In part reflecting the growing American interest in Japan and in part following up on the programmatic success of the Japan Foundation, Washington formed the Japan–United States Friendship Commission in 1975. Initially proposed as an act of Congress by Senator Jacob K. Javits of New York and Congressman Marvin L. Esch of Michigan in 1972, the Friendship Commission was the brainchild of Edwin Reischauer, Yale historian John Whitney Hall, and Stanford's Robert Ward. After being stalled in

Congress for three years, the act was passed and was signed into law on October 20, 1975, by President Gerald Ford.

It was no accident that the Friendship Commission was officially formed just as Emperor Hirohito commenced his first visit to the United States. This was, of course, the first visit by a Japanese emperor to America, and it came on the thirtieth anniversary of the end of World War II. As a public relations event, Hirohito's visit was intended unequivocally to convey that Japan was an equal to the United States and would be playing a correspondingly larger role in the world. The emperor's state tour garnered enormous media attention and included several highly public events, including a visit to Colonial Williamsburg outside of Washington, D.C., and a stop at Disneyland, where the seventy-five-year-old, formerly considered a semidivine descendant of the gods, was photographed with Mickey Mouse. The emperor's visit also included the traditional elite gatherings, notably President Ford's white-tie state dinner at the White House, an event that underscored once again Japan's position in the first rank of U.S. allies.

The new Japan–United States Friendship Commission embodied a growing official commitment to cultural exchange. Despite government support, the Friendship Commission was of moderate size: its initial funding comprised only $18 million from the United States and $12.5 million from Japan.[26] The commission was designed to be an official effort to sponsor pure cultural relations, such as artistic exchanges and language- and area-studies programs, which had seen enormous growth in the 1960s. The first American chairman was John Whitney Hall, whose fellow commissioners were drawn from the Joint Committee on United States–Japan Cultural and Economic Cooperation, an advisory body formed back in 1968, consisting of twelve members from both countries, plus four U.S. members of Congress and the chairs of the National Endowment for the Arts and the National Endowment for the Humanities. Hall, however, insisted that the commission itself be independent from any official public diplomacy oversight by U.S. or Japanese government bodies.

Throughout the 1970s and 1980s, the Friendship Commission served as both a stabilizer and a barometer of U.S.-Japan cultural relations, particularly of the state of organized study of each country. When initial budgeting targets were set in the late 1970s, 40 percent of the Friendship Commission's budget went to Japanese studies in the United States, but only 20 percent to American studies in Japan, reflecting the underdeveloped state of academic programs on America in Japanese universities. By the mid-1990s, the ratio had dramatically widened, with 38 percent of the Friendship Commission's budget allocated to Japanese studies in America, but a mere 8 percent for American studies in Japan.[27] Indeed, in Japan there continued to be only two major American-studies centers, at the University of Tokyo and Doshisha University in Kyoto, compared with the dozens of programs in nearly all leading U.S. universities. Yet academic studies were but a portion of the Friendship Commission's focus, as roughly 15–20 percent of its budget supported performance and visual arts, in addition to translations, grassroots exchanges, and professional development and exchanges. In many ways the seed money for much of the expansion of cultural exchange during the 1970s and 1980s was provided in tightly targeted fashion by the Friendship Commission, combined with funds from the Japan Foundation.

The Continued Role of Nongovernmental Exchange Organizations Old and New

Despite new support from both the Japanese and American governments, cultural exchange was not dependent solely on official patronage. Following on the commitments of the 1960s, major philanthropic organizations continued their support for various programs during the succeeding decade. The Ford Foundation, for example, was instrumental in funding some of the more important exchange organizations, such as International House and the Japan Center for International Exchange (about which more will be said later). By the end of the decade, however, the foundation had dramatically shifted its focus to the developing world and closed its Tokyo office in 1979. By the time it did so, however, the Ford Foundation had distributed $3.8 million to Japan-focused activities. The Rockefeller Brothers Fund, similarly, donated $2.2 million from 1970 to 1979, much of it for educational purposes, such as a high school exchange program, translations into English of Japanese articles, and the Shimoda

Conference series, which brought together high-level academic and government experts from both countries.[28]

Such funding sources allowed many established institutions to continue their activities during the turbulent economic shocks of the 1970s. The International House in Tokyo, for example, continued to function under the firm leadership of Matsumoto Shigeharu. The important place I-House occupied in unofficial relations was captured in a photograph taken at its thirtieth-anniversary banquet in 1982, in which Matsumoto sits at a table surrounded by Harvard historian and former ambassador Edwin Reischauer, Princeton historian Marius Jansen, and Yale's John Whitney Hall, the Big Three of Japanese historical studies in the United States. Indeed, in the 1970s and 1980s, I-House expanded the number and variety of its events, drawing more participants from America than ever before. Though now competing with an abundance of programs sponsored not just by the Japan Foundation but also by the major universities in Japan, particularly Tokyo, Kyoto, Keio, and Waseda, I-House remained one unofficial center for American academics in Japan and a regular meeting place for groups and organizations devoted to U.S.-Japan relations. Perhaps more importantly, it served as a primary venue in Japan for American academics in all social science disciplines. It thus complemented Japanese academic visits to the United States by introducing the work of American scholars to Japanese audiences.

The world of cultural exchange was larger than academia, however, and during the 1970s and 1980s, the vibrancy of exchange was highlighted by the growth of privately supported organizations in addition to publicly supported ones, such as the Japan Foundation. The Japan Society of New York not only continued to function but grew in size, adding to its activities more directly targeted corporate and young business leader–oriented programs. In 1971, in part through the continuing philanthropy of John D. Rockefeller 3rd, the Japan Society built a new four-story building a block from the United Nations in midtown Manhattan. This allowed the society to expand its exhibit space and classroom capacity and to create a performance stage and auditorium. As a result, the Japan Society in New York regularly hosted major performing arts series and film festivals, attracting crowds in the hundreds and thousands.[29] In most major cities in the United States, moreover, local Japan America societies functioned on a more or less regular basis, though often with just a few part-time staff and volunteers, usually holding annual Japan festivals in the spring or summer. Given these widespread activities, a new national umbrella organization, the National Association of Japan America Societies (NAJAS), emerged to try and deepen and coordinate resources.

The formation of NAJAS reflected the continuing interlinked nature of exchange organizations in the U.S. The society began as a committee formed as early as 1960 to celebrate the centennial of the 1859 commercial treaty between Japan and the United States. The committee was chaired by John D. Rockefeller 3rd, who had resuscitated the Japan Society of New York eight years previously. After sporadic meetings throughout the 1960s and early 1970s, a formal meeting was held in Washington, D.C., which lead to regular gatherings every other year. Once the organization had proved its durability, the Japan–United States Friendship Commission stepped in to provide start-up funding for programming and administrative needs. With this backing, the National Association of Japan America Societies officially formed in 1979, during which time the number of local Japan and Japan America societies continued to grow, ultimately reaching forty throughout the United States by the 1990s. In the succeeding decades, however, NAJAS's role remained limited and its mission little defined beyond serving as a clearinghouse of information on Japan-related activities of its various chapters. The real work of cultural exchange continued to be done by the small, local societies.

The growth of local societies depended of course on philanthropic and corporate sources of funding and also increasingly on the funds provided by semi-public organizations. The support function of the Japan–United States Friendship Commission often proved important, as in the case of the venerable Japan Society of Boston, which received Friendship Commission funds in 1980 to hire more staff as the society transitioned into a full-time operating structure. The Friendship Commission's work at both the national and local level helped broaden the base of exchange activities in the United States. For those in states with smaller metropolitan areas, such as Mississippi or Arizona, any exposure to Japanese culture, outside of academic programs at state universities, depended on a functioning Japan America society. This spread of exchange throughout the United States was fueled, of course, by increasing fascination with the Japanese economy, but as in the prewar years, it was up to locally staffed associations to provide the actual programming, be it a cherry blossom festival, a touring performance group, or a current events symposium. It was natural for the local societies to leverage the Japanese-studies professionals in their areas, and many of the societies interacted with their regions' colleges and universities. One example in a much larger metropolitan region was the Japan America Society of Chicago, which provided modest scholarships to Illinois-based graduate students working on Japan and thereby offered funds sometime not available from students' home institutions. Even more important than the limited funds were the opportunities for the budding professionals to integrate into the larger network of cultural exchange.[30]

Perhaps most importantly during this period, new private exchange groups emerged in the 1970s and 1980s as the Japanese economy and bilateral interest grew apace. One of the key organizations in this phase was the Japan Center for International Exchange (JCIE), formed in January 1970 by Yamamoto Tadashi. Yamamoto was a protégé of Kosaka Tokusaburo, a pioneer in private diplomacy in Japan, and had served as the executive secretary of the Japan Council for International Understanding. Before founding JCIE, Yamamoto had organized the major private international exchange programs between Japan and the United States under Kosaka's auspices. These programs included the Japanese-American Teacher Exchange Program in 1964, the Shimoda Conference series in 1967, and the U.S.-Japan Parliamentary Exchange Program in 1968.

Yamamoto became well known in international exchange for his ubiquitous activities and connections. A close friend of David Rockefeller, the former chairman of both the Council on Foreign Relations and Chase Manhattan Bank, Yamamoto helped him form the Trilateral Commission in 1973. The Commission was designed to bring together leading U.S., Japanese, and European politicians, business executives, and academics for private, Track II discussions (as did the earlier Shimoda Conference between Japan and the United States). Yamamoto's JCIE served as the Japanese secretariat of the Trilateral Commission from its inception to the commission's reorganization into an Asian secretariat.

The Japan Center for International Exchange began an ambitious schedule of programming, propelling itself to the first rank of nonprofit, nongovernmental institutions dedicated to U.S.-Japan exchange. Part of Yamamoto's influence derived from JCIE's continuing focus on leader exchanges; he pulled in luminaries such as Henry Kissinger; Donald Rumsfeld, then a U.S. representative and the future U.S. secretary of defense in two different administrations; and future prime minister Miyazawa Kiichi for various JCIE-sponsored programs. A number of U.S. academics also became deeply involved in JCIE projects over the years, foremost among them Herbert Passin, former head of Columbia University's Department of Sociology, and Gerald Curtis, a political scientist also at Columbia. JCIE also began to focus increasingly on people-to-people exchanges and research projects, including a major, multiyear study of postwar philanthropy and one on the development of local government in Japan. And while America was a large part of JCIE's focus—the center established a New York office to coordinated activities in the United States—it also created nongovernmental links with the Association for Southeast Asian Nations (ASEAN), Korea, Europe, and even Israel, which had almost no official or nonofficial contacts with Japan.[31]

By the time JCIE observed its twenty-fifth anniversary, in the dawn of the 1990s, the Cold War had ended and U.S.-Japan relations were increasingly driven by long-term economic conflicts. While not abandoning his emphasis on U.S.-Japan exchange, Yamamoto shifted his interest to the evolution of civil society in Asia and the U.S.-Japan expertise that could help facilitate this process. One of the center's main projects developed into CivilNet, which focused on promoting Japanese and Asian civil society. In this sense, Yamamoto and JCIE served a key role as facilitators, making connections between groups and among individuals who were hitherto underserved or who did not neatly fit into the established parameters of cultural exchange.

Another addition to the panoply of exchange groups during the last decade of the Cold War was the United States–Japan Foundation (USJF), begun in 1980. The USJF was not a formal exchange group but became an important funder for Japanese global outreach. The USJF was founded by Robin Chandler Duke, her husband, Ambassador Angier Biddle Duke, and the Japanese entrepreneur Sasakawa Ryoichi, with $44 million in support coming from Sasakawa's Japan Shipbuilding Industry Foundation (now known as the Nippon Foundation). Sasakawa was a controversial figure in certain circles, particularly due to claims about his ties to Japanese nationalist groups and the fact that much of his later fortune came from founding Japan's Speedboat Racing Association.

Yet Sasakawa was also a private philanthropist of rare breed in Japan. In addition to his $44 million gift to found the USJF, he donated $25 million to United Nations activities, most notably to the World Health Organization, UNICEF, UNESCO, the Office of the UN High Commissioner for Refugees, and the UN Fund for Population Activities. In addition, American schools, including Morehouse College and Duke University, each received gifts of $6 million from Sasakawa. In September 1986, he established the Sasakawa Peace Foundation with a grant of ¥50 billion, aiming "to contribute to the welfare of humankind and the sound development of the international community, and thus to world peace" through international exchange activities.[32] While Sasakawa never won over his critics, he was perhaps the largest single Japanese philanthropist since Shibusawa Eiichi in the first decades of the twentieth century. Sasakawa followed a venerable American tradition of philanthropic industrialists, such as John D. Rockefeller and Andrew Carnegie, both of whom had been distrusted, if not excoriated, despite their giving away millions of dollars to charitable interests.

The United States–Japan Foundation added its philanthropic weight to a variety of causes, taking up demand not filled by the Friendship Commission and the Japan Foundation. Like both of these organizations, the USJF had a portfolio of activities divided among education, policy, and the arts. Unlike Japan Foundation funding, however, USJF grants went almost exclusively to established groups, such as the Asia Society in New York; academic programs, such as Tufts University's Fletcher School of Law and Diplomacy; and production groups, such as public television stations. In its early years, the USJF's largest grants went to policy studies, such as a three-year project by the Atlantic Council of the United States on the U.S.-Japan energy relationship, a project that ran from 1982 to 1985 and received over $240,000.[33] Throughout the 1980s, the USJF funded a wide variety of programs in American universities, as well as business leader–exchange programs and scientific organizations, such as the Woods Hole Oceanographic Institute. The foundation also provided support to many Japanese organizations, such as Yamamoto's JCIE, the Asia Pacific Association of Japan, and NHK International for a one-hour television special in 1985, "Big Bird in Japan."[34] As the USJF matured, however, and budget limitations became more apparent, it began increasingly to focus on educational issues, concentrating much of its resources on teacher training, Japanese programming in American precollegiate schools, and American programming in Japanese elementary and secondary schools. It was hoped this focus would bring greater returns on investment, so to speak, by engaging future generations in Japanese-American relations.

The growing institutionalization of U.S.-Japan cultural exchange, supported by the organizations discussed above, led to thousands of more American students studying Japanese history and language, numerous artistic exchanges, and the publication of hundreds of scholarly books on each country. Professional societies grew in size and influence, and the older exchange organizations benefited from the sustained attention paid to Japanese-American relations. As a result, more Americans than ever before knew something, no matter how trivial, about Japan. At the same time, however, there was an explosion in direct contact between the two countries on a variety of levels, from Japanese corporations expanding into small-town America to Americans embracing Japanese popular culture and purchasing household goods made in Japan. This, too, was a kind of cultural exchange, and it led to a complex and often stormy U.S.-Japan relationship in the 1980s and beyond.

Japan as the Future: Global Economic Power, Popular Culture, and American Backlash in the 1980s

By the mid-1980s, the U.S.-Japan relationship was very different from what it had been two decades previously. The political bond between the two countries had deepened as the Cold War dragged on and Tokyo remained Washington's key Asian ally. This bond continued despite a steady buildup of U.S.-China relations, which had been normalized by President Jimmy Carter in 1979. When President Ronald Reagan came to office in 1981, he focused on Japan in his Asian policy and soon found a Pacific soul mate in Japanese Prime Minister Nakasone Yasuhiro, who began his term in 1982. Nakasone followed a series of Liberal Democratic Party (LDP) nonentities as premier and became perhaps the most influential prime minister since the LDP kingmaker Tanaka Kakuei back in the early 1970s.

Nakasone was committed to building up Japan's political and military strength commensurately with the country's economic power, thus hoping to fulfill the long-held predictions of pundits like Herman Kahn.[35] Reagan, who had made his foreign policy priority the escalation of pressure on the Soviet Union in order to roll back Communism, immediately identified with Nakasone's willingness to increase Japan's security posture. In a series of agreements, Tokyo sought to beef up Japan's military capabilities by buying top-of-the-line American technology and agreed to expand Japanese responsibilities under the Mutual Security Treaty (which had hitherto relegated the country to the most basic elements of self-defense), most notably by taking on the responsibility for patrolling the sea lanes up to a one-thousand-mile radius from the home islands and providing rear support for American troops in the case of armed conflict. These actions seemed to indicate that Japan was evolving from a country in its postwar phase to a "normal nation," a phrase made famous in the following decade by LDP maverick politician Ozawa Ichirō. Further, although not as celebrated as the bond between Reagan and the British prime minister, Margaret Thatcher, the "Ron-Yasu" relationship helped make Nakasone the first Japanese leader known to more than a handful of Americans.

It was Japan's spectacular economic growth, however, that truly gave the country its influence in the 1980s. The effects of that growth on relations with America were much more complex than the generally warm political-military relationship between Washington and Tokyo. Japan's emergence as an economic superpower tied the two countries more closely together than ever, embedded Japan firmly in the American consciousness, and yet also generated serious tensions between them. There was good reason for such changes, as Japan was without question the global economic success story in the post–World War II era. The country's gross domestic product grew at annual rates of 6 to 10 percent from the 1950s through the 1980s, and Japan's once modest cities were transformed through massive building programs. Per capita income also rocketed, making Japanese consumers among the wealthiest in the world. Exports were the driving engine of growth, and Japan's current account surplus reached the billions of dollars in the 1980s. By the early 1980s, indeed, Japanese-made consumer goods were edging out American and European products in everything from transistor radios to automobiles.

In May 1985, Tokyo was invited to a meeting of the Group of Seven (G7), the annual economic gathering of the leading Western industrial nations. The invitation was a symbol of the new global status of Japan and was no less important than its inclusion at the Paris peace talks ending the Great War back in 1919. The invitation also was recognition that Japan's economic surpluses were becoming a political issue in America and an economic drain on countries around the world. In September of that same year, five members of the G7 signed the Plaza Accord, which Reagan administration officials thought would devalue the dollar vis-à-vis the yen and help cut America's trade deficit with Japan, which was to reach $59 billion the following year. The appreciation of the yen indeed made Japanese goods more expensive, but that did not stop exporters from taking short-term losses to increase their market share in the United States. In fact, Japanese exports to America in the years following the Plaza Accord increased over 20 percent, and the resulting flood of cash into Japan coincidentally ignited an asset boom, mainly in land prices.[36]

The failure of the Plaza Accords to restrain the yen propelled Japan into the "bubble economy" of the 1980s. Land prices skyrocketed in urban areas, leading firms to borrow capital based on the inflated value of their holdings. At one point in the late 1980s, the land under the Imperial Palace in central Tokyo was officially valued more than the entire state of California; to sober observers, this was a symbol not of Japan's strength but of how out of balance the system had become. The Tokyo Stock Exchange witnessed a similar spiral in asset prices, regardless of the profitability of the listed firms, and by 1990 the exchange represented 60 percent of the world's stock market capitalization. The resulting influx of cash into the economy found an outlet in overseas investment, particularly in America.

These political and economic shifts caused swings in cultural relations between Japan and the United States. In contrast to the cultural exchange of the 1960s, however, the irruption of Japan into the American cultural landscape in the 1980s was a double-edged sword. Even amid the economic scandals noted above, Japanese liquid capital was perceived as an unstoppable economic strength, the proof of predictions made back in the 1960s and 1970s by writers such as Herman Kahn. Aggressive investing by Japanese during a time of U.S. recession in the early 1980s led to growing fears that America would soon lose its economic primacy to Japan, which was a threat to America's future as serious as that posed by the Soviet Union's machinations in the Western hemisphere.

Japan seemed everywhere in the mid- and late 1980s, which would have amazed earlier generations of Japanophiles used to the country being considered an insignificant global player. What received the most attention was the buying spree that Japanese corporations went on, first by acquiring American businesses, as when Sony purchased entertainment giant MCA, and then by snapping up American landmarks. The October 1989 purchase by a Japanese investment group of New York City's Rockefeller Center had the impact of a small earthquake in the American media. The Rock, as it was called, not only sat in a prime location in midtown Manhattan, but it also was the very symbol of U.S. capitalist strength and an ever-present reminder of the power of American industrialists, like that of the building's namesake, John D. Rockefeller Jr. The unsettling feeling that the student had outstripped the teacher was evident in media coverage of the Rock's sale, with the *New York Times* snidely remarking that the Mitsubishi Estate Company had bought "New York cachet" with its purchase.[37] The circus atmosphere was commented on by conservative icon William F. Buckley, who noted that the press approached the Rockefeller Center story in a "tone of voice . . . such as would have been appropriate in response to a bulletin in 1945 that the Japanese had reoccupied Okinawa."[38] On top of this, a Japanese group then bought Pebble Beach Golf Links in California, another symbol of American wealth and the playground of America's elite set. Such purchases were not accidental, for while there was, of course, no Japanese grand strategy to emasculate America, prizes such as Rockefeller Center were attractive to Japanese investors who wanted to own the most recognizable, most profitable properties in the world.

For most Americans, however, the most visible face of Japan was the flood of Japanese consumer goods into their everyday lives. Economics intersected with culture, as Japan became the major exporter of key products to America, thus leading Americans to see Japan in a new light, one that was not always positive. Sony became a household name for its portable tape recorders and in 1979 introduced the Walkman personal cassette-tape player. Up to that time, of course, taped music could be played only on large, immobile stereo systems or bulky tape players. The Walkman revolutionized entertainment technology, and the nation was overrun by headset-sporting consumers absorbed in their music regardless of public venue. Within twenty years, by the turn of the century, over 185 million Walkman units had been sold worldwide, the majority of them in America.[39] Sony, along with Panasonic and others, also challenged American radio and television set manufacturers, eclipsing Zenith, RCA, and the like within just a matter of years.

Perhaps the greatest consumer prize of all was the quintessential American product, the automobile. Japanese automakers launched a direct challenge to the supposedly unassailable American production of cars in the 1970s and 1980s, after a rocky start a decade earlier. Toyota Motor Corporation, along with companies such as Honda and Nissan, rolled out affordable compact automobiles, responding more quickly than American carmakers to the oil crises of the 1970s and permanently higher gasoline prices.[40] The Japanese concept of smaller, more fuel-efficient cars turned the American automotive industry, with its large, gas-guzzling models, on its head. Within just thirty years, by 2009, Toyota had become the largest automaker in the world, while former American giants such as General Motors and Chrysler went bankrupt. To American consumers, Japanese goods now meant quality, not cheapness, as well as functionality and efficiency. Yet as much as Americans eagerly voted with their pocketbooks and poured cash into the coffers of Japanese producers, thinly veiled worries about the loss of American competitiveness and the reach of Japan into everyday American life were taking root.

The result was a popular backlash against Japan and Japanese goods at the same time that they were more popular than ever. News media jumped on this nativist bandwagon early on, portraying the Japanese nation as a conglomerate buying up America and taking away American jobs during a recession. Those who claimed that the power of negative cultural images could bring about strife were soon proved right. By the 1980s, the tone in the United States turned decidedly ugly, and the decade began with a tragedy that showed how fraught the situation had become. Latent racism on the part of some Americans was already at a boiling point, and in June 1982, a young man named Vincent Chin was beaten to death with baseball bats outside a bar in Detroit, Michigan, after his bachelor party. Chin's murderers were two white Americans who blamed the Japanese for layoffs of Detroit autoworkers. The fact that Chin was not Japanese, but rather a Chinese American immigrant, only added to the crime's senselessness.

Throughout the decade, Americans became increasingly suspicious of Japan and its challenge to American supremacy. A leading periodical, *Time* magazine, swung between extremes in these years: in 1981 it featured a stylized samurai on its cover with the headline "How Japan Does It: The World's Toughest Competitor"; just six years later, *Time* portrayed the United States and Japan as sumo wrestlers facing off under the headline "Trade Wars: The U.S Gets Tough with Japan."[41] The depth of suspicion among Americans was captured in a 1990 best-selling book, *Agents of Influence*, by economist Pat Choate. Choate claimed that Japan "purchased political influence" in America through a well-funded network of intellectuals, opinion leaders, lobbyists, and other cheerleaders throughout American society.[42] Choate's book was popular in no small part because he named the names of those he saw as "agents" of Japan in the United States, and he included a seven-page appendix of "Japan's registered foreign agents in America," noting throughout the work those who were unregistered yet who in his view played key roles in pushing Tokyo's policy goals or points of view in America. Intellectual and cultural exchange groups, such as the Japan Society, also came under Choate's fire for acting as public relations outlets for Japanese companies or the government.

Such distrust and fear was mixed with thinly veiled admiration of Japan throughout American society. The Harvard Business School went so far as to assign a seventeenth-century work of samurai philosophy to its students; this text, the *Book of Five Rings*, by master swordsman Miyamoto Musashi, was believed to be a Rosetta stone for interpreting the mind-set and success of the Japanese businessman. Those businessmen were homogenized by specialist and lay Americans alike into a monolithic

group called "salarymen," lemmings who sacrificed all for the parent
company and who threw their lives away due to overwork as easily as the
samurai on the battlefield centuries before had eagerly given all for his
feudal lord. The transformation of Japan into a nation of modern, predatory samurai spread through a media frenzy and films such as the futuris-
tic thriller *Blade Runner* (1982), which portrayed an America dominated
by Japanese cultural influences;1989's *Black Rain,* a gangster movie pit-
ting two American cops against bloodthirsty Japanese *yakuza* mobsters;
and Michael Crichton's 1992 novel *Rising Sun,* about predatory Japanese
corporations that kill to gain their objectives.

While such tragedies as the Chin murder did not happen again, symbolic violence against Japan was rampant during the decade. Autoworkers smashed Japanese cars with sledgehammers around the country, while
U.S. congressmen destroyed a Toshiba radio on the Capitol grounds after the manufacturer was convicted of selling sensitive technology to the
Soviet Union in July 1987.[43] The theme was picked up by authors George
Friedman and Meredith LeBard in their 1991 book, *The Coming War
with Japan,* which identified Japan's resurgent nationalism and economic strength as the new geopolitical threat to America that one day
may have to be settled by force of arms.

The spectrum spanning Herman Kahn through Chalmers Johnson to
Freidman and LeBard in the space of just two decades testifies not merely
to a lack of confidence among Americans at the time but also to the lack of
understanding between the two societies. As such, it could be seen as a
direct refutation of the claims of the cultural exchange community that
the efforts of such groups were bringing the two countries closer together.
Equally, it raised questions about whether cross-cultural "understanding" was a chimera, subordinate as always to political and economic realities. In other words, the very same shortcomings of cultural exchange that
were revealed in the 1930s returned in the 1980s and 1990s.

Matters came to a head as the twentieth century entered its last decade.
The political and security basis of the U.S.-Japan relationship was called
into the question by the effective end of the Cold War, when the Berlin Wall
was torn down in 1989. Seemingly overnight, Americans moved past their
four-decade struggle with the Soviet Union and began to think about a
post–Cold War world. Without the specter of a worldwide Communist

movement, the defense of key allies might not be as crucial, and America might not have to permanently deploy its sons and daughters around the world. If this were the case, what would remain to link Tokyo and Washington together, since their economic relations were going from bad to worse?

Ironically, such a break from military commitments was soon revealed to be a fantasy, and the first post–Cold War crisis tested the worth of Japan as an ally and raised a host of disturbing questions in the minds of both Americans and Japanese. On August 2, 1990, Iraqi dictator Saddam Hussein's army invaded the neighboring country of Kuwait. President George H. W. Bush soon committed the United States to removing Iraqi forces from the oil-rich country. As the United States embarked on its largest military mission buildup since the Vietnam War, eventually moving half a million troops to the Middle East as part of an international coalition, Bush asked Tokyo to provide substantial funds for the mission.[44] Since 12 percent of Japan's oil came from Iraq, not to mention the billions owed it by Baghdad for loans, Tokyo provided little immediate support, despite Prime Minister Kaifu Toshiki's promises to Bush. This Japanese reluctance to join the largest allied military operation in decades immediately caused pundits and policy makers alike to question if Japan had any value to America.

Tensions between the two countries had already been strained by Tokyo's refusal to follow the American clampdown on business and aid to China after the 1989 Tiananmen Square massacre. Tokyo's response to Operation Desert Storm solidified popular American views that Japan was a free rider, a country that was dependent on Washington for security yet unwilling to support its key ally and perhaps which did not even share core American values. Japanese views were similarly negative, seeing America as a fading giant, yet one willing to wield the stick of military power to get its way. Although Tokyo ultimately paid over $12 billion dollars to fund the Gulf War, the public relations damage had been done. The symbolic low point of the relationship may well have been President George H. W. Bush's January 1992 visit to Japan. Derided for being the "Salesman in Chief" by attending the opening of a Toys'R'Us branch in Tokyo, Bush became sick at a formal dinner while sitting next to Prime Minister Miyazawa Kiichi. The incident was broadcast worldwide and seemed to encapsulate the woes of transpacific ties.

Yet even as political relations were trending downward, both Americans and Japanese suddenly had to struggle to make sense of the abrupt end to the Japanese economic miracle. By 1989, the Tokyo Stock Exchange was capitalized at a higher value than the New York market, and an explosion in Japanese asset prices was tied to an unsustainable rise in land values from the mid-1980s on. Economic reality finally caught up with the Japanese market at the end of 1990, as stock prices plummeted and the bubble broke. Over the next fifteen years, land prices declined annually, down 40 percent from their high in 1991, and the stock market dropped by 80 percent, leading to a decadelong economic slump. While few initially thought that this was more than a temporary bump in the road for Japan's economic juggernaut, the downturn nonetheless punctured Japan's inflated view of its unique society, which was proved no longer immune from the economic cycles that plagued Western nations. Insult was added to injury in Japanese eyes by strong U.S. economic growth during the balance of the 1990s.

As the last decade of the twentieth century dawned, the U.S.-Japan relationship seemed in disarray, and decades' worth of cultural exchange seemed as though it might turn out to be as impotent as the failed efforts of the 1930s. If the two countries were to continue to view each other as allies, then relations would have to be reset somehow, and cultural exchange organizations would play their role in the effort to do so, with new government support for some groups even as others faced the perpetual struggle to maintain their independence.

Resetting U.S.-Japan Cultural Exchange in the 1990s

In response to this new, unsettled, and disturbing constellation of events, the Japanese government once again focused on public diplomacy, as much to repair Japan's relationship with America as to defend its own policies. In late February 1991, just as the U.S.-led coalition was driving the Iraqis out of Kuwait in a mere one-hundred-hour ground war, the Japan Foundation held in Tokyo a two-day symposium, titled Challenges and Opportunities for U.S.-Japan Exchange in the New Era, to celebrate the thirtieth anniversary of the U.S.-Japan alliance. The symposium marked the launch of a new cultural exchange organization, run through the Japan Foundation, but semiautonomous in its funding and activities.

In English, the new organization was called the Center for Global Partnership (CGP), but its Japanese name more clearly revealed the focus its activities: the Japan-America Center.

The Center for Global Partnership was the brainchild of Abe Shintarō, the foreign minister under Nakasone Yasuhiro in the mid-1980s, and its first director was the veteran bureaucrat Kusuda Minoru. Over $370 million was put into an endowment created within the Japan Foundation, an investment designed to promote a "shared endeavor to formulate values appropriate to this new age," as Kusuda put it in his first executive director's message.[45] The CGP was not merely an attempt to restabilize U.S.-Japan cultural relations (and by extension provide capital, so to speak, for political relations); it was in many ways the apotheosis of cultural exchange organizations, devoted solely to becoming the nerve center behind U.S.-Japan intellectual and cultural interaction.

For nearly a century, cultural relations had become increasingly formalized and at the same time more important to national goals and policies. Cultural ties had helped guide the important early years of Japanese and American interaction as each became a global power around 1900. Leaders of cultural exchange had attempted, and failed, to address the tensions leading to anti-immigration legislation in the U.S. during the 1920s and to geopolitical competition in east Asia in the 1930s and 1940s. Yet cultural exchange was also crucial to reestablishing cordial relations after World War II and the U.S. Occupation of Japan. By 1990, U.S.-Japan relations were inconceivable without the sustained, thick network of cultural exchange organizations that operated at local and national levels, providing venues for elites, students, and interested individuals. And these groups played an increasingly important role in attempting to spread each nation's values and explain policies to the other.

The blueprint established by the Center for Global Partnership recognized this reality. The CGP presumed to focus in particular on the following goals: strengthening intellectual exchange, creating opinion-leader networks, and training specialists. The second of these goals would serve to maintain the tradition of high-level, elite contact between Japan and America and yet would run into the difficulty of expanding such networks beyond those already involved in U.S.-Japan exchange. The center would focus on further developing the infrastructure of exchange by expanding bilateral contacts and sponsoring research projects.[46] In CGP's first year, 46 percent of its approximately $8.6 million in total grants went to intellectual exchange. Of that amount, nearly $4 million went to policy-oriented research by established groups (mainly think tanks) and most of the rest to "dialogues," primarily binational and multinational conferences.[47] The marquee program of the new center was the Abe Fellowship, which awarded yearlong research grants for midcareer academics and professionals from both Japan and the United States. The Abe Fellowship required its American recipients to reside in Japan, and vice versa, for much of the grant period; this, it was hoped, would institutionalize intellectual exchange between experts in both countries on a regular basis. With this initial slate of funding, the CGP became perhaps the most prolific funder in the community of U.S.-Japan exchange organizations. Its cultural exchange grants blanketed the United States, from the Des Moines Metro Opera (for a tour in Japan) to the Japan/Montana Women's Link program for state representatives.[48]

The Center for Global Partnership's establishment reflected a belief by Tokyo that the role of public opinion and cultural interchange was central to the functioning of U.S.-Japan relations. In an era of growing mistrust, in fact, this kind of interchange might be more directly effective than macro-economic tools or policy changes, of which most Americans remained unaware. At the same time, of course, the attempt to develop, nurture, and guide public opinion was at best an inexact science, and the results the government wanted could be observed only indirectly, in light of the broad-based state of relations between the two countries. From an historical viewpoint, indeed, the creation of CGP was the culmination of a process stretching back to 1898 and the formation of the American Friends' Association. For the intended recipients of CGP largesse, its formation was hoped to be the solution to the eternally vexing question of where to find resources for projects and activities connected with Japan-U.S. relations.

Trading Places: Japan's Fall, China's Rise, and American Ambivalence

Just as CGP was developing its programming base during the 1990s, however, Japan was slipping farther and farther into recession. What observers had assumed was a minor blip in the unstoppable growth of the Japanese economy turned out to be a systemic slowdown caused by a host of inefficient and opaque practices covered up during the decades of Japan's economic successes after World War II.[49] Suddenly, the maze of regulatory restrictions on Japanese businesses, limits on foreign owner-ship, endemic collusion and bid rigging, not to mention the massive over-sight failures of Japan's financial institutions, coalesced to provide a very different image of Japan in the United States. At the same time, America's economic boom, inaugurated in the early 1980s under the administration of President Ronald Reagan, recovered from a minor recession and kicked into high gear during the presidency of Bill Clinton. Within just a few years, Japanese triumphalism and simmering resentment by Americans would almost entirely reverse themselves.

Japan's fall from grace was swift and stunning. The country was bat-tered during the 1990s not merely by economic recession. One corrosive result of the decades of growth was an explosion of corruption, already a seemingly permanent feature of Japan's political landscape, corruption which reached endemic proportions during the bubble. The LDP had been battered by scandal during the 1970s, when former prime minister Tanaka was convicted of accepting bribes from the Lockheed Corpora-tion in return for pushing Japan Airlines to buy Lockheed airplanes. Later fund-raising scandals involving Japan's leading politicians in the late 1980s tarnished Japan's image in America and more importantly resulted in a revolt by Japanese voters in 1993, which ended the LDP's thirty-eight-year monopoly on power and brought in a short-lived reformist government. The next decade and a half would witness a seesaw battle between the LDP and various opposition parties to control the Diet. Ex-cept for the strong leadership of LDP Prime Minister Koizumi Jun'ichiro from 2001 to 2006, politics in Japan during the 1990s and first decade of the twenty-first century seemed to mirror the uncertain state of the econ-omy: the concept of "reform" was much bruited about, but little actual change occurred, even after the formation of one main opposition party, the Democratic Party of Japan, in 2003.

It had been the myth of Japanese organizational and bureaucratic superi-ority that had driven years of fascination with Japan, but by the early 1990s a challenge to this myth began emerging. Emblematic of this dramatic reversal of fortune was *The Sun Also Sets,* a best-selling book of 1991 by future editor of the *Economist* magazine Bill Emmott. Coming out just as the economic recession began to take hold, Emmott's treatise critiqued Japanese postwar economic policy and directly challenged those who still saw Japan as the next great power or as a threat to U.S. economic supremacy.[50] Indirectly, the book argued that Japanese culture did not create a miraculous environment freeing the country from the bounds of economic reality, and Emmott built on the case made a year earlier by the Dutch journalist Karl van Wolferen, whose *The Enigma of Japanese Power* made the more explicit charge that Japanese political culture was in fact a major impediment to the continued economic growth and vitality of the nation.[51] Reaction to Emmott, Van Wolferen, and others, including journalist James Fallows and former U.S. trade official Clyde Prestowitz, author of 1993's *Trading Places,* was heated, indicating that these writers had challenged not just received economic beliefs but a more fundamental wisdom about the essence of Japanese culture. Defenders of the idea of Japan's uniqueness heavily criticized Van Wolferen, in particular, and in return were labeled as tools of the Japanese government and members of the "Chrysanthemum Club" by authors such as Pat Choate, in his *Agents of Influence.* The emotionalism of the debate on Japan revealed not merely the perceived stakes of the economic competition between Japan and the United States but also the depth of intellectual investment on both sides. Such bitter public debate would have been familiar to a reader of critical journalist Carl Crow eight decades previously.

If Emmott and Van Wolferen were seen by some as intellectual outsiders at the beginning of the decade, their views gained ground as the bedrock presumptions of Japanese strength were put under enormous stress in the 1990s and revealed to be riddled with weaknesses. The midpoint of the decade was a particularly rough year. On January 17, 1995, a massive earthquake devastated Kobe, one of Japan's main cities and largest ports, killing nearly sixty-five hundred persons in the city and its environs. Widespread anger over the failure of early warning systems and of supposedly earthquake-proof buildings was followed by equally strong criticisms over the disorganized and ineffective local- and national-government disaster relief. Americans were stunned at the feeble government response and even more so at much-publicized reports that Japan's largest *yakuza* organization, the Yamaguchi-gumi, was the most effective provider of relief supplies, including food and diapers, on the streets of Kobe in the days after the quake.[52]

Barely two months later, on March 20, 1995, the country was rocked by a domestic terrorism attack. A millennial cult called the Aum Shinrikyo (Supreme Truth) unleashed five coordinated sarin gas attacks on the Tokyo metropolitan subway system, the world's busiest, during the morning rush hour. A dozen commuters and subway workers died, and over a thousand others were injured. Once the press revealed the government's inaction in response to previous, smaller attacks by the Aum cult—inaction that allowed the cult to build up to its mass attack—the impression of bureaucratic incompetency was overwhelming. Again, Japan's self-esteem and image in America suffered serious blows as these natural and manmade disasters piled up, and Americans began to wonder about the darker side of a society that could germinate a terrorist group like Aum Shinrikyo.

With a deepening recession taking hold, Japan began to slip off the front pages in America, the once fearsome challenge of Japan dismissed and its attractions increasingly ignored. After putting the Aum Shinrikyo cult's leader on its April 1995 cover, *Time* magazine did not headline Japan for over a decade, until August 2005, and then only to bring up one of the darkest moments in Japanese history on the fiftieth anniversary of the atomic bombings of Hiroshima and Nagasaki. Japan, once universally seen as the wave of the future, had suddenly returned to its immediate postwar state of helpless victim, and a more nuanced and critical view of the country was cemented in the American consciousness.

If this shift in the cultural zeitgeist was not striking enough on its own, the years of what some had called "Japan bashing" during the economic confrontations of the 1980s now became labeled as "Japan passing," as Americans began focusing on a newly ascendant China. Few initially recognized how complete the shift ultimately would become, but by decade's end, the historical pendulum of American interest in Asia had once again swung between its two traditional poles. It was, after all, dreams of the China trade that had first brought Americans to Japan, even if the small country had soon eclipsed its older cousin on the world stage. Indeed, Japan's growth through the late nineteenth and twentieth centuries was regularly contrasted with China's tragic history of civil war, invasion, Communist revolution, and social disruption during the Great Leap Forward and the Cultural Revolution. Yet by the last decade of the twentieth century, China's post-Mao-era reforms, guided largely by leader Deng Xioaping, brought economic reform amid continuing political repression. For American business interests, the undeniable profits to be had soon outweighed any qualms about dealing with an authoritarian leadership that in June 1989 had massacred thousands of its own students who were protesting for greater democracy. The George H. W. Bush administration calculated that it was better to engage the rising political and military power of Beijing than to try and contain it and thus quietly reopened relations with China's rulers just months after the Tiananmen massacre. Bush's successor, Bill Clinton, sought to make the change in American focus permanent by declaring a "strategic partnership" between Beijing and Washington.

Over the next decade, American pundits, policy makers, intellectuals, and businesspeople would become preoccupied with China. Writers switched seamlessly from celebrating or decrying Japan to putting the same breathless focus on China. Books with titles ranging from *The China Threat* to *Rising Star* and from *The Writing on the Wall: Why We Must Embrace China as a Partner or Face It as an Enemy* to *China: Fragile Superpower* overloaded both bookshelves and readers in America. In just a few years, the country transferred its desires and fears to a different Asian power. Indeed, the period best could be summed up by the title of journalist James Mann's study of modern U.S.-China relations: *About Face*.[53] As if to confirm China's new ascendance, Beijing took a page out of Japan's cultural exchange playbook and aggressively promoted cultural ties with American youth. Starting in the middle of the first decade of the twenty-first century, the Chinese government opened over fifty-five Confucius Institutes at American colleges and universities. These institutes, which now number more than the combined offices of the Japan Foundation and the Japan America society network, teach the Chinese language and run a wide variety of cultural events, and hold the goal of mainstreaming Chinese culture among American audiences.

For Japanese policy makers and Japan watchers in the United States, this apparent shift was the culmination of fears that had been growing since Richard Nixon had secretly decided to reach out to China back in the early 1970s. The symbolic nadir of this new reality came in July 1998, when Bill Clinton made a nine-day state visit to China and chose not to stop in Japan on either end of the trip. This was the first time that an American president had failed to visit Japan when going to China, and the repercussions were deep, although in public the two allies were quick to reassert their close relationship. Secretary of State Madeleine Albright was dispatched to Tokyo after Clinton left Beijing, to assure the Japanese that their ties with Washington remained strong and that "relations with China were not a zero-sum game." Despite Albright's visit, the sense of unease in Tokyo and among Japan specialists in America only grew.[54]

Such concerns flourished despite the fact that Clinton and Japanese Prime Minister Hashimoto Ryutaro had signed a major joint declaration on the future of the alliance back in 1996 and had agreed to expand bilateral security cooperation. The new worries revealed the importance of the nonpolitical aspects of the U.S.-Japan relationship. There seemed to be at the core of the relationship a connection deeper than simple politics, one in which the Japanese reacted strongly to perceptions based not solely on pure power calculations. For some, the apparent U.S. estimation of Japan was as significant a factor as the political and security arrangements that continued to tie them together even after the end of the Cold War.[55]

With Japan no longer threatening to become the next great power and with its vaunted bureaucratic system being unable to solve the country's problems, Japanese reconsidered their previous dismissal of America's numerous social problems. As in the nineteenth century, some politicians and intellectuals in Japan began to talk of how to reform their country. From financial regulation to the length of the school year, Japanese recognized that areas that had seemed unquestioned postwar successes in fact had stopped responding to changing conditions and now needed to be updated. Works with forthright titles like *Japan's Lost Decade* or *Japanese Foreign Policy at the Crossroads* signaled a new wave of critical self-introspection, even if long-standing social practice and cultural norms hindered any radical reform.[56]

From a different perspective, however, one could argue that the U.S.-Japan relationship was maturing once the unrealistic expectations of the

1970s and 1980s had abruptly ended. It is undoubtedly true that many Americans took pleasure in Japan's comeuppance and harped on the country's failings; others recognized that Japan's continuing economic power, global role, and societal stability had not fundamentally changed or perhaps had simply realistically adjusted to levels that the country could maintain. Thus, critics could point out numerous failings among Japan's political class, economic regulations, social patterns, and the like, while still stressing that compared with other countries, including China, Japan played and would continue to play a major role in the world, in areas such as overseas financial aid and later in humanitarian relief.[57]

This view, and the larger resetting of expectations in the U.S.-Japan relationship that accompanied it, was if anything strengthened during the unexpectedly vigorous rule of Prime Minister Koizumi Jun'ichiro, from 2001 through 2006. Not since Nakasone Yasuhiro back in the 1980s had a Japanese premier so attracted attention in America, and his relationship with President George W. Bush brought back memories of the Ron-Yasu friendship of two decades before. Koizumi, indeed, went Nakasone one better, by equally captivating both Americans and his compatriots with bold reform plans and brash policies to reinvigorate Japan's economy and increase its role on the global stage. His policies of tackling bad bank assets, increasing foreign direct investment, and continuing the financial reform policies started in the late 1990s led to positive economic growth in Japan during much of his term.

Koizumi, however, became best known for his steadfast support for American antiterrorist operations after the al-Qaeda attacks of September 11, 2001. Avoiding the missteps and fatal irresolution that Japanese leaders showed during the Gulf War, Koizumi moved to centralize decision making in the prime minister's office and pushed through Japan's parliament special measures laws that allowed for the dispatch of Self-Defense Force (SDF) members to Afghanistan, Iraq, and the Indian Ocean. This was the first time that Japanese troops had been deployed to a combat zone since the end of World War II, and it seemed to mark a new phase in Japan's global activities, even though the SDF limited its activities to reconstruction assistance, logistical supply, and maritime refueling.[58] Some Japan observers went so far as to call this use of troops a "resurgence" of Japanese power, raising old visions of Japan's moving beyond postwar restrictions on the use of force and finally playing a security and political role commensurate with its political power.[59]

The limits of Japan's new orientation soon became clear, however, as Koizumi was followed by a succession of weak premiers, who brought about the diminution of the Liberal Democratic Party's hold on power and ushered in a period of political paralysis starting in July 2007, when the opposition Democratic Party of Japan captured control of the Upper House of the National Diet. Over the next two years, paralysis transformed into a political earthquake that swept the LDP from power in August 2009 and led to the accession of the Democratic Party of Japan under Prime Minister Hatoyama Yukio, in the first full turnover of power to an opposition party in over a half century. Nevertheless, a somewhat more generous picture of Japan had emerged during the first decade of the twenty-first century, in part due to Koizumi's leadership and in part due to recognition by many Americans that Japan, constitutional restraints and political stagnation notwithstanding, remained a valued and trusted ally in a volatile world. If the U.S.-Japan relationship was indeed "maturing" during these years, the cultural exchange organizations that helped maintain nonofficial relations between the two countries remained an important ingredient in shaping public opinion in the two countries.

Maintaining, let alone expanding, the activities of cultural exchange groups during the 1990s and beyond was a difficult undertaking in the wake of Japan's extended economic stagnation. Indeed, by the middle of the first decade of the twenty-first century, money for traditional academic, cultural, and intellectual programs had been cut by major funders such as the Japan Foundation. By 1996, just half a decade after its founding, the Center for Global Partnership saw its endowment revenue drop by one-third, as long-term interest rates in Japan fell.[60] As a result, the CGP, like other organizations, revised program guidelines and concentrated its shrinking resources on a narrower range of activities. Such reorientation occurred in conjunction with a tapering off of public and professional interest in Japan, a tapering off that ironically may have helped reduce the demand on resources but did little to assuage the worry of exchange leaders that Japan was being relegated to the back burner of American foreign interest.

In response to this decline in interest and resources, groups like CGP sought to address post–Cold War issues that might even serve as a new basis for U.S.-Japan global cooperation. Three broad areas made up the redefined CGP program orientation starting in 2000: intellectual exchange, regional and grassroots exchange, and joint-sponsorship projects. Within intellectual exchange, priority was given to the subfields of international economic relations, international security issues, civil society, sustainable development, and health care and aging societies; grassroots programs targeted funds for youth exchange and nonprofit organization exchanges. This resulted in over $780,000 in grants to U.S. universities, nonprofit groups, and other organizations in 2002, monies that were administered through CGP's Tokyo and New York offices.[61]

By 2010, CGP had further restructured its programming to focus on "building global partnerships, cultivation of individuals in the U.S.-Japan relationship to sustain global partnerships, and expanding and deepening the understanding of Japan in the United States."[62] Its institutional grants division, after distributing over $680,000 to U.S. groups in 2008, was narrowed down to supporting collaborative projects related to global stability and "overcoming the challenges of globalization."[63] The center also reorganized its fellowships funding, continuing the flagship Abe Fellowship for established scholars and starting three new programs: the Security Studies Fellowship program for young scholars; the Japan Outreach Initiative, which placed an average of four Japanese volunteers per year, mainly in the U.S. South, "to promote awareness and understanding of Japan in regions of the United States with relatively few Japan-related activities . . . and to nurture new leaders in the field of grassroots exchange"; and the short-lived NPO Fellowship, which aimed at developing young leaders in Japan's nonprofit sector who would later act as bridges between the two countries.[64] At the same time, traditional funding for a broad range of academic research by American scholars and graduate students continued to be run directly through the Japan Foundation's Japanese Studies Fellowships, and some in the Japan studies community worried that the separate institutional identity of the Center for Global Partnership was at risk of being lost and the Center would be absorbed back into the Japan Foundation.[65]

To some degree the funding activities of leading organizations such as the Japan Foundation indeed seemed concentrated on a smaller circle of individuals and organizations, but that reflected the reality that Japanese studies and programming in the United States had become ever more specialized. What the foundation hoped to do with this new approach was integrate the U.S.-Japan relationship into larger global issues and thereby maintain Japan's relevance in foreign eyes.[66] Whereas in previous decades much of the focus of such grants was for research on the bilateral relationship itself, the concept of a Japan-U.S. global partnership increasingly came to define the funding objectives of major organizations like the Japan Foundation during the 1990s and 2000s. This change dovetailed with the approach of other established exchange organizations, such as the British Council, whose two U.S. offices also ran programs on global development, climate change, and community issues.[67]

The fact that Japan no longer was perceived by Americans as the next great power resulted in a rebalancing of exchange programs away from harder security and political issues and toward more social and traditional cultural concerns. In a way, exchange between Japan and the United States was returning to its original, century-old focus on education and material culture. The end of the twentieth century and the beginning of the twenty-first witnessed a resurgence of American interest in popular culture, for example, and program managers at foundations and exchange groups alike quickly responded to capture a new audience, and to make up for the drifting away of others now looking toward other countries.

Educational Exchange and Focusing on the Grass Roots: Returning to the Past

To a large degree, this resurgence of interest in cultural exchange reflected the success of American academic programs on Japan, which, as before, was not mirrored in Japan and for which substantial funding continued to be sought. Japanese largesse during the 1970s and 1980s had built up a large community of Japan-studies departments in American colleges and universities. While some may question whether Japanese studies were cultural exchange, U.S. college courses introduced more Americans to facets of Japan than did any other means. On top of that, thousands of American students studied Japanese language for some period of time in Japan itself, which was indeed a direct form of exchange and much of which was funded by major organizations such as the Japan Foundation. Private initiatives, such as the Japan-America Student Conference for college students, also continued their activities, and JASC celebrated its seventieth anniversary in 2004, although interest in the program had clearly begun to wane with the changing foreign interests of American college students. This led to the establishment of the new Korea-America Student Conference in 2008.

During the 1990s, academic exchange slowly spread beyond higher education, as Japanese language and culture classes were offered in more primary and secondary schools in America (although these were soon outstripped by Chinese-language courses). In part, funding organizations that backed such classes were attempting to offset the declining interest in Japan among adults and university students, and their attempts to engage an even younger generation met with mixed results. Special summer programs, such as at the Governor's Honors Academy of West Virginia, provided short, intensive language and culture programs to selected high school students who already had some exposure to Japanese but who did not have the opportunity to participate regularly in Japanese cultural activities. Building on sister-city relationships, public schools in the United States hosted visiting delegations of Japanese secondary school students, who often visited multiple schools, many rural, during their visits.[68] Yet such programs and visits were also part of a much larger foreign exchange movement in American schools, in which representatives of dozens of countries stimulated the growth of numerous language and study abroad programs. In such conditions, Japanese often did not stand out from the diverse crowd of foreign exchange participants.

Funding organizations continued to play a significant role in promoting Japan-oriented classes, in part to attempt to interest a new generation in Japanese issues. The United States–Japan Foundation, for example, saw a reversal of its funding priorities during these years, spending $9 million on educational grants and $7 million on policy studies by the second half of the 1990s.[69] These included programs to connect Japanese-language students at Evanston Township High School, in Evanston, Illinois, with counterparts at a high school in Niigata, Japan, and fellowships for non-native-speaking precollege teachers of Japanese to attend language training at Middlebury College. In 2000, extending the outreach focus of the organization, the USFJ began a new program aimed at early career professionals, the U.S.-Japan Leadership Program, which aimed at building a transpacific network of fellows with a diverse range of policy expertise.[70]

The attempt at broadening the scope of U.S.-Japan exchange by organizations such as the Japan Foundation and others was a reflection of the maturation of Japan's nonprofit sector. By 2000, there were over 13,500 foundations in Japan promoting nonprofit activities at home and abroad. A survey by the Japan Foundation of 615 foundations found that they had disbursed ¥47 billion ($360 million) in 1998, though the vast majority each gave out less than $400,000 in grants.[71] Covering the gamut of activities, from scientific collaboration to health promotion and nature conservation, these organizations included small groups, such as the International Institute for Children's Literature in Osaka, which sponsored the International Brothers Grimm Award for non-Japanese making outstanding contributions to the field of children's literature, and the Satoh Artcraft Research and Scholarship Foundation, which provided $10,000 grants "to contribute to the enhancement of Japanese culture by awarding grants for research and creative activities in the fine arts and crafts" by non-Japanese.[72] Few of these organizations concentrated solely on Americans or U.S.-related causes, but they nonetheless were part of the larger circle of intellectual and artistic exchange that dominated U.S.-Japan organizations. If Japan was indeed being bypassed by China in American eyes by the early twenty-first century, the irony was that Japan now had a fully developed community of exchange groups and funding organizations. The country was, by any measure, a mature player in the loosely organized world of nonprofit activities and cultural exchange.

This strengthening of grassroots relations through a variety of forums and initiatives continued to develop during the economically lean years of the 1990s and the early part of the following decade. Using limited funds for locally oriented activities might have raised eyebrows among those used to promoting high-level U.S.-Japan connections, such as academic or parliamentary exchanges, but such grassroots events had long been a central feature of U.S.-Japan cultural relations. Official and quasi-official funders from Japan and the United States continued to have the objective of swaying and influencing public opinion in both countries, but these funders did not limit their focus to the elites. Rather, these organizations worked with local leaders and educators, facilitating the activities of those whose goals were traditionally cosmopolitan and at most incidentally linked to broader policy considerations. Such a relationship of dependency was not new in U.S.-Japan cultural exchange, but the rationing of resources meant taking a harder look at which programs or groups would receive funding.

Among such grassroots activities that continued to receive public funding, the sister-cities network was one that had long attracted Japanese support. A People-to-People program was developed in September 1956 as a part of President Dwight D. Eisenhower's citizen diplomacy initiative. For Japan, the program seemed an ideal way to help reintegrate the country into the global community after World War II, but to do so at a very different level from that pursued by International House of Japan or the Fulbright Scholarships. Here, the goal would be to build links among localities in both countries and hopefully promote sorely needed goodwill and better understanding. The first U.S.-Japan sister-city relationship began in 1955 as an unofficial pairing between Saint Paul, Minnesota, and Nagasaki, which was still recovering from the effects of the atomic bombing a decade previously. Once the formal sister-cities program began, as an outgrowth of Eisenhower's People-to-People initiative, the two leading port cities of Kobe and San Francisco entered into a relationship in 1956, the same year that Japan joined the United Nations.[73]

Half a century later, Japan was the most active global participant in the sister-cities network. Japanese local and prefectural-level governments had 239 different partnerships around the world, and nearly 110 with American counterparts in 2009.[74] Outside of Sister Cities International, the formal sister-cities program, over 300 other localities in Japan maintained some form of affiliation with American towns and cities. Tokyo supported the program by establishing the Council of Local Authorities for International Relations (CLAIR), which played a coordinating role with American localities, and by budgeting approximately $16 million annually to fund sports exchanges, goodwill visits, annual festivals, and student programs, not to mention tourist packages.[75] Yet as one CLAIR director noted, it was easier to set up a sister-cities relationship than it was to keep it growing and active over the years, especially when the work of running the exchanges often was left to overburdened local officials in Japan rather than to volunteers, as was usually the case in America.[76] Despite such difficulties, sister-cities relationships played significant roles in bringing together hundreds of smaller Japanese and American towns and supplemented the limited number of local Japan-America societies that sponsored similar events, such as annual festivals and student exchanges.

Yet if most U.S.-Japan cultural exchange followed well-trod paths, one innovative program married a grassroots focus with precollegiate education in Japan, becoming one of the most successful initiatives yet in the long relationship. Beginning in 1987, the Japan Exchange and Teaching (JET) program placed native speakers of English into public primary and secondary schools in Japan as assistants to language teachers.[77] Run by the Ministry of Education in Tokyo, the program explicitly aimed at internationalizing Japan's youth and promoting intercultural understanding, especially in rural areas. While the program eventually brought on Chinese, Korean, French, and other speakers, the overwhelming bulk of assistants taught English, and half of those consistently were from America.

Participants in JET primarily were young college graduates who signed on for one-year contracts, with the option to renew for two further years. Selected through a multistage, competitive application process in their home countries, they were paid a monthly salary and assigned to a home school that provided housing, usually in the town in which they taught. The majority of "JETs," as the program's participants were commonly called, did not speak Japanese and had usually not had any experience living in the country. JETs were placed throughout Japan, from the megalopolises of Tokyo and Osaka to tiny hamlets in the mountains or fishing villages on islands off the mainland.[78] The JET teaching assistants were encouraged to enter into local life where they lived, usually through participation in school events, such as athletic festivals, summer and New Year's holiday celebrations, and official school ceremonies.

The reality of promoting both English-language competency and mutual understanding, of course, was more complex than merely shipping eager young Americans to Japan. Success depended on the chemistry among participants, their supervisory teachers, the students, and the school communities at large. JETs were not professional teachers and had no specialized training; for many of them, moreover, the program was their first job out of college. That raised questions as to how effective the JETs were in teaching English, while for their part, many JETs complained of being little more than "human tape recorders," endlessly repeating stock phrases for students to memorize. Language was obviously a barrier for the JETs, and some did not fare well being isolated from other Americans and Westerners in small villages. While it was overstating the issue to say that many Japanese had never before met Americans (or Westerners) until they encountered a JET, it was usually the case that few Japanese had had the opportunity to get to know Americans particularly well or for an extended period of time. JETs were often treated as minor local celebrities and surrounded by schoolchildren whenever the young foreigners went through town.

Despite doubts about the program's pedagogical impact, both participants and the Japanese government consider JET a success on the whole. Even with the decline in interest in Japan, an average of five thousand foreigners a year were hired for JET in the first decade of the twenty-first century, usually half of them Americans. Since the program's inception, over twenty thousand Americans have become alumni of the program, and informal surveys indicate that many of those went on to work professionally in some Japan-related field, be it academia, nonprofits, or business. Many other JETs remained involved in their local Japan-America societies or in sister-city relationships. Hundreds of Japanese communities have now had over two decades of constant exposure to young Americans (and other Westerners), and most of these communities eagerly anticipate receiving a new assistant teacher each year. Central government control of the program seems not to have made any less tangible the unique grassroots connections formed by JETs and their local communities, nor does the clear government interest in promoting U.S.-Japan relations through the program sidetrack JET's hopes of improving English-language instruction, which is the primary goal in the eyes of most Japanese and American participants.

Continuing Criticism of Cultural Exchange

Despite success at maintaining or expanding cultural exchange, suspicion of programs like JET continued to dog the U.S.-Japan relationship. If

anything, the criticisms increased after the collapse of the Japanese economic bubble, the recovery of the U.S. economy, and the decline of Japanese influence in America and around the globe. Many of the critiques
mirrored earlier arguments, with most commentators either decrying the
superficiality of exchange or believing it was manipulated by the government (usually Japan's) for state ends. Most criticisms have at their core
the belief that cultural exchange activities have done little, if anything, to
actually promote better understanding, empathy, or free inquiry into each
other's societies. Worse, according to the critics, these activities may have
contributed to reifying the very cultural stereotypes that cultural cosmopolitans hoped to bury.

More substantive criticisms took aim in particular at intellectual exchange and the side of cultural relations devoted to academic research.
Works such as those by Ivan Hall, a Harvard-trained historian, focused
on claims of discrimination against foreigners working in Japanese academia as well as on Tokyo's success in co-opting American intellectuals.
These scholars "collaborate," in Hall's words, in disseminating positive
images of Japan that provide Japanese policy makers with an edge in
maintaining protectionist economic policies.[79] Such charges mirrored
those made decades earlier by journalist Carl Crow and others, excoriat-
ing pro-Japan Americans for blocking disinterested debate about Tokyo's
aims and policy. These criticisms not only cut to the heart of questions of
intellectual integrity and personal intentions, but also remained issues
that could not be resolved to either side's satisfaction. Other scholars,
such as Japanese historian Takeshi Matsuda, made reverse claims, namely,
that American cultural policy served to keep Japan in a state of "permanent dependency" that suited Washington's political objectives in Asia.
Matsuda's 2007 revisionist history, titled *Soft Power and Its Perils*, argued
that early postwar American policy included a "cultural offensive" that
established in Japan a conformist, pro-American intellectual community
that served to justify American political domination of Japan's political
class.[80]

Much of the evidence offered by such critics points to the lack of academic criticism of Japan by those who received funds directly or indirectly from Japanese sources. By extension, similar claims could be made
that traditional cultural exchange organizations promoted only positive

views of Japan through their arts and performances exhibitions or lecture series. In short, in the eyes of its critics, cultural exchange largely remained, as in years past, mere propaganda that stifled dissenting views.

Yet a closer look at cultural exchange during the 1990s and especially in the first years of the twenty-first century revealed a far more complex landscape. Venerable organizations, such as the Japan Society of New York, hosted lectures on sex and violence in contemporary Japan, Japanese social protest movements, Tokyo's political dysfunction, and the difficulties of economic reform.[81] Similarly, Japanese funding organizations, such as the Center for Global Partnership, provided financial assistance to American and Japanese scholars alike to explore topics ranging from Japan's declining marriage rate to a comparison of discrimination against the Japanese *buraku* and American black communities.[82] The Center's flagship Abe Fellowship funded research for a book exposing Japan's lost generation—who became so-called shut-ins as a result of the social rigidity and conformity that the author argued continues to stifle the country's economic, political, and social progress.[83] Numerous American academic studies of discrimination against Japan's ethnic minorities or marginalized groups keenly laid out problems in Japanese history and society. Indeed, Takeshi Matsuda's scathing critique of postwar American cultural policy in Japan was published by the congressionally established Woodrow Wilson International Center for Scholars in Washington, D.C, an organization that received support in part from American taxpayers. If intellectual works had to compete both in the marketplace of ideas and in the marketplace of funding, there was ample evidence that studies critical of Japan and programs exposing problems in Japanese society received not only support but also receptive forums in which their arguments were presented and debated.

The Triumph of Popular Culture and the Reinvention of Japan

Such battles over intellectual independence, the integrity of research, and the manipulation of cultural exchange by government bodies took place at a level far removed from that of most producers and consumers of cultural exchange. Exchange activities remained, in the late twentieth and early twenty-first centuries, distinctly nonpolitical in the eyes of those most directly involved. Groups large and small continued to organize exchange with goals little more than responding to the interests and needs of themselves and their audience. Few practitioners of cultural exchange could have envisioned, however, the sudden resurgence in American interest in one aspect of Japan: its popular culture. As in the 1950s, Japanese pop culture surprisingly took America by storm during the 1990s. Just at the moment when professionals in both countries began to decry the declining interest of Japan in America (and to a lesser degree, of America in Japan), American youth began flooding to Japanese cultural products that had been around for decades but that now became an overwhelming sensation.

Perhaps the defining and driving feature of this new pop culture phenomenon was the impact of *anime* (Japanese animated features) and *manga* (comic books). The two had been a staple of life in Japan since before World War II, but young American consumers became addicted to both starting in the late 1980s, just as Japan's economic bubble was popping. Both *anime* and *manga* covered a vast array of topics and were far from the typical superhero or comedic fare familiar to most Americans. From teen angst themes of romance and sports competition to the sensitive and fantastical offerings of *anime* master Miyazaki Hayao, both *manga* and animated films soon became as well known to American youth as to their Japanese counterparts.

Among the first true megahits that ignited the *anime* boom was the gritty 1988 science fiction offering, *Akira*. Adapted from a bestselling *manga* of the same name, this film about a post-apocalyptic Tokyo encapsulated fears about nuclear war, environmental damage, and the costs of technology. Like many of its genre, *Akira* included characters with fantasy powers, such as ESP, and captured the mood of some Japanese who were beginning to question the path their country had taken in its climb to seeming invincibility. The economic collapse that followed immediately on *Akira*'s release fueled films and comic books that had even darker visions of the future, as the country began to realize how dramatically its fortunes had changed in such a short period of time. This questioning of Japan's past and future, and the treatment of weighty moral issues, became the main theme in the works of Miyazaki, the Walt Disney of Japanese animation producers. His films, including *Tonari no Totoro* (My

Neighbor Totoro, 1998) and *Mononoke-hime* (Princess Mononoke, 1997), were critical hits that included visions of monsters and spirits alongside probing critiques of society. What Japanese did not expect, however, was that American children would respond just as strongly as Japanese youth to *anime* themes. During the 1990s, the lag time between *anime* being released in Japan and America dwindled dramatically, so that young consumers on both sides of the Pacific were watching, and often reading, the same things simultaneously.

In the two decades after both *Akira* and *My Neighbor Totoro* came out, hundreds of animation titles were available on DVD in America, U.S. television broadcast numerous *anime* series, and *manga* comic book series flooded bookstores from New York to Los Angeles. Quickly taking advantage of the audience demand, American animators from studios like Pixar transformed their production to imitate Japanese styles, themes, and even production methods. Producers like Miyazaki became cultural icons in America and were subject to the same type of flattering profiles as 1950s directors such as Akira Kurosawa.[84] Just as powerfully, marketing departments produced every type of merchandise tie-in imaginable, from trading cards to stuffed animals, which cluttered children's rooms in Osaka and Chicago. Sanrio, the enterprise responsible for the powerhouse Hello Kitty product line, became a billion-dollar company through its domestic and foreign sales of items connected to the character.[85]

Japan's new cultural muscle was not limited to the world of children's fantasy. Through the 1990s and especially after 2000, Americans found themselves rooting for Japanese on the baseball field and in the cinema, thus bringing Japan back closer to the center of American popular culture. When pitcher Hideo Nomo broke in with the Los Angeles Dodgers in 1995, it had been thirty years since a Japanese player made it to the American big leagues. A decade later, no fewer than forty Japanese were playing or had played for American ball clubs. Americans, of course, had played for years in the Japanese professional baseball league, often on their way down in their careers (though not always, as witnessed by the success of Cecil Fielder in returning to the Detroit Tigers after several years in Japan). The ubiquity of older American players on Japanese teams was the subject of at least one Hollywood movie, *Mr. Baseball,* which starred well-known actor Tom Selleck and which itself was a comedic reflection on the clash of cultures between Japan and America that had been more seriously dealt with in baseball books like Robert Whiting's classics *The Chrysanthemum and the Bat* and *You Gotta Have Wa.*[86]

Few American sports experts believed that Japanese could perform consistently at a major league level, due to their size, their training, and the hyper team-oriented nature of Japanese baseball. While Nomo may have paved the way, however, the real boom began in 2001, when a lanky twenty-eight-year-old Japanese outfielder joined the Seattle Mariners. Ichiro Suzuki became not merely a transpacific phenomenon but one of the best players of his era. In his first year, he not only got more hits than any player in seventy-one years but was named both the American League Most Valuable Player and the Rookie of the Year, only the second player ever to achieve that double distinction. In 2004, he garnered 262 hits and broke George Sisler's 1920 record for most hits in a season, finishing with a .372 batting average. In his first eight seasons in the majors, Ichiro never hit below .303, leading many to laud his work ethic in comparison with that of a growing number of American stars who were embroiled in drug and steroids scandals. Ichiro soon found himself competing for American and Japanese attention with New York Yankees' slugger Hideki Matsui, whose numbers were less spectacular but whose power and massive fan following in Japan brought droves of Japanese tourists to New York to watch him in action. Japanese television broadcast Mariners and Yankees games live in the middle of the night, and the exploits of Ichiro and Matsui often led off evening newscasts, especially during the postseason races.

It may not be fair to describe Ichiro and Matsui as cultural emissaries, though the term might be applied less self-consciously to Japanese masters of traditional arts, such as pottery and dance. Nonetheless, due to their success and that of their fellow countrymen, no longer would Japanese be considered as being too small to play American ball or lacking in the skill level of their U.S. counterparts. As the first decade of the twenty-first century progressed, these Japanese big leaguers were joined by a handful of players from Korea and Taiwan, thus reducing somewhat the Japanese players' uniqueness. Nonetheless, the acceptance of Japanese ballplayers by American fans seemed representative of the degree to which each country saw the other as "normal," or at least the degree to which each rapidly absorbed those individuals and products fitting easily into their own culture.

Yet such normalization could be interpreted in different ways, as witnessed by Japan's reemergence in two American-made films that appeared in late 2003. One, Sofia Coppola's sleeper hit *Lost in Translation*, was a minutely drawn study of an unexpected expatriate relationship between an older man and younger woman, which took place (for the most part) during nighttime Tokyo. The other, *The Last Samurai*, was a sprawling historical epoch placing a psychically wounded American ex-soldier, played by Tom Cruise, in the midst of the aftermath of the Meiji Restoration and the struggle to determine Japan's future. Yet both films, wittingly or not, indulged in stereotypes that treated Japan more as object than subject, and both played on Japan's supposed exoticism, as did a later film, 2005's *Memoirs of a Geisha*. This is especially true of *Lost in Translation*, a sensitive movie that nonetheless portrays Tokyo as a miasmic kaleidoscope of nocturnal partying, bizarre customs, and perpetual adolescence. *The Last Samurai*, for its part, embraced an antimodernist philosophy, which is embodied by the wise and patient samurai leader, played by veteran actor Ken Watanabe; this leader is upheld as an ideal of Japanese society before its corruption by industrialization and Western ways of fighting. Such stereotypes appealed more to American moviegoers than did portrayals of Japan by the Japanese themselves, whose films were relegated to art house status in America, a far cry from the acclaim lavished on Kurosawa or Mizoguchi in the 1950s and 1960s.

On the other side of the Pacific, of course, Japanese audiences flocked to American megahits like 1997's *Titanic* or 2002's *Spider-Man*, and U.S. stars made the obligatory trip to Tokyo for packed press conferences and public screenings since their films regularly earned more in Asia than back home. Moreover, as Japanese cable television expanded after 2000, American television shows finally found a regular audience in Tokyo, Osaka, and other large cities. This entertainment dynamic was little changed from earlier decades, in which Japanese-themed cultural products in America retained their exotic cachet, while in Japan, lifestyles in dining, recreation, and the like were increasingly indistinguishable from those in America. Twenty-first-century "exchange" in Japan meant the adoption of cultural forms that could hardly be considered foreign anymore yet still seemed a bit apart from what many in Japan and abroad considered to be "traditionally" Japanese.

The new wave of American interest in Japanese popular culture, no matter how superficial, did not escape the notice of groups that had long thought of themselves as the main conduit for exchange between Japan and America. Anything that raised the profile of Japan was an unexpected gift to those who had spent the previous decade worrying over the future of their endeavor, and they moved quickly to take advantage of the opportunity. Japan Society of New York, facing increasing competition from the Korea Society, the New York Chinese Cultural Center, and the Asia Society, found it fairly easy to incorporate pop culture into its performing arts and gallery programs, in part because the organization had long presented avant-garde works to the New York community. Blockbuster exhibitions, such as 2005's Little Boy: The Arts of Japan's Exploding Subculture, curated by Takashi Murakami, gave new gravitas to what had long been considered the province of children and adolescents. The announcement for the Little Boy exhibition celebrated it quite accurately as "the subculture of 'geeks' or 'pop culture fanatics'—a fantasy world where apocalyptic imagery, fetishistic commerce, and artistic vanguards meet."[87] Such was not what the Japan Society had been known to promote during its previous years, but the audience response made it clear that a new era had dawned. The society further explored the phenomenon with professional lectures, such as "Otaku Unmasked: The Life, Death and Rebirth of Japan's Pop Culture" in November 2005. Other exchange groups across the country vied to host Japanese sports and movie stars, such as Ichiro Suzuki and Ken Watanabe.

Japanese pop culture even seemed to bring American academics back onto the same page as the traditional exchange organizations after decades of little interaction between the two. Japanese-studies programs in U.S. universities and colleges followed the demand of their students, turning away from traditional courses on economics and politics. Instead, from the 1990s onward, academic programs sprouted courses on animation, *manga* as literature, and the landscape of Japan's pop culture, while professors of art and literature produced dozens of books on pop culture.[88] Many of these studies asserted that comics and animation could not be understood simply as things of interest to adolescents. Rather, claimed the specialists, comics and animation now played a global role that far transcended their surface appearance. One author wrote, "What interests me in these new global flows of Japanese children's properties are the ways in which fantasy, capitalism, and globalism are conjoined and (re)configured."[89] If Japan were no longer the economic engine of the future, let alone a political power, American intellectuals nevertheless invested the country with perhaps an even more grandiose influence in the life of consumers and cultural producers around the globe. This idea, that Japan's major role in the world was now as purveyor of pop cultural products and arbiter of international taste, was summed up in the title of a 2002 *Foreign Policy* article—"Japan's Gross National Cool"—which neatly underscored the lack of Japan's economic importance but gave the country a new, postmodern edge.[90]

Ultimately, even the Japanese government joined the bandwagon, fully embracing the new buzz phrase "soft power," which suggested that a country's ability to pursue national ends through co-optation or its attraction to others was as powerful a tool of foreign policy as economic or military power.[91] Tokyo's public diplomacy organs, primarily within the Ministry of Foreign Affairs, saw the resurgent global interest in Japan's popular culture as a new tool for promoting Japan's image abroad. As China's economic, political, and military power grew apace after 2000, Japanese diplomats and policy makers became increasingly concerned that American (and world) interest would continue to shift from Tokyo to Beijing. Fascination with *anime* and *manga* could be used not only to strengthen American involvement with Japan, so the argument went but also to strengthen Japan's role around the globe, particularly in Europe and Asia, where a large consumer class was snapping up pop culture–related goods. By the end of the first decade of the twenty-first century, the Ministry of Foreign Affairs explained that, "aiming to further the understanding and trust of Japan," it was "using pop-culture, in addition to traditional culture and art, as its *primary* tools for cultural diplomacy."[92]

Using soft power as statecraft was not a new idea, for in many ways the pre–World War II Society for the Promotion of International Culture had used government funds for the same purpose. What was new, however, was the Foreign Ministry's direct involvement at the highest levels in the promotion of pop culture as a key pillar of Japanese diplomacy. Foreign

Minister Asō Tarō, a confirmed *manga* fan who later served as prime minister in 2008–2009, put the official imprimatur on "pop-culture diplomacy" by creating the International Manga Award in July 2007 as a way to encourage and tap into the global *manga* community. His inaugural statement on the Foreign Ministry's Web site waxed, "Manga is about love. Manga is about friendship. Manga is about growing-up. Manga is about everything-it knows absolutely no boundaries. Manga, in a word, is the most universal unifier of the hearts and minds that are young or young at heart."[93]

Unlike the claims of American academics, who saw in *manga* (and *anime*) deep truths about the rootedness of particularist identities or the triumph of global capitalism, Aso chose to stress the unifying, even childlike, nature of Japanese comic books. Over 150 Americans heeded Aso's call and entered the *manga* contest in its first three years, though none of them won or placed as runners-up.[94]

One year after inaugurating the *manga* awards, the Ministry of Foreign Affairs capitalized on the equally strong popularity of Japanese animation by designating one of the most popular animation characters, the feline Doraemon, as Japan's first "*Anime* ambassador." The character would be sent around the world to promote positive images of Japan at festivals, *anime* gatherings, and the like, and would be later joined by the ubiquitous Hello Kitty. The final piece of the ministry's outreach came in early 2009, when "with a view to promoting understanding of and confidence in Japan . . . [through] more active use of Japan's pop culture," the Public Diplomacy Department named three "Trend Communicators of Japanese Pop Culture," or "*Kawaii* (Cute) Ambassadors," who specialized in costume fashions favored by young Japanese women. These cultural ambassadors were to engage in public relations activities and work on cultural projects with Japanese embassies abroad, as well as with the programs of the Japan Foundation, thus making more explicit the link between the government and the semiprivate exchange organizations.

Whether the world of pop culture fans, many of them preteens, would respond in any meaningful way to the Japanese government's approach was impossible to know. Cultural exchange had always contained within it three main divergent streams: government-supported programs, private exchange organizations, and the mass of unregulated, uncharted individual activities. The attempt by Tokyo to take advantage of Japan's pop culture sought more explicitly than in the past to link all three streams together, but that also reflected the trend in exchange since the formation of the Japan Foundation back in 1972. Yet the new approach was not without risk, for there was strong reason to doubt that adolescent-oriented pop culture had the lasting intellectual and artistic appeal of Japan's great traditional arts. Those forms, such as ikebana flower arranging, the tea ceremony, and traditional dance, had for generations entranced foreigners young and old and led to lifelong personal engagements with Japanese art. Nor, despite academic asseverations, would all observers agree that *manga* reflected complex truths about Japanese society and the human condition to the same degree as works by master novelists such as Natsume Soseki or Yasunari Kawabata.

Regardless of such unaddressed, perhaps unarticulated, concerns, the world of Japan-U.S. cultural exchange in the early twenty-first century fully embraced the new focus on pop culture. Those interested in promoting U.S.-Japan relations fixed on the image of a benign Japan whose importance lay in bringing peoples together through its culture. Exhibits of traditional masterworks of art continued to be staged, and perceptive analyses of Japan's economic and political developments still appeared, but the weight of exchange activities shifted to the successfully commercialized youth-oriented culture. Along with a new government policy focus on nontraditional issues, such as climate change, health policy, and civil society, Japanese cultural leaders worked with American counterparts to showcase a vision of Japan that was uniquely personal: what was important about Japan, and the U.S.-Japan relationship, was how it affected the lives of individuals. Long gone were the claims that Japan would change the world through its economic or political strength. Rather, Americans and Japanese would come together to enrich personal lives and solve problems created by the rampant globalization that had made both countries so powerful in the first place. Even academics, skeptical of Japanese government programs and the importance of cultural exchange, would nonetheless identify the new cultural power of Japan as its most important export to America and the world.

The popular acceptance of such views was symbolized by a November 2008 *Time* magazine cover story, which proclaimed that the "world's renewed love affair" with Japan was due to its new focus on culture and the ethic of social responsibility. The soft side of Japan, compared with its threatening 1980s economic domination, had propelled Japan to become the world's second-most admired country after Germany, according to the article.[95] Indeed, as an element of national power, cultural exchange had never seemed stronger in the U.S.-Japan relationship, whether it was promoted by the government, private organizations, or individuals. As always, however, those cultural relations took place in a diverse environment of competing foreign exchange groups, national organizations, and fickle American interest in other countries.

Whether or not a sustainable balance had been reached between traditional and pop culture, little disturbed the flow of cultural exchange between the two countries at the beginning of the second decade of the twenty-first century. The need to jointly address political and economic issues or to continue intellectual exchange was recognized, but such exchange increasingly seemed less important to the great questions of the day. Japanese appeared content playing a respected yet secondary role in the world, while Americans no longer thought that the future was Japanese or that the country was crucial to American foreign policy. A mature relationship had been reached, according to some, while to others the Japan-America relationship was mired in secondary concerns. Above all, the cross-Pacific ties seemed anchored by cultural connections. The long-held dream of cultural cosmopolitans had seemingly come true, and they now occupied the commanding heights of the U.S.-Japan relationship, though in a world far different from what they had long envisioned.

Conclusion

WERE BARON KANEKO Kentarō to walk into the Japan Foundation headquarters today or visit an exhibition at the Japan Society of New York, he might not believe his eyes. The man who, more than any other, developed the modern idea of cultural exchange would be dumbfounded at the scale and scope of U.S.-Japan cultural exchange in the twenty-first century. From humble beginnings of occasional dinners and scattered meetings, the industry of cultural exchange has grown to produce hundreds of exhibitions, speeches, research projects, and books every year. Highly educated professionals in Japan and America teach courses, write about topics, and organize events related to the culture of the other country. Thousands of Americans participate in Japanese festivals in their home cities, while Japanese life has become ever more indistinguishable from life in America.

Even more so would Ranald MacDonald and Nakahama Manjirō be astounded, not merely at the changes in each country but at the very fact that so much is known, that so many people followed them across the Pacific, and that experts on each land would often play very public roles and be celebrated, and sometimes castigated, for their knowledge. The difference between the early nineteenth century and our day, the briefest moment in time, is nowhere more clearly exposed than in comparing

Manjirō's Edo with today's Tokyo, or MacDonald's America with the current community of Japan studies in colleges and universities.

Industrialization in both countries did not merely produced more educated individuals and higher standards of living for most citizens but also spread the technology that allowed each culture to interact with the other far more fully and regularly than ever before. Industrialization also created a middle class that amassed knowledge and valued the experience of encountering other cultures. Once the wealthy noble adventurers had enticed their fellow citizens, the development of formal exchange organizations was a natural expression of the cultural interests of the modern nation-state. If organized exchange found its first support among social elites and local businesspeople who sought to promote better relations for trade purposes, U.S.-Japan cultural exchange swiftly expanded to include activities such as art exhibitions, traveling lectures, and study abroad programs. Scholars of each country found outlets to publish their work, and eventually comprehensive Japan-studies programs developed in the United States, while Japanese intellectuals congregated at institutions like the International House in Tokyo. Even more impressively, thousands of regular Japanese and Americans attended cultural events in big cities and smaller towns, thanks to the generosity of private foundations and to government funds.

In truth, of course, the world of cultural exchange was always intertwined with political issues and economic trends. Both governments attempted to use cultural policy to promote positive images of their societies before and after World War II. The crisis that led to the war proved impervious to the attempts by cultural leaders to maintain good relations. Once the guns fell silent, cultural products were soon commoditized into consumer goods, which then created images of each country that were designed to garner profit and not necessarily promote better understanding. These realities provided strong ammunition to critics of exchange, who saw it largely as the tool of diplomats or industrialists and who viewed those who promoted positive images of the other culture as dupes or malicious agents. Such arguments can never be resolved to the satisfaction of partisans on both sides, nor can they fully represent the truth of cultural exchange between the two nations.

Cultural relations between Japan and the United States have been of a

depth as well as breadth rare between nations. At their base, these relations were animated by a cosmopolitan impulse among a diverse group of
individuals who saw in their efforts something of value to their personal
lives as well as to their own culture. Many simply found pleasure in the
tea ceremony or jazz piano, while others sought to show how cultural encounter could enrich peoples separated by vast distances, language, and
experience. The idea that cultural boundaries could be softened by the
conscious attempt to bring two societies together, and that good-faith efforts to promote better mutual understanding have their own intrinsic
value as well as the potential to bring about better political relations between states, has been a hallmark of the U.S.-Japan relationship since its
beginning. The demands of culture have been no less present throughout
that intense history than have those of economics and politics, even when
the lofty hopes of advocates of cultural exchange have been disap-
pointed.

Today, those who wish to engage with the culture of the other have a
bounty of opportunities to do so. The vast majority of such individuals
are unconcerned with the larger political or economic questions between
Japan and the United States. They benefit from the years of labor of
specialists and the commitment of numerous members of exchange societies in each country. Yet it is their continuing demand for cultural experiences, for exchange in the purest sense of the word, which is the motivating
force for the ongoing existence of the world of U.S.-Japan cultural exchange.

The cultural exchange organizations continue to exist uneasily with
the professional academic world and the influence of foundations and
governments. Yet they, too, have become professional to a degree that en-
sures their ability to raise funds, protect their interests, and attract tal-
ented individuals to staff their offices and run their programs. The
division between specialists and interested amateurs remains, though the
two interact in a variety of ways that prevent a complete split between
them. The business community in both countries also consistently provides major financial support, and often hours of volunteer work, without
which the exchange organizations would not be able to exist. The fight
for adequate support, as well as independence, will no doubt continue,
but there is little danger that the world of cultural exchange faces any dire

threats to its future. Although Japan and the United States are no longer as focused on each other as in decades past, they not only remain close allies, but will likely face challenges in the years ahead that will require trust, mutual effort, and not a small amount of mutual understanding.

After a century and a half, the continued striving of Pacific cosmopolitans has created a unique community, in which the two peoples continue to attempt to integrate something of the other, no matter how little, into their own lives and societies. That attempt will remain of value as long as Japanese and Americans continue to encounter each other in an imperfect world.

Notes

1. SHADOWS AND TRINKETS

1. Today, the work of Japanese and Western scholars alike has advanced to the point where the commonly used Japanese word for isolation *(sakoku)* now regularly appears in quotation marks; see, e.g., Kawakatsu Heita, ed., *"Sakoku" to kaikoku* (Tokyo: Dōbunkan, 2000); see also Ronald P. Toby's detailed discussion of the etymology of the term in *State and Diplomacy in Early Modern Japan: Asia in the Development of the Tokugawa Bakufu* (Stanford: Stanford University Press, 1991), pp. 12–22.

2. See Mark Mancall, *China at the Center: 300 Years of Foreign Policy* (New York: Free Press, 1984); the classic exposition of the "Chinese world order" is John King Fairbank, *Trade and Diplomacy on the China Coast* (Cambridge, Mass.: Harvard University Press, 1954).

3. Shimizu Hajime, "Sakoku jidai ni kōken shita nan'yō bōeki" in Kawakatsu Heita, ed., *"Sakoku" to kaikoku* (Tokyo: Dōbunkan, 2000), pp. 45–56.

4. A major study is Mancall, *China at the Center*. See also John King Fairbank, *China: A New History* (Cambridge, Mass.: Harvard University Press, 1991), pp. 112–113, and Joanna Waley-Cohen, *The Sextants of Beijing: Global Currents in Chinese History* (New York: W. W. Norton, 1996), pp. 14–15.

5. Katō Eiichi, *Bakuhansei kokka no seiritsu to taigai kankei* (Kyoto: Shibunkaku, 1998), pp. 27–28.

6. See Toby, *State and Diplomacy*, esp. chap. 2; Katō, *Bakuhansei kokka*, pp. 18–19.

7. A good review is Ōba Osamu, *Edo jidai no Nichū mitsuwa* (Tōbō Shoten, 1980), chap. 1. In English, see C. R. Boxer, *The Christian Century in Japan* (Berkeley: University of California Press, 1951).

8. See Toby, *State and Diplomacy*, pp. 36–37, 48–49, where he calculates that for the period 1607–1811 there was a total of twelve Korean embassies and eighteen Ryukyuan embassies, which were dispatched often on the occasion of a new shogun's installment.

9. A classic formulation is E. Herbert Norman, *Japan's Emergence as a Modern State: Political and Economic Problems of the Meiji Period* (New York: International Secretariat, Institute of Pacific Relations, 1940), most recently reissued by University of British Columbia Press in 2000.

10. See Ronald P. Toby, "Carnival of the Aliens: Korean Embassies in Edo-Period Art and Popular Culture," *Monumenta Nipponica* 41, no. 4 (Winter 1986): 415–456. Also, see Ronald P. Toby, "Kindai bunka toshite no ikoku shisetsu—tasha to Nihon no aidentiti," in Kawakatsu Heita, ed., *"Sakoku" to kaikoku* (Tokyo: Dōbunkan, 2000), pp. 77–91.

11. See Grant K. Goodman, *The Dutch Experience in Japan* (London: Athlone Press, 1986).

12. A good discussion is Kate Wildman Nakai, "The Naturalization of Confucianism in Tokugawa Japan: The Problem of Sinocentrism," *Harvard Journal of Asiatic Studies* 40, no. 1 (1980): 157–199.

13. Shiba Yoshinobu, "Tōjinami to sakoku," in Kawakatsu Heita, ed., *"Sakoku" to kaikoku* (Tokyo: Dōbunkan, 2000), pp. 92–104.

14. Yamaguchi Osamu, *Nichū kōshōshi bunka kōryū no ni-sen nen* (Tōbō: Shoten, 1996), p. 121.

15. Yamaguchi, *Nichū kōshōshi*, pp. 125–126.

16. Toby, "Kindai bunka," pp. 80–81.

17. The following is based on Ōba, *Edo jidai*, pp. 160–170.

18. Ōba, *Edo jidai*, chap. 8.

19. Yamaguchi, *Nichū kōshōshi*, pp. 116–120; Ōba, *Edo jidai*, chap. 8.

20. A recent study is Suzuki Eiichi, *Kokugaku shisō no shiteki kenkyū* (Tokyo: Yoshikawa Kobunkan, 2002). In English, see Peter Nosco, *Remembering Paradise: Nativism and Nostalgia in Eighteenth-century Japan* (Cambridge, Mass.: Council on East Asian Studies, Harvard University, 1990), and Harry D. Harootunian, *Things Seen and Unseen: Discourse and Ideology in Tokugawa Nativism* (Chicago: University of Chicago Press, 1988).

21. Ōba, *Edo jidai*, chaps. 2–3.

22. The major study is *Sakoku jidai Nihonjin no kaigai chishiki: Sekai chiri—seiyōshi ni kan suru bunken kaidai* (Tokyo: Kaikoku Hyakunen Kinen Bunka Jigyōkai Hen, 1953), pp. 344–355.

23. Marius Jansen, *China in the Tokugawa World* (Cambridge, Mass.: Harvard University Press, 1992), pp. 74–75.

24. See Satō Shōsuke, *Yōgakushi kenkyū josetsu: Yōgaku to hōken kenryoku* (Tokyo: Iwanami Shoten, 1964), esp. part 1.

25. Timon Screech, *The Western Scientific Gaze and Popular Imagery in Later Edo Japan* (Cambridge: Cambridge University Press, 1996).

26. For an overview of Japanese knowledge of geography pre-Meiji, see Ayusawa Shintarō, *Sakoku jidai no sekai chirigaku* (Tokyo: Hara Shobō, 1980). An earlier work is Fujita Motoharu, *Nihon chirigaku shi* (Tokyo, 1932). See also Ronald P. Toby, "From Three

Realms to Many: An Ethnography of the Other in Early Modern Japan," unpublished paper. *Bankoku* literally means "ten thousand countries."

27. See Fukui Tamotsu, *Edo bakufu kankōbutsu* (Tokyo: Yūshōdō, 1985), which discusses many of the books published by the Tenmonkata and succeeding translation institutes. I have used Ronald Toby's translation for the title of *Bankoku sōzu*.

28. Donald Keene, *The Japanese Discovery of Europe, 1720–1830*, 2nd ed. (Stanford, Calif.: Stanford University Press, 1969).

29. *Sakoku jidai Nihonjin*, pp. 110–111.

30. Quoted in Sakamaki Shunzo, *Japan and the United States, 1790–1853* (Tokyo: Asiatic Society of Japan, 1939), p. 114.

31. Quoted in Sakamaki, *Japan and the United States*, pp. 129–142.

32. See listing in *Sakoku jidai Nihonjin*, pp. 461–474.

33. A meditation on this point is at Hannah Arendt, *On Revolution* (New York: Viking, 1963), chap. 1

34. See Richard Pells, *Not Like Us: How Europeans Have Loved, Hated, and Transformed American Culture since World War II* (New York: Basic Books, 1996), chap. 1.

35. For Astor, see Alex Madsen, *John Jacob Astor: America's First Multimillionaire* (New York: Wiley, 2001).

36. David M. Pletcher, *The Diplomacy of Involvement: American Economic Expansion across the Pacific, 1784–1900* (Columbia: University of Missouri Press, 2001), p. 11.

37. Michael H. Hunt, *The Making of a Special Relationship: The United States and China to 1914* (New York: Columbia University Press, 1983), esp. chap. 1.

38. Van Wyck Brooks, *The Flowering of New England, 1815–1865* (New York: E. P. Dutton, 1940), p. 8.

39. For a general discussion of Asia in the mind of early America, see Akira Iriye, *Across the Pacific: An Inner History of American–East Asian Relations* (New York: Harcourt, Brace, and World, 1967), chap. 1.

40. Among the many writings on this subject, see Simon Kow, "The Idea of China in Modern Political Thought: Leibniz and Montesquieu," www.cpsa-acsp.ca/papers-2005/kow.pdf (accessed October 30, 2008).

41. American Philosophical Society, "Proposals For enlarging the Plan of the American Society, held at Philadelphia, for Promoting Useful Knowledge," *Pennsylvania Gazette*, March 17, 1768.

42. "Dissertation on the Chinese," *New York Magazine, or Literary Repository*, November 1792, pp. 685–689; accessed at APS Online.

43. See the *Pennsylvania Gazette* of July 16, 1767, for just such an advertisement.

44. *Pennsylvania Gazette*, August 22, 1787.

45. See Sakamaki, *Japan and the United States*, p. 4; quote from Foster Rhea Dulles, *Yankees and Samurai: America's Role in the Emergence of Modern Japan: 1791–1900* (New York: Harper and Row, 1965), pp. 1–5.

46. See E.S.W., "The First Voyage to Japan," in *Historical Collections of the Essex Institute*, vol. 2 (June 1860), and the account in Dulles, *Yankees and Samurai*, pp. 8–10.

47. "Advantages of Opening a Trade to Japan," *Providence Gazette and Country Journal*, September 13, 1794.

48. For an account of Benyowski, see Keene, *The Japanese Discovery of Europe*, chap. 3.

49. *Farmers' Cabinet,* October 30, 1830.
50. See Peter Booth Wiley, *Yankees in the Land of the Gods,* chap. 1.
51. For an account, see Dulles, *Yankees and Samurai,* pp. 18–22.
52. A recent, though severely edited, edition is Engelbert Kaempfer, *Kaempfer's Japan: Tokugawa Culture Observed,* ed., trans., and annotated by Beatrice M. Bodart-Bailey (Honolulu: University of Hawai'i Press, 1999).
53. See *Manners and customs of the Japanese, in the nineteenth century : from the accounts of Dutch residents in Japan and from the German work of Philipp Franz von Siebold* (Rutland, Vt.: C. E. Tuttle Co., 1973).

2. NOBLE ADVENTURERS

1. The most recent translation is John Manjirō, *Drifting toward the Southeast: The Story of Five Japanese Castaways,* Told in 1852 by John Manjirō, trans. Junya Nagakuni and Junji Kitadai (New Bedford, Mass.: Spinner Publications, 2003).
2. See Agawa Naoyuki, *Amerika ga mitsukarimashitaka—senzen hen* (Tokyo: Toshi Shuppan, 1998), pp. 8–20.
3. See Ranald MacDonald, *Ranald MacDonald: The Narrative of His Early Life on the Columbia under the Hudson's Bay Company's Regime, of His Experiences in the Pacific Whale Fishery, and of His Great Adventure to Japan; With a Sketch of His Later Life on the Western Frontier, 1824–1894,* ed. and annotated by William S. Lewis and Naojiro Murakami (Portland: Oregon Historical Society, 1990).
4. Nor were the men of the *Lagoda* the first, for six survivors of the wreck of the whaler *Lawrence* had already been held and released by the time MacDonald landed. See Foster Rhea Dulles, *Yankees and Samurai: America's Role in the Emergence of Modern Japan* (New York: Harper and Row, 1965), pp. 30–38.
5. Quoted in Dulles, *Yankees and Samurai,* p. 38.
6. See *Farmers' Cabinet,* August 15, 1850.
7. "Castaway in Japan," *New York Times,* September 16, 1923, p. BR14.
8. See Koriyama Yoshimitsu, *Bakumatsu Nichirō kankei-shi kenkyū* (Tokyo: Kokusho kankōkai, 1975), pp. 248–253.
9. Most of the following comes from Joseph Heco, *The Narrative of a Japanese: What He Has Seen and the People He Has Met in the Course of the Last Forty Years,* 2 vols., ed. James Murdoch (Yokohama: Yokohama Printing and Publishing, 1894).
10. Ibid. Heco's memoir was probably composed from a contemporary diary, as long sections of narrative are interspersed with shorter, essentially daily, entries.
11. See F. L. Hawks, *Narrative of the Expedition of an American Squadron to the China Seas and Japan, Performed in the Years 1852, 1853, and 1854: Under the command of Commodore M. C. Perry, United States Navy, by Order of the Government of the United States; Compiled from the Original Notes and Journals of Commodore Perry and His Officers, at His Request, and under His Supervision* (Washington: A. O. P. Nicholson, Printer, 1856).
12. See Heco's account in *Narrative of a Japanese,* pp. 336–346.
13. See Marius B. Jansen, "New Materials for the Intellectual History of Nineteenth-

century Japan," *Harvard Journal of Asiatic Studies* 20 (December 1957): 567–597; see also Michael R. Auslin, *Negotiating with Imperialism: The Unequal Treaties and the Culture of Japanese Diplomacy* (Cambridge, Mass.: Harvard University Press, 2004), pp. 135–142.

14. James L. Huffman, *Creating a Public: People and Press in Meiji Japan* (Honolulu: University of Hawai'i Press, 1997), p. 30.

15. See the collection, *Josefu Hiko Kaigai shinbun* (Tokyo: Waseda Daigaku Shuppanbu, 1977); examples from the paper are available in *Nihon shoki shinbun zenshū* (Tokyo: Perikansha, 1988).

16. A readable account, told primarily from the American side, is Peter Booth Wiley, *Yankees in the Land of the Gods: Commodore Perry and the Opening of Japan* (New York: Penguin, 1990).

17. "The Japan Expedition," *New York Times,* March 11, 1852, p. 2, and "Latest Intelligence," *New York Times,* August 22, 1853, p. 1.

18. For more on this, see Auslin, *Negotiating with Imperialism,* chaps. 1–2.

19. See ibid., chap. 1.

20. Examples of such prints can be found in *Nichibei kōryū no akebono: Kurofune kitaru* (Tokyo: Edo-Tokyo Hakubutsukan, 1999), pp. 133–135.

21. The reference appears in "The Advocate," chap. 24 of *Moby-Dick* (1851).

22. See Auslin, *Negotiating with Imperialism,* chap. 2, for a full discussion.

23. A comprehensive cultural study is Masao Miyoshi, *As We Saw Them* (Tokyo: Kodansha, 1979). Embassy official Muragaki Norimasa's diary was translated into English as *The First Japanese Embassy to the United States of America* (Tokyo: America-Japan Society, 1920).

24. "About the Strangers," *New York Times,* May 18, 1860, p. 8; a letter condemning her fellow females by "A True American Woman" appeared in the June 28, 1860, edition on p. 2.

25. Walt Whitman, "A Broadway Pageant," in *Walt Whitman's Drum-Taps* (New York, 1865).

26. The best studies are William G. Beasley, *The Meiji Restoration* (Stanford, Calif.: Stanford University Press, 1972), and Conrad Totman, *The Collapse of the Tokugawa Bakufu, 1862–1868* (Honolulu: University of Hawai'i Press, 1980).

27. See Ian Nish, ed., *The Iwakura Mission to America and Europe: A New Assessment* (London: Routledge, 1998).

28. See Ken Gewertz, "History of the Japanese at Harvard," *Harvard University Gazette,* February 26, 2004, www.news.harvard.edu/gazette/2004/02.26/11-japan.html (accessed June 21, 2005).

29. Yumoto Kōichi, *Meiji jibutsu kigen jiten* (Tokyo: Kashiwa Shobo, 1996), pp. 142–143.

30. Kurt Singer, *Mirror, Sword and Jewel: The Geometry of Japanese Life* (Tokyo: Kodansha, 1973), p. 34.

31. Yumoto, *Meiji jibutsu,* pp. 256–257.

32. Ibid., p. 290.

33. *Shinbun zasshi,* March 19, 1872, reprinted in *Bakumatsu Meiji shinbun zenshū,* pp. 107–108.

34. Yumoto, *Meiji jibutsu,* pp. 146–147.

35. *Shinbun zasshi,* mid-April 1872, reprinted in *Bakumatsu Meiji shinbun zenshū* (Tokyo: Sekai Bunko, 1960–61), pp. 307–308.

36. There is a voluminous literature on the Iwakura Mission. Kume's entire text has recently been translated into English as *The Iwakura Embassy, 1871–1873: A True Account of the Ambassador Extraordinary and Plenipotentiary's Journeys of Observation through the United States and Europe,* ed. Graham Healey and Chushichi Tsuzuki (Princeton, N.J.: Princeton University Press, 2002); see also Nish, *Iwakura Mission.*

37. See Shunsuke Kamei, "The Sacred Land of Liberty: Images of America in Nineteenth Century Japan," in Akira Iriye, *Mutual Images: Essays in American-Japanese Relations* (Cambridge, Mass.: Harvard University Press, 1975), p. 63.

38. Nihon Eigo Gakushi Gakkai, ed., *Eigo kotohajime* (Tokyo: Ensaikuropedia Buritanika, 1976), p. 258.

39. Ibid., p. 258.

40. An excellent study is Kenneth B. Pyle, *The New Generation in Meiji Japan: Problems of Cultural Identity, 1885–1895* (Stanford: Stanford University Press, 1969).

41. Kamei, "Sacred Land of Liberty," pp. 55–72.

42. A recent translation is Mori Arinori, *Mori Arinori's Life and Resources in America,* ed. John E. Van Sant (Lanham, Md.: Lexington Books, 2004), while the major biography in English is Ivan P. Hall, *Mori Arinori* (Cambridge, Mass.: Harvard University Press, 1973).

43. An English translation of the Meirokusha's occasional journal can be found at Willliam Braisted, *Meiroku Zasshi: Journal of the Japanese Enlightenment* (Cambridge, Mass.: Harvard University Press, 1976).

44. See William G. Beasley, *Japan Encounters the Barbarian* (New Haven: Yale University Press, 1995).

45. See the announcement from the *Shinbun zasshi,* March 19, 1872, reprinted in *Bakumatsu Meiji shinbun zenshū,* vol. 6 (Tokyo: Sekai Bunko, 1973), p. 109.

46. Hanami Sakumi, *Danshaku Yamakawa sensei den* (Tokyo: Iwanami Shoten, 1939), pp. 68–79.

47. A brief overview is Dorothy Robins-Mowry, "Westernizing Influences in the Early Modernization of Japanese Women's Education," in *Foreign Employees in Nineteenth-Century Japan,* ed. Edward R. Beauchamp and Akira Iriye (Boulder, Colo.: Westview Press, 1990), pp. 121–136).

48. See Kuno Akiko, *Rokumeikan no kifujin Ōyama Sutematsu: Nihon hatsu no joshi ryūgakusei* (Tokyo: Chuo Koronsha, 1988); a slightly redacted version in English is Akiko Kuno, *Unexpected Destinations* (Tokyo: Kodansha International, 1993).

49. A standard biography is Yoshikawa Riichi, *Tsuda Umeko den* (Tokyo: Tsuda-juku Dōsōkai, 1956). In English, see Barbara Rose, *Tsuda Umeko and Women's Education in Japan* (New Haven, Conn.: Yale University Press, 1992).

50. Robins-Mowry, "Westernizing Influences," p. 126.

51. U.S. Bureau of the Census, *Historical Statistics of the United States: Colonial Times to 1970,* Bicentennial Edition, part 1 (Washington, D.C.: U.S. Department of Commerce, 1975), p. 14. Immigration numbers are from George Thomas Kurian, ed., *Datapedia of the United States: American History in Numbers,* 3rd ed. (Lanham, Md.: Bernan Press, 2004).

52. Roger Daniels, *Asian America: Chinese and Japanese in the United States since 1850* (Seattle: University of Washington Press, 1988), p. 69.

53. See Hilary Conroy, *The Japanese Frontier in Hawaii, 1868–1898* (Berkeley: University of California Press, 1953), introduction.

54. Daniels, *Asian America*, p. 101.

55. U.S. Bureau of the Census, *Historical Statistics of the United States*, part 1, p. 14. If the figures are to be believed, fewer than three hundred were born in the United States. This would accord, however, with the gender imbalance noted above.

56. See Donald T. Hara Jr., *"Undesirables": Early Immigrants and the Anti-Japanese Movement in San Francisco, 1892–1893* (New York: Arno Press 1978).

57. For a broad overview, see Akira Iriye, *Across the Pacific: An Inner History of American–East Asian Relations* (New York: Harcourt, Brace and World, 1967), esp. chaps. 1–3.

58. "Japan," *Atlantic Monthly*, June 1860, p. 722.

59. "Progress in Japan," *New York Times*, April 2, 1873, p.4.

60. Some might give the title to Sir George Sansom's *Japan: A Short Cultural History*, which has been continuously in print since 1931, although Sansom revised it only once.

61. William Elliot Griffis, *The Mikado's Empire*, 9th ed. (New York: Harper and Brothers, 1900), p. 8.

62. Sidney L. Gulick, *Evolution of the Japanese: Social and Psychic* (New York: Fleming H. Revell, 1903).

63. Eliza Ruhamah Scidmore, *Jinrikisha Days in Japan* (New York: Harper and Brothers, 1891).

64. See Neil Harris, "All the World a Melting Pot? Japan at American Fairs, 1876–1904," in Akira Iriye, *Mutual Images: Essays in American-Japanese Relations* (Cambridge, Mass.: Harvard University Press, 1975), p. 31.

65. Data taken from Raymond W. Goldsmith, *The Financial Development of Japan, 1868–1977* (New Haven, Conn.: Yale University Press, 1983), chap. 1.

66. Much of this is from Thomas Lawton, "Yamanaka Sadajirō: Advocate for Asian Art," in *Orientations* (January 1995): 80–93.

67. Quoted in Lawton, "Yamanaka Sadajirō," p. 82.

68. See Aaron M. Cohen, "Otojirō Kawakami and Yacco Sada: Japanese Actors in America at the Turn of the Twentieth Century," *Nanzan Review of American Studies* 25 (2003): 31–51.

69. *Frederick Douglass's Newspaper*, August 13, 1852, www.accessible.com/accessible/text/freedom/00000339/00033968.htm.

70. See Gilbert Anthony Williams, *The Christian Recorder, Newspaper of the African Methodist Episcopal Church: History of a Forum for Ideas, 1854–1902* (Jefferson, N.C.: McFarland, 1996).

71. *Christian Recorder*, July 25, 1863, www.accessible.com/accessible/text/freedom/00000587/00058750.htm.

72. *Christian Recorder*, August 17, 1861, www.accessible.com/accessible/text/freedom/00000429/00042955.htm.

73. *Christian Recorder*, September 4, 1873, www.accessible.com/accessible/text/freedom/00000974/00097454.htm.

74. Rutherford Alcock, *Capital of the Tycoon*, vol. 2 (London: 1863), p. 386.

75. The 1872 figure for Kobe is from *Kobe to kyōryūchi* (Kobe: Kobe Shinbun Sōgō Shuppan Senta, 2005), p. 59; the 1893 figures for Yokohama and Kobe are from *Kobe-Yokohama: Kaika monogatari* (Kobe: Kobe Shiritsu Hakubutsukan, 1999), p. 5.

76. The key resources in English on the *yatoi* are Hazel Jones, *Live Machines: Hired Foreigners and Meiji Japan* (Vancouver: University of British Columbia Press, 1980), and Edward R. Beauchamp and Akira Iriye, eds., *Foreign Employees in Nineteenth-century Japan* (Boulder, Colo.: Westview Press, 1990). The literature in Japanese is vast; see, in particular, the seventeen-volume series, Umetani Noboru, ed., *Oyatoi gaikokujin* (Tokyo: Kajima Kenkyujo Shuppankai, 1968–1976), which is divided into specialities by volume.

77. There is no modern biography of Verbeck in English. A brief article on his Nagasaki days is Lane R. Earns, "A Miner in the Deep and Dark Places: 'Guido Verbeck in Nagasaki, 1856–1869," www.uwosh.edu/home_pages/faculty_staff/earns/verbeck.html (accessed November 17, 2010). There is also William Elliot Griffis's biography of him, *Verbeck of Japan: A Citizen of No Country; A Life Story of Foundation Work Inaugurated by Guido Fridolin Verbeck* (New York: Fleming H. Revell, 1900). In Japanese, see Ohashi Akio, *Meiji Ishin to aru oyatoi gaikokujin: Furubekki no shogai* (Tokyo: Shin Jinbutsu Oraisha, 1988).

78. See also the brief account in Nihon, *Eigo kotohajime*, pp. 143–145.

79. John M. Maki, *A Yankee in Hokkaido: The Life of William Smith Clark* (Lanham and New York: Lexington Books, 2003).

80. On House, see James L. Huffman, *A Yankee in Meiji Japan* (Lanham, MD: Rowman and Littlefield, 2004).

81. Again, the only major biography of Hepburn is by the indefatigable William Elliot Griffis: *Hepburn of Japan and His Wife and Helpmates: A Life Story of Toil for Christ* (Philadelphia : Westminster Press, 1913).

82. Nihon, *Eigo kotohajime*, pp. 139–142.

83. Ibid., p. 140.

84. See Dwight Whitney Learned, *Skeleton of Lectures on Economics* (Yokohama: R. Meiklejohn, 1889).

85. See Brian Platt, *Burning and Building: Schooling and State Formation in Japan, 1750–1890* (Cambridge, Mass.: Harvard University Asia Center, 2004).

86. This group is the subject of Christopher Benfey's *The Great Wave* (New York: Vintage, 2003).

3. THE BIRTH OF EXCHANGE

1. See Kristin Hoganson, "Cosmopolitan Domesticity: Importing the American Dream, 1865–1920," *American Historical Review* 107 (February 2002), no. 1: 55–83.

2. "Japan's Wars with China," *New York Times,* April 18, 1895, p. 7.

3. "Noted Vassar Graduate," *New York Times,* December 2, 1894, p. 18.

4. See Mary Ann Heiss, "The Evolution of the Imperial Idea and U.S. National Identity," *Diplomatic History* 26, no. 4 (Fall 2002): 524–525.

5. Joseph C. Kiger, *American Learned Societies* (Washington, D.C.: Public Affairs Press, 1963), pp. 10, 14–15.

6. For a discussion of the effects of this growth on American culture, see Jean V. Matthews, *Toward a New Society: American Thought and Culture, 1800–1830* (Boston: Twayne Publishers, 1991), esp. chaps. 4–5.

7. Kiger, *American Learned Societies,* p. 191.

8. Ibid., pp. 191–192.

9. See Thomas Lawton and Linda Merrill, *Freer: A Legacy of Art* (Washington, D.C.: Freer Gallery of Art, 1993), and Thomas Lawton and Thomas W. Lentz, *Beyond the Legacy* (Washington, D.C.: Smithsonian Institution, 1998).

10. Akira Iriye, "A Century of NGOs," *Diplomatic History*, vol. 23, no. 3 (Summer 1999), pp. 422–423. See also Akira Iriye, *Global Community: The Role of International Organizations in the Making of the Contemporary World* (Berkeley: University of California Press, 2002). On transnational movements, see John Boli and George M. Thomas, *Constructing World Culture: International Nongovernmental Organizations since 1875* (Stanford, Calif.: Stanford University Press, 1999).

11. Raymond B. Fosdick, *The Story of the Rockefeller Foundation* (New York: Harper and Brothers, 1952), p. 15.

12. Volker R. Berghahn, *America and the Intellectual Cold Wars in Europe: Shepard Stone Between Philanthropy, Academy, and Diplomacy* (Princeton: Princeton University Press, 2001) pp. 397–398.

13. Elihu Root, "A Requisite for the Success of Popular Diplomacy," *Foreign Affairs* 1, no. 1 (September 1922); reprinted in James F. Hoge, Jr., and Fareed Zakaria, eds., *The American Encounter: The United States and the Making of the Modern World* (New York: Basic Books, 1997), pp. 11–17.

14. *Beiyū kyōkaishi* (Tokyo, privately published, 1912), p. 5.

15. Ibid.

16. Ibid., pp. 10–11.

17. There is no biography, and little writing of any kind, on Kaneko in English. In Japanese, see Takase Nobuhiko, *Kaneko Kentarō jijoden* (Tokyo: Nihon Daigaku Seishin Bunka Kenkyu jo, 2003–2004), and the journal *Kaneko Kentaro kenkyu* (2001–).

18. *Beiyū kyōkai shi,* pp. 86–107.

19. See Matsumura Masayoshi, *Nichi-Ro sensō to Kaneko Kentarō: Kōhō gaikō no kenkyū* (Tokyo: Shin'yūdō, 1987).

20. "The Yellow Peril Is the Golden Opportunity for Japan," *North American Review*, November 1904, p. 647.

21. This is also a point raised by Akira Iriye, "A Century of NGOs," p. 432.

22. *American Asiatic Association 40th Annual Meeting* (1937): 21.

23. Constitution of the American Asiatic Association, section 5, article 2.

24. *American Asiatic Association 40th Annual Meeting* (1937): 21.

25. *Journal of the American Asiatic Association* 4 (May 1905): 101–103.

26. *Journal of the American Asiatic Association* 5 (June 1905): 324.

27. See, for examples of such articles, the *Journal of the American Asiatic Association* 5 (June 1905).

28. *American Asiatic Association 40th Annual Meeting* (1937): 26.

29. *Journal of the American Asiatic Association* 5 (June 1905): 130.

30. U.S. Bureau of the Census, *Historical Statistics of the United States: Colonial Times to 1970*, Bicentennial Edition, part 1 (Washington, D.C.: U.S. Department of Commerce, 1975), p. 14.

31. For a biography of Arai in English, see Haru M. Reischauer, *Samurai and Silk: A Japanese and American Heritage* (Cambridge, Mass.: Harvard University Press, 1986).

32. The only English biography of Takamine is K. K. Kawakami, *Jokichi Takamine: A Record of His American Achievements* (New York: W. E. Rudge, 1928). For a study of his relationship to Caroline Takamine, see Iinuma Nobuko, *Takamine Jōkichi to sono tsuma* (Tokyo: Shin Jinbutsu Oraisha, 1993).

33. "Japanese Residents Organize Social Club," *New York Times*, May 14, 1905, p. 14.

34. "Anglo-Japanese Alliance," *New York Times*, June 2 1095, p. 2; "Japanese Naval Heroes Tell of Their Victory," *New York Times*, August 1, 1905, p. 2; "Japanese Exultant at Dinner to Envoys," *New York Times*, August 2, 1905, p. 2..

35. *Yomiuri Shinbun*, September 6, 1908, p. 2.

36. See Robert S. Schwantes, *Japanese and Americans: A Century of Cultural Relations* (New York: Harper and Brothers, 1955), p. 290. The organization is now known as the Japan Society of Northern California.

37. See Schwantes, *Japanese and Americans*, p. 290.

38. "The Japan Society," *New York Times*, May 21, 1907, p. 8.

39. Japan Society of New York archives, notes of Executive Committee meetings, June 12, 1907, unboxed (held at Japan Society of New York; hereafter, JSEC notes); JSEC notes, October 16, 1908.

40. Proposal agreed to at March meeting, JSEC notes, March 28, 1911.

41. JSEC notes, January 12, 1916.

42. JSEC notes, December 19, 1911.

43. JSEC notes, April, 10, 1918.

44. Minutes, Japan Society of New York, Annual Meeting, February 28, 1911 (held at Japan Society of New York; hereafter, JSAM minutes).

45. JSEC notes, January 19, 1909.

46. "Art at Home and Abroad," *New York Times*, April 23, 1911, p. SM15.

47. JSEC notes, December 19, 1911; JSAM minutes, February 7, 1912.

48. Inazo Nitobe, *The Japanese Nation: Its Land, Its People, and Its Life: With Special Consideration to Its Relations with the United States* (New York: G. P. Putnam's Sons, 1912).

49. This claim was made in JSAM minutes, February 28, 1918.

50. JSEC notes, February 23, 1916.

51. JSEC notes, January 8, 1918.

52. Schwantes, *Japanese and Americans*, p. 291.

53. William Elliot Griffis, *Some of Japan's Contributions to Civilization* (New York: Japan Society, n.d.), copy held at Kobe University Library, Kobe, Japan.

54. Nippon Yusen Kaisha, *The Charm of the East: Guide to Japan and China for the Use of Passengers by the N.Y.K. Steamers* (Tokyo: Nippon Yusen Kaisha, 1919).

55. Imperial Japanese Government Railways, *An Official Guide to Eastern Asia: Transcontinental Connections between Europe and Asia* (Tokyo: Imperial Japanese Govern-

ment Railways, 1913–1915). For a general study of the role of the railways in promoting tourism, see Nakagawa Koichi, *Kankō no bunkashi* (Tokyo: Chikuma Shobo, 1985).

56. Nagai Kafu, "Ō-Bei no seikatsu to Nihon no seikatsu," *Shinchō,* January 1909, pp. 48–51.

57. Hanako, "Shumi ooki Beikoku no daidokoro seikatsu," *Shukujo gahō,* April 1914, pp. 152–157.

58. *Shin-Nippon,* October 1911.

59. Ōkuma Shigenobu, "Nichi-Bei ryōkoku no rekishiteki yūgi," *Shin-Nippon,* October 1911, pp. 5–12.

60. Kaneko Kentarō, "Beikokujin no tokushoku," *Shinchō,* October 1911, pp. 13–16.

61. Carl Crow, "The Two Japans: The Land of Facts v. the Land of Press Agents; Keeping Up Appearances for the Foreigners and How It Is Done," *McBride's Magazine,* March 1916, p. 140.

62. Jackson Fleming, "Japan and World Order," *Asia* 18 (August 1918): 634–637.

63. Gertrude Emerson, "'Bitter Learning' in Japan: A Study in Human Documents," *Asia* (October 1918): 851–858, and (November 1918): 937–944.

64. In English, see Neil Harris, "All the World a Melting Pot? Japan at American Fairs, 1876–1904," in Akira Iriye, *Mutual Images: Essays in American-Japanese Relations* (Cambridge, Mass.: Harvard University Press, 1975), pp. 24–54.

65. A brief history can be found at http://www.nationalcherryblossomfestival.org/cms/ index.php?id=574 (accessed November 17, 2010).

66. See brief history at http://www.bbg.org/discover/gardens/japanese_garden/#/tabs-2 (accessed November 18, 2010).

67. Invitation in Japan Society of New York archives, JSEC file for 1914.

68. See Joseph Bucklin Bishop, *A. Barton Hepburn: His Life and Service to His Time* (New York: Scribner's and Sons, 1923), pp. 295–316.

69. Incredibly, no full-scale biography of Shibusawa exists in English. His autobiography has been partially translated by Teruko Craig as *The Autobiography of Shibusawa Eiichi: From Peasant to Entrepreneur* (Tokyo: University of Tokyo Press, 1994). In Japanese, see the fifty-eight-volume *Shibusawa Eiichi denki shiryō* (Tokyo: Shibusawa Eiichi Denki Shiryō Kankōkai, 1955–1965), and numerous shorter collections and biographies, including Akashi Teruo, ed., *Seien Shibusawa Eiichi: Shiso to genko* (Tokyo: Shibusawa Seien Kinen Zaidan Ryūmonsha, 1951), and *Shibusawa Eiichi jijoden: denki Shibusawa Eiichi* (Tokyo: Ōzorasha, 1998).

70. The best study of this trip and Shibusawa's internationalist activities in general is Kimura Masato, *Shibusawa Eiichi: Minkan keizai gaikō no sōshisha* (Tokyo: Chuo Koronsha, 1991).

71. "Commerce Chamber Welcomes Japanese," *New York Times,* October 15, 1909, p. 18.

72. See the discussion in Schwantes, *Japanese and Americans,* pp. 299–300.

73. For an account of the dinner, see *America-Japan Society Bulletin* (hereafter, *AJS Bulletin*), no. 2 (June 1918).

74. *AJS Bulletin,* no. 3 (October 1918).

75. America-Japan Society of Tokyo archives (hereafter AJS), "Articles of Incorporation" (1927), reprinted in *America-Japan Society List of Members* (1935).

76. *AJS Bulletin,* no. 3 (October 1918).

77. *AJS Bulletin,* no. 4 (April 1919).

78. For a reappraisal, see Bruce A. Elleman, *Wilson and China: A Revised History of the Shandong Question* (Armonk, N.Y.: M. E. Sharpe, 2002), pp. 15–20, 53–70.

79. Speech reprinted in *America-Japan* (July 1920): 16.

80. Editorial in *America-Japan* (June 1921).

81. Hara Takashi, "Fusion of Oriental and Occidental Cultures: A Basis of Permanent Peace," *America-Japan* (January 1921): 79.

82. A classic account is Akira Iriye, *Pacific Estrangement: Japanese and American Expansion, 1897–1911* (Cambridge, Mass.: Harvard University Press, 1972).

83. A discussion is in Roger Daniels, *Asian America: Chinese and Japanese in the United States since 1850* (Seattle: University of Washington Press, 1988), chap. 4.

84. See Daniels, *Asian America,* pp. 139–142.

85. Text of telegram to President Woodrow Wilson, JSEC notes, April 25, 1913.

86. Copies held in Japan Society of New York archives.

87. JSEC notes, June 6, 1918.

88. Statement in JSEC notes, December 2, 1918.

89. JSAM minutes, February 27, 1920.

90. In reference to new proposed legislation to close loopholes in the 1913 Act, JSEC notes, October 14, 1920.

91. Resolution of Executive Committee, in JSEC notes, April 3, 1924.

92. Kaneko Kentarō, *America-Japan* (May 1921).

93. Lead editorial by J. T. Swift, *America-Japan,* (October 1920): 1–10.

94. Hugh Byas, "Race Contact: A Worldwide Problem," *America-Japan* (October 1920): 38.

95. See *Osaka Mainichi,* April 7, 1924, and *Jiji Shinpō,* April 13, 1924.

96. Matsui quoted in *Jiji Shinpō,* April 16, 1924; Hanihara quoted in *Osaka Mainichi,* April 17, 1924.

97. *Tokyo Nichinichi,* July 2, 1924.

98. *AJS Special Bulletin,* no. 1, July 1925.

4. STORM ON THE HORIZON

1. The best study remains Akira Iriye, *Pacific Estrangement: Japanese and American Expansion, 1897–1911* (Cambridge, Mass.: Harvard University Press, 1972).

2. Joseph Kiger, *American Learned Societies* (Washington, D.C.: Public Affairs Press, 1963), p. 197. See also Library, Archives, League of Nations file, www.unog.ch/leagueofnations for a brief review (accessed November 17, 2010).

3. Akira Iriye, "A Century of NGOs," *Diplomatic History* 23, no. 3 (Summer 1999): 425.

4. See Christy Jo Snider, "The Influence of Transnational Peace Groups on U.S. Foreign Policy Decision-Makers during the 1930s: Incorporating NGOs into the UN," *Diplomatic History* 27, no. 3 (June 2003): 377–404.

5. On these activities, see Matsumura Masayoshi, "Washintonu kaigi to Nihon no kōhō gaikō," *Gaimushō chōsa geppō* 1 (2002):47–76, and Matsumura, "Japan Calling: The

Origins and Early Days of the Ministry of Foreign Affairs Information Department in the Early 1920s," *Transactions of the Asiatic Society of Japan* 16 (2001): 51–70.

6. See Frank Ninkovich, *The Diplomacy of Ideas: U.S. Foreign Policy and Cultural Relations, 1938–1950* (Cambridge: Cambridge University Press, 1981), chap. 2.

7. Report from the Japan Society of New York Annual Meeting, January 9, 1924 (held at Japan Society of New York; hereafter, JSAM report).

8. JSAM minutes, January 14, 1925.

9. Minutes from the Japan Society of New York Director's Meeting April 3, 1924, (hereafter, JSDM minutes).

10. *Japan Society News Bulletin,* March 1926, p. 7.

11. "Japanese Prince Lauds Amity," *New York Times,* November 4, 1930, pp. 28, 33, for two different stories; JSDM minutes, December 29, 1930.

12. America-Japan Society of Tokyo, *Ninth Annual Report* (Tokyo: America-Japan Society of Tokyo, 1926). p. 11.

13. Ibid., p. 2.

14. America-Japan Society of Tokyo, *Tenth Annual Report* (Tokyo: America-Japan Society of Tokyo, 1927), p. 10.

15. *AJS Special Bulletin,* no. 4 (February 1927): 35.

16. *Yomiuri Shinbun,* January 24, 1927, p. 3.

17. *Yomiuri Shinbun,* February 1, 1929, p. 3.

18. America-Japan Society of Tokyo, *Tenth Annual Report,* p. 16.

19. Up to this time, even military leaders who served as premier had been heads of political parties, such as Tanaka Giichi, president of the Seiyūkai.

20. "Japanese Sailors Cheer Babe Ruth," *New York Times,* September 30, 1927, p. 10.

21. A brief history can be found at Tomoko Nakashima, "The Formative Years of the Transpacific Networks Promoting Japanese Studies in America," *Tōkyō Daigaku Amerika taiheiyō kenkyū* 4 (March 2004): 113–115.

22. An overview is Marius B. Jansen, "History: General Survey," in *Japanese Studies in the United States,* part 1, *History and Present Condition* (Tokyo: Japan Foundation, 1988), pp. 7–26.

23. Louis V. Ledoux, *The Art of Japan* (New York: Japan Society, 1927); Harold G. Henderson and Louis V. Ledoux, *The Surviving Works of Sharaku* (New York: Society for Japanese Studies, 1939). Estimate of membership in the Society for Japanese Studies from Jansen, *Japanese Studies in the United States,* part 1, p. 16.

24. The trees are still there, though the pine is sickly. Every May, the U.S. Embassy holds a brief ceremony marking the tree planting.

25. There is a large body of literature on the IPR. The major recent study is Tomoko Akami, *Internationalizing the Pacific: The United States, Japan, and the Institute of Pacific Relations in War and Peace, 1919–45* (London: Routledge, 2002). See also Michiyo Yamaoka, ed., *The Institute of Pacific Relations: Pioneer International Nongovernmental Organization in the Asia-Pacific Region* (Tokyo: Institute of Asia-Pacific Studies, Waseda University, 1999). A firsthand account is William L. Holland, *Remembering the Institute of Pacific Relations: The Memoirs of William L. Holland,* ed. and introduced by Paul F. Hooper (Tokyo: Ryukei Shyosha, 1995).

26. America-Japan Society of Tokyo, *Fifteenth Annual Report* (Tokyo: America-Japan Society of Tokyo, 1932), p. 10.

27. Snider, "Influence of Transnational Peace Groups," p. 391.

28. "Matsuoka Arrives; Says Japan Makes Plea to No Nation," *New York Times*, March 25, 1933, p. 1.

29. *Yale Daily News*, March 25, 1933, p. 1.

30. *Yomiuri Shinbun*, March 31, 1933, p. 2.

31. "Ishii Would Alter League Covenant," *New York Times*, June 1, 1933.

32. JSAM report, January 11, 1933.

33. "Hospital at Tokyo to Open New Units," *New York Times*, June 4, 1933.

34. America-Japan Society of Tokyo, *Seventeenth Annual Report* (Tokyo: America-Japan Society of Tokyo, 1934), p. 1.

35. The only work on Kabayama is a volume of remembrances, *Kabayama Aisuke Ō* (Tokyo: Kokusai Bunka Shinkōkai, 1955); see esp. pp. 78–83.

36. U.S. Bureau of the Census, *Historical Statistics of the United States: Colonial Times to 1970*, Bicentennial Edition, part 1 (Washington, D.C.: U.S. Department of Commerce, 1975), p. 14.

37. *Yomiuri Shinbun*, February 13, 1935, p. 7; see also *First Annual Report* (Eighteenth Annual) of the "new" America-Japan Society of Tokyo (Tokyo: America-Japan Society of Tokyo, 1935), p. 4.

38. America-Japan Society of Tokyo, *Second Annual Report* (Tokyo: America-Japan Society of Tokyo, 1936), p. 4.

39. *AJS Bulletin* 2, no 1 (1938): .

40. *America-Japan Society List of Members* (Tokyo, America-Japan Society, January 1936).

41. Ibid.

42. This information is taken from *Nichibei gakusei kaigi 70-shunen kinen shi* (Tokyo: Japan-America Student Conference, 2005), and *The Japan-America Student Conference: Celebrating Seventy Years* (Tokyo: Japan-American Student Conference, 2004).

43. *Yomiuri Shinbun*, November 5, 1931, p. 8, and November 6, 1931, p. 8.

44. See the special insert in the *Yomiuri Shinbun* of October 14, 1934; see also *Yomiuri Shinbun*, November 1, 1934, p. 7, and December 2, 1934, p. 7.

45. Julia Ruth, letter, *Yomiuri Shinbun*, November 12, 1934, p. 9.

46. See Hatano Masaru, "Nichibei yakyū kōryū—puro yakyū no seikatsu to kōryū ni kaketa otoko," in *Nichibei bunka kōryūshi: Karera ga kaeta mono to nokoshita mono*, ed. Hatano Masaru (Tokyo: Gakuyō shobō, 2005), pp. 66–69.

47. "Japan's Sea Policy Defended by Saito," *New York Times*, February 1, 1936, p. 7, and the *New York Herald Tribune*, February 1, 1936, p. 1.

48. *New York Times*, February 1, 1936, p. 7.

49. Untitled draft for a league of nations, Inquiry Papers, Series 3, Box 11, Folder 156, Sterling Memorial Library, Yale University.

50. The standard history of the League of Nations is F. P. Walters, *A History of the League of Nations*, 2 vols. (London: Oxford University Press, 1960). See also F. S. Northedge, *The League of Nations: Its Life and Times, 1920–1946* (Leicester: Leicester University Press, 1986).

51. Archibald MacLeish, introduction to *The Cultural Approach: Another Way in International Relations* by Ruth Emily McMurry and Muna Lee (Chapel Hill: University of North Carolina Press, 1947), pp. v3rd–ix.

52. John M. Mitchell, "The Historical Development of International Cultural Relations," in *Between Understanding and Misunderstanding: Problems and Prospects for International Cultural Exchange* (New York: Greenwood Press, 1990), p. 4. See also Mitchell, *International Cultural Relations* (London: Allen and Unwin, 1986), chap. 1.

53. See Frank A. Ninkovich, *The Diplomacy of Ideas: U.S. Foreign Policy and Cultural Relations, 1938–1950* (Cambridge: Cambridge University Press, 1981), chap. 2.

54. "Setsuritsu keika oyobi Shōwa 9-nendo jigyō hōkokusho," p. 4, Kokusai Bunka Shinkōkai Archives, Japan Foundation Library, Tokyo.

55. Ibid., pp. 6–7, 10.

56. See the *Yomiuri Shinbun* of April 19, 1934, p. 2, for example.

57. "Setsuritsu keika," p. 17.

58. Ibid., p. 13.

59. Ibid., pp. 13–16.

60. Kokusai Bunka Shinkōkai, *KBS 30-nen no ayumi* (Tokyo: Kokusai Bunka Shinkōkai, 1964), p. 15.

61. Ibid., p. 17.

62. Ibid., p. 20.

63. John Henry Wigmore's original 1892 study had been published under the auspices of the Asiatic Society of Japan. His drastically expanded version appeared as *Law and Justice in Tokugawa Japan: Materials for the History of Japanese Law and Justice under the Tokugawa Shogunate, 1603–1867* (Tokyo: Kokusai Bunka Shinkōkai, 1941–1943).

64. "Setsuritsu keika," p. 55.

65. Mimiya Miyako's report is found at ibid., pp. 167–183.

66. See the *Yomiuri Shinbun* of May 12, 1935, p. 7, and May 15, 1935, pp. 7, 9.

67. "Setsuritsu keika," pp. 64–65.

68. See, for example, Jessamyn Abel, *Warring Internationalisms: Multilateral Thinking in Japan, 1933–1964* (PhD diss., Columbia University, 2004), esp. chap. 2.

69. See the *Yomiuri Shinbun* of February 3, 1935, p. 2, for a story on the staging of Chūshingura.

70. Kwame Anthony Appiah, "Cosmopolitan Patriots," in Martha C. Nussbaum, *For Love of Country: Debating the Limits of Patriotism* (Boston: Beacon Press, 1996), pp. 21–29.

71. The ship's name is pronounced "pa-NIGH."

72. *AJS Bulletin* 2, no. 1 (1938).

73. *AJS Bulletin* 4 (December 1940), p 1.

74. "Kabayama Plans Tour," *New York Times*, February 27, 1941, p. 6.

75. Miyata Torao, ed., "Sōsetsuki no Rikkyō Daigaku Amerika kenkyūjo: shiryō shū," *Rikkyō Amerika kenkyū shirizu*, no. 16 (1984) and no. 17 (1985).

76. *Bulletin of the Museum of Fine Arts* (December 1939), p. 117.

77. "Gets Books on Japan; Bates Receives Seven Volumes for Phelps Collection," *New York Times*, June 1, 1941.

78. The *New York Times* ran a laudatory obituary titled "Count Kaneko Dies; Peace Advocate," on May 17, 1942, p. 47.

5. OUT OF THE ASHES

1. See John Dower's classic treatment, *War Without Mercy: Race and Power in the Pacific War* (New York: Pantheon, 1987).

2. John F. Embree, *The Japanese,* War Background Studies, no. 7 (Washington, D.C.: Smithsonian Institution, 1943).

3. U.S. Navy, Pacific Fleet and Pacific Ocean Areas, *Guide to the Western Pacific: For the Use of the Army, Navy and Marine Corps of the United States,* 2nd ed., CinCPAC-CinCPOA Bulletin, no. 126–44 (Washington, D.C.: U.S. Navy: 1945).

4. This is not to dismiss the real suffering during the first years of Occupation. Revisionist views are in John W. Dower, *Embracing Defeat: Japan in the Wake of World War II* (New York: W. W. Norton, 1999), and Robert Whiting, *Tokyo Underworld* (New York: Vintage, 2000).

5. There is a large body of literature on the Occupation, ranging from paeans to condemnation. See, in addition to Dower's *Embracing Defeat,* Kazuo Kawai, *Japan's American Interlude* (Chicago: University of Chicago Press, 1960), and Robert E. Ward and Sakamoto Yoshikazu, eds., *Democratizing Japan: The Allied Occupation* (Honolulu: University of Hawai'i Press, 1987).

6. See, among others, the account in Tetsuya Kataoka, *The Price of a Constitution: The Origin of Japan's Postwar Politics* (New York: Crane Russak, 1991), chap. 2.

7. The censored pages form the bulk of the Gordon W. Prange Collection, University of Maryland, College Park.

8. See Kyoko Hirano, *Mr. Smith Goes to Tokyo: The Japanese Cinema under the American Occupation, 1945–1952* (Washington, D.C.: Smithsonian Institute, 1992). Also worthwhile is Mark Sandler, ed., *The Confusion Era: Art and Culture of Japan during the Occupation, 1945–1952* (Seattle: University of Washington Press, 1997).

9. Quote is from Prime Minister Nakasone Yasuhiro, in Henry Scott Stokes, "Dip In Nakasone Backing Tied to Arms Stand," *New York Times,* February 20, 1983, p. 21.

10. Kataoka, *Price of a Constitution,* chap. 4; see also Richard B. Finn, *Winners in Peace: MacArthur, Yoshida, and Postwar Japan* (Berkeley: University of California Press, 1992), chaps. 14–16.

11. See Howard Schoenberger, *Aftermath of War: Americans and the Remaking of Japan, 1945–1952* (Kent, Ohio: Kent State University Press, 1989).

12. See Penny M. Von Eschen, *Satchmo Blows Up the World: Jazz Ambassadors Play the Cold War* (Cambridge, Mass.: Harvard University Press, 2004).

13. Suzuki Daisetsu, "Amerika no seikatsu to bunka," *Kaizō,* September 1952, p. 24.

14. *Shūkan Asahi,* June 24, 1949, pp. 3–4.

15. The original treasures were the mirror, sword, and jewel.

16. For a popular account of Rikidozan, see Whiting, *Tokyo Underworld,* pp. 101–113.

17. Suzuki, "Amerika no seikatsu to bunka," p. 29.

18. Mishima Yukio, "Bunka bōei ron," *Chūō Koron* 83(7) (July 1968), pp. 95–117. I would like to thank John Treat for bringing this article to my attention.

19. Ironically, the very products derided during the 1950s became highly collectible even as early as the 1970s. See, for an example, Marion Klamkin, *Made in Occupied Japan: A Collector's Guide* (New York: Crown Books, 1976).

20. James Kelly, "No Jade, No Peonies," *New York Times*, November 30, 1952, p. BR47.

21. Bosley Crowther, "The Screen in Review: 'Ugetsu' from Japan Offered at Plaza," *New York Times*, September 8, 1954, p. 40.

22. Bosley Crowther, "This Week: 'Ugetsu,'" *New York Times*, September 12, 1954, p. X1.

23. In the skit, Sid Caesar plays a Japanese warlord trying to win the hand of the daughter (Nanette Fabray) of the king (Howard Morris) and having to fight an evil samurai (Carl Reiner) to do it. The spoof is included in *The Sid Caesar Collection: The Fan Favorites* (Creative Light Entertainment), disk 2. Sid Caesar and Carl Reiner, telephone interviews with author, April 2007.

24. A collection of thirty of these songs was released under the title *Welcome to Chinatown: Oriental "Popcorn" Tracks, Vol. 1*, compact disc, Marginal, 1995.

25. This was the label for Sapporo Beer, Japan's oldest continuously produced brand, which was started in 1876 and was among the first exported to the United States.

26. See Japan Center for International Exchange, *The Role of Private Institutions in International Relations: Lessons from Trans-Atlantic Relations and Challenges for Japan* (Tokyo: Japan Center for International Exchange, 1991), p. 22.

27. This is the argument of Waldemar Nielsen, former vice president of the Ford Foundation, who asserts that the collaboration actually began in the days just before World War II, as the foundations realized the risk to the capitalist system from fascist and communist challengers. Quoted in Volker Berghahn, "Philanthropy and Diplomacy in the 'American Century,'" in *Diplomatic History* 23, no. 3 (Summer 1999): 399. For an extended study, see Volker Berghahn, *America and the Intellectual Cold Wars in Europe: Shepard Stone between Philanthropy, Academy, and Diplomacy* (Princeton, N.J.: Princeton University Press, 2001). A critical and irreverent view was taken by Dwight MacDonald in *Ford Foundation: The Men and the Millions* (New York: Reynal, 1956).

28. On the council in this period, see Michael Wala, *The Council on Foreign Relations and American Foreign Policy in the Early Cold War* (Providence, R.I.: Berghahn Books, 1994), and Robert D. Schulzinger, *The Wise Men of Foreign Affairs* (New York: Columbia University Press, 1984); also useful is Walter Isaacson and Evan Thomas, *The Wise Men: Six Friends and the World They Made* (New York: Simon and Schuster, 1986). A critical view can be found in Laurence H. Shoup and William Minter, *Imperial Brain Trust: The Council on Foreign Relations and United States Foreign Policy* (New York: Monthly Review Press, 1977).

29. See Japan Center for International Exchange, *Role of Private Institutions*, pp. 23–31.

30. "The Fulbright Program, 1946–1996: An Online Exhibit," www.uark.edu/depts/speccoll/fulbrightexhibit/history.html (accessed November 15, 2010). For a history, see National Humanities Center, *Fulbright at Fifty* (Research Triangle Park, N.C.: National Humanities Center, 1997).

31. The author was a Fulbright Scholar in Japan as a graduate student during 1997–1998.

32. "Japanese Students in the U.S., 1954–2003," in Institute for International Education, *Open Doors 2004* (New York: Institute for International Education, 2004).

33. For an overview, see David F. Krugler, *The Voice of America and the Domestic Propaganda Battles, 1945–1953* (Columbia: University of Missouri Press, 2000).

34. A list of participants appears in International Visitor Program, *A Look Back at a Half-Century of the International Visitor Program* (Tokyo: U.S. Embassy, 2004).

35. By 2005, the number of American Centers had declined to five. In 1997, USIA was folded into the State Department, ending the USIA's independence and diluting the influence of public diplomacy abroad. William Morgan, Minister-Counsellor for Public Affairs, U.S. Embassy, interview with author, Tokyo, March 7, 2005.

36. *Asahi Shinbun,* March 13, 1961, p. 1.

37. Dewey Talks to Reporters in Tokyo," *New York Times*, July 5, 1951, p. 5; "Dewey Tours Japan," *New York Times*, July 7, 1951, p. 3.

38. "Japan to Celebrate Century Since Perry," *New York Times,* October 12, 1951, p. 47.

39. The best source on John D. Rockefeller 3rd's interest and activities in Asia is John Ensor Harr and Peter J. Johnson, *The Rockefeller Conscience: An American Family in Public and in Private* (New York: Scribner, 1991). The Rockefeller Archive Center, Sleepy Hollow, New York, contains all of John D. Rockefeller 3rd's papers relating to Japan as well as to his organizational activities.

40. "Japan Society Election," *New York Times,* March 26, 1952, p. 27. This aspiration is carved into a wooden plaque on display in the lobby of the Japan Society's New York headquarters.

41. "Japanese Envoy in Trade Appeal," *New York Times,* June 18, 1952, p. 3.

42. "Dulles Asks Japan to Step Up Defense," *New York Times,* September 18, 1953, p. 3.

43. "Art Preview Honors Japan's Ambassador," *New York Times,* March 27, 1953, p. 48.

44. "Study Aid Given to 25 Japanese," *New York Times,* August 1, 1953, p. 9.

45. Compiled from biographical information in *Tsuisō Matsumoto Shigeharu* (Tokyo: Kokusai Bunka Kaikan, 1989).

46. International House of Japan, *Summary Report of the Initial Five Years of the International House of Japan, Inc.* (Tokyo: Kokusai Bunka Kaikan, 1957), p. 10.

47. Ibid., p. 56.

48. International House of Japan, *The International House of Japan, Inc.: Challenge, Response, Progress, 1952–1962* (Tokyo: Kokusai Bunka Kaikan, 1962), pp. 18–20.

49. International House of Japan, *Summary Report,* p. 89.

50. Ibid., p. 15.

51. Ibid., p. 46.

52. Figures from International House of Japan, *Challenge, Response, Progress,* p. 53. In 2003, total membership was 4,151, of whom 1,430 were foreigners (*Annual Report* 2003).

53. *Asahi Shinbun,* May 22, 1953, p. 3.

54. *Asahi Shinbun,* September 6, 1960, p. 11.

55. International House of Japan, *Challenge, Response, Progress,* p. 41.

56. There is no history of the school, but its archives are being collected by David Hays at the University of Colorado at Boulder; see http://uclibraries.colorado.edu/archives/collections/jlsp/index.htm (accessed November 15, 2010). The Pacific Basin Institute

at Pomona College, for years under the direction of Frank Gibney until his death in 2006, is making video testimonies of the teachers and alumni of the program; information is available at www.pomona.edu/pbi/oralhistory/oralhistory.shtml (accessed November 15, 2010).

57. A critical analysis, especially in relation to east Asian studies, can be found at Masao Miyoshi and Harry Harootunian, eds., *Learning Places: The Afterlives of Area Studies* (Durham, N.C.: Duke University Press, 2002).

58. Marius B. Jansen, "History: General Survey," in *Japanese Studies in the United States, part 1, History and Present Condition* (Tokyo: Japan Foundation, 1988), p. 21.

59. See Kimberly Gould Ashizawa, "Understanding the 'Other': Foundation Support for Japanese Studies in the United States," in Yamamoto Tadashi et al., eds., *Philanthropy and Reconciliation: Rebuilding Postwar U.S.-Japan Relations* (Tokyo: Japan Center for International Exchange, 2006), pp. 213–246.

60. Jansen, "History: General Survey," p. 21.

61. Ibid., p. 22.

62. Ibid, p. 23. The titles (all by Princeton University Press) were *Changing Japanese Attitudes Toward Modernization,* edited by Marius B. Jansen (1965); *The State and Economic Enterprise in Japan: Essays in the Political Economy of Growth,* edited by William W. Lockwood (1965); *Aspects of Social Change in Modern Japan,* edited by R. P. Dore (1967); *Political Development in Modern Japan,* edited by Robert E. Ward (1968); *Dilemmas of Growth in Prewar Japan,* edited by James William Morley (1971); and *Tradition and Modernization in Japanese Culture,* edited by Donald H. Shively (1971).

63. A critical view of American studies in Japan is in Takeshi Matsuda, *Soft Power and Its Perils: U.S. Cultural Policy in Early Postwar Japan and Permanent Dependency* (Washington, D.C.: Woodrow Wilson Center Press, 2007), which argues that the United States supported the domestic position of intellectual elites, who were in turn submissive to U.S. policy in Asia.

64. For an overview that explores in detail the types of support received, see James Gannon, "Promoting the Study of the United States in Japan," in Yamamoto Tadashi et al., eds., *Philanthropy and Reconciliation: Rebuilding Postwar U.S.-Japan Relations* (Tokyo: Japan Center for International Exchange, 2006), pp. 187–211.

6. NEW CHALLENGES, NEW HOPES

1. An extended review of détente is in Gordon S. Barrass, *The Great Cold War: A Journey through the Hall of Mirrors* (Stanford, Calif.: Stanford University Press, 2009), pp. 151–237.

2. A brief review is in Walter LaFeber, *The Clash: U.S.-Japan Relations throughout History* (New York: W. W. Norton, 1997), pp. 352–358.

3. See Jacob Schlesinger, *Shadow Shoguns* (Stanford, Calif.: Stanford University Press, 1999).

4. Michael Schaller, *Altered States: The United States and Japan Since the Occupation* (New York: Oxford University Press, 1997), pp. 245–247.

5. Andrew Gordon, *A Modern History of Japan: From Tokugawa Times to the Present* (New York: Oxford University Press, 2003), pp. 287–288.

6. See LaFeber, *The Clash,* pp. 350–351.

7. Japan Foundation, *Annual Report 1973* (Tokyo: Japan Foundation, 1973), p. 1.

8. Matsumura Masayoshi, *Kokusai kōryūshi: Kingendai Nihon no kōhō bunka gaikō to minkan kōryū,* 2nd ed. (Tokyo: Chijinkan, 2002), pp. 362–363.

9. Japan Foundation, *Annual Report 1973,* p. 1.

10. Ibid., p. 2.

11. Ibid.

12. Ibid., p. 5.

13. Ibid., p. 27.

14. "Toward the Japanese Century," *Time,* March 2, 1970, http://www.time.com/time/magazine/article/0,9171,904215,00.html (accessed November 18, 2010).

15. Herman Kahn, *The Emerging Japanese Superstate: Challenge and Response* (Englewood Cliffs, N.J.: Prentice-Hall, 1970), p. ix.

16. Chalmers Johnson, *MITI and the Japanese Miracle: The Growth of Industrial Policy, 1925–1975* (Stanford, Calif.: Stanford University Press, 1982).

17. Japan Foundation, *Annual Report 1973,* p. 30.

18. Ibid., p. 30.

19. Ibid., pp. 45, 12.

20. Japan Foundation, *Annual Report 1975* (Tokyo: Japan Foundation, 1975), p. 32; Japan Foundation, *Annual Report 1982–83* (Tokyo: Japan Foundation, 1983), p. 20.

21. Japan Foundation, *Annual Report 1976* (Tokyo: Japan Foundation, 1976) p. 39.

22. Japan Foundation, *Annual Report 1982–83,* p. 20.

23. Japan Foundation, *Annual Report 1984–85* (Tokyo: Japan Foundation, 1985), p. 47.

24. Japan Foundation, *Annual Report 1975,* p. 1.

25. See numerous studies, including Richard T. Arndt, *The First Resort of Kings: American Cultural Diplomacy in the Twentieth Century* (Washington, D.C.: Potomac Books, 2005); David Caute, *The Dancer Defects: The Struggle for Cultural Supremacy during the Cold War* (Oxford: Oxford University Press, 2003); and Yale Richmond, *Cultural Exchange and the Cold War: Raising the Iron Curtain* (University Park: Pennsylvania State University Press, 2003).

26. Francis B. Tenny, *The Japan–United States Friendship Commission: A History of the Commission Commemorating the 20th Anniversary, 1975–1995* (Washington, D.C.: Japan–United States Friendship Commission, 1995), p. 5.

27. Tenny, *Japan–United States Friendship Commission,* pp. 8–15.

28. Figures for both Ford and Rockefeller funding from Nichibei Zaidan, *Nichibei taiwa: Nichibeikan no sōshikiteki kōryū katsudō ni tsuite* (Tokyo: Nichibei Zaidan, 1981), pp. 26–27.

29. For a review, see Michael R. Auslin, *Japan Society: Celebrating a Century, 1907–2007* (New York: Japan Society, 2007), pp. 72–74.

30. The author received such a scholarship from the Japan America Society of Chicago in 1995.

31. Much of the above information taken from *JCIE: Twenty-fifth Anniversary 1992–1994*

Program Report, and *Japan Center for International Exchange 1999–2000 Annual Report.*

32. Foundation description at Sasakawa Peace Foundation, http://www.spf.org/e/profile/index.html (accessed November 18, 2010).

33. *United States–Japan Foundation 20th Anniversary* (2000), p. 31.

34. Ibid., pp. 36, 38.

35. For a brief review, see Kenneth B. Pyle, *Japan Rising: The Resurgence of Japanese Power and Purpose* (New York: Public Affairs, 2007), pp. 270–277.

36. A brief review can be found in LaFeber, *The Clash,* pp. 376–377; see also Gillian Tett, *Saving the Sun: How Wall Street Mavericks Shook Up Japan's Financial World and Made Billions* (New York: Harper Collins, 2003), part 1.

37. Robert J. Cole, "Japanese Buy New York Cachet With Deal For Rockefeller Center," *New York Times,* October 31, 1989, p. A1.

38. William F. Buckley, Jr., "The Japs Capture Rockefeller Center," *National Review,* December 8, 1989, p. 53.

39. Information at Sony, www.sony.net/SonyInfo/News/Press/199907/99-059 (accessed November 15, 2010).

40. See David Halberstam, *The Reckoning* (New York: William Morrow, 1986).

41. See *Time* of March 30, 1981, and April 13, 1987, respectively.

42. Pat Choate, *Agents of Influence: How Japan Manipulates America's Political and Economic System* (New York: Simon and Schuster, 1990), p. xv.

43. "When Japan-Bashing Goes Too Far," *New York Times,* July 6, 1987, p. 30.

44. A recap can be found in LaFeber, *The Clash,* pp. 385–389.

45. *Annual Report JFY 1991,* Japan Foundation Center for Global Partnership, p. 3.

46. Center for Global Partnership, *Challenges and Opportunities for U.S.-Japan Exchange in the New Era: Report of the International Symposium* (Tokyo: Japan Foundation Center for Global Partnership, 1991), pp. 8–12.

47. CGP *Annual Report 1991* (Tokyo: Japan Foundation Center for Global Partnership, 1991) pp. 6, 10.

48. Ibid., pp. 31–34.

49. For good overviews, see Bill Emmott, *The Sun Also Sets: The Limits to Japan's Economic Power* (New York: Touchstone, 1991), and Tett, *Saving the Sun.*

50. Emmott, *The Sun Also Sets.*

51. Karl van Wolferen, *The Enigma of Japanese Power: People and Politics in a Stateless Nation* (New York: Vintage, 1990).

52. Nicholas D. Kristof, "The Quake That Hurt Kobe Helps Its Criminals," *New York Times,* June 6, 1995, p. A3.

53. Among hundreds of such books, see Bill Gertz, *The China Threat: How the People's Republic Targets America* (Washington, D.C.: Regnery, 2000); Bates Gill, *Rising Star: China's New Security Diplomacy* (Washington, D.C.: Brookings Institution Press, 2007); Will Hutton, *The Writing on the Wall: Why We Must Embrace China as a Partner or Face It as an Enemy* (New York: Free Press, 2006); Susan L. Shirk, *China: Fragile Superpower* (Oxford: Oxford University Press, 2007); James Mann, *About Face: A History of America's Curious Relationship with China, from Nixon to Clinton* (New York: Vintage, 2000).

54. Nicholas D. Kristof, "Albright Hugs Wary Tokyo Smarting From Beijing Trip," *New York Times*, July 5, 1998, p. A4.

55. A recounting of the political issues of these years is in Yoichi Funabashi, *Alliance Adrift* (New York: Council on Foreign Relations Press, 1999).

56. Yoshikawa Hiroshi, *Tenkanki no Nihon Keizai* (Tokyo: Iwanami shoten, 1999); in English, Hiroshi Yoshikawa, *Japan's Lost Decade* (Tokyo: International House of Japan, 2001); Yutaka Kawashima: *Japanese Foreign Policy at the Crossroads: Challenges and Options for the Twenty-first Century* (Washington, D.C.: Brookings Institute Press, 2003).

57. For one overview, see Dennis D. Trinidad, "Japan's ODA at the Crossroads: Disbursement Patterns of Japan's Development Assistance to Southeast Asia," *Asian Perspective* 31, no. 2 (2007): 95–125.

58. An overview is in Tomohito Shinoda, *Koizumi Diplomacy: Japan's* Kantei *Approach to Foreign and Defense Affairs* (Seattle: University of Washington Press, 2007).

59. See Kenneth B. Pyle, *Japan Rising: The Resurgence of Japanese Power and Purpose* (New York: Public Affairs, 2007).

60. *CGP Newsletter,* Summer 2002, p. 8.

61. Ibid., pp. 18–26.

62. See CGP guidelines at https://www.jpf.go.jp/cgp/e/grant/dl/CGP_Guidelines2011e .pdf (accessed on November 15, 2010).

63. See grant guidelines at https://www.jpf.go.jp/cgp/e/grant/index.html (accessed November 18, 2010).

64. CGP Grant Program, http://www.jpf.go.jp/cgp/e/fellow/index.html (accessed November 16, 2010).

65. Information on that program can be found at Japanese Studies Fellowships, www.jpf .go.jp/e/intel/study/fellowship/index.html (accessed November 15, 2010). The author received a Japan Foundation Fellowship for intensive language study in Japan during 1995–1996. Comments on the status of CGP from various American academics and nonprofit executives in private conversations.

66. CGP database located at www.jpf.go.jp/cgp/e/grant/db.html (accessed).

67. See http://www.britishcouncil.org/usa.htm (accessed on November 15, 2010).

68. See, for example, the *Richmond Times Dispatch,* March 27, 2009, for an account of the visit of Saitama prefecture high school students to rural Virginia public schools.

69. *The United States–Japan Foundation 20th Anniversary* (2000), pp. 28, 50.

70. The author was a USJLP delegate in 2005–2006.

71. *Directory of Grant-Making Foundations in Japan 2000* (Tokyo: Center for Global Partnership, 2000), p. 12.

72. Ibid, pp. 100, 211.

73. See http://www.sister-cities.org/about/history.cfm (accessed on November 15, 2010).

74. Information from Sister Cities International, www.sister-cities.org/about/statistics.cfm (accessed November 15, 2010).

75. Naofumi Hida, Director of Japan Local Government Center, speech, Second Japan-U.S. Sister City Conference, New York, July 18, 2002, p. 6, available at www.sister-cities .org/conference/Toledo/JapanHida.pdf (accessed July 7, 2009).

76. Ibid., p. 8.

77. The author participated in the JET program in Hyogo prefecture in 1991–1992 and has remained in contact with the program since then.

78. The JET program has been the subject of a number of studies and memoirs, including David L. McConnell, *Importing Diversity: Inside Japan's JET Program* (Berkeley: University of California Press, 2000), and Bruce Feiler, *Learning to Bow: Inside the Heart of Japan* (New York: Harper Perennial, 2004).

79. Ivan P. Hall, interview, 2002, *JapanReview.net*, www.japanreview.net/interview_ivan_hall.htm (accessed November 16, 2010). Hall's provocative works include *Cartels of the Mind: Japan's Closed Intellectual Shop* (New York: W. W. Norton, 1997), and *Bamboozled! How America Loses the Intellectual Game with Japan and Its Implications for Our Future in Asia* (New York: East Gate Books, 2002).

80. Takeshi Matsuda, *Soft Power and Its Perils: U.S. Cultural Policy in Early Postwar Japan and Permanent Dependency* (Washington, D.C.: Woodrow Wilson Center Press, 2007).

81. See programs from the *Japan Society Annual Report, 2007–2008* (New York: Japan Society of New York, 2008); *Japan Society Annual Report 2008–2009* (New York: Japan Society of New York, 2009).

82. See the list of Abe Fellows of the Center for Global Partnership, http://www.jpf.go.jp/cgp/e/fellow/abe/index.html (accessed November 16, 2010), esp. Miho Iwasawa (2007–2008) and Eric Brown (2006–2007) as examples.

83. Michael Zielenziger, *Shutting Out the Sun: How Japan Created Its Own Lost Generation* (New York: Doubleday, 2006).

84. See, for example, Margaret Talbot, "Letter from Japan: The Auteur of Anime," *New Yorker*, January 17, 2005, pp. 64–75.

85. Ken Belson and Brian Bremner, *Hello Kitty: The Remarkable Story of Sanrio and the Billion Dollar Feline Phenomenon* (Singapore: John Wiley and Sons, 2004).

86. Robert Whiting is the dean of commentators on Japanese-American baseball. His works include *The Chrysanthemum and the Bat: Baseball Samurai Style* (Avon Books, 1983); *You Gotta Have Wa* (New York: Vintage, 1989); and *The Samurai Way of Baseball: The Impact of Ichiro and the New Wave from Japan* (New York: Grand Central Publishing, 2005).

87. See announcement archived at Japan Society of New York, www.japansociety.org/little_boy_the_arts_of_japans_exploding_subculture (accessed July 13, 2009).

88. See, for example, Tufts University's Susan J. Napier, *Anime from* Akira *to* Howl's Moving Castle: *Experiencing Contemporary Japanese Animation*, rev. and updated ed. (New York: Palgrave Macmillan, 2005); MIT's Ian Condry, *Hip-Hop Japan: Rap and the Paths of Cultural Globalization* (Durham, N.C.: Duke University Press, 2006).

89. Anne Allison, *Millennial Monsters: Japanese Toys and the Global Imagination* (Berkeley: University of California Press, 2006), p. 4. Allison is a professor of cultural anthropology at Duke University.

90. Douglas McGray, "Japan's Gross National Cool," *Foreign Policy* (June/July 2002), pp. 44–54.

91. The term originated with academic Joseph Nye; see his *Soft Power: The Means to Success in World Politics* (New York: Public Affairs, 2005).

92. Japan Ministry of Foreign Affairs, "Pop-Culture Diplomacy," www.mofa.go.jp/policy/culture/exchange/pop/index.html (accessed on July 15, 2009; emphasis added).

93. Ministry of Foreign Affairs of Japan, "International Manga Award," www.mofa.go.jp/policy/culture/exchange/pop/manga/index.html (accessed July 15, 2009).

94. The winners came primarily from Asia, though a handful were from Europe. Numbers of participants from each year's recap are available online, ibid.

95. Hannah Beech, "Japan Reaches Out," *Time,* November 20, 2008, http://www.time.com/time/magazine/article/0,9171,1860765,00.html (accessed November 18, 2010.

Acknowledgments

In writing a book with the sweep of this one, I incurred many debts over a good number of years. Both Yale University and the American Enterprise Institute gave me valuable time to research and write, and Kobe University kindly offered me an office where I largely composed the first draft in the summer of 2005. Funding for the initial research was generously provided by the Smith Richardson Foundation's Junior Faculty Research Grant, and research funds from the Council on East Asian Studies at Yale and Japan Studies at AEI were crucial for follow up needs.

My thanks go to those who helped at various stages in the research and writing of this book, or simply gave welcome moral support. They include Agawa Naoyuki, Tomoko Akami, Kimberly Gould Ashizawa, Andrew Barshay, Thomas Bender, Volker Berghan, John Brademas, Ted Bromund, Arthur Brooks, Sid Caesar, Chano Jun'ichi, Gerry Curtis, Mark Davidson, Chris DeMuth, Fred Dickinson, Roger Dingman, Alan Divack, Kevin Doak, Gretchen Hobbs Donaldson, Frank Ellsworth, Martin Fackler, Fujimura Satoshi, Glenn Fukushima, Eric Gangloff, James Gannon, Sheldon Garon, Nathan Glazer, Andrew Gordon, Jonathan Green, Peter Grilli, Sayuri Guthrie-Shimizu, David P. Janes, Ellen Hammond, Hara Hideki, Daniel Headrick, James Huffman, Cappy Hurst, Iida Noriko, Inoue Jun, Iokibe Makoto, Akira Iriye, Itô Eiichi, Itô Misako, Peter Johnson, Ben Karp, Ambassador Kato Ryozo, Dan Kevles, Kitaoka Shin'ichi, Koide Izumi, Koshikawa Kazuhiko, Kuno Akiko, Kurita Junko, Walter LaFeber, Jane Levin, Richard Levin, Matthew Louchheim, Minh Luong, Mabuni Yuka, Kathryn Malizia, Erez Manela, Matsumoto Hiroshi, Matsumoto Kenji, Matsumura Masayoshi, Marlene Mayo, Maria Menocal, Norman Mineta, Tosh Minohara, Rico Mochizuki, Bill Morgan, Murata Akihiko, Frank Ninkovich, Fred Notehelfer, Ambassador Okawara Yoshio, Ôkubo Naoko, Ôkubo Toshihiro, Ôkubo Yoko, George R. Packard, Danielle Pletka, Thierry Porte, Christopher Poston, Emily Putze, Ken Pyle, Stuart Reider, Carl Reiner, Susanne

Roberts, David Rockefeller, Walter Roberts, Zachary Safir, Motoatsu Sakurai, Dick Samuels, John Schrecker, Sam Shepherd, Nick Shulz, Benjamin Seiver, Martha Seiver, Shono Keiji, Cynthia Sternau, Susa Yuko, Taida Hideya, Tevi Troy, Ronald Toby, Tokugawa Iehiro, Tokugawa Tsunenari, James Ulak, Umeeda Masako, Cecil Uyehara, Arthur Waldron, Joanna Waley-Cohen, Steven C. Wheatley, John K. Wheeler, George M. Wilson, Steven Whitfield, Yamaji Hidetoshi, Yamamoto Tadashi, Yokoyama Yuka, Marilyn Young, and Barry Zorthian. My apologies to any friends or associates whose names I have omitted from this list.

Conrad Totman took his sharp pencil to an early draft, resulting in much soul-searching and rewriting. Valuable help was given by my research assistants, Jeremy Ershow, Leslie Forgach, Chihiro Ikegami, Naoko Kozuki, and Risa Suzuki.

I am grateful to many institutions or groups which provided research materials or venues for discussing this work, including the America-Japan Society of Tokyo, the Smithsonian Institution's Freer Gallery of Art, Harvard University Archives, Harvard University's Widenor Memorial Library, International House of Japan, Inc., International Security Studies at Yale, Japan America Society of St. Louis, Japan America Student Conference, Inc., Japan Center for International Exchange, Japan Foundation Center for Global Partnership, Japan Society of New York, Kobe City Museum, Kobe University Library, Library of Congress, Maneki restaurant (Seattle, WA), Montgomery County (MD) Public Libraries, National Association of Japan America Societies, Nippon Club (N.Y.), Shibusawa Eiichi Memorial Foundation, Sony Corporation of America, Toyota Motor North America, University of Maryland's Center for East Asian Studies, University of Missouri-St. Louis, University of Pennsylvania's Center for East Asian Studies, University of Tokyo, United States-Japan Foundation, United States-Japan Friendship Commission, U.S. Department of State, Washington and Southeast Japan Seminar, Yale University's Sterling Memorial Library, and the Yokohama Archives of History.

As always, my parents, Donald and Myra Auslin, and my in-laws, Tetsuo and Yoshiko Ueyama gave unconditional support for my work. It was my father's experiences in the U.S. Army in Japan in the 1950s that got me first interested in U.S.-Japan relations, and led directly to this book. Benjamin Auslin provided inspiration, diversion, and unconditional love. Nothing that I do would be possible without Ginko Auslin—as a partner, critic, and helper she is unsurpassed.

A personal note should be inserted here. Like many of the individuals in this book, I have been a beneficiary of government, corporate, and foundation funding throughout my career as student, professor, and policy analyst. However, I received no funding for the research or writing of this book from any of the organizations that I discuss in these pages. As always, any errors in fact or interpretation are solely of my own making.

Index

Harvard University Press is a member of Green Press Initiative (greenpressinitiative.org), a nonprofit organization working to help publishers and printers increase their use of recycled paper and decrease their use of fiber derived from endangered forests. This book was printed on recycled paper containing 30% post-consumer waste and processed chlorine free.